THE THIN
BLUE LINE

International Peacekeeping
and Its Future

A STUDY SPONSORED BY THE INTERNATIONAL PEACE ACADEMY
WITH THE SUPPORT OF THE CHARLES F. KETTERING FOUNDATION

THE THIN
BLUE LINE

INTERNATIONAL PEACEKEEPING
AND ITS FUTURE

INDAR JIT RIKHYE
MICHAEL HARBOTTLE
BJØRN EGGE

NEW HAVEN AND LONDON, YALE UNIVERSITY PRESS

Published with assistance from
the Louis Stern Memorial Fund.

Designed by Sally Sullivan
and set in Times Roman type.
Printed in the United States of America by
Vail-Ballou Press, Inc., Binghamton, N.Y.

Published in Great Britain, Europe, Africa, and Asia
(except Japan) by Yale University Press, Ltd., London.
Distributed in Latin America by Kaiman & Polon,
Inc., New York City; in Australia and New Zealand
by Book & Film Services, Artarmon, N.S.W.,
Australia; and in Japan by
Harper & Row, Publishers, Tokyo Office.

TO
MRS. ARTHUR M. YOUNG
WHOSE IMAGINATION CREATED
THE INTERNATIONAL PEACE ACADEMY

In recent years, we have found ourselves locked in fruitless debates about the inauguration of the peacekeeping operations and over the degree of control the Security Council would exercise over peacekeeping machinery—an impasse which has insured only that permanent peacekeeping machinery would not come into being. Each peacekeeping unit we have formed has been an improvization growing out of argument and controversy.

We should delay no longer. The time has come to agree on peacekeeping guidelines so that this organization can act swiftly, confidently and effectively in future crises.

—U.S. Secretary of State Henry Kissinger,
in an address to the UN General Assembly,
24 September 1973.

Contents

PART III: PEACEKEEPING PRESENT

MAPS   *Following page 210*

Preface

This book was commissioned by the International Peace Academy as a contribution to the further development of the organization, mechanisms, and human skills required for international peacekeeping. The Academy, founded in 1971 following preliminary efforts begun in 1967, has as its aim the advancement of practical education in peacekeeping and in mediation, negotiation, and peaceful action for human rights and social development in conflict situations. It is not a research institute nor a center for theoretical study. It is essentially a decentralized international educational institution which directs its attention to the practical needs of the peacekeeper, peacemaker, and peace builder for solving problems on the ground. In the words of former United Nations Secretary-General U Thant, "The International Peace Academy is one of the enterprises which deserve full support by the international community, governmental or non-governmental, organizational or individual."

It is noteworthy that more than forty former participants in the Academy's seminars are currently holding appointments in their countries' delegations at the United Nations, in departments of their national Ministries of Foreign Affairs dealing with United Nations matters, and with United Nations peacekeeping forces and missions. Among the latter there is a consensus that what they learned through Academy training projects has helped them in performing the role they are now being called upon to fulfill.

This book distills the authors' personal experience as United Nations peacekeepers, together with their collective experience in education and training for peacekeeping assignments, into workable ideas for the future of international peacekeeping. All three have brought their particular knowledge and skills to the preparation of the book and have collaborated to present an agreed analysis and evaluation of future possibilities. They indicate how the skills and techniques that are needed in peacekeeping can be more widely understood and developed, so that despite the political limitations and organizational and administrative problems that plague them, peacekeeping operations can be managed more effectively and economically.

In parallel with the operational requirements, there are the organizational difficulties that prevail within the United Nations itself, stemming as they do from political differences. These difficulties require attention, and the authors suggest ways and means by which they may be overcome or at least simplified so that a more responsive and durable collective security system might evolve. They have taken care to see that their proposals are realistic, falling within the framework of the existing Charter of the United Nations and taking into account current world political trends and geopolitical attitudes.

The "thin blue line" of the title more than aptly describes the size and capacity of those United Nations peacekeeping forces and observer missions that have exercised truce supervision or been interposed between hostile forces in interstate and domestic disputes since 1946—a thin thread that, more often than not, has by its presence provided a defusing of tensions and a deescalation of violent conflict.

When considering the future of international peacekeeping and how it can be made more effective as an instrument for ending hostilities, the authors have turned to the history of UN and other multinational peacekeeping operations. The first part of this book, therefore, contains a comprehensive review covering United Nations, regional, and non-UN multinational initiatives. The comparative results derived from this case study clearly indicate that despite political and mechanical difficulties, the United Nations is at present the international institution best organized and equipped to mount and maintain such operations with a reasonable chance of success.

This should not be taken as meaning that the other levels of intervention should not be encouraged or developed to acquire a greater potential. The authors argue that there would be considerable advantage in developing a viable peacekeeping capability under regional arrangements to deal with continental domestic disputes, with the United Nations intervening only if invited to do so. In such cases the United Nations' role would be limited to support unless a regional organization found itself unable to deal with the situation itself.

Part III of the book, which has been added as an epilogue, deals with the latest United Nations peacekeeping operation in the Middle

East up to the time of the disengagement of the Egyptian and Israeli forces along the Suez Canal during January and February 1974. It does not cover the UN force's subsequent deployment and manning of the buffer zone established in the Sinai as a result of the disengagement agreement of 18 January 1974. Since the original manuscript had been completed before the new United Nations Emergency Force came into existence, the authors felt that the addition of this postscript would place the latest peacekeeping initiative in its proper perspective in relation to the rest of the book. In their view, it helps to emphasize the lessons that still need to be learned, while underlining the essential prerequisites of efficient peacekeeping machinery, including preparation and preparedness. The contribution that experience made to UNEF II's initial operational achievements is clearly apparent in this final chapter, as is the necessity for the widest possible development of training in peacekeeping procedures and techniques.

In writing the book, each of the authors assumed responsibility for the initial drafting of specific chapters which were then revised in the light of the comments and suggestions by the other two. The whole manuscript was styled by Michael Harbottle for publication.

Acknowledgments to those who gave their professional time and talents, their advice and comments, are made elsewhere. However, the authors wish to express here their particular indebtedness to Dr. Yashpal Tandon, lecturer in international relations and political science at the University of Dar-es-Salaam, Tanzania, for his constructive and helpful advice and for the major contribution he made to that part of the book dealing with the identification of conflict and the future possibilities for its control.

Acknowledgments

The authors wish to place on record the debt of appreciation they owe to the International Peace Academy for making possible the creation of this book; to Mrs. Arthur M. Young, founding member and an honorary chairman of the Academy, to whom the book is dedicated; to Abraham Wilson, founding member and treasurer-counsel; to Phillips Ruopp, a vice-president of the Academy; and to Mildred Robbins, a member of the Academy's International Board of Directors. All have given generously of their time and talents to the development of the Academy and its programs.

The Academy and the authors are deeply grateful to the Charles F. Kettering Foundation of Dayton, Ohio, for its generosity in helping to fund the preparation of the manuscript and for its continuing support of the Academy's work. The encouragement and material assistance received have been significant and the personal thanks of the authors go to James M. Read, vice-president for program management, and William P. Shaw of the International Affairs Program.

In June 1973, a conference was held at Sir George Williams University, Montreal, to which the Academy invited a number of consultants to discuss with the authors the first draft of the manuscript. The consultants who attended were: Gordon Hawkins, director of the Center for Foreign Policy Studies at Dalhousie University, Nova Scotia, who acted as conference chairman; Lieutenant General E. L. M. Burns (Ret.),* former chief of staff of UNTSO and first commander of UNEF; Paris Arnopoulos,* Political Science Department, Sir George Williams University; Brigadier General George Bell (Ret.), former director-general of Military Plans and Operations, National Defence Headquarters, Canada; Major General F. S. Carpenter (Ret.),* Royal Canadian Air Force and former commandant of the Canadian National Defence College; David Cox, Department of Political Science,

---

* All former resource staff or participants of the International Peace Academy's seminars.

xv

Queen's University, Kingston, Ontario; Gordon E. Cox,* Department of Political Science, York University, Ontario; Leo Gross, Fletcher School of Law and Diplomacy, Tufts University, Boston, Massachusetts; Robert W. Reford, executive director, Canadian Institute of International Affairs; Lieutenant Colonel Douglas Rogers (Ret.),* formerly of the Canadian Armed Forces; Henry Wiseman,* Department of Political Science, Guelph University, Hamilton, Ontario. Their combined contribution was deeply appreciated by the authors.

Finally, it is the wish of the Academy and of the authors to record their special thanks and appreciation to Eirwen Harbottle for typing the original and final manuscripts, and for her valuable and painstaking work in checking and correcting the grammar, construction, and syntax; and to Lauranne Pazhoor and Anne Denvir of the Academy's New York office for the thorough and patient manner in which they handled the secretarial and clerical work involved in the book's production.

To all of these admirable individuals the authors and the Academy say thank you.

PART I

PEACEKEEPING PAST

1

A Reason and a Purpose

In a personal message to the inaugural seminar of the International Peace Academy in Vienna in 1970, UN Secretary-General U Thant raised a number of issues which in his view had an important bearing on the development of an effective international peacekeeping apparatus within the framework of the United Nations. They were:

1. The fact that peacekeeping missions often can only be undertaken at the request of or with the consent of governments who reserved their right of option to request their removal at any time desired by them
2. The continuing debate over the specific provisions of the UN Charter under which peacekeeping missions are undertaken
3. The question of a greater involvement of the Security Council and the Military Staff Committee in the day-to-day direction and administration of peacekeeping operations
4. The practicability of preplanning for peacekeeping missions and the extent to which the Military Staff Committee should be responsible
5. The freedom of action for the secretary-general to offer his good offices without being dependent on the prior approval of the Security Council, General Assembly, or any other competent principal organ
6. The need for a firmer attitude in regard to financial dues and the requirement that permanent member governments of the Security Council should be expected to make appropriate financial contributions toward the cost of any peacekeeping mission for whose establishment they have voted in the Security Council
7. The desirability of establishing standby UN peacekeeping forces

The concerns of U Thant in 1970 still represent the fundamental issues that will need to be resolved along with others before a sound and effective machinery can be structured to meet the requirements of international conflict control, with all its aspects of violence, and provide the framework within which disputes can be settled peacefully. Until this happens, any realistic system of collective security and safeguards will remain an unfulfilled wish.

However, it is not the machinery alone that requires attention. Past experiences emphasize the practical problems that arise in the execution of multinational peacekeeping operations when they have to be engineered on an ad hoc basis. Inevitably, the wide extremes of military knowledge and professionalism among the contingents of the various contributing nations, who by and large have been the smaller nations of the world, make the processes of mounting a peacekeeping force extremely complex in terms of organization and manpower resources.

In this book we explore the future possibilities of peacekeeping in its third-party context and suggest practical solutions to some of the issues raised by U Thant. In so doing a careful analysis is made of existing procedures and organizations and of the major case studies of the past, which provide valuable pointers to the requirements of the future. Since this study is directed at the potential of peacekeeping forces and their role in third-party interventions of a peaceful nature, the one enforcement operation of the United Nations—Korea—has not been included among the case studies that have been used for analysis, even though it is the single instance where the Security Council acted in strict accordance with Chapter VII of the Charter. But as the antecedents and the nature of that operation can be considered exceptional in the context of UN peacekeeping, it has not been given a place in our assessment of the possibilities for collective action.

Analysis inevitably plays an important part in the construction of a work of this kind—analysis not only of practical experience but also of the structural framework within which the practical concepts need to be set. We have therefore separated the content into two main parts and an epilogue. The first part deals with the existing procedural and organic mechanisms that control the operation of peacekeeping forces and missions, and the second with the future prospects of international peacekeeping interventions and how they might be given greater credibility. In our analysis of existing mechanisms we study the constraints imposed by the UN Charter and the interpolitical attitudes of the big powers toward its interpretation and implementation, and we suggest how in some instances these might be overcome. We also propose how the UN organs could be reappraised and made more flexible in an attempt to rejuvenate the peacekeeping process. Finally in the first part we make a detailed analysis of the case studies of the "peacekeeping past," both within and outside the framework of the United Nations, and draw from them the lessons that are essential to any diagnosis of the "peacekeeping future." In the second part of the book our aim has been to present what we believe are viable concepts for the development and improvement of the international peacekeeping system so that it can materially contribute to international collective security. Part III, described as an epilogue, studies the latest UN peacekeeping operation in the Middle East in its initial stages and provides an updated commentary on its positive as well as its negative aspects, so giving substance to the proposals and suggestions put forward in the earlier parts of the book.

Since this book is directed at a multiprofessional as well as an academic audience, it is important that we properly state the theoretical premiss on which we base our beliefs in the value of peaceful interventions. The early chapters of each part are intended to establish this essential base, from which the rest can evolve; for the prevailing attitudes and aspirations within the political complex of the United Nations and their influence on the future of peacekeeping at the international level are relevant to what follows.

The ideas that we will be presenting have been developed in the course of a series of studies on the control of conflict in the international arena that have been carried out by the International Peace Academy over the last four years. During that period there were no new UN peacekeeping operations, and those that had existed before remained unchanged.[1] The deadlock between the superpowers over matters of procedure and principle and the inflexibility of their positions in the Security Council have prevented any real progress in developing new concepts for peacekeeping. The failure of many UN member states to use the instruments of peacekeeping within the United Nations and their negative attitude toward international peace-

---

1. The second UNEF operation in the Middle East was mounted after the conclusion of the Peace Academy's 1973 peacekeeping seminar in Vienna, Austria.

keeping in general have been obstacles to the United Nations becoming a positive and practical influence in the settlement of disputes. Its potential has been ignored and often bypassed. Perhaps the present UNEF operation will change all this, but it is too early yet to say.

One might consider that all this mounts up to one very good reason why there is little point in a book of this kind. But there is a significant difference between what is possible and what is desired, what is impracticable and what is practicable. In our view the need for a definitive security system is recognized and appreciated by the majority of states. The initiatives that brought UNEF II into being certainly strengthen the belief that the kind of collective security system envisaged by us is both possible and credible. Whatever shape it takes, clearly it must have a practical relevance to present and future political trends on a global plane. To be credible it must be firmly founded on the UN Charter as it was drafted—otherwise one would be experimenting in "cloud-cuckoo-land" with a system without substance. Recognizing these qualifications, we have put forward a set of ideas regarding both the formulating machinery and the contributing agents in the practical field, which together could provide a foundation on which future peacekeeping operations could be mounted with much greater efficiency and effectiveness than formerly. Such a foundation could also provide a basis on which subsidiary organizations other than the United Nations could build their peacekeeping structures.

We make the point here at the beginning, and we repeat it later on, that most nations feel there should be a global conflict control system through collective security and that its present lack is a matter of great concern to the middle and small nation-states. But because of a lack of confidence in the United Nations' ability to maintain international peace and security, those who are its members have tended to look elsewhere for means of settling their disputes—even though their failure to support the United Nations in the development and strengthening of its peacekeeping machinery makes the rejection of a UN intervention inevitable. It is a vicious circle which requires a major collective initiative and strong intent to break. The world if it is to survive must come to terms with itself as to whether conflict and violence are to become the cornerstones of contemporary life and the accepted social patterns for the future, or whether a comprehensive effort is to be made to reach solutions based on peaceful approaches, which not only limit violence but remove it as a means of conflict control. Youth, as the legatees of the future, are unwilling to accept as their inheritance the status quo of a violent world. This factor alone must influence attitudes and policies of nations in the years to come.

2

Peacekeeping—A
Third-Party Role

Conflict has no single form, nor do its various manifestations fall into any single descriptive category. The different levels of conflict and their individual characteristics, ranging from full-scale war to domestic and intercommunal disputes, need to be recognized by those concerned with conflict abatement and resolution. At the top of the scale, power politics and the need to protect national security interests (real or perceived) are the generally accepted causes of war; while at the lower levels, racial, religious, ethnic, or economic and social differences form the structural bases from which conflict and physical violence erupt. It stands to reason, therefore, that there can be no stereotyped methodology for controlling and ending conflict—if there is to be a cure, the doctor's prescription must suit the ailment.

Apart from some rare instances where more peaceful efforts have been used, warlike demonstrations, whether in the international or national context, have generally been remedied by the "use of the sword"—or in UN terms, "enforcement action designed to maintain peace and security." At the higher levels of the conflict spectrum these means are likely to remain in use, for it is at these levels that big power interests are more deeply involved, and any attempt at physical interventions by middle and small nation-states to influence a peaceful settlement are neither realistic nor viable. However, the same argument does not necessarily apply to the lower levels of the spectrum, where there appears to be a greater possibility for third-party interventions and more flexible circumstances within which peace initiatives of all kinds can be developed. Therefore, while recognizing that all conflict problems are not solvable by peaceful means, a case does exist for a different approach to the resolution of conflict—not a substitute for enforcement but an alternative treatment for certain forms of conflict.

It is a recognized fact that we live in a world of "conflicts"— some active, some temporarily quiescent, and some dormant. Conflict in this context includes every interstate, intrastate, communal, and nationalistic confrontation presently conceived and extant. These conflicts have their base in the structural causes set down above but have reached the point where they have erupted into manifest expressions of violence, from acts of terrorism and insurgency, to direct armed-force engagements between armies or between armies and guerrilla or resistance movements. In comparison to the major level of conflict these "small wars" have occupied the world stage since the end of World War II. Estimates of how many there have been vary and depend upon the individual assessor's definition of war, ranging in number between the forties and a hundred, but a broad consensus would seem to put the figure around the fifty mark.[1] It is, however, reasonable to suggest that on any one day in any one year one can count twice on the fingers of both hands the tally of conflicts manifest at that moment around the world.

It is important that the significance and prevalence of small wars be borne in mind and their effects studied in contrast to the deterrent strategies of the superpowers, which are aimed at avoiding a nuclear holocaust. Traditional military states that have or have access to nuclear warheads, the United States and the Soviet Union included, are only too well aware of the price that would have to be paid in terms of massive and mutual destruction were a nuclear war to erupt, and it is their credibility and the effectiveness of their deterrents that are the major factors in reducing the chances of a nuclear war. It is not therefore in this rarefied realm of conflict that we set our concepts for peacekeeping, but rather at those levels at which the opportunities for peacekeeping through third-party intervention are more real and where the danger of conflict escalation from minor to major proportions cannot be ignored, but must be promptly and adequately treated.

Since the essential theme of this book is that peacekeeping in the

---

1. Two examples: A recent research analysis by the Institute of Strategic Studies put the estimate at 1.5 conflicts per year since 1945. Professor Istvan Kende, professor of modern history at the Karl Marx University, Budapest, records ninety-seven international disputes between 1945 and 1970.

UN sense does have a valuable and constructive contribution to make to the resolution of conflict—and case study shows that the claim is fully justified—it seems appropriate to define exactly what we mean by the term *peacekeeping,* for it has connotations that suit a number of variables in conflict action. It is an interesting fact that the Charter of the United Nations does not use the word anywhere in its 111 articles, yet it has acquired a common usage in describing the military operations of the United Nations over the past three decades. This, therefore, makes it even more important that the distinction be drawn between the interpretation of *peacekeeping* in this context and the type of operations to which the word is applied outside the United Nations.

It is only in recent years that the word *peacekeeping* has replaced the hitherto more commonly applied phrase *keeping the peace* to describe the latter type of operations. The substitution of one word for three may be admirable in the semantic sense, but in precise terms the two are not analogous; for *keeping the peace* implies a more aggressive action than *peacekeeping,* which denotes the more impartial role in conflict of a referee.

Peacekeeping outside the United Nations has been made to mean whatever those applying it have wished it to mean, from total suppressive action to the use of minimum force in the control of violence. The degree of force is really irrelevant; the operation in either case is of an enforcement nature in which the degree of force used inevitably escalates in direct ratio to the resistance encountered—the greater the force the more determined the resistance is likely to become. Some operations have been brutal, bloody, but quickly completed; others, adhering more closely to the principle of minimum force, have probably been less bloody but have dragged on over a greater period of years. Whatever their character, these security actions are inaccurately described as peacekeeping operations. They may bring a halt to manifest violence, but under the surface the structural conflict remains unresolved, its reemergence simply deferred to a later date.

We are not concerned here with peacekeeping in the context just described, but in its true sense of peaceful intervention, where a third party acts in the capacity of an impartial referee to *assist* in the settlement of a dispute between two or more other parties. This is the concept of peacekeeping on which the UN operations in the Middle East, the Congo, and Cyprus have been structured; which motivated its observer missions in the Balkans, Palestine, Kashmir, Lebanon, and Yemen; and which made acceptable the setting up of the eight-month interregnum in West New Guinea to cover the period between the hand-over of responsibility from the Netherlands to Indonesia. Only once has the United Nations embarked upon an enforcement operation, and that was in the Korean War of 1950—the single instance where the United Nations acted to all practical purposes in accordance with the provisions of Chapter VII of its Charter. By definition, therefore, though not in Charter terms, the role of the United Nations peacekeeping operations has been "the prevention, containment, moderation and termination of hostilities between or within states, through the medium of a peaceful third party intervention organized and directed internationally, using multinational forces of soldiers, police and civilians to restore and maintain peace." [2]

The essence of this characterization of the role of international peacekeeping lies in the fact that enforcement plays no part in it. It is a concept of peaceful action, not of persuasion by force, where the fundamental principles are those of objectivity and nonalignment with the parties to the dispute, ideally to the extent of total detachment from the controversial issues at stake. The "weapons" of the peacekeeper in achieving his objectives are those of negotiation, mediation, quiet diplomacy and reasoning, tact and the patience of a Job—*not* the self-loading rifle. To many this is a negative and unsuitable role to ask a soldier to perform, for he is not trained to fulfill it. This can be disproved by looking at the facts, but what is important is that without this impartiality and without the correct attitude and approach on the part of the third party, the chances of the intervention remaining peaceful become less likely. The success of any multinational third-party intervention into a conflict hinges on this basic principle. Disregard it and one will forfeit the confidence, respect, and trust of both sides and thereby the cooperation, understanding, and recognition that are vital to the complete and successful performance of the peacekeeper's mandate.

Any practical concept has to have a theoretical framework on which to construct its working principles and machinery, so that their

2. Definition used by the International Peace Academy in its study of international control of violence; *Report from Vienna: An Appraisal of the International Peace Academy Committee's 1970 Pilot Projects.*

application and implementation are maximal in effect. The premiss on which this study is based is that it is possible for international violence to be controlled and for peace to be kept without necessarily having to resort to enforcement measures. This is admittedly not a hypothesis that is accepted by everyone—there are certainly those who consider the use of force as the only effective medicine to cure violence and, as such, beneficial to the system. This viewpoint cannot be dismissed lightly, and some of the arguments in its favor are discussed later on. One cannot be doctrinaire or dogmatic on this issue, and this book sets out to present the pragmatic alternatives to force. Broadly speaking in the general context of interstate and intrastate conflict, it is worth repeating that force and counterforce, violence and counterviolence, do tend to exacerbate and prolong conflicts rather than to reduce them; and that military action in support of law enforcement, even of a purely policing nature, stiffens rather than overcomes resistance. It certainly does not remove the structural causes, the roots of the conflict, which remain and are nurtured for a later day when history will repeat itself.

Looked at in this way, some may question whether one form of military intervention is likely to be any more successful than another. The evidence is that for certain levels and types of conflict peaceful intervention can better and more quickly achieve the desired stabilizing effect and develop a less violent and tension-ridden atmosphere. But if this is the sole instrument used, and it is allowed to operate in isolation from any other instrument or agent of conflict resolution, then its effect will be as counterproductive as any other kind of military intervention and, like it, will only succeed in preserving the status quo. The military is just one of the instruments that can be used in the settlement of disputes; its effectiveness will depend upon the degree to which it can aid the total peace-finding effort by its stabilizing and peacekeeping operations. In fulfilling its responsibilities in this respect its primary aim is to provide an atmosphere as stable and tension-free as possible in which the peacemaker and the peace builder (the political and socioeconomic instruments) are better able to deal with the problems that are the roots of the conflict and that need to be resolved if a lasting peaceful resolution is to be found. As stated, it is our contention that in intercommunal and intrastate conflicts—and in some interstate disputes—the peaceful rather than the enforcement approach is more likely to provide the level of stability and calm that is required for the other instruments of conflict settlement to carry out their roles more successfully. The use of the phrase "more likely to" is relative and, as already pointed out, applies to particular settings, levels, and characteristics of conflict. It is, however, intended to emphasize the point that "peaceful means" constitute a positive alternative to enforcement and should be recognized as viable and more productive instruments for use in conflict resolution in certain defined contexts. Peacekeeping and the international control of violence are synonymous terms when used in this context.

International control of violence embraces a wider spectrum than the relatively narrow compass of military peacekeeping. Treatment of conflict is as important during its precursive and postcare stages as it is during its manifest phase—the open violence. It is therefore most necessary to look at the scenario of conflict as a whole, for processes of prevention, containment, and rehabilitation to complete recovery are interrelated and often cannot be separated. It is a combined operation involving all those agencies needed and available to contribute to the prevention and containment of conflict and the reestablishment of stability in community life. It becomes more of a relief operation for a man-made disaster than a military operation—with the role of particular agencies varying in degree to suit the different characteristics of the "disaster." In essence, therefore, the theory of conflict control is that the use of military and other professional techniques, adjusted to meet the requirements of nonviolent application and in conjunction with other skills and agencies, often can prove a more effective contribution to conflict control than direct enforcement measures.

The question of choice therefore exists—not a clear-cut choice between two methods of treating conflict as a single entity, but rather a choice of "which treatment for which conflict." [3] However, not everyone accepts this criterion. As has already been said, there are those who sincerely believe that counterviolence does have its place in the "prevention, containment, moderation and termination" of violence, and that in certain areas of the world the nonviolent approach simply will not work. They insist that in such areas violence has to be met with violence, if violence is to be suppressed, and they see this counterviolence as the only kind of treatment that the opposition will

---

3. Dealt with more fully in chapters 12 and 15.

understand and respond to. There are others who take a less rigid position but who tend to look at the problem from a traditionally conservative standpoint, viewing enforcement measures as a necessary purgative, cleansing the bowels of discontent and rebellion at regular intervals and returning the "body" to its comfortable condition of status quo ante, after which the medicine is locked away safely in the medicine chest in readiness for the next assault upon the sensibilities of the constitution.

Conflict has also been viewed as a means of population control; the contention being that without violent war and the resultant loss of life, the population explosion would inevitably leave ever increasing discontent and violence in its wake. A process of extermination is therefore considered helpful in reducing the environmental problems and is encouraged as a life-and-death cycle repeating itself in the best interests of humanity. This view defies humanity and as a solution has little credibility. Admittedly it may reduce a population problem in a specific area—but so do famine, floods, earthquakes, disease, and other disaster phenomena. Statistically the overall effect is likely to be minuscule.

For their different reasons these various groups believe that there is no choice, either because an alternative to counterviolence does not exist or because the alternative alone cannot provide the answer. It is easier to challenge the first of these two beliefs, for there is already a growing division of opinion as to the efficacy of counterviolence. This division exists not only between states but also within states and regional organizations, with moderating voices becoming more numerous, and responsible leaders placing greater emphasis on peaceful rather than violent settlement of disputes—at least as a first resort. Those who dismiss the peaceful alternative as having no credibility believe that sooner or later, whatever its mandate, a military peacekeeping force will become an enforcement agent, either because its peaceful methods fail or, more likely, because it will become committed to maintaining law and order. This opinion stems largely from the many examples from colonial history where the administering power has employed armed force in internal security situations as a means of maintaining law and order. In this capacity any intervention will be in support of the local law-and-order authorities and will quickly assume a partial image. Once this happens, the interveners are aligned on one side in the dispute and can no longer exercise with credibility their third-party role. They therefore become the target for violent attack and are quickly forced onto the offensive.

This kind of law enforcement action, however necessary it may be, inevitably suffers in time from a physical and moral handicap. The UN or international peacekeeping intervention has a far better chance of maintaining its impartial image because of its terms of reference— avoiding direct involvement in the issues at stake and barring the use of forceful methods to impose solutions or decisions on any of the parties to the dispute. Were it to default in either way, the intervention most certainly would lose its credibility. This then is the difference in technique between peaceful intervention and enforcement, and it is no wonder that there are those, particularly soldiers, who are skeptical of the virtues and values of nonviolent action in the context of military operations, and who have never considered peaceful peacekeeping as a realistic and viable alternative. Armies are recruited and trained to fight. The threat to national security and peace is the motivation behind all national defense policies; and the danger of armed-force confrontation in Europe, with its nuclear configuration, understandably assumes in international politics a primacy and priority far removed from the substance of small wars and intercommunal conflicts. It would, however, be unrealistic in today's political climate not to recognize that there are dangers other than the East-West confrontation in Europe and that the development of alternative treatments at all levels of conflict could provide defense safeguards against unwitting and dangerous escalation.

All wars are important and potentially dangerous to mankind, needing careful and appropriate treatment. Conflict treatment might be said to have become a science. The philosophy behind the technique of peacekeeping and the correct psychological approach and attitude of those involved in practicing the technique are all important. Whereas the major confrontations are conflicts between armed forces, at the other end of the scale it is more a matter of conflicts between people, where the wrong judgment in deciding upon the treatment to be used could bring about the directly opposite effect to that which was intended and an escalation of the conflict to a point where it threatened international peace.

So far we have been concerned only with those who argue the case for enforcement; but one should not ignore those who are critical of peacekeeping operations in any form, whether enforced or peaceful, because they see them as being wholly counterproductive—as simply preserving the status quo and failing to solve any of the problems. The theoretician, studying the whole framework of conflict, is primarily concerned with its structure and the underlying causes of violence from which manifest violence emerges. He sees physical violence as the visible expression of the root problem and the natural and rightful outcome, which he considers should not be suppressed by any means, however peaceful or impartial, but rather should be encouraged. As the Irish say, "A kettle that boils over often cleans the hearth." The theoretician's view is that only through free expression can come the social and economic changes that resolve or at least ameliorate the basic conflict problem. In his opinion the control of violence simply prolongs the conflict and delays its resolution, merely anesthetizing the wound but doing nothing to cure the festering sore. He does not see conflict being resolved without bloodshed, recognizing it to be inevitable, however regrettable, that many people must die before the needed change can be achieved.

It is important to recognize the depth of the division of opinion between the practitioner and the theoretician on this point. It is also important to be wholly aware of the reality of what the theoretician is saying. Peacekeeping by itself inevitably tends to prolong rather than to resolve conflict. By the very nature of its purpose peacekeeping contains and constrains violence; it has no other function. It aims to induce an atmosphere of calm in which a peaceful settlement can be negotiated. Already in this chapter the point has been made that peacekeeping represents a valuable agency for peace and need not necessarily hinder the development of social change—providing that it is used not in isolation but in support of and in interrelation to those other agencies of peacemaking and peace building. The later pages of this book will show that the role of the peacekeeping agency overlaps in many respects with those of the other two. One can therefore answer the theoretician fairly by admitting to the inherent dangers of peacekeeping and recognizing the need to be fully aware of them, but at the same time making the point that, properly used and developed in conjunction with other agencies in the field of conflict resolution, peacekeeping need not have a stultifying and counterproductive effect but can play an important role in the peaceful settlement of disputes.

Theory and practice are not irreconcilable; they are important to each other because together and only together can constructive progress be made in the research and development necessary to the requirements of conflict resolution. A lack of communication in this sector of international study could affect the degree to which the objectives of international control of violence can be achieved. The practitioner's experience is important to the development of new theoretical concepts for conflict resolution. Equally, there has to be a theoretical framework for the practitioner to work within; unless he understands what lies at the root of the conflict in which he is involved, he will not correctly adjust his attitude, approach, and actions to the problems that arise to confront him. Whatever either may be inclined to assert, both the practitioner and the theoretician are dependent upon each other. Their roles are complementary and as such could be damagingly unproductive if separated into watertight compartments; only by developing together can they pursue a continuing, productive, and progressive effectiveness—an ever forward movement in the development of skills and techniques. Theory and research alone are incomplete without practical application. A thesis or a report will not of itself produce the remedy—the draughtsman only outlines the design, it needs the man or woman at the workbench to bring it to life.

It would be unrealistic not to accept that skepticism and prejudice exist in the minds of those who find it hard to believe that peaceful peacekeeping is a role for the military to fulfill, and that it represents a counterproductive approach to the settlement of disputes. On the one hand, there is doubt that it can effectively control violence; and on the other, there is a real conviction that far from helping to end conflict, the actions of peacekeeping forces only prolong it and preserve its causes. Too often these doubts and criticisms have been encouraged by weaknesses and deficiencies in the operational handling of peacekeeping forces, but even more so, through a basic misunderstanding and misconception of the nature and extent of the role that they are called upon to perform. It is a sad fact that far too many people all too quickly dismiss this concept of peacekeeping as ineffectual and unsuccessful. Yet if one makes a careful assessment of the contribution that this kind of peacekeeping has made to the maintenance of world peace over the last quarter century, it becomes clear that this contribution can be evaluated in degrees of success—not in terms of failure. It is therefore unjustifiable that this remarkable and sustained effort of peaceful intervention should be held in such little regard by such a large percentage of public opinion throughout the world. Despite its record of quieting explosive situations, reducing armed confrontation, dissipating tension, cooling tempers, and providing a degree of military as well as economic and social stability in conflict areas, people are still only too ready to disregard its virtues and to emphasize its weaknesses, ignoring the need to investigate all possible avenues for effective conflict control and resolution. The machinery for conducting international peacekeeping operations is not as efficient and effective as it could be; in fact, it is remarkable in the given circumstances that it works at all. What is certain though is that it is not an instrument that should be summarily discarded, but warrants a closer understanding of its workings and its potentialities and a more generous attitude toward its failings. Perhaps then the looked for improvements will materialize.

Our purpose in this chapter has been to show that a peaceful approach to the control of violence is both practical and productive and deserves every bit as much consideration as other more forceful means. In fact we have pointed the finger firmly at the need to develop and perfect an alternative means of dealing with violence and conflict in which enforcement plays no part. Many national leaders have declared both inside and outside the United Nations that disputes must be settled by peaceful means and not by armed action. If this is the criterion on which future conflict action will be based, then we must be sure that the machinery devised for peacekeeping is equal to the requirement. Not only, therefore, is it our intention in this book to substantiate the case for a peaceful alternative to enforcement and counterviolence, but also to suggest how the alternative can be developed to provide a more viable and effective instrument for dealing with conflicts of the future.

3

The United Nations Charter and Control of Conflict

On 14 August 1941, when Prime Minister Winston Churchill and President Franklin Roosevelt presented to the world their Atlantic Charter and in it declared that all nations "must come to the abandonment of the use of force," the first positive step was taken toward the establishment of the United Nations. The antecedents that helped to precipitate this reaffirmation of the need for an effective world organization went back to the 1930s when the impotent League of Nations had failed to intervene to stop Mussolini's invasion of Ethiopia and Hitler's take-over of Austria and seizure of Czechoslovakia. World War II materially reemphasized the conviction which was to find expression initially in the Atlantic Charter and thereafter in the signing by twenty-six countries of the Declaration of the United Nations on 1 January 1942 at Washington, D.C., and in the declarations of the Allied heads of state at the Teheran and Moscow conferences in 1943. At Dumbarton Oaks in 1944 the first draft blueprint for the establishment of an international organization was prepared. This was later approved by Roosevelt, Churchill, and Stalin at their Yalta Conference in February of the following year. On 25 April 1945 delegates from fifty countries met at San Francisco and between that date and 26 June 1945 drew up and finally agreed upon the Charter of the United Nations and the Statute of a new International Court of Justice.

The basic objective of the UN Charter, as outlined in the Preamble, is "to save succeeding generations from the scourge of war" and "to establish conditions under which justice and respect for the obligations arising from treaties and other sources of international law can be maintained . . ." The purposes and principles of the United Nations, contained in Article 1 of the Charter, are: "to maintain international peace and security . . . and to bring about by peaceful means, and in conformity with the principles of justice and international law, adjustment or settlement of international disputes or situations which might lead to a breach of the peace.''

Article 2(3) requires ''all States to settle their international disputes by peaceful means,'' while 2(5) makes it obligatory for states to ''refrain in their international relations from threat or use of force against the territorial integrity or political independence of any state.'' While recognizing the sovereign equality of states, the Charter legally strips them of their sovereign prerogative to wage war. However, the Charter does not impair their ''inherent right of individual or collective self-defense'' (Article 51). In fact, this twilight zone between state sovereignty and international obligations has proved to be a constant source of controversy and a major problem in the management of international affairs. There is the common assumption that an international organization should give aid and protection to every nation, but that at the same time it should not in any way inhibit any nation's exercise of sovereign responsibility, however questionable that responsibility may be.

The major architects of the Charter, the five big powers, were the first to take advantage of this contradiction, thereby setting a pattern that has continued to dilute the ability of the United Nations to become an effective world security system. Whenever their interests have been involved, they have acted, using force on occasions, to safeguard these interests. Other nations have followed their example. The inviolability of national sovereign rights has provided the cover for their violations of international laws and of the UN Charter, including the waging of war, despite the provisions of its Article 2. Though the Charter provides for reviews of its provisions at periodic intervals, no such review has ever taken place. So far there has been no determined consideration of possible variations or improvements in techniques of conflict or violence control [1]—no revision of the Charter nor of the United Nations' institutions as they now stand.

UN membership is regulated through the provisions of Articles 3, 4, and 5. Nations who were not members of the United Nations as original signatories of the Charter require the approval of the General

1. The Uniting for Peace Resolution approved by the General Assembly in 1950 was an attempt which, though implemented, has not been legally ratified as an amendment to the Charter. For its origin and purpose see pp. 29–31.

Assembly upon the recommendations of the Security Council before they can be admitted as members. There have been notable instances where important states have not been elected or considered for election—the two Germanys are a case in point. It was to be expected that Germany, Italy, and Japan would not be admitted, at least in the first instance, since they were the "enemies" of World War II. When the world community was ready to accept them into the United Nations, Italy and Japan were eligible, but since Germany was a divided country of two states, each remaining unrecognized by the other, the question of membership of the Federal Republic of Germany and the Socialist Republic of Germany could only be settled after a relationship between the two had been established and the important question of whether or not they were to remain divided had been decided. There were other equally serious questions to be settled, relating to Berlin, the border between the two states, and particularly that of the frontier with Poland. The gradual thawing of the cold war between East and West, the resultant easing of tensions in Europe, and the bold policies of the federal chancellor, Willy Brandt, led to a détente and resolution of the outstanding problems that Europe had inherited with the end of World War II. Although a number of issues remain unresolved, the essential relationship has been established, and the two Germanys became UN members during the 1973 General Assembly session. It can be expected that eventually North and South Korea will be similarly treated.

In a similar fashion the United Nations denied the People's Republic of China its due representation by continuing to permit Chiang Kai-shek's regime, which controls only the island of Taiwan, to fill China's seat for more than twenty years. By thus excluding the most populous nation in the world, the United Nations denied itself the opportunity to do the very thing that is at the heart of the Charter—"to be a center for harmonizing the actions of the nations." Although many UN members would have preferred the representation of Peking, the United States led the fight to retain Chiang Kai-shek's Kuomintang delegation and keep out the People's Republic of China. The cost of this exclusion to the United States in terms of men and money has been considerable; a candid consideration of past history illustrates this. The United States had a long tradition of trade with China, and during World War II Roosevelt encouraged the impression that Chiang Kai-shek was playing a vital role on the side of the United

States against Japan. What with strong public sentiment and an effective Chiang Kai-shek lobby in Washington, no United States president could afford to take the political risk of recognizing realities. Since the United Nations came into existence, two major wars have been fought in Asia in which both the United States and the People's Republic of China played dominant roles—the Korean and Indochina wars. Had China been a member of the United Nations, there would have been opportunities for contacts, for dialogue, and for the harmonizing of relations with other member states, leading toward a settlement of these disputes, maybe before they had reached the proportions of full-scale war. The consequences of China's absence from the United Nations over all these years, and particularly during these two crisis periods, surely are incalculable.

More recently the Security Council has failed to agree (a People's Republic of China veto) on UN membership for the newly emerged state of Bangladesh on the Indian subcontinent. In terms of population alone this country of 75 million people deserves a place among the UN member states. In contrast, membership has been given to several so-called microstates with minuscule populations whose presence in the world organization cannot influence developments beyond their size and geopolitical position. Election to the United Nations resembles a bargaining game in which the obstructive and destructive influence of big powers can be, and is, employed to deny membership to one state while others with less contribution to make are elected. The relevant difference between Bangladesh and the microstates is that there are conflicting great power interests in Bangladesh. Until these are rationalized, it is likely that Bangladesh will continue to be denied UN membership, whereas other lesser states will be more fortunate on the grounds that they have contributed to the global strategic strength of the great powers by providing them with valuable "facilities." The denial of membership to Bangladesh simply further delays the United Nations in its aim of becoming a truly representative world forum where relations among nations can be harmonized.

Any idealism that war might generate in terms of finding an alternative to man killing man does not last for long—even the catastrophe of World War II was no exception. Nations, their leaders, and their people soon return to normal patterns of human and social behavior—often laying the foundations for new conflicts that develop into new wars. In cases of the mass violation of human rights, governments have appeared heartless, even when their people have shown concern, and have refused to act either because their interests have been involved with those perpetrating the violence or because their interests are not involved and they see no reason to intervene. The divergence of views among governments in regard to matters affecting sovereignty and their efforts to protect or advance their interests has meant a weakening of the United Nations' influence and of its ability to settle disputes. Not surprisingly therefore, nations, big and small, often disregard the Charter and engage in war as a means of achieving their ends—looking upon the United Nations as nothing more than another channel for diplomacy available to them were they to choose to use it. Cynically, it might be said that the act of aggression has on occasion been committed as a step toward involving the United Nations in diplomatic action. Nations have been known to attack their enemies, counting on the fact that the UN Security Council would act to stop the war, thus conceding to the aggressor nation territorial and perhaps economic advantage.[2] Member states, when wishing to pursue their own interests, turn a blind eye to the Charter, though they express themselves as its strong supporters when its advocacy is to their gain or advantage.[3] Even when member states, particularly the major powers, decide to support the United Nations' capability to resolve conflicts, they provide that support in varying degrees, ranging from abstention to full support. The degree of support may change after a peacemaking or peacekeeping effort is authorized, thereby placing political, financial, and administrative restrictions on its implementation. By disregarding the Charter and using it only when and to the extent that it suits their purpose to do so, member states at the same time misuse the machinery that is available for the peaceful resolution of conflicts.

On some major issues the United Nations has declined to act because the permanent members have refused to take action or have threatened to veto if the case were brought to the Security Council. Although the Security Council was already engaged in considering the Syrian complaint of a threat of invasion by Israel in April and May 1967, the Council did not agree to consider U Thant's reports with regard to the withdrawal of UNEF. Similarly, when the secretary-

2. Israel in 1956 and 1967.
3. United States in Santo Domingo, 1965; India and Pakistan, 1948, 1965, 1971; United Kingdom and France, 1956; etc.

general informed the president of the Security Council of the high incidence of violations of human rights in East Pakistan and the imminent threat of war on the Indian subcontinent,[4] the Council,
hamstrung by threats of veto, would not meet to consider this issue.
Thus, often the members and particularly the big powers themselves
refuse to act and therefore fail to use the UN institutions to keep and
make peace.

The Security Council is empowered with the primary responsibility
for maintaining international peace and security. The Charter grants it
specific powers under Chapters VI and VII for settlement of international disputes. The General Assembly has no such authority or responsibility vested in it by the Charter, though by the provisions of
Article 11 it may "discuss any questions relating to the maintenance
of peace and security" and "may make recommendations with regard
to any such questions to the state or states concerned or to the Security Council or to both." However, this mandate is somewhat qualified in Article 12, which makes clear that so long as the Security
Council is exercising its prerogative in any dispute, the General Assembly shall not make any recommendations regarding the settlement
of that dispute except when requested to do so by the Security Council. It does have a limited prerogative under Article 14 to "recommend measures for the peaceful adjustment of any situation . . .
which it deems likely to impair the general welfare and . . . friendly
relations between nations." Different interpretations of these provisions of the Charter and their application to the UN peacekeeping
operations have been a continuing source of controversy and have
been one of the main causes of the financial difficulties that have
plagued UN peacekeeping operations.

By virtue of its primary responsibility, the Security Council can investigate any dispute or situation that might threaten international
peace and security and may recommend means of settlement. The
Council is authorized by the Charter to take any appropriate action
necessary to "give effect to its decisions" (Article 41). If through
peaceful methods it fails in its purpose, then the Security Council is
empowered to take enforcement action as a collective security measure to secure international peace (Article 42). To support the capability of the United Nations to implement any enforcement action au-

4. Secretary-General's Memorandum to the Security Council, 20 July 1971.

thorized by the Security Council, detailed provision was made in the Charter. This includes the requirement that member states provide armed forces and other military assistance and facilities for use by the United Nations (Article 43), but this provision has never been effectively activated. Some member states have made voluntary offers of forces and material assistance, but these have not been pursuant upon Article 43. There has been no earmarking of forces or facilities under the provisions of the article, and it has remained moribund. It is important and relevant to the future of peacekeeping to consider why the requirements of the Charter in respect to the provision of peacekeeping forces for international collective security have been ignored.

Article 43   Article 43 specifically calls for the earmarking of armed forces for use at the direction of the Security Council as the latter may deem necessary for the maintenance of international peace and security. It requires that agreements "shall be concluded between the Security Council and groups of Members," and that such agreements "shall govern the numbers and types of forces, their degree of readiness and general location, and the nature of the facilities and assistance to be provided." By the very nature of such formal agreements a special relationship is created between all member states and a single organ of the United Nations—the Security Council. In these unique circumstances provided by the provisions of Article 43, the Security Council would have the right by solemn treaty to exercise its authority over the deployment and operational responsibilities of the armed forces of those sovereign states who agreed to earmark forces. It is not therefore surprising that member states have been reluctant to implement Article 43, although acceptance of the Charter does carry with it a responsibility toward its provisions. It is, however, worth considering that were member states to enter into such solemn treaties as are required by Article 43, this might favorably affect agreements and undertakings in other fields—including even the most complex issue of all, finance.

When the Charter was drafted, the articles relating to the maintenance of international peace and security were directed primarily at preventing German and Japanese militarism from ever again holding the world to ransom. This motivation no longer exists, and since it is recognized that none of the big powers could be militarily contained in such a way as prescribed in Article 43, no great incentive exists for the smaller member states, on whose shoulders for obvious political reasons the burden of peacekeeping operations will inevitably fall, to bind themselves by treaty to the authority of the Security Council— and of the big powers. They have, however, accepted the onus of the peacekeeping role, and many member states have made forces and facilities available to the United Nations on a voluntary basis, thereby broadening the potential resources from which the United Nations can draw; but the basic problems remain unresolved and have tended to hamper the effectiveness of the peacekeeping machine. The nonactivation of Article 43 alone has seriously affected the operational flexibility of the United Nations and has necessitated successive UN operations being mounted on an ad hoc basis.

In an effort to overcome the Article 43 deadlock and problems related to the machinery of international peacekeeping, a number of initiatives have been taken both inside and outside the United Nations in the past two decades. Trygve Lie when secretary-general sought to obtain the approval of the Security Council for the formation of a UN Guard, while Dag Hammarskjöld's goal was to develop a concept of peacekeeping using the experience of the 1956 UNEF in the Middle East on which to build; neither received much encouragement. The General Assembly, as part of its Uniting for Peace Resolution, set up the Collective Measures Committee in an attempt to create a collective security system for peacekeeping. Its purpose was to report back to the Assembly on the methods that might be used collectively to maintain peace. The committee is still in existence but has been no more fruitful than the Special Committee on Peacekeeping Operations,[5] which was established in 1965 by the General Assembly during its Nineteenth Session in the wake of the Article 19 crisis over the nonpayment of dues by member states. It was directed to resolve all outstanding questions concerning the authorization, financing, and conduct of peacekeeping missions. Outside the United Nations, some countries have taken unilateral action to increase their ability in peacekeeping, while the Nordic countries have taken both unilateral and collective initiatives for the same purpose.

There is a possibility that as a result of current thinking and position changing on the part of the superpowers, the relevance of Article

5. Committee of Thirty-three. See p. 35.

43 might assume a new prominence. At the Twenty-fifth Anniversary Session of the General Assembly in 1970 a resolution calling for the strengthening of international security revived the idea of Article 43. The article contains the only obligation for a member state to participate in any way in the military actions of the United Nations, and thereby defines a nation's liability in so far as military action is concerned. The fact that Article 43 was singled out for special consideration in the 1970 resolution is considered significant because it is this article that provides the United Nations with the instrument whereby it can use force under Article 42.

As long as the UN system is made up of sovereign states, it cannot operate without consent; yet this should not necessarily mean that consent need be sought and given at every stage of each operation. In effect, a semipower of veto does exist in that member states, despite their agreements with the Security Council as provided for in Article 43, can always withhold their forces if they are opposed to the operation to which they are called upon to contribute. Essentially, the dual requirement to respect the sovereignty of member states and to implement the principles and purposes of the UN Charter remains the basic issue. Some provision is made in the Charter to cover this requirement. Article 44 permits non–Council members contributing under Article 43 to participate in Council decisions on the employment of their contingents.

It is generally accepted that it would be difficult for the United Nations to make contingency plans, even though such planning is usually a standard procedure for any organization that could be involved in military operations. At the same time it is inconceivable that a government would allow its forces to be used for an operation that it opposes; although it is conceivable that it could forgo its right of refusal were the purpose and force requirement of the operation to be limited. The questions relating to command and control of the forces provided naturally constitute a major issue in this context; one which has yet to be decided.

Article 43 was never intended to create levels of membership between those governments that have qualified themselves for participation and those that have not. It is essential that the United Nations be free to call upon other governments which, though not committed under Article 43, nonetheless are prepared to participate in one way or another. A rationalization of Article 43 is therefore desirable if any improvement, however short-term in concept, is to be made in the implementation of the Charter structure for peacekeeping. Putting pressure on member states, big or small, to activate Article 43 by entering into blanket agreements is unlikely to serve any useful purpose; rather an attempt should be made to change the focus from "what" to "how." Since there is no power in the Charter under which the Security Council can force a settlement, settlements have to be made by the parties to the dispute. Any enforcement action that is taken is directed at maintaining the peace, rather than at effecting a settlement; and the emphasis is naturally on *what* manpower and material requirements are needed for the achievement of this purpose. Article 43 and its implications are therefore usually discussed in the strict context of such requirements, whereas a more constructive purpose for these discussions, inside the diplomatic forum, would be to create assurances and guidelines on *how* the manpower and materials provided would be used. The detail of operational rosters and planning and the organizational charting of manpower and materials required would then become subsidiary to the main issue of application. To obtain this shift in emphasis will require an expression of willingness, at least on the part of some countries, to sign Article 43-type arrangements. Article 43 agreements between member states and the Security Council, if realistically worded and constituted, could provide a workable basis on which member states could make their commitments to future peacekeeping.

It is doubtful whether Article 43 was really meant to have teeth. It is also questionable whether this collective security system was ever intended to apply to the five permanent members of the Security Council. At least in the transitional period during the first years of the United Nations and before Article 43 could be fully implemented, the "Big Five" were empowered under Article 106, in consultation with one another and as occasion required with other UN members, to take such joint action as might be necessary to maintain international peace and security. What is certain is that the grant of the veto power to them was tantamount to ensuring that the collective security system could never be used against any of them. In purely specific terms the collective security system has operated only once, and that was during the Korean War in 1950. This single instance was made possible by the Russian representative walking out of the Council in January 1950 in protest against the seating, as president in rotation, of the Kuomintang Chinese representative, whose eligibility the USSR did not recognize.

Uniting for
Peace Resolution

The United States' vigorous opposition to permitting the People's Republic of China's representative to attend the discussions on the Korean crisis had been a contributing factor in the Soviet attitude in the Security Council at this time. The validity of the Council's decision to authorize the UN operation in Korea, reached only because of the absence of USSR from the Council, has since been seriously questioned. It became clear that once the Soviet delegation reseated itself it would veto any decision related to the Korean operation so that it could not proceed. In order to circumvent that obstacle, the United States took the matter to the General Assembly, which prima facie was contrary to Article 12 of the Charter. Recognizing that the Security Council lacked the necessary unanimity to fulfill its responsibilities as required by the Charter, the General Assembly drew up and approved the Uniting for Peace Resolution,[6] which permitted it to take whatever action it felt was necessary for the maintenance of international peace and security. In so far as Korea was concerned, the immediate effect was to sanction the continuance of the UN operation.

This controversial initiative by the Assembly has had a far-reaching impact, for better or for worse, on the working system of the United Nations. While reaffirming the importance of the Security Council's primary responsibility for the maintenance of international peace and security, the resolution pointed out that "failure of the Security Council to discharge its responsibilities . . . does not relieve Member States of their obligation or the United Nations of its responsibility under the Charter." It was therefore resolved that "if the Security Council, because of lack of unanimity of the permanent members, fails to exercise its primary responsibility for the maintenance of international peace and security in any case where there appears to be a threat to the peace, breach of the peace, or acts of aggression, the General Assembly shall consider the matter immediately with a view to making appropriate recommendations to the Members for collective measures." The Soviet Union and other socialist countries

6. United Nations General Assembly Resolution 377(V), 3 November 1950.

challenged the validity of the resolution, pointing to the "primary responsibility" assigned to the Security Council in Article 24 of the
Charter and to the explicit limitations placed on the General Assembly on such matters in the terms of Article 12. The supporters of the
resolution, led by the United States, on the other hand, argued that
the General Assembly could take action under "residuary powers"
when the Security Council becomes ineffective or veto-bound.

Korea became a turning point for the United Nations, from which
it developed in a direction quite different from that which was envisaged in the Charter. In this first major challenge to the Security
Council—the North Korean invasion across the thirty-eighth
parallel—the lack of unanimity among Council members led the
United States to take advantage of the absence of the Soviet representative and obtain approval for UN enforcement measures as specifically provided for by the Charter. When the Russian representative
returned to the Security Council to denounce this action, it was already too late to stop the operation, though the USSR had the power to
negate any continuing action. In realization of this, the United States
persuaded the General Assembly to act. There is some irony in the
fact that despite the USSR's consistent challenge to the Assembly's authority to act in the event of a veto or threatened veto in the Security
Council, it has itself on one occasion requested the General Assembly to meet under the Uniting for Peace Resolution; that was after the
conclusion of the Middle East Six-Day War in June 1967. In addition, the initiative of the delegate of another communist state, Yugoslavia, under the same resolution brought the issue of the Suez invasion by the Anglo-French forces before a special emergency
session of the Assembly in 1956, when the Security Council was
blocked by the vetoes of Britain and France and unable to deal with
the crisis. Other occasions when the Uniting for Peace Resolution has
been activated were the Hungarian crisis of 1956, that between Jordan and Lebanon in 1958, and the Congo crisis in 1960. Uniting for
Peace remains a clear affirmation of the world community, represented in the General Assembly, that it will act when there is a stalemate in the Security Council, despite the dictates of Article 12 of the
Charter, which are provided for in the wording of the General Assembly resolution. This is one of the anomalies that exist between the
authoritative provisions of the Charter and the hard facts of political
reality as they have developed since the Charter was written. One

might argue that this affirmation of intent by the world community within the United Nations is more important and should be more telling than the authoritarian responsibilities vested in the neofeudal persons of the big powers.

Collective Security and the Veto It would appear that on the basis of past experience a fairly clear distinction has emerged between the "enforcement action" provided for in Chapter VII of the Charter and the type of peacekeeping operations that followed the Korean War and that pertain more closely to the purposes and spirit of the Charter. Enforcement action has been superseded by two distinct categories of peacekeeping operations: (1) peace observation groups, such as those deployed in Greece (1947), Palestine (1948), Indonesia (1948), Kashmir (1949), and Lebanon (1958); and (2) the force level peacekeeping operations of the Middle East (1956 and 1973), the Congo (1960), and Cyprus (1964).

The experience of the last three decades of UN operations also indicates that the collective security scheme, based on the assumption that the big powers, acting in unison, would deal with any threat to peace and security regardless of its source, has not stood the test of time. Though the major burden for its failure has been placed on the existence of veto power (most frequently used by the Soviet Union), the problem is much more complex. In fact, no country and much less any superpower, could agree to an enforcement action that might directly or indirectly jeopardize its own national interest.

The big powers' unanimity rule was provided because it was hoped that they would act in unison against an enemy of peace and thus their common enemy. An agreement among the veto powers would preclude counteractions and in fact would guarantee their support, thereby preventing international fiascos. The United Nations, as a world body without the support of the big powers or even of only one, could lack the resources to implement its resolutions. Certainly, force level operations could not have been accomplished without assistance from the big powers. Above all, it is only the will of the big powers, with their ability to exercise political, economic, and military influence, that can make the United Nations an effective instrument of peace.

The Charter envisaged the use of conventional military methods—

the waging of war by the United Nations to counter aggression—but apart from Korea, its members have not authorized any enforcement actions. Peacekeeping operations, developed since Korea, cannot be confused with action under Chapter VII of the Charter. The interventions have been peaceful, and the forces involved have operated with the consent or at the request of the parties directly involved.

In the existing international power configuration, enforcement action appears to be inconceivable. The quarter century after World War II has been an unending scenario of local and civil wars. The role of the United Nations has, therefore, been one of low-profile action. At the same time, the Charter system has exhibited some flexibility. In place of the intended collective security system we have witnessed increasing peacekeeping operations in action, varied in context and in degrees of objective and mounted in certain instances under regional arrangements. The termination of the Vietnam War has inevitably led to another venture in international peacekeeping operations—one of more challenging dimensions. The International Commission for Control and Supervision is a multinational ad hoc truce observation and supervisory operation with no enforcement authority. It was mounted independently of the United Nations, by agreement between the United States and the governments of North and South Vietnam, and therefore does not draw its authority from the United Nations. The collective security system has, for the time being, given way to other forms of peacekeeping, which have in the main been undertaken by the United Nations whose presence in trouble spots has provided a buffer between the hostile parties, prevented or stopped fighting, supervised cease-fire lines, and possibly kept the big powers from getting involved.

As already pointed out, this evolution from peace enforcement to peacekeeping reflects a significant structural and functional transformation within the principal organs of the United Nations; one which has not been acceptable to all member states, with the result that they have defaulted in their financial obligations to subscribe to the costs of peacekeeping operations. So far the controversy remains unresolved, and despite the advisory opinion given by the International Court of Justice there is a shortfall in payments of dues causing considerable financial embarrassment to the world body. The latter, however, has been able to continue its role in the field of peacekeeping, even after the storm that stalemated the General Assembly of 1965 when the United States pressed for and the USSR hotly contested the implementation of Article 19, which deprives a member state of its vote in the General Assembly for two years if it is more than two years in arrears with its dues. Despite these difficulties a new functional relationship seems to be emerging. Even the United States has new thoughts about the United Nations' decision-making process. In the Special Committee on Peacekeeping Operations, the United States has indicated that it increasingly favors authority remaining in the Security Council, where it retains the veto power, rather than in the General Assembly, where its influence is unpredictable. However, having reaffirmed the primary responsibility of the Council, the United States continues to uphold the Assembly's authority to act when the Council is paralyzed and to apportion the costs of peacekeeping operations.

At the signing of the Charter it was not envisaged that the future would bring disagreement rather than unanimity among the veto-holding powers, but this is what has happened. Too often the Security Council has failed to act to prevent war because of disagreement or because it was known that one permanent member or another would use its veto power to render the Council powerless to act. The authority and resources of at least one or more big power are prerequisites to ensure the implementation of UN decisions.

Although the Special Committee on Peacekeeping Operations still has to report its recommendations, it is certain that the political effectiveness and economic feasibility of UN peacekeeping operations always will depend to a large extent upon big power agreement. Even so the Charter as written provides many possibilities for initiating new and innovative peacekeeping initiatives, and these should not be ignored. For though there is little likelihood of the Charter being reviewed, it would seem that underlying all issues a genuine and strong resolve exists among most member states of the United Nations to overcome the enormous difficulties and to realize the long-desired objective of establishing a world security system.

4

The Peacekeeping Organs of
the United Nations—
An Analysis of Their Potential

The United Nations, the latest attempt to build an effective peacekeeping institution, has followed a long and tortuous path, the end of which has not yet been reached. It is relevant therefore to look more specifically at the responsibilities of the primary functional components of the United Nations as created by the Charter and to evaluate their performances in terms of their potential for the future.

Security Council　　　　　　　　After the disappointment with the League of Nations it was hoped that in the United Nations a more durable and effective organization had been constructed. At its focal point is the Security Council. In exact terms the Council's functional mandate is "the primary responsibility for the maintenance of international peace and security." The Charter requires the Council to assume this responsibility on behalf of the members of the United Nations (Article 24 [1]). The Charter is detailed in its instructions to the Security Council including those specific to voting procedures (Article 27). It is from this article that much of the frustration and limitation of the Council's decision making has come. Though in concept an authoritative body, the Security Council has lost much of its credibility through the lack of unison among its five permanent members, who have been more often divided than united in the United Nations' three decades of existence. As noted in chapter 3, the use of the veto on several important occasions has prevented the United Nations from becoming an effective instrument of peace.

The clear inability of the Security Council to fulfill its mandate other than when its five permanent members are in agreement could permanently stultify any positive UN attempt to establish any kind of collective security system or conflict control system in the future. In an endeavor to overcome this impasse, and consequent upon the Article 19 crisis in 1965, the Special Committee on Peacekeeping Operations was established, consisting of thirty-three members including the five permanent members. It started by reviewing Security Council approved observer operations and then went on to deal with the more complex force level operations.

Some relatively minor understandings have been reached, and certain concrete proposals have been and are under consideration, but so far as the major issues are concerned the committee has found it impracticable to deal effectively with them until the superpowers have narrowed those areas of disagreement that need to be resolved before any constructive progress can be made. The committee has therefore put these issues aside for direct consideration by the United States and the Soviet Union. They include the recognition of the Security Council as the authoritative body in respect to peacekeeping operations and the question of command and control of all such operations. It is over the latter issue that there is most divergence between the superpowers, with the Soviet Union insisting upon an operational committee acting under the direction of the Security Council, and the United States firmly adhering to its opinion that the secretary-general, as in the past, should be responsible for the day-to-day conduct of operations. So long as this issue remains open, it will continue to confound the deliberations of the Committee of Thirty-three and hinder progress toward the development of new concepts for improving the machinery of peacekeeping. There are hopeful signs of a new move toward a greater flexibility of approach and attitude on the part of the United States and the USSR.

The entry of the People's Republic of China into the United Nations and its effect on current UN consideration of peacekeeping procedures, previously dominated by the United States and the Soviet Union, introduced a new and vital ingredient of uncertainty and a renewed skepticism about the viability of a concept of peacekeeping that had been gaining strength before China's entry. Yet another consideration is the emergence of new centers of power already evident among states who are not permanent members of the Security Council, but who would almost certainly insist on a voice commensurate with their enhanced status. Japan, with broadening support, is a candidate for a permanent seat on the Security Council. India, with the second largest population in the world and with a new status in the subcontinent, Nigeria and Brazil, respectively the largest states in Africa and Latin America, are among nations under consideration for permanent membership though not necessarily with a veto authority. It is also becoming increasingly self-evident that for the great powers, as for all industrialized states, other priorities will compete for attention with peacekeeping in the future. Domestic concerns are perhaps foremost among these; while internationally, collective security will share center stage with environment management, population and resource control, trade, and other world problems.

At yet another level, there is evidence of even more insistent doubt about the underlying objectives of peacekeeping. Since 1945 the relationship between international violence and political change has become more complex and is less likely to yield a broad international political consensus for peacekeeping. There are those who question whether a status quo should be protected by peacekeepers against destabilizing violence; whether efforts to clamp down on conflicts are presumptively more conducive to justice than indifference would be; whether a concept of peacekeeping that stresses violence reduction over conflict prevention and resolution can long retain the support of large segments of the UN membership; whether peacekeeping as traditionally defined can be allowed to take precedence over the other, perhaps more compelling commitments covered in Article 55—those of economic development, modernization, and the advancement of human rights. UNEF II may provide some of the answers.

These doubts do not seriously challenge the established thesis that points to the continued use of the Security Council as the control system for UN peace maintenance. The generally accepted definition of peacekeeping is compatible with the flexibility of the relevant Charter language. Though the Charter does not use the word *peacekeeping*, the recurring phrase "the maintenance of international peace and security" is broad enough to cover it. Moreover, under Article 42, the Security Council is empowered "to take such action by air, sea, or land forces as may be necessary to maintain or restore international peace and security." This includes what are known today, in law and practice, as peacekeeping operations. Not only is this central role for the Security Council compatible with the intent of the drafters of the Charter, it is likely that the political realities of emerging relations among the permanent members of the Security Council will respond better to it.

Some nations take issue with this emphasis on the exclusive role of the Security Council. They argue that, notwithstanding the fact that the Charter is specific in this respect, the maintenance of peace is not the primary purpose of the world organization; rather, they contend that the Charter was intended as a blueprint for world order and as the framework on which to build "peace in depth." They also insist that the General Assembly cannot be left without any responsibility in regard to peacekeeping. Even though authorization would come from the Council, the Assembly should, within the terms of the Charter, play a backup role in urging member states to help in the whole process of resolving disputes.

The Security Council still lacks a satisfactory set of principles on which it can evolve and effect a sound workable system for crisis control and management. Consequently the Council lacks a comprehensive peace maintenance and peacemaking strategy and an overall set of guidelines that can be tailored and adopted to specific contingencies. In tackling this deficiency the Council must deal with three main issues, all of which will influence the type of response needed for any particular crisis. The first of these requires that short-term norms be set down to meet the immediate emergency, which may be the supervision of a cease-fire, the observing of a withdrawal of armed forces, the investigation of border violations, and so on. Within this same context it would also be necessary to determine the technical short-term arrangements and action necessary for dealing with such matters as the traffic of arms, involvement of mercenaries in a conflict between or within states, and local communications between disputing parties. Second, the Council has to decide how these norms can be made politically and legally binding. Third, and possibly most difficult, the Council must agree on precisely how it will obtain acceptance of the principles and compliance with their implementation, and what action it should take in the face of noncompliance or an ambiguous response from the parties concerned.

The Council must insist on the acceptance by the involved parties of any effort directed at finding longer-term solutions to the root causes of their conflict. Violence control measures must be accompanied by a genuine and wholehearted commitment to conflict resolution. To date the success of peaceful settlement agents operating with peacekeeping missions or forces has been peripheral and undistinguished; perhaps the provisions of Article 33 need to be more readily and energetically applied.[1]

The four big powers, excluding China, appear to have narrowed their differences with regard to developing peacekeeping institutions to a degree where agreement might become possible. The seating of the People's Republic of China in the United Nations has, however, altered the big powers' balance in the Security Council. China has allied itself with the "Third World" nations and is an advocate of change through the use of force where necessary. With new alliances and changing patterns in the world power structure, nations like Japan, the Federal Republic of Germany, India, Nigeria, and Brazil are playing an increasingly large role in world affairs. All these nations would not only like to see a stronger world organization but are committed to it.

Military Staff Committee   Since the creators of the Charter were concerned to ensure that there would be no fresh upsurge of German and Japanese militarism, it is not surprising that they built into the Charter certain provisions to cope with this potential problem. Among these was the establishment of a Military Staff Committee, to be composed of the chiefs of staff of the permanent members of the Security Council or their representatives. Article 47 established the Military Staff Committee for the purpose of advising and assisting "the Security Council on all questions relating to the Security Council's military requirements for the maintenance of international peace and security, the employment and command of forces placed at its disposal, the regulation of armaments and possible disarmament." At first the committee was taken very seriously; the manner of its establishment was a major item on the agenda for the first meeting of the Security Council. At the Twenty-third Session of the Security Council in February 1946, after considering a report from the committee on its Rules of Procedure and its Statute, the Security Council adopted a directive to the committee which read, in part, as follows:

1. Article 33 requires parties to any dispute that is likely to endanger international peace and security to first seek to resolve the dispute by all peaceful means available to them.

"The Council directs the Committee, as its first task, to examine, from the military point of view, provisions contained in Article 43 of the Charter." To facilitate its work the staff of the committee was considerably increased, but nevertheless it worked on the Article 43 study for a year without agreement. In February 1947 the Security Council indicated its impatience and set a deadline for April. The committee met that deadline by submitting an unagreed paper. It was deadlocked on sixteen points, but the main issues centered on the composition of the armed forces' contribution made by the Big Five (which Russia insisted should be exactly matched), and the size of the force that the Security Council would have. All five were in disagreement on this latter point.[2]

From that point on the Military Staff Committee was never again called upon to function as its Charter mandate required it to do. The developing mutual distrust between East and West that built up over the succeeding years, and the meticulous efforts that were made to ensure that neither side obtained a military advantage over the other, negated any real chance of the Military Staff Committee becoming a cohesive strategical component. It was evident that amid the divergence and suspicion of the developing cold war, any collective security concept was beyond reach. The Military Staff Committee became an early victim of the changing political world climate.

This premature setback does not mean that the committee is defunct. It is there to be reactivated to carry out its original function as defined by the Charter. This is not wishful thinking; it is only realistic to accept that any reconstruction of the UN peacekeeping machinery must include the Military Staff Committee in one form or another. Of course there are a number of prejudices and problems to be resolved before the committee could become properly functional once again. Possibly the most fundamental of these prejudices is the mistaken belief that military professionalism in UN peacekeeping is unsatisfactory. It is a prejudice that arises from misplaced interpretations of the role that the military might attempt to play in what, in the United Nations, is generally considered to be a politico-civilian scenario. This prevailing misunderstanding could be dispelled if military professionalism were integrated with the nonmilitary components within the UN framework; the Military Staff Committee could be used to pro-

2. Andrew Boyd, *Fifteen Men on a Powder Keg,* pp. 79–80.

vide that professionalism. The committee should not, however, be incorporated into the chain of operational command; by the nature of its Charter mandate and its structure it is not eminently suitable to take responsibility for operational management of UN peacekeeping forces. So long as the committee stays outside the chain of command and simply functions in its capacity as adviser to the Security Council, the latter as it might deem necessary could direct it to support the secretary-general. If the Charter were redrafted today, the drafters would most probably combine Chapters VI and VII or seek another approach. While elaborate machinery is available for enforcement actions through Article 43-type agreements, no such blueprint exists for the provision of professionally equipped UN fact-finding machinery.

It is generally accepted that peacekeeping cannot be improved in any fundamental way without a political consensus that can be subscribed to by the permanent Council members and by a healthy majority in the General Assembly. Given such a consensus, it is argued that a revived Military Staff Committee, with a sound and integrated international staff, organized and competent as required by the Charter, but also under orders from the Security Council to support the secretary-general in peacekeeping matters, could make a badly needed contribution to planning and preparing for peacekeeping operations, at whatever level of intensity those operations take place, now and in the future. A number of channels of activity spring immediately to mind. The committee could be expected to study different typologies of operations (not contingency planning), so that there would be a better understanding of the kinds of instruments that can be used by the United Nations in the operational field and of what would be necessary in the way of preparation. It could establish training standards as the Nordic countries have successfully done. It could assess, in collaboration with the nations concerned, the operational preparedness of contributing nations based on firsthand studies of those forces or facilities that have been offered under Article 43-type agreements. It could also perform a highly useful advisory role in terms of administration and procurement, particularly by analyzing logistic, supply, transportation, and special equipment requirements.

To assist the Military Staff Committee there needs to be a backup of data information. A method for providing this within the UN framework is suggested in chapter 13. It could be the responsibility of the committee to coordinate the data made available from a documentation of UN conflict control activities and research—concerned with the employment of good offices, mediation, conciliation commissions, and so on.[3]

The committee could be required to prepare the drafts for agreements under Article 43 beginning with observer, fact-finding, and other less spectacular assignments. In so doing it could give guidance to member states who are considering the establishment of systems for earmarking part of their armed forces for UN duty. Besides handling primarily matters of military concern, the committee could have an important supporting role in the coordination of military action and conflict control, through nonmilitary initiatives such as mediation and other efforts aimed at solving basic underlying conflict problems.

No doubt all this will require an organic restructuring of the committee to give it a broader base, so as to allow representation from other member states, particularly some with comprehensive UN peacekeeping experience. A precedent for this already exists in Article 47(2), which allows the committee to invite any non–committee member state to be "associated with it when the efficient discharge of the Committee's responsibilities requires the participation of that Member in its work." It need be only a short step from here to a broader-based committee, and it need not stop there. The Soviet Union in its UN Memorandum of 20 March 1972 advocated the demilitarizing of the Military Staff Committee, which was a considerable shift from its previous position of insisting that the very lightest controls were to be exercised by the committee over operational command and decision making. The United States has also adopted a less rigid posture, and now no longer insists that the secretary-general's military advisory staff should be strengthened. The United States remains, however, strongly opposed to the idea of the Military Staff Committee having any important functions entrusted to it or being given a place in the UN peacekeeping command apparatus. It sees the committee's responsibilities as being purely of an advisory nature to the Security Council.

These modified views of the two superpowers could lead to a removal of those obstacles that have impeded the development of an effective conflict control system for so long. China of course remains the unknown quantity for the present, but the concept of a broader-

---

3. Material has been collected by the secretariat over the last three years to form a historical record of UN peacekeeping, but purely from the standpoint of the secretary-general.

based Military Staff Committee in the full sense of the term—a committee of interprofessional skills and of multinational composition—
could emerge as a result of this position changing. Certainly such
changes could make the committee's contribution to planning and
coordination very real indeed.

Any new role for the Military Staff Committee must inevitably
hinge on the ultimate decision about the role of the secretary-general.
While still firmly of the opinion that the secretary-general should
remain responsible for day-to-day direction of peacekeeping operations, the United States does not place exclusive reliance on his being
the sole operational executive for peacekeeping. It is a little ironic
that the secretary-general has achieved his present peacekeeping responsibilities because of the basic failure of the UN collective security
system to provide an alternative. Peacekeeping experience over the
past three decades has underlined the dominant fact that the Military
Staff Committee has been excluded from any executive or support
role in peacekeeping operations or missions. This further reflects the
failure of the big powers to agree on the committee's role within the
UN system—and makes understandable the prominence that the secretary-general has achieved in the management of those operations
mounted under the mandates of the Security Council or the General
Assembly. U Thant himself, in his final annual report before retiring
from the post of secretary-general, welcomed the move to reexamine
possible roles for the Military Staff Committee in the peacekeeping
context.[4]

It would seem that three principal issues need to be resolved if the
committee is to become an active force. First, the operational authority and latitude of the secretary-general will have to be clearly defined or at the least clarified; second, the principles governing the role
of other international civil servants will have to be spelled out unmis-
takably so far as the execution of peacekeeping mandates are concerned; and third, the difficulties of running peacekeeping operations
by a committee must be universally recognized and analyzed. From a
military point of view one cannot separate the operational direction
from the support organization that is required to coordinate the logistic, administrative, and manpower requirements of the field force. To
do so would be to endanger the whole operation. Whether or not the

4. Secretary-General's Report to the Twenty-sixth Session of the General Assembly,
A/8401/Supp. 1, October 1971.

secretary-general directs the operation, he remains, as head of the secretariat, the essential coordinator of supply and demand and the anchor man between the field force and the Security Council. He must play an important role in the day-to-day operation. It is the settlement of this fundamental question of command and control that is paramount and a prerequisite to the future structuring of UN peacekeeping.

Future Framework   In any event, the Security Council, as the recognized authority, would lay down the basic mandates, and these in turn could be elaborated and converted into operational terms by the Military Staff Committee or some other planning body created for that purpose.[5] Actual execution and implementation could then be carried out by the secretary-general. Alternatively, the Security Council could issue their mandates directly to the force commander appointed by it. The Council in this case presumably would instruct the secretary-general and the secretariat to provide all necessary administrative and secretariat support to the force commander for the performance of his responsibilities. The idea that command responsibilities should rest with the Military Staff Committee should be discarded as being an outdated residue from the committee's original design, based on the Allies' experience of World War II, in which the committee was intended to service the UN's collective security forces which never materialized. In the context of future peacekeeping needs, the Military Staff Committee needs to be coupled with new Security Council arrangements. Under Article 29, one of a group of articles coming under the procedural provisions in the Charter, the Security Council may establish such subsidiary organs as it deems necessary for the performance of its functions. It would be appropriate for the Security Council to set up a committee (a subsidiary organ) composed of the five permanent members and other member states contributing peacekeeping contingents. Because the establishment of subsidiary organs is a procedural matter, it is not subject to the veto. Both the committee and the secretary-general could receive military advice from the Military Staff Committee, which would in turn be expanded to include military officers from states participating

5. See later in this chapter and also chapter 13.

in the peacekeeping operations, who would be co-opted on a rotating basis. This committee of the Council would then, in effect, monitor the actions of the secretary-general who would act as the administrative agent and manager of the peacekeeping operation on behalf of the Security Council.

Whatever new or renovated peacekeeping structures emerge, overall peacekeeping capabilities will not be strengthened unless certain related problems are resolved as well. Foremost among these is the question of financing, which today represents one of the major handicaps to effective UN peacekeeping. With the development of a functional structure such as that suggested here and its acceptance by the majority of members including the superpowers, it could be that much of the reserve and disinclination of the non-paying countries would disappear and they would be willing to pay their dues.

Renewed interest in the peacekeeping potential of the Security Council and the Military Staff Committee has generated the possibility of activating Article 43. It is questionable whether Article 43 as it stands could be acceptable to member states; it needs to be qualified by a more specific description of the undertakings that they would be required to make. The medium- and small-sized states, who can be expected to be the main contributors, must be capable of responding to the varied requirements of peacekeeping. To help them do so would necessitate breaking down the different functional skills of peacekeeping into separate categories such as investigations into alleged aggression and other related fact-finding services; verification and supervision of cease-fire or withdrawal of forces agreements; provision of interposition and intermediary forces; provision of monitoring and supervisory teams to cover plebiscites and other special situations calling for third-party assistance. For each of these categories, specially tailored organizational structures, equipment tables, and standing operating procedures for earmarking and training would need to be prepared, so that the rapid mobilization of the standby resources would be possible in all cases. It is to be hoped that member states would be willing to make advance commitments to serve the United Nations, within all or any of the categories required, always subject to the respective governments' right to ultimate approval for the release of their national contingents for UN duty.

The requirement should not be limited to military forces only. One should remember that civilian police skills can be equally beneficial in appropriate circumstances, ranging from traditional guard and security duties to the more active investigative and violence control services that have already been performed by the UN riot-control police in the Congo and by regular civilian police serving with the operation in Cyprus. Nor should Article 43 be exclusive in its implication. Permanent members of the Security Council should be as much subject to its provisions as any other members. The idea of permanent members being excluded from any renegotiated undertakings under Article 43 should be dropped; instead, they should be required to make whatever commitments are deemed acceptable to host countries, probably in the form of technical and logistical support for the field operations and of initial transportation facilities.

Day-to-day operations will demonstrate, as they have in the past, whether the range of technical and operating problems have been satisfactorily resolved between UN headquarters and the field command and among the several components of the field structure. Understandings need to be developed and, as circumstances change, periodically clarified in regard to the content of the force mandate and its translation into military directives; the handling in the field of information and public relations activities; the extent to which commanders are authorized to use force; the intended duration of the operation; the requirements for experts and professional field staff; the harmonization of diverse needs and perspectives of the multinational contributors to the peacekeeping force; and the vitally important conduct of civil-military relations. It will very much depend upon the future workability of the central organization and of its peacekeeping organs in particular whether the goals that need to be achieved in functional procedures and operational effectiveness can be realized. China is the one great imponderable, and whether there is to be a positive realization of these goals will be largely subject to its performance in the United Nations.

China's attitude so far has been uncompromising. Its participation in deliberations of the Committee of Thirty-three has yet to materialize. China has so far declined to join with the other four big powers in their private meetings to resolve problems related to peace. Its reluctance to do so is understandable, as it has not been at the United Nations very long and is certainly unfamiliar with developments in the field of peacekeeping. China retains its own approach to future structures of the world, which is somewhat different from what the other four powers had more or less agreed upon. There is no doubt that at least for the time being, until China has come to a better understanding with its Security Council colleagues, its entry into the United Nations is likely to inhibit any agreement among them and further delay progress toward establishing a framework for peace-keeping operations that would embrace a practical relevance for Article 43 and the redevelopment of the Military Staff Committee. It is to be hoped that the period of China's adjustment will not last long; for delay can only blunt the progress noticeable in the months before China's arrival in the United Nations. It is, however, proper to point out that although agreement on peacekeeping procedures might have been reached more quickly without China, its significance would have been much reduced. Therefore, in view of the possibility of a continuing deadlock in the Council over the main questions relating to peacekeeping operations, medium and small powers must continue to support pragmatically the development of a world system for the maintenance or restoration of international peace. In a later chapter the idea of specially prepared peace contingents, trained in the skills of mediation, negotiation, and conciliation and in the process of peaceful social change, is discussed. Such contingents would be more broadly based than those of the more traditional peacekeeping forces normally made available to the United Nations. Their inclusion could mitigate the criticism that peacekeeping operations merely freeze a conflict to a point where it becomes unsolvable and is in constant danger of eruption.

It is certain that the permanent members will continue not only to adhere to but to insist upon the Security Council's dominant role in international peacekeeping to the extent that all operations and missions will be under its direct control. We have attempted in the preceding paragraphs to suggest a functional framework on which the Security Council and the United Nations as a whole could better fulfill their peacekeeping role.

5

Case Study 1—Middle East (UNEF 1956)

No analysis of the future of international peacekeeping can ignore the experience and the lessons learned from the past. This then is the moment to consider the specific case studies available to us and to set down the conclusions that can be drawn from them. Future structures and the viability of future operations will depend on realistic factors, not only in terms of political credibility but also in the practical character of their application. Since this book is concerned with the peaceful settlement of disputes, the case studies we use are those involving peaceful intervention. We analyze in detail the three force level operations in the Middle East, the Congo, and Cyprus and the contribution made by the observer and supervisory missions of the United Nations, as well as those mounted under regional and multinational (non-UN) arrangements.[1]

The following six chapters are therefore concerned with these case studies. Since each of the three force level operations was so different from the others, a separate chapter is devoted to each. As there has been a fundamental common denominator to all of the UN observer and supervisory missions, it is possible to consider them as an entity under one heading; the regional and multinational operations are treated in the same way. Our object is to summarize the causes of the conflicts, explain the nature and effect of the UN intervention, and point out those factors that have a particular and important relevance to the future. No specific attempt has been made in individual chapters to interrelate the operations one to another, though in some instances comparisons are remarked upon, for it is considered that the comments and conclusions on each operation stand on their own and

---

1. The UNEF operation of October 1973 constitutes part III of this book.

can be measured in terms of their application to the development of the techniques and character of international conflict control which forms the subject of later chapters.

No one who has carefully studied the performance of these international peacekeeping forces in a role closely dictated and controlled by the mandate that they have been given by the Security Council or General Assembly can lightly dismiss the contribution that any of them has made to the control of violence. They have all been successful, though to varying degrees. The fact that these successes were not fully exploited through political initiatives does not diminish their importance or credibility. In any future system for the treatment and control of conflict this deficiency of the past has to be corrected so that no agency for peace is allowed to operate in a vacuum.

The United Nations Emergency Force (UNEF) for the Middle East was established by a resolution of the United Nations General Assembly on 6 November 1956. Its initial function was "to enter into Egyptian territory with the consent of the Egyptian Government in order to maintain quiet during and after the withdrawal of foreign troops" [2]— the foreign troops were the British, French, and Israelis. The events that led to the armed action against Egypt by Israel, and subsequently by Britain and France, can be traced to the "Palestine problem" and the nationalization of the Suez Canal by Egypt. These background events are important to an understanding of the causes of the aggression against Egypt in 1956, and a brief summary of those causes is a necessary preface to what followed.

The Palestine problem had its seeds in the mandate exercised by Britain between 1920 and 1948, which included provision for the establishment in Palestine of a national home for the Jews, without prejudicing the legal rights of the existing inhabitants, an undertaking echoing the firm pledge contained in the Balfour Declaration of 1917. Despite this, Britain's White Paper on Palestine in 1939 strictly controlled the immigration of Jews into Palestine, at a time when many thousands of them were attempting to escape from Nazi Germany. When World War II came to an end, and with it a widespread movement to bring about a large-scale immigration of displaced Jews into

2. UN Document A/3296, Report of Secretary-General submitted to and adopted by the General Assembly on 2 November 1956 in pursuance of General Assembly Resolution 997(ES-1), paragraph 5.

Palestine, the pressure from Zionists everywhere for the establishment of a Jewish state in Palestine became insistent. Arab aspirations were opposed to the formation of such a state, but the Jews were determined to see it happen. Inevitably violence flared both between Jew and Arab and between the Jewish underground fighters and the British. Intense diplomatic and political endeavor failed to provide any solution, and in April 1947 Britain took the issue to the United Nations. The move resulted in the establishment of a Special Committee on Palestine (UNSCOP), but no great advance toward a settlement of the dispute was made, due to the considerable divisions of opinion both among the committee members and among the Palestinean people themselves. Britain, prepared to wait no longer, declared that it would end its mandate on 15 May 1949. When the moment arrived for Britain to fulfill its intention, the state of Israel was proclaimed, followed almost immediately by the outbreak of hostilities along the whole of its newly defined boundaries with its Arab neighbors. After many vicissitudes, including the breakdown of two truce agreements arranged and supervised by the United Nations and the assassination of UN Mediator Count Bernadotte by an activist Jewish group, Ralph Bunche of the United Nations, who had succeeded Bernadotte, finally managed in 1949 to arrange a series of armistice agreements acceptable to Israel and each of the Arab states involved. These armistice lines now became the frontiers of the new state of Israel and not surprisingly caused a massive exodus of Arab refugees (800,000) from Israel into the adjoining Arab states and the Gaza Strip.

During 1955 and 1956 hostility between Israel and Egypt steadily increased. The *fedayeen* (Arab ''commandos'') based in the Gaza Strip carried out intensified raids into Israel, and there were many violations of armistice lines elsewhere, though not of the same magnitude. These raids and increased political tension, aggravated by the possibility of a military alliance between Jordan, Egypt, and Syria, constituted in Israel's view a direct threat to its security and occasioned the inevitable result. On 29 October 1956 Israel invaded the Sinai.

But the Israeli-Arab confrontation was not the only dispute that had been raising political sandstorms at this time. While Gamal Abdel Nasser firmly established his leadership in Egypt and the Arab world, Britain took the first step toward establishing a politico-military alliance, later to become known as the Central Treaty Organization (CENTO), to protect its interests in the Middle East and to ensure its retention of control over the Suez Canal. By 1954 Britain had agreed with Egypt to withdraw its troops from the canal zone on condition that the storage depots and other facilities there would remain available to the West in the event of major crises. The United States, taking advantage of this withdrawal, stepped in and increased its aid to Egypt; however, with the establishment of the Baghdad Pact and the signing of bilateral treaties between the United States and Iran, Iraq, and Turkey, the United States' policy changed, and Egypt was the one that suffered. It is not surprising that this reversal of policy rankled with Nasser, who saw in the new treaties an anti-Egyptian rather than an anti-Soviet alliance.[3] The changed policy of the United States also meant a reduction in arms supplies for Egypt.

The arms situation became worse when on 28 February 1955 the Israelis carried out a major raid into the Gaza Strip as a reprisal to the increasing terrorist acts by Egyptian-trained fedayeen based there. This visible demonstration of Israel's arms superiority increased the pressure on Egypt to obtain more arms. Britain and France were reluctant to supply Nasser with arms; France especially was concerned at Egypt's support for the Algerian rebels. Since Egypt could not expect supplies from Britain and France, it turned to Czechoslovakia and successfully negotiated for a large shipment of modern tanks, jet fighters, and bombers. This profitable maneuver upset the Arab-Israeli military balance and certainly constituted a major diplomatic coup by the Soviet Union.

It was in this climate that the United States on 19 July 1956 cancelled the loan to Egypt that it had promised for the building of the Aswan Dam; the net result was that Nasser announced the nationalization of the Suez Canal seven days later so that he could use the dues accruing from user nation's payments to raise the necessary funds for the construction of the dam. This reaction by Nasser was a direct threat to the West and could not be expected to go unheeded. The great importance of the Suez Canal to Europe, especially to Britain and France, and the arbitrary fashion in which this international waterway had been nationalized, threatened the main trade route to the East. Britain and France, being the most concerned, reacted

3. Higgins, *United Nations Peacekeeping; 1946–67*, vol. 1, *The Middle East*, p. 222.

strongly. In late September and in October a series of meetings, some in secrecy, took place in Paris at prime minister and foreign minister level. To at least one of these meetings came the Israeli army chief of staff and a senior official of the Ministry of Defense. One outcome of these meetings was that Britain and France sent elements of their armed forces to Cyprus and to Malta. There seems little doubt now that Britain and France collaborated with Israel in planning the coming battle and that there was collusion from the start not to press for a settlement through the United Nations. On 29 October 1956 Israel invaded the Sinai, and in four days its advance reached to within fifteen miles of the canal. Israel also occupied Sharm el Sheikh, which gave it control of the Straits of Tiran at the narrow entrance to the Gulf of Aqaba.

Meanwhile, as part of the political charade, Britain and France issued an ultimatum on 30 October calling upon both Israel and Egypt to cease fighting and to withdraw their armies ten miles from either bank of the canal. In the case of Egypt the ultimatum had an added request that it allow a combined Anglo-French force to be stationed temporarily at the canal to separate the belligerents and ensure the safety of canal shipping. Since the Israeli forces were still more than ten miles from the canal and the Anglo-French move had been prearranged, Israel's acceptance of the ultimatum was a matter of course, but Egypt's anticipated refusal opened the way to the Anglo-French offensive, which began on the night of 31 October with air attacks against Egyptian air bases followed by air and seaborne landings at Port Said.

Since Britain and France vetoed any move to bring a halt to the fighting, the Security Council was in deadlock. Sensing that no action could be expected from that body, the General Assembly, acting under its own Uniting for Peace Resolution, initiated and approved on 2 November resolutions calling for an immediate cease-fire and the withdrawal of all forces behind armistice lines,[4] and for the secretary-general to submit plans for the setting up of an international peacekeeping force.[5] Israel, having achieved its prescribed objectives of destroying the fedayeen bases in the Gaza Strip and securing Sharm el Sheikh at the entrance of the Gulf of Aqaba, was willing to accept a cease-fire. But the Anglo-French offensive had not secured

4. General Assembly Resolution 997(ES-1), 2 November 1956.
5. General Assembly Resolution 998(ES-1), 2 November 1956.

the desired control over the canal, still less had Nasser been deposed, so neither Britain nor France showed any enthusiasm to bring the fight to an end. However, on 7 November, with the understanding that an effective international force would be provided in the area, they indicated that they would accept a UN intervention. By this time their combined forces had reached a point just north of Qantara on the Suez Canal.

The eventual shape of the UN Emergency Force turned out to be somewhat different from what had been originally proposed. Egypt, the host country, was permitted the discretion of saying which member states would be acceptable as contingent contributors to UNEF. Naturally this limited the number of nations, both medium and small, from which the force could be formed. Early on it was agreed that it would be undesirable for the permanent members of the Security Council to be among the contributors. In any event Britain and France were clearly unacceptable. The outline organization finally agreed upon for UNEF was a headquarters to which would be attached eight units of battalion size. These units would be administered by the UNEF headquarters. Since only Canada and India could offer administrative and technical troops, it was decided that it would be more useful if Canada contributed the bulk of them. India also agreed to supply certain elements of the service corps, ordnance, provost, and signal personnel; while Norway offered to supply a medical company to organize a hospital. Egypt's agreement to Canada's participation was by no means unqualified. At first an infantry regiment was to be included in Canada's contingent. The regiment chosen was the Queen's Own Rifles of Canada. This apparently close allegiance to the Queen of England, implicit in the regiment's title and the fact that the Canadian army wore the same uniform as the British, made Canada's credentials at first unacceptable to Egypt. It was only at the insistence of Denmark, which indicated that it would not participate if Canada were not included in the force, that Egypt eventually agreed to Canada's participation in a support role.

On 12 November 1956 the designated force commander, General Burns of Canada, then chief of staff of UNTSO, arrived in Cairo from Jerusalem accompanied by a small staff. About the same time contingents' advance parties began to arrive at Capodichino near Naples. Troops from the contributing countries were flown to Italy by United States Air Transport Command and from there they were moved to

Abu Sueir near Ismailia by a neutral commercial airline, Swissair. By this time, the secretary-general had set up a military advisory committee at UN headquarters in New York,[6] consisting of representatives from the contributing nations.

Shortly after the cease-fire had taken effect, the Egyptians complained that fighting was still going on in Port Said. Since it was not possible at that stage to send any members of the force along the Suez Canal route, it was arranged for some observers from the United Nations Truce Supervision Organization in Palestine to move by sea from Haifa to Port Said. These officers established the first link between the invading forces and UNEF, and shortly afterward the first troops in the form of a Danish company were able to move to Port Said.

The next step was to separate the combatants, and to achieve this a Norwegian company was interposed between the Anglo-French forces and the Egyptians. Then, so as to effect a smooth withdrawal of the Anglo-French forces, it was arranged that UNEF troops would gradually take over the responsibility for guarding vulnerable points at Port Said and Port Fuad. Arrangements were also made for UNEF to replace the Anglo-French forces at El Cap, the farthest point of their advance along the Suez Canal, while other elements of the force were to move into the Sinai along several roads, to follow up the Israelis who had announced a withdrawal of 50 kilometers. These plans were soon put into effect, and despite some delay a smooth withdrawal of the Anglo-French forces from Egypt was completed on 22 December.

At this juncture UNEF was experiencing considerable administrative difficulties. The British command had done what it could to help, but there were six battalion-size units on the ground practically without transport except for a few jeeps that had been flown in; the problem of feeding the troops was becoming increasingly difficult, for they had only the rations that they had brought in with them and these were fast being exhausted. At that time there was neither a logistic staff nor any logistic installations to maintain the troops. Normally, whenever a force is introduced into a theater of operations, administrative troops either are on the ground or are introduced rapidly behind the leading elements. This first experience of the United Nations

6. Established by General Assembly Resolution 1001(ES-1), 7 November 1956.

to create a peacekeeping force of its own started in reverse. These logistic difficulties did not make it any easier for UNEF to fulfill its role of assisting the civil administration in maintaining law and order and developing a working cooperation with the Egyptian authorities.

UNEF at the start consisted of contingents from Brazil, Canada, Colombia, Finland, India, Indonesia, Sweden, Yugoslavia, and a mixed contingent from Denmark and Norway. Although not initially sanctioned in the authorizing resolution of 7 November, which envisaged UNEF remaining in the Port Said area only until the withdrawal of all foreign troops from there, the force mandate was subsequently extended to allow it to follow up the Israeli withdrawal into the Sinai.[7] This extension of its role necessitated a regrouping so that the Israeli withdrawal would be followed up at all points and along all routes. At the same time UNEF had to leave behind in the canal zone some elements to provide security for the salvage operations in the canal, where Nasser had sunk blockships, and to look after UNEF's base installations.

The move of UNEF through the Sinai was extremely difficult, since the Israelis had carried out a systematic destruction of all road and rail communications as they withdrew. Furthermore, there were a large number of unmarked minefields, mostly of Egyptian origin. However, by late February 1957 UNEF was able to take over the Sinai with the exception of the Sharm el Sheikh area. After protracted negotiations, Israel announced on 1 March 1957 its intention to withdraw from Sharm el Sheikh and the Gaza Strip. This necessitated a redeployment of UNEF up to and along the Egyptian-Israel frontier and 1948 armistice line.

The new task of UNEF was to help maintain peaceful conditions along the armistice demarcation line in the Gaza Strip and along the international frontier in the Sinai. This involved preventing the violation of both by the armed forces of either Egypt or Israel; illegal crossings by civilians of either side; seizure of cattle or sheep by either party from across the demarcation line; and violation of territorial waters and air space.

There were a number of factors that affected the deployment of the force in the Gaza Strip. Each battalion had to conform as far as possible to the five administrative districts. A number of observation posts

7. General Assembly Resolution 1125(XI), 2 February 1957.

had to be established along the armistice demarcation line. The distance between these posts depended on visibility and on the nature of the terrain—in general about 500 meters between each. In certain open areas, particularly the southern part of the Gaza Strip, fixed observation posts were not necessary, and instead mobile patrolling provided adequate coverage. A 500-meter zone was established along the armistice demarcation line which was forbidden to local inhabitants, except for purely agricultural purposes. Thus, the general deployment plan in the Gaza Strip was to have a line of observation posts, backed by platoon camps located within the 500-meter zone. Company camps were located farther back, their siting being dependent upon the road communications available to the platoon camps. Battalion headquarters were invariably located at the civil administration headquarters.

In the Sinai the situation was somewhat different and demanded a more flexible solution. The northern part of the international frontier, being open and firm surfaced, was easy to patrol with vehicles. From opposite the El Auja neutral zone up to the Gulf of Aqaba the country was rugged and broken, and movement was confined to an unpaved road which ran through a series of communication centers that provided the bases for the mobile patrols. The length of the international frontier was about 180 kilometers from Rafah to the Gulf of Aqaba; to cover such a great distance mobile patrols and air reconnaissance were the only practical answer.

UNEF headquarters was at Gaza. It was structured on the pattern of an American divisional headquarters. Since the headquarters was required to carry out all functions normally performed by different echelons of command in the field, it was large for the size of the force. In order to keep in line with UN specialized field agencies, most of the administrative functions that were normally carried out by higher echelons in the army were vested in officials from the UN secretariat who were an integral part of the headquarters. While often these functions overlapped with those of the military staff, it could generally be said that there was a functional distinction. In order to maintain contact with Egypt and other neighboring countries for purposes of a political nature or to facilitate the administration of the force, UNEF liaison officers were located at Beirut, Cairo, Gaza, Pisa, and Tel Aviv. The fusion of military and civilian activities required considerable understanding as well as knowledge on the part of the

Figure 1. First United Nations Emergency Force

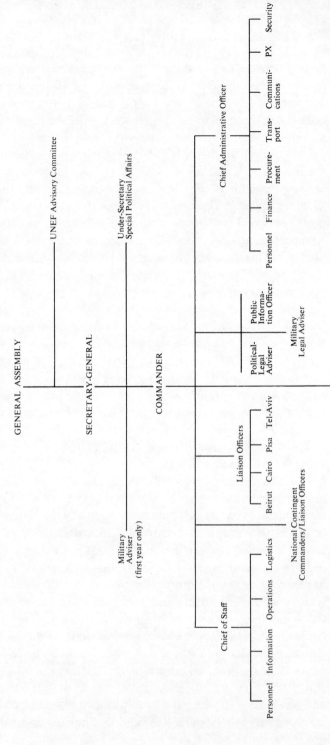

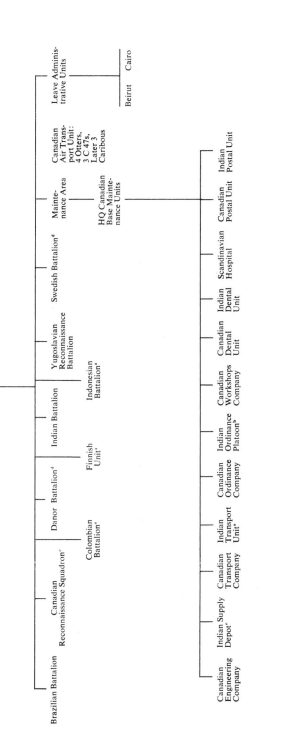

Brazilian Battalion · Canadian Reconnaissance Squadron · Danor Battalion[d] · Indian Battalion · Yugoslavian Reconnaissance Battalion · Swedish Battalion[d] · Maintenance Area · Canadian Air Transport Unit: 4 Otters, 3 C 47s, Later 3 Caribous · Leave Administrative Units

Colombian Battalion[c] · Finnish Unit[a] · Indonesian Battalion[a] · HQ Canadian Base Maintenance Units · Beirut · Cairo

Canadian Engineering Company · Indian Supply Depot[c] · Canadian Transport Company · Indian Transport Unit[a] · Canadian Ordinance Company · Indian Ordinance Platoon[b] · Canadian Workshops Company · Canadian Dental Unit · Indian Dental Unit · Scandinavian Hospital · Canadian Postal Unit · Indian Postal Unit

[a] Withdrawn 1958.
[b] Withdrawn 1959.
[c] Withdrawn 1965.
[d] Only one battalion from Scandinavia from 1966.
[e] Withdrawn 1966.

commander, who was the only officer in the force operating in both a military and civilian capacity. Such understanding and knowledge were needed equally by the senior military and civilian officials, if the working relationship between the two was to be effective and smooth running.

UNEF by mid-1957 had shrunk to seven national contingents (Brazilian, Canadian, Danish, Indian, Norwegian, Swedish, and Yugoslav); those of Colombia, Finland, and Indonesia having been withdrawn from the force soon after its advance into the Sinai and its deployment along the frontier and armistice demarcation line. To offset this strength decrease, the contingents from Denmark/Norway (DANOR), India, and Sweden had been reinforced. All contingents were directly under and responsible to the commander for operations, logistic support, and matters connected with general discipline, while retaining their individual identity and organizational unity. For all other purposes, units were under the command of their respective national contingent commanders.

Once UNEF moved into the Gaza Strip and along the international frontier, both the Israelis and the Arabs came to know peaceful conditions in this area. The Israelis, on the one hand, and the Egyptians and Palestinians in the Gaza Strip, on the other, went about their routine business without disturbance. Similarly, the movement of shipping through the Gulf of Aqaba to the Israeli port of Eilat and the Jordan port of Aqaba was restored to normal. The presence of the force provided protection to both Egypt and Israel. In the case of Israel, before UNEF's arrival in the area the kibbutzim situated in the vicinity of where UNEF subsequently established its camps had lived in a state of constant emergency. Little work could be done on their farms, and a disproportionate amount of manpower was committed to security. In the case of Egypt, at least two divisions were deployed in this area. While the presence of UNEF did not provide a physical stop to either side's aggressive intentions, there was no doubt about its moral force, since as an instrument of the United Nations it had the support of its member nations. It certainly enjoyed excellent relations and understanding with the local inhabitants, including Palestinian refugees, and contributed to the local economy in many ways.

Over the ten years that UNEF kept peace along Egypt's border with Israel, President Nasser was engaged in a complicated game aimed at furthering Egypt's position of leadership among the Arabs. He assisted in the establishment of revolutionary socialist regimes in Syria and Iraq and denounced the monarchies of Jordan and Saudi Arabia as being conservative, corrupt, and unpatriotic. While the level of hostility conducted by the radio-press war among the Arab rivals varied with circumstances, President Nasser and Egypt gained prestige in Arab eyes throughout the region. Along with the political campaigning for the leadership of the Arab world, Nasser's resolve was to increase Egypt's military superiority over all the other Arab states in order that it should become the most important factor in the event of any future conflict with Israel. These considerations put President Nasser in a delicate and precarious position at home, where more important matters were in need of attention, particularly Egypt's economy and the rapidly growing population.

While UNEF kept the Gaza Strip and the international frontier along the Sinai relatively quiet, Arab guerrilla raids into Israel from Jordan, Syria, and Lebanon increased in pace and intensity with the establishment of the Palestine Liberation Organization in 1964. In turn, Israel stepped up its retaliatory raids. In November 1966 Egypt signed a Mutual Defense Pact with Syria. The Syrian government, led by the Ba'ath party, had for some time shown its impatience to liberate Palestine by openly supporting Palestinian commando raids into Israel from Syrian territory, inviting heavy retaliation by Israel. That retaliation had come in October when, reacting to Arab guerrilla activity from Jordan, Israel had heavily punished Jordanian forces at Samu. From then on the political and military situation in the Middle East became progressively worse. As a result of the increased level of guerrilla activity from Syria, there were continuous counterraids by Israeli forces leading to an air battle in April 1967 in which Israel knocked out four of the six MIG 21's of the Syrian air force. Syria, without an effective air cover, felt threatened and invoked the Mutual Defense Pact with Egypt. For Nasser it was the point of no return. In order to maintain his leadership among the Arab nations, he had to accept the challenge and stop the accusations of his rival Arab monarchies that "he was hiding his armies behind UNEF's skirt."

On 13 May he ordered his forces to move into the Sinai in strength. On 16 May, in order to avoid a UNEF involvement in any possible future clash with Israeli forces along the international frontier in the Sinai, his chief of staff, General Fawzi, in a letter to the commander of UNEF,[8] requested the withdrawal of all UN troops manning observation posts along Egypt's borders. When this letter was handed to the commander of UNEF, it was made clear to him that he must order the immediate withdrawal of UNEF troops from El-Sabha and Sharm el Sheikh, since UAR forces must gain control of those two places that very night. The UNEF commander correctly replied that he did not have the authority to withdraw his troops from these positions as he could do so only on instructions from the secretary-general; therefore, he must continue with UNEF operations in Sinai as hitherto.

On receiving the force commander's message informing him of General Fawzi's request, the secretary-general asked the permanent representative of the UAR to obtain his government's clarification of the situation, pointing out that any request for withdrawal of the force must come directly to the secretary-general from the government of the UAR. On the morning of 17 May 1967, UAR forces arrived on the international frontier and occupied all UNEF observation posts. At noon the same day, the chief of staff of the UAR liaison staff conveyed to the commander of UNEF a request from General Fawzi for the withdrawal of Yugoslav detachments in the Sinai within twenty-four hours and added that the UNEF commander might take "forty-eight hours or so" to withdraw UNEF detachments from Sharm el Sheikh. The commander of UNEF repeated that any such move required instructions from the secretary-general.

Meanwhile in New York, the secretary-general met with the UNEF Advisory Committee, but they were unable to arrive at any consensus of action. For some unexplained reason the committee did not agree to refer the question to the General Assembly, which it was empowered to do under its founding resolution.[9] The Security Council, although already in session on the Middle East question, was threatened by a Russian veto and was therefore powerless to act. The secretary-general, faced by the failure of the Advisory Committee to fulfill its mandate, considered that he had no alternative but to give orders for the withdrawal of UNEF.[10] He pointed out to the UAR government that UNEF could not modify its role and responsibilities as

8. Major General I. J. Rikhye.
9. General Assembly Resolution 1001(ES-1), 7 November 1956.
10. Secretary-General's Report to Security Council, S/7906, 18 May 1967.

defined by the General Assembly. It therefore had to remain and carry out its duties according to its mandate or withdraw completely. The order to withdraw was given by the secretary-general on 18 May.[11]

Before the evacuation could be completed, Israel launched its offensive into Gaza and the Sinai. Some of the UN contingents were still in the combat area and became caught up in the fighting. Shooting first and asking questions afterward, the Israelis inflicted serious casualties upon the Indian units still maintaining their positions in the Gaza Strip, killing fourteen soldiers and wounding twenty. No justification can be pleaded for these attacks, and the Israelis never attempted to excuse themselves—so far as they were concerned, anybody in uniform facing them was an enemy. This tragic end to what had been a remarkably successful effort at peacekeeping was an unjust reward for those countries that had borne the burden of the task for more than ten years.

The decision to withdraw UNEF has been characterized in some quarters as hasty and precipitous, and some have even suggested that it took President Nasser by surprise. What is often forgotten is that the establishment of UNEF by the General Assembly was delayed because of Egypt's reluctance to permit the arrival of the force on its soil. Egypt was assured that its sovereignty would be respected and that any request for the withdrawal of the force would be honored. The siting of UNEF solely on Egyptian territory was necessary because of Israel's refusal to permit the force to be positioned anywhere on territory under its control. Opinions have also been expressed that the withdrawal of UNEF should have been delayed to allow for consultation and negotiation and that efforts should have been made to resist the UAR request or to bring pressure on the UAR to reconsider its decision. Criticism of the secretary-general's actions at this time appear to stem from a basic misunderstanding of the circumstances under which UNEF had first been established. Within the prescribed limits of the initiatives available to him, U Thant took all necessary steps to carry out a wide range of consultation, including an attempt to make a personal appeal to President Nasser, which was brusquely rejected by Egypt's foreign minister on the grounds that such an appeal would be unwise and unavailing. Though a subsequent proposal

11. Secretary-General's Report of Withdrawal of UNEF, A/6730/Add., 26 June 1967.

to visit Cairo was accepted and took place, by then it was too late to alter anything. Since the Security Council members, including the president, had failed to take action although in session at the time, there was little or no point in the secretary-general's attempting to do what the Council itself had failed to do; in any event since the Council had disagreed on the setting up of UNEF in the first instance, it is realistic to suppose that there would have been even less unanimity of opinion about its withdrawal. The Advisory Committee's decision not to refer the question to the General Assembly, which was also in emergency session, remains one of the mysteries, as does the lack of action on the part of member states to exercise their right to call a meeting of the Assembly. But had such initiatives been taken, it is doubtful that they would have resulted in a different answer. So far as Egypt was concerned, there was no compromise. It had always believed that any request by Egypt for the withdrawal of UNEF would be honored. In the words of the Egyptian foreign minister in the General Assembly on 27 November 1957, "the General Assembly Resolution of 7 November 1956 still stands, together with its endorsement of the principle that the General Assembly could not request UNEF to be stationed or operate on the territory of a given country without the consent of the government of that country."

There was little doubt that the withdrawal of UNEF would inevitably lead to war between Israel and Egypt, which would envelop all other Arab states as well. The United Nations, tied to a policy of the supremacy of the sovereignty of nations, had to respect Egypt's wishes once it had requested withdrawal of the force. The Security Council is so structured that a consensus among the five great powers is a prerequisite to any action, and it was certain in this case that Russia would use its veto. The Soviet position was that it was Egypt's sovereign right to require the withdrawal of the UN presence. Any enforcement action by the Security Council with UNEF was out of the question because of the arrangements that had been arrived at by the United Nations with the contributing states. India and Yugoslavia together had made it clear to the secretary-general at the UNEF Advisory Committee meeting that Egypt was within its rights to request the withdrawal of the force and that the United Nations had no alternative but to respect the sovereign right of Egypt to do so.

There is no doubt that the withdrawal of UNEF and the Six-Day War were serious setbacks to the UN's image as an international peacekeeping authority. But any loss in credibility stemmed from a false and unrealistic understanding of the role of peacekeeping forces and the clearly defined limits of their capability. Had there been correct recognition, greater justice would have been done to UNEF's achievements and less ill-informed criticism would have been levelled at the United Nations and against the secretary-general in particular.

UNEF, the first peacekeeping force of its kind established by the United Nations, was delicately structured. As a first attempt at multinational force level operations based on third-party intervention, it was a remarkable success. Unfortunately, its success soothed the breasts of those whose job it was to work for a peaceful political settlement of the dispute—the Security Council—who not surprisingly turned their attention to more strident problems, where peace was not being so successfully kept, with the result that at a time when political initiatives were needed and had a chance of succeeding in a relatively quiet military atmosphere, no initiatives were forthcoming. UNEF's withdrawal was sown of the seeds of this indifference and complacency—and because of the opportunity missed, its achievements were in vain. UNEF deserved better than it got.

When evaluating the effectiveness of UNEF and its achievements, it should be remembered that it was the first of the force level operations conducted by the United Nations based on the principle of third-party peaceful intervention rather than enforcement. There were no guidelines from history, no standing procedures, no previous practical experience for the planners to follow—all that the United Nations had in the way of examples were the observer missions of Palestine (UNTSO) and Kashmir (UNMOGIP), and these were operations of a very different character. This was a first for the organization itself, as well as for the national contingents that made up UNEF.

Account must also be taken of the speed with which UNEF became operational, not of its own choosing, but because interventions of this kind need to be swiftly undertaken in a rapidly deteriorating conflict situation. Although later the first ONUC troops arrived in the Congo within forty-eight hours, the eight-day response by UNEF was more remarkable because of its being the first time that anything like it had been attempted. No machinery existed for mounting peacekeeping operations, and though the Korean crisis brought a quick response from a wide group of countries, the central command structure was already in being and operational before the first non-American contingents arrived in Korea, and the contributing countries did not need to be vetted by the host country for political suitability before being accepted. By the time that the Congo explosion occurred, some vital lessons had been learned from the UNEF experience. However unsatisfactory and inadequate ad hoc procedures for mounting peacekeeping operations may be, UNEF showed that a multinational force can be gathered and deployed in a relatively short time and become operationally effective without too much delay. There is therefore nothing wrong or impractical about the concept of force level operations of this kind; what is needed (and the Congo and Cyprus operations have also borne out this point) is a properly structured machinery for ensuring that any force when deployed is properly balanced from the start with a fully operational logistic support. Speed is all very well in an emergency, but nothing is gained if too much haste negates the immediate effectiveness of a force through inadequate administrative backing. No force can be deemed operational when six of its battalions arrive to find themselves in the desert without transport or medical supplies and with only ten days' rations—as was the experience of UNEF in the sand dunes around Port Said.

UNEF was designed to fulfill a wholly military task; it did not have, as its successors did later, a political component to contend with immediate political problems and to act as the representative of the secretary-general in the field. This lack of a politico-diplomatic input had the effect of relegating political initiatives to the periphery and might be said to have been the missing link that, had it been there, might have inspired greater attention to the international political action needed to bring about a peaceful settlement of the Middle East dispute. In fact, UNEF's force commander had no mandate to concern himself with political matters, and so this on-the-spot representation and coverage were missing during UNEF's stay in Egypt. It is possible that a mission to the Middle East, similar to the one carried out by Ambassador Gunnar Jarring on behalf of the Security Council from 1967 onward,[12] might have achieved greater positive results had it

12. Ambassador Jarring's mission continued spasmodically right through until the outbreak of hostilities in 1973. His mandate was to try to find a modus vivendi between Israel and its Arab neighbors based on the requirements of Security Council Resolution 242 of 22 November 1967, which called for an Israeli withdrawal from the occupied territories and the recognition by the Arab countries of the lawful existence of Israel.

been operative during the period when UNEF was keeping the peace between Egypt and Israel. Certainly subsequent experience from Cyprus would suggest that it might have, underlining as UNFICYP has, the importance of the interrelationship among the essential instruments of conflict control. In comparison to the situation in Cyprus, UNEF's force commander had to conduct his operation with one hand tied behind his back, having as his only counselor the legal and political adviser who headed a small political staff and who was more concerned with the legal and political aspects of UNEF's presence and status than with the major political scene.

The evaluation of UNEF falls primarily into two parts—the early days of 1956–57 and the events leading up to and including its withdrawal in the summer of 1967. The years between followed a prescribed pattern in which the role and operational character of UNEF remained unchanged, except for some reductions in its size. From 1957 to 1967 UNEF might be described as a forgotten army, and commentators tend to forget the contribution that it made during those years in their emotional recriminations of its last days. Although its contribution during the ten years could be described as having no lasting effect, and although it could be said that whatever UNEF's achievements may have been, they disappeared altogether in the Israeli army's advances on the first day of the Six-Day War, there is no denying the fact that something happened in those intervening years in the Gaza Strip and Sinai that had not been possible or even envisaged for decades before the arrival of UNEF. What this was can best be described by quoting from Secretary-General U Thant's final report on the UNEF operation.

When, in March 1957, UNEF reached the International Frontier in Sinai and the Armistic Demarcation Line in the Gaza Strip . . ., it was deployed along what had been only four months before one of the most troubled borders anywhere in the world. With UNEF's deployment there, that line became and remained almost completely quiet. The terrorising raids of the fedayeen across the line into Israel became a thing of the past. Infiltration across the line from either side was almost ended. Fields near the line on both sides, which for long had been left uncultivated because it was near suicidal to come into view in the open fields, were now being worked right up to the line itself and on both sides of it. Costly irrigation systems were extensively installed. Heavy investments in new citrus orchards and in other cash crops were made. A new prosperity came to the area in UNEF's decade. Above all, because of UNEF's effective buffer role, there was security as there was no longer a military confrontation between the armed forces of Israel and the United Arab Republic, and clashes between those forces practically ceased. In consequence, there was throughout Gaza and Sinai an unaccustomed quiet for more than ten years. This was due very largely, if not entirely to the presence of UNEF.[13]

This then was no counterproductive preservation of the status quo—a criticism so often levelled at the peacekeeper—but rather a positive contribution to achieving reconciliation through communication. Though it cannot be claimed that this peaceful economic breakthrough affected the hearts and minds of Arab and Jew in the area, the lesson that stands out clearly is that, within the military framework of international peacekeeping, there are opportunities and initiatives for action that can make a constructive contribution to solving some of the structural problems that beset efforts to find a political settlement of the dispute. This brings us back to the point that no single effort can be expected to achieve much in isolation, but when interrelated with other agencies, the combined effort that results has a better chance of success. The point has already been made that the reduction in tension and the decrease in violence achieved by UNEF had the effect of lessening the sense of urgency for arriving at a political solution. As the secretary-general made clear in his final report on UNEF,

> The ability of (a peacekeeping) operation to re-establish and maintain quiet for an extended period may come to be mistaken for a solution of the basic problem. This can only increase the sense of shock when, ultimately and inexorably, it is demonstrated that problems of conflict may lie dormant even for longer periods, but they do not necessarily solve themselves by the passage of time, and the day may come [perhaps *will* would be a more appropriate word than *may*] when they will explode anew. Peacekeeping operations can serve their purpose if they are accompanied by serious and persistent efforts to find solutions to problems which required the peacekeeping in the first place.[14]

13. Secretary-General's Report to the General Assembly, A/6672/Add. 1, 12 July 1967.
14. Ibid.

Nothing that has happened since in the Congo and Cyprus has modified this premiss to any degree.

UNEF's relationship with the local Arab authorities, with whom it had to work, and with the population, whom it had come to serve, remained excellent throughout. The need for good relations is a salient factor in the success or failure of any third-party peacekeeping force, for it helps to generate the confidence and trust with which the force is viewed and to strengthen the mutual understanding and persuasive power with which the peacekeeper can settle disagreements at their source before they escalate into something far more serious. One limitation in UNEF's case was that the relationship was one-sided because of Israel's refusal to accept the presence of UN troops on its territory. Another limitation was that since coercion and force were not the methods used to keep the peace, the UN soldiers were faced with a concept of soldiering that was a contradiction of their basic military training. Bearing these limitations in mind, the successes achieved by UNEF in the highly explosive arena of the Middle East provide a major lesson for the future use of international forces.

The tragedy of UNEF was its ending—undeserved and unwarranted, born of political indolence. It was almost inevitable that the operation should have ended as it did, when year succeeded year without any determined effort to take advantage of the cooler and quieter atmosphere existing as a result of UNEF's presence to find and encourage a formula for peace. With Israel's refusal to accommodate UN soldiers on its territory, it could only be a matter of time before pressures within and among the Arab states reached a stage where President Nasser and the Egyptian government found themselves faced with having to honor their pledges and fulfill the role that they had carved for Egypt—that of champion of the Arab world. From that moment on UNEF's days were numbered, for so long as it remained, it acted as a physical obstacle to any military action that Egypt and its allies might choose to take. When the ultimatum came and the withdrawal of UNEF took place, the world voiced its bitterness and disgust and railed against the perfidy of UNEF withdrawing at the moment when it was most needed. The words to describe this reaction have been carefully chosen, for they illustrate only too clearly how, at the moment of crisis, criticism is directed at the organization (personified in the secretary-general) and at the particular agency in question, as if they and not the member states were to blame. How conveniently public opinion in any country ignores the fact that the fundamental fault lies with the inability of member states, their own included, to react sufficiently and quickly enough as a world body to prevent conflict! Public opinion prefers a single recognizable scapegoat. So long as the UN force on the ground is keeping conflict under control, it tends to be ignored and forgotten, but as soon as there is a violent flare-up that the UN force is unable to control, it can become the immediate object of scorn, derision, and frustration. The operations in the Middle East, the Congo, and Cyprus bear this out. Proper regard is not paid to the fact that renewed violence stems from the failure of others to take advantage of the breathing space provided by the peacekeeping force for developing the political initiatives aimed at bringing about a peaceful settlement of the dispute. It is a salutary thought for the practitioners of peace that their worst enemy is public opinion and that their greatest need is the support and confidence of world opinion.

One important factor arising out of UNEF's withdrawal, which could be described as the most important lesson for the future construction of peacekeeping forces, is the fashion of the withdrawal itself. Once Egypt withdrew its consent to UNEF's presence, UNEF had no legal right to operate or remain on Egyptian territory; the safeguards for UN soldiers provided for in the Status of Force Agreement were no longer operative. In his final report U Thant pointed to the fact that,

The experience acquired with the withdrawal of UNEF most certainly points up the desirability of having all conditions relating to the presence and the withdrawal of a peacekeeping operation clearly defined in advance of its entry onto the territory of a host country. In most instances, however, this is unlikely to prove to be practicable for the reason that the critical situation which demands the presence of the operation is likely to require that presence so urgently that time cannot be taken to negotiate agreements on detailed conditions in advance of the entry. Moreover, it remains an open question as to whether in the present stage of the development of international order, any host country would be inclined to accept formal limitations on its sovereignty with regard to the exercise of its consent for the presence of an international force. Its attitude in this regard is bound to be influenced by the knowledge that there can never be certainty about the action on a given matter such as the presence of a United Nations force, which the Security Council or the General Assembly might take at some future date, since the decisions of these political bodies are always subject to political considerations.[15]

While appreciating the weight of the secretary-general's comment that a host country "may not be inclined to accept formal limitations on its sovereignty with regard to the exercise of its consent for the presence of an international force," it is an undeniable fact that so long as the consent or request principle remains without any built-in safeguards, both the credibility and viability of multinational peacekeeping forces come into question. And yet it does not seem unreasonable to require of a host country certain basic undertakings, as part of the overall consent/request agreement, that would ensure a notice period of sufficient length (and not more than six months) to allow for negotiation of a new mandate under which a force, maybe of different character and role, might remain in its operational area; or, if a new agreement cannot be reached, to allow sufficient time in which the force can make an orderly and safe withdrawal. It does not seem to threaten or trespass upon the sovereignty of a host state to request such an undertaking at the time when the initial agreements are being drawn up at the outset of the operation. UNEF certainly demonstrated the dangers consequent upon the lack of the necessary safeguards. However, one cannot disregard the possibility of a host country subsequently abrogating the initial agreement to accept a notice period and demanding the instant withdrawal of the peacekeeping force. Since it is the Security Council that exercises the authority for the maintenance of peace and security under the Charter, it should be the Council's decision whether or not to comply with such a demand. Contributing countries will be unlikely to offer contingents for peacekeeping forces, so long as they feel that their troops will suffer the same undignified fate of their UNEF predecessors. India and Yugoslavia made it abundantly clear to the secretary-general at the meeting of the UNEF Advisory Committee after the receipt of Egypt's ultimatum, that they could no longer continue to keep their contingents with UNEF against the wishes of Egypt. So long as the uncertainty of tenure exists, member states will not be so inclined as they

15. Ibid.

might have been in the past to support the United Nations in its peacekeeping endeavors.

Israel's adamant refusal from the start to permit UNEF on its territory was a significant handicap to the total potential of the force. It added to its operational difficulties and at the time of the withdrawal made impossible any idea of a side-stepping maneuver to allow UNEF to continue in being. Obviously it is desirable that all parties to a dispute should accept the presence of a peacekeeping force, but with the precedent set by Israel the desirable will not always be achieved. However, UNEF proved that, whatever may be the disadvantages, it is still both practical and possible to maintain a viable peacekeeping presence despite the consequences of such a refusal by one of the disputants.

In a military sense much was learned from the UNEF operation that has been applied with advantage in successive operations, particularly in Cyprus. Possibly the most far-reaching experience of all was the development of operational procedures and wide-ranging techniques for use by multinational forces, not organized on an international treaty basis but drawn from a world club of national armies, where military experience and professionalism vary to extremes and where the character of the role is based on concepts strange to the ways of soldiers. UNEF can take credit for being the pioneer of this development.

6

Case Study 2—Congo (ONUC)

The UN Congo Operation was the largest third-party peacekeeping effort ever to be authorized by any international organization. During its four years of operation, from 1960 to 1964, a total of over 93,000 men from thirty-five countries served in ONUC. The operation took a death toll of 126 men and an equal number of wounded, and its total cost was $411 million. As a conflict the Congo presented the UN force with a situation of unprecedented size, seriousness, and complexity. (Territorially alone, the Belgian Congo—now Zaire—was the size of Western Europe.) Internal and external factors of a political and legal nature confronted the international organization with problems difficult to cope with, even for experienced national statesmen. For international civil servants and military officers, the task bordered on the impossible.

The emergence of nationalist movements that could be found in most colonial territories after the end of World War II was as manifest in the Belgian Congo as anywhere else. Although with the passage of time and the decolonization policies of other colonial powers, the Congo's ultimate self-determination and independence were inevitable, Belgium was not willing to listen to the new voices of nationalism and made little attempt to prepare the country and its population for the day when Belgium would hand over its responsibilities to them. This day came on 30 June 1960, and it found the Congolese people unprepared to run their own affairs. They had no experience of civil administration except at the lowest levels, and this inexperience was found in every department of government and in the armed forces. The Force Publique (later to change its name to Armée Nationale Congolaise, ANC) at the time of independence had a strength of approximately 28,000 and, as the national security force, combined the functions of an army and a constabulary. It was officered by 1,100 Europeans of whom the great majority were Belgians. No

Congolese held a rank higher than that of warrant officer, and prospects for him to be promoted to commissioned rank were nonexistent.

The almost total absence of any preparation of the Congolese for their public responsibilities stemmed from the Belgians' belief that many of their nationals would be retained in their existing appointments by the Congolese government. This belief appears to have been particularly common among officers of the Force Publique. In the event, this was not the case, except, as will be seen later, in Katanga Province. Belgian expectations were therefore short-lived.

Two days after Independence Day, on 2 July 1960, intertribal fighting broke out in Leopoldville and Luluabourg. This was not wholly unexpected, since tribal aspirations for power in the newly independent state had been apparent for some time. However, what was not foreseen was the mutiny of elements of the Force Publique three days later. On 5 July the Congolese soldiers in the garrisons of Thysville and Leopoldville rose against their Belgian officers and imprisoned them (some of them later died at their captors' hands). The grounds for the mutiny were simply the soldiers' complaints over pay and promotion, but these were enough to cause a complete breakdown in law and order. Disorders spread throughout the country, property was destroyed, and a number of Europeans were killed or injured. The situation was most serious for the 100,000 Belgian citizens living in isolated areas of the Congo. Many fled from Leopoldville across the Congo River to Brazzaville. Belgian authorities tried to persuade Prime Minister Patrice Lumumba and other Congolese officials to permit Belgian metropolitan troops, which were still stationed in the Congo, to restore order, but permission was not given and the disorders continued to spread. The Belgian government decided that it could no longer sit back and ignore the plight of its nationals by taking no steps to go to their rescue. On 9 July military reinforcements were flown from Brussels to the two bases at Kitona and Kamina retained by Belgium under the terms of the Treaty of Friendship signed on the eve of independence on 29 June. Within twenty-four hours of arriving they had opposed the mutineers at a number of placed including Elisabethville, Jadotville, and Kamina and had restored order. Despite the protests of the Congolese government, the military buildup continued until by 19 July there were 10,000 Belgian troops in the Congo.

In the meanwhile two significant events had taken place—almost simultaneously on 11 July. The first was an appeal by Prime Minister Lumumba to the United Nations for assistance in restoring the fast deteriorating law-and-order situation, largely brought about through the breakdown in discipline within the ANC. The second event, the declaration of secession by Katanga Province, extended the Congo crisis far beyond the extremities of a mere domestic squabble and brought about the most controversial of all UN peacekeeping operations. The provincial head of Katanga, Moise Tshombe, based the right to secede on the grounds that communist influence was responsible for the breakdown in law and order, and that Katanga could not go along with the communist line being followed by Lumumba. He appealed to Belgium for military aid. The fact that Katanga provided 50 percent of the Congo's revenue at that time, through its mineral wealth in copper, radium, uranium, zinc, and other minerals, made this action of secession not only unconstitutional but an illegal confiscation of national wealth.

Facing the disintegration of the country, the Congolese government cabled the secretary-general of the United Nations on 12 July for the urgent dispatch of military assistance to protect the national territory of the Congo against the present external aggression (of Belgium), which they interpreted as a threat to international peace. The aggression so far as they were concerned was Belgium's dispatch of metropolitan troops to the Congo and its apparent involvement in the plot leading to Katanga's secession. This appeal for help was followed the next day by another telegram declaring that the military assistance was needed to protect Congolese territory, rather than to restore the internal situation. This second telegram stated that if a UN force made up of contingents from neutral countries were not dispatched without delay, the government would be obliged to seek help elsewhere. On 14 July the Congolese leaders addressed a message to the Soviet premier begging the USSR to interest itself in the events taking place in the Congo as a result of Western aggression.

The secretary-general of the United Nations, acting at the request of Prime Minister Lumumba, sought an urgent meeting of the Security Council to consider the situation. The Council met on 13 July, when Dag Hammarskjöld urged immediate action and advised that all necessary steps be taken in consultation with the government of the Congo to provide the government with military assistance until such a time when its national security forces were, in the opinion of the government, able to meet fully their responsibilities. The Council, though not condemning Belgium as "aggressor," did call upon Belgium to withdraw its troops, and authorized the secretary-general to provide the military assistance required.[1] Along with the military assistance the Security Council approved the setting up of a technical assistance program asked for by Lumumba in his first approach to the UN on 11 July. Hammarskjöld was satisfied that these provisions provided sufficient guarantees for Belgium to withdraw its troops. In this he was only partly right.

Steps were immediately taken to implement the provisions of the resolution. The secretary-general developed the organizational concept that became the modus operandi for the ONUC operation. The concept was based as far as possible on the intent implicit in the Security Council resolution and defined by its members. Hammarskjöld saw ONUC as a combined effort in which the political, military, and technical assistance aspects would all be welded into an integrated organization with the common purpose of restoring law and order and of enabling the Congolese people to find their own destiny under their own government. The designation of a top political officer with the rank of under–secretary-general (acting as the special representative of the secretary-general) to head the entire civilian and military operation represented an important departure from UN practice; never before in UN history had an important military operation and a very substantial civilian activity been linked in a common organization under a single leadership. There are reasons to believe that Hammarskjöld's dream of the ideal international peacekeeping operation was imbedded in this concept. Here, for the first time, was an opportunity to prove to the world that a new kind of international conflict control could be implemented. The integrated efforts of military, political, and economic forces would constitute the new way of dealing with international disputes. The military would assist in creating the peaceful environment necessary to start political conciliatory efforts, and the technical assistance program would start the process of creating favorable social and economic conditions, which are a necessary prerequisite for peaceful development of any nation. The initial hope and expectation on the military side was that a relatively small emergency force of perhaps 3,000 men could restore law and order in

1. Security Council Resolution S/4387, 14 July 1960.

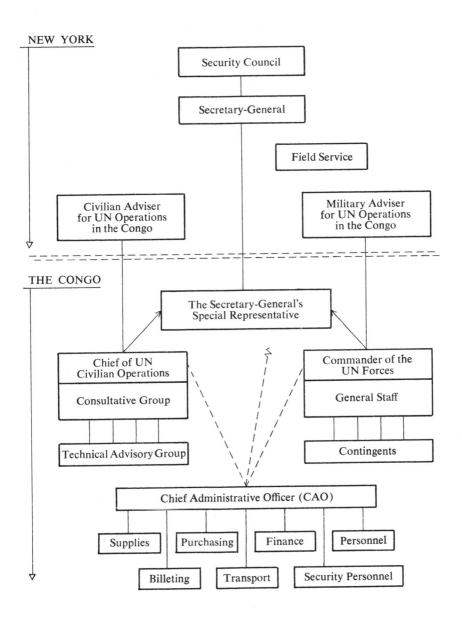

NEW YORK

Security Council

Secretary-General

Field Service

Civilian Adviser
for UN Operations
in the Congo

Military Adviser
for UN Operations
in the Congo

THE CONGO

The Secretary-General's
Special Representative

Chief of UN
Civilian Operations

Consultative Group

Commander of the
UN Forces

General Staff

Technical Advisory Group

Contingents

Chief Administrative Officer (CAO)

Supplies

Purchasing

Finance

Personnel

Billeting

Transport

Security Personnel

Figure 2. The Central Administration of UN Operations in the Congo

a reasonably short time. But this expectation soon faded in the face of continued violence and political conflict throughout the Congo. It quickly became evident that to cope with the very complex situation that existed in the country a sizable force would be required.

Tunisian and Ghanaian troops were the first to arrive in the Congo, only forty-eight hours after the resolution establishing ONUC had been approved by the Security Council. The force commander and the nucleus of officers needed for the headquarters staff were drawn in the first instance from UNTSO (United Nations Truce Supervision Organization) in the Middle East; later the various staff appointments were filled by officers from those countries providing contingents. The Swedish battalion in UNEF was temporarily assigned to ONUC. By the end of the month over 11,000 troops from eight countries were assembled in the Congo. By the end of August the number had risen to 16,000.

Tshombe in the meantime had refused admittance of UN troops into Katanga, stating that he would rely for military assistance on the Belgian military forces already there. He went so far as to add that he would use force to prevent the entry of UN troops. Despite this threat, on 12 August 1960, when some three hundred of the Swedish UN contingent entered Katanga along with the secretary-general himself, the "invasion" passed off peacefully. It did not, however, please Prime Minister Lumumba, who accused the secretary-general of connivance with Tshombe against the Congolese government in that Hammarskjöld had forestalled the latter from taking military action against Katanga. In any event Lumumba's days were numbered. The internal situation was deteriorating fast. In Kasai Province at Bakwanga, the massive and powerful Baluba tribe had followed in Katanga's footsteps, and its king, Albert Kalonji, had proclaimed independent statehood for his tribe. Lumumba, while appealing to other African states to assist him in overthrowing Katanga, also approached the Soviet Union to assist in airlifting Congolese troops to attack Kasai. Lumumba had clearly become too great a liability. He was deposed as prime minister by President Joseph Kasavubu, but at his own request he was permitted to remain in his own house guarded by UN (Ghanaian) troops.

The struggle for power within the leadership in the Congo made the work of restoration that much harder for the United Nations. President Kasavubu, having dismissed Lumumba, was himself dismissed by Lumumba though both continued in office. Into this confusion in government control stepped Army Chief of Staff Colonel Joseph Mobutu, who dissolved the National Assembly and suspended the political leaders. In their place he appointed a College of Commissioners made up of graduates and students called home from their studies abroad to take over the duties of government. Mobutu's own position was tenuous, since he had acted without a public mandate. Kasavubu and Lumumba were still the constitutionally elected president and prime minister and were recognized as such by the United Nations, who never accorded recognition to the College of Commissioners. The latter was never a substitute for government. The Senate continued to sit and conduct its business, while Kasavubu and Joseph Ileo, who had been appointed prime minister in place of Lumumba, carried out their duties as usual. But Mobutu's star did not wane; he remained in the political wings, later to become Zaire's first president. However, in October 1960 the confusion over leadership had reached a bizarre state with the detained Lumumba still the declared prime minister, Kasavubu and Ileo continuing to carry out their duties despite their suspension by Mobutu, and Mobutu himself acting out the role of kingmaker without public support. Mobutu was particularly critical of the United Nations' continued support of Lumumba and its interference in protecting him from arrest. This confrontation with the army chief did not make for good relations between the ANC and ONUC, and many clashes and gun fights took place with casualties on both sides. Although ONUC had no mandate to involve itself in the internal and domestic issues of the Congo, the virtual breakdown in ordered government made it inevitable that the United Nations would find itself the target for attack from quarters other than the ANC—the tribal factions in the areas of ONUC's operations who were still engaged in intertribal war.

In November 1960, a pro-Lumumba group set itself up in power in Stanleyville, the capital of Orientale Province. This new regime led by a former deputy prime minister, Antoine Gizenga, and deposed army commander in chief, General Victor Lundula, was recognized by a number of countries including the USSR. Lumumba slipped unnoticed out of his house in Leopoldville and ostensibly went to join them. He never arrived and on 1 December was arrested by Mobutu's soldiers and brought back to the capital. For a month he remained in prison there, but at the beginning of January 1961 Lumumba was handed over by Mobutu to his archenemy Tshombe. On 13 February it was announced that he had been shot dead in an escape bid along with two other political leaders and prominent Lumumbists who had escaped with him. The worldwide reaction to the news was strong and outspoken, and one week later, on 21 February, the Security Council approved a resolution deploring the murders and urging

[1] that the United Nations take all appropriate measures to prevent the occurrence of civil war in the Congo, including arrangements for cease-fires, the halting of all military operations, the prevention of clashes, and the use of force, if necessary, in the last resort.

[2] that measures be taken for the immediate withdrawal and evacuation from the Congo of all Belgian and other foreign military and para-military personnel and political advisors not under the United Nations command, and mercenaries.[2]

The resolution also urged the convening of the National Assembly and the taking of necessary protective measures in that connection.

The second part of this resolution was particularly relevant to Katanga, where large numbers of mercenaries, not only from Belgium, were being inducted into the Katanga gendarmerie. This mercenary menace was to become a major factor in determining the United Nations' subsequent actions in and against Katanga, which now became the focal point of ONUC's attention. Although there were to be further serious attacks on UN troops, the most serious perhaps being when thirty-eight Ghanaian and four European soldiers were killed in an attack by the ANC at Port-Francqui in April 1961, the main military action from here on was to be directed at ending Katanga's secession.

The chief purpose in reconvening the National Assembly was to re-establish normal political life in the Congo. The purpose was achieved, largely due to the UN's good offices and to the security guarantees for the delegates provided by ONUC. Thanks to these measures, the assembly was able to meet and conduct its business. Cyrille Adoula was elected prime minister on 2 August and continued in that office throughout the remainder of ONUC's stay in the Congo. Gizenga in Stanleyville recognized the Adoula government shortly af-

2. Security Council Resolution S/4741, 21 February 1961.

terward when normal political control of the country's affairs was resumed.

With a new political incentive in Leopoldville, it was possible for ONUC to concentrate more directly on implementing the provisions of the Security Council's resolution of 21 February 1961. The problem of mercenaries had got worse rather than better, and efforts to expel those apprehended had not proved effective since most of them had gone into hiding. Later, many of them reappeared in Katanga. The resolution of 21 February had called for their expulsion, but Tshombe had so far disregarded it. On 28 August, in a surprise move (Operation Rum Punch), ONUC rounded up 338 of the 442 European officers who were known to be serving with the Katangese forces and who occupied certain key positions in the provincial capital Elisabethville.[3] The next day Tshombe capitulated to the expulsion demand, broadcasting an endorsement to this effect. But Tshombe's action was wholly deceptive, for within a very short while the officers were back again leading his gendarmerie. The Belgian consul who had undertaken to expel the mercenaries who had been arrested failed to fulfill his obligations, with the result that only a small proportion were ever repatriated and most of these found their way back to the Congo.

Two weeks later a second intervention by ONUC (Operation MORTHOR [4] —otherwise known as Round ONE) resulted in eight days of severe fighting. The initiative for this operation was not the secretary-general's, but that of Mahmoud Khiary of Tunisia, the head of the UN civilian operation, and Conor Cruise O'Brien, the UN representative at Elisabethville. (Hammarskjöld was not to realize the full implications of Operation MORTHOR until he arrived in the Congo on 13 September,[5] by which time the operation had run into serious difficulties.) The objective, so far as these two men were concerned, was to bring about the end of Katanga's secession, and the plan was to secure the main radio and telegraph installations and the offices of the Sureté and Ministry of Information.[6] The central government had on 9 September prepared warrants of arrest for Tshombe and four of his senior ministers; these were handed to Khiary on 11 September,

3. Security Council Document S/4940/Add. 1, p. 106, 14 September 1961.
4. The Hindu word for "smash."
5. Urquhart, *Hammarskjøld,* p. 571. See also Secretary-General's Report to the Security Council.
6. O'Brien, *To Katanga and Back.*

who took them himself to O'Brien. Tshombe was to be arrested in
the last resort, but it was hoped that he would cooperate with the representative of the central government, who it was intended should
take over (administrative) authority for the province.

This collaboration with the Adoula government over the arrest of
Tshombe and the others was a direct departure from the prescribed
limits of ONUC's mandate. The use of force as a means to end secession did not accord with the instructions governing the use of force
by ONUC that were operative at that time. It was not surprising therefore that international reaction was to deplore the UN action. The
operation failed. Tshombe and three of the ministers avoided arrest;
the UN troops were subsequently forced to hand back the objectives
they had secured; and ONUC's military posture was badly shaken, not
least by the fate of a 200-strong company of the Irish contingent
which was encircled at Jadotville, forced to surrender, and held cap-
tive for five weeks before being released on 25 October. The controversy over the rights and wrongs of Round ONE that has continued
over the years has colored the attitudes of member states toward the
future use of the UN peacekeeping instrument and has no doubt had a
major influence on the deliberations of the Committee of Thirty-three
and their deadlock over the role of the secretary-general.

Round ONE solved nothing; the situation if anything became worse.
Tshombe resumed where he had left off as if nothing had happened,
and the mercenaries continued to operate in large numbers in
Katanga. The tragic death of Hammarskjöld, killed in an air crash at
Ndola, Northern Rhodesia, on 18 September when flying to meet
Tshombe, cast a dark shadow over the Congo scene and dimmed
hopes of an early settlement of the Katanga problem. Nevertheless
his successor as secretary-general, U Thant, wasted no time in authorizing his officials in the Congo to take every possible measure for
the restoration of law and order and the United Nations' freedom of
action in Elisabethville. On 24 November the Security Council approved what could be described as the strongest and most direct authorization for the use of force ever issued by that body, in a resolution that gave the secretary-general authority to "take vigorous
action, including the use of requisite measure of force, if necessary,
for the immediate apprehension, detention pending legal action
and/or deportation of all foreign military and para-military personnel
and political advisors not under the United Nations Command, and

mercenaries as laid down in paragraph A.2 of the Security Council Resolution of February 21st, 1961." The resolution further requested the secretary-general to "take all necessary measures to prevent the entry or return of such elements under whatever guise and also of arms, equipment or other material in support of such activities." The resolution also requested "all States to refrain from the supply of arms, equipment or other material which could be used for warlike purposes, and to take the necessary measures to prevent their nationals from doing the same, and also to deny transportation and transit facilities for such supplies across their territories, except in accordance with the decisions, policies and purposes of the United Nations." [7]

But despite this forceful resolution, the situation continued to deteriorate. In December 1961, following a skirmish between the gendarmerie and UN troops on the outskirts of the city—occasioned when the latter attempted to remove a roadblock—ONUC launched a second operation (Round TWO) in Elisabethville. This fared no better than its predecessor but lasted twice as long; in the process severe casualties in UN terms were suffered by both sides. This second failure drew a further storm of criticism because (1) it failed to end Katangan secession, and (2) it was considered that the UN force had gone beyond its declared principle of "force only in self-defense." U Thant strongly denied the second charge, pointing to the harassment that the UN troops had suffered at the hands of the mercenaries and gendarmerie over a long period. The use of force by ONUC can be justified on the grounds that it was retaliatory in reply to a prolonged period of violence against UN persons and positions. People may consider that this puts too fine a point on what is retaliatory and what constitutes self-defense. The fact of the matter is that acting in self-defense can be premeditated as well as instantaneous. Using force without provocation is quite a different matter from using force to secure one's positions and safety against provoked and continuing attack. In the case of Round TWO, the use of force seems to have been wholly justified; but it resulted in the death of 206 Katangan and 6 non-Congolese soldiers, and 50 civilians were killed or wounded. This is a large casualty list for a defensive action, but it was largely brought about by the actions of the mercenary leaders who were responsible for ordering the Katangan soldiers to attack the ONUC troops and positions. Later

7. Security Council Resolution S/5002, 24 November 1961.

on in Cyprus, UNFICYP's terms of reference with regard to the use of force were more clearly defined, but even so there were occasions when a more explicit definition would have helped. What Round TWO in Katanga showed was that a more clearly defined UN policy on the use of force is needed.

Round TWO was concluded with the signing of the Kitona Accord, by which Tshombe recognized President Kasavubu as head of state, recognized the indissoluble unity of the republic and the central government's authority over all parts of it, and agreed to the placing of the Katangan gendarmerie under the authority of the president. In effect this represented the end of secession, but within twenty-four hours the Katanga cabinet reneged on the agreement by declaring that it was not competent to authorize President Tshombe to make such an agreement; a few days later fighting between ONUC and the Katangese flared up again in the north of the province.

Despite subsequent meetings between Adoula and Tshombe, the deadlock over the Katanga issue persisted throughout 1962. In an attempt to break the deadlock, the secretary-general proposed a four-phased program of national reconciliation to achieve a new federal constitution which would provide for a just division of revenues between the central and provincial governments, a reconstruction in the composition of the central government to allow for representation from all political and provincial groups, and a unification of the Congolese armed forces. This Plan for National Reconciliation, as U Thant termed it, was accepted in principle by Adoula, and Tshombe intimated that he was prepared to accept, but once again he defaulted when it came to the point of implementing the terms, doing nothing to halt the armed action of his forces against ONUC and the ANC. Warned by the secretary-general that the program would be implemented despite his inaction, Tshombe made no move. So on 27 December 1962, Round THREE, the final chapter of the secession issue, began and, after only thirty-six hours of fighting, ended with ONUC in complete control of Elisabethville. Secession was at an end, and although there was to be a period of consolidation and another eighteen months of tough peacekeeping for ONUC, the central government gradually gained control over the situation.

ONUC withdrew from the Congo on 30 June 1964, after a four-year operation of a most complex and difficult kind. Had its length, manpower commitment, and financial cost been foreseen, there is not much doubt that it would never have taken place—the cost alone would have dissuaded the member states from embarking upon the operation in the first instance. The balance sheet of achievement is difficult to draw up. Those who were lukewarm at the start were the first to raise their voices at any sign of ONUC's exceeding what they considered to be the limits of its mandate. As the operation proceeded, the limitations of the UN machinery for managing such an enterprise became increasingly evident. The extent of the multinationality of the force and the wide extremes of military experience and characteristics of the various contingents imposed problems and markedly affected the conduct of operations. The precipitous haste with which the force was collected and deployed posed an unprecedented command and control problem for the commander and his staff—a problem made more difficult by the fact that the headquarters staff itself was put together piecemeal as the operation proceeded and was not fully manned until six months after its start. Add to this the size of the territory to be covered, making overall coordination impossible, and the differing loyalties governing the actions of certain of the contingents, and it is a wonder that anything at all was achieved.

Looking at the credit side, the first question to be asked is What did the UN intervention achieve? Dag Hammarskjöld's purpose was for ONUC to restore law and order and enable the Congolese people to find their own destiny under their own government. In structuring the force the Security Council had provided for both requirements—a military force for the first and a civilian technical assistance program for the second. Hammarskjöld's hope was that the two elements would become fully integrated and complementary to each other. Although it cannot be said that the required integration was successfully achieved at this first attempt, it was a brave effort and only faltered because of the lack of understanding on the part of both soldier and civilian of the needs of the other and their failure to recognize that to be effective in both spheres there needed to be an openhanded interrelationship between the two. This is a matter of experience, and the mistakes of the Congo need not be repeated, provided this need is recognized from the start, and operating procedures are designed to meet it. When ONUC arrived in the Congo, it was faced with a rapidly deteriorating security situation and a complete breakdown in the civilian machinery of government—public services, communications, and supply—a serious health issue, a critical disruption in the economy of the country, the total collapse of the social security and judicial systems and of the administration of labor. As the military operation got under way, the civilian operation was able to start picking up the pieces. Reporting to the secretary-general in September 1960, his special representative in the Congo, Rajeshwar Dayal, wrote:

> On attaining independence . . . the country would have been faced even in normal circumstances with many economic, social, political, military and administrative problems. . . . The almost complete lack of trained civil servants, executives and professional people among the Congolese and the striking absence of administrative and political experience . . . created a serious situation for the young republic. But this situation was made worse by a complete failure (on the part of Belgium) to arrange for any organized hand-over to the Congolese of the administrative machinery of government and essential services.[8]

In answer, therefore, to the question: What did the United Nations achieve? there is enough evidence to show that had the United Nations not intervened, the Congo would have become the cauldron into which other African states, the United States, the Soviet Union, and other big powers would have been drawn on one side or the other, and the Congolese themselves would not have acquired the stability on which to build their independent nation-state. That is the justification for the UN operation, whatever mistakes were made. Mongi Slim, former foreign minister of Tunisia, giving the Hammarskjöld Memorial Lecture at Columbia University in 1963, said: "Much controversy arose on the merits of such operations with many pros and cons. But what can be asserted beyond any doubt is that the UN presence prevented the cold war from settling in the Congo, that the unity of the Congo was reestablished thanks in large measure to the UN's efforts and that the UN helped to avoid an impending chaos that threatened peace and security, not only in the Congo but in the whole of the African continent."[9]

In planning the structure of ONUC, the secretary-general was influ-

8. First Report by Rajeshwar Dayal, Special Representative in the Congo, to the Secretary-General, 21 September 1960.

9. Cordier and Foote, *The Quest for Peace.*

enced by his desire to respect the political requirements for African solidarity and indiscrimination. The initial recruitment of national contingents was carried out without great difficulty, with the majority of the troops coming from African states; though there was a sizable contribution from Europe and Asia. After a time, differences in political outlook began to show among the contributing countries; some of them, disagreeing with the secretary-general on matters of policy affecting the role of ONUC, withdrew their contingents. However, the replacements for the withdrawn troops, provided mostly by strengthening existing contingents from other countries, created a more stable and competent force. Of the 93,000 men from thirty-five states who served in ONUC during the four years of the operation, the majority (82.4 percent) came from nineteen Afro-Asian states, with most of the technical units and specialists being provided by the Western countries. Yugoslavia contributed a small contingent during the first few months, while the Congo itself made available an ANC battalion, which served in the force for a period of eighteen months.

The command structure placed the secretary-general's special representative (later to be known by the title of "officer in charge") at the head of the operation, with the force commander and the chief of UN civil operations subordinate to him. The latter were complementary to each other and, though they had their own distinct channels of communication, met daily to coordinate. In spite of this there appears to have been little cross flow of information or close liaison at the lower working levels, the tendency being for each component to operate within its own watertight compartment, with the result that there was little coordination between them. The force commander had a multinational headquarters staff at Leopoldville, but owing to a lack of standard operating procedures and an uneven level of professionalism in method and experience among the staff members, even here coordination and general efficiency left much to be desired. However, in spite of deficiencies in some sectors of the system, the military command structure worked reasonably well, both at force level and at the regional level, where staffs were either single-nation or multinational, dependent upon the composition of the regional force. Some national contingents kept in direct contact with their home governments, which is understandable, but there is no evidence that contingent commanders took instructions from their governments that conflicted with UN policies.

To maintain such a force as ONUC was a major problem. There was a central logistic organization, but the lower echelons were inadequate and insufficient. In the case of UNEF, which was admittedly a much smaller manpower commitment, individual contingents were expected to provide their own particular requirements from their own resources, though Canada assumed the role of logistic coordinator and purveyor of general stores, equipment, and maintenance facilities. In the Congo it was necessary to establish a central maintenance base from which shipments could be made to the various regional districts from where they were distributed down to units. Clearly such a system could only cater for the major items of an operational character, since road and air communications were poor and inadequate, resulting in considerable delays. Dietary considerations were high on the list of importance and a matter of particular concern. Contingents had their different dietary needs, and each had to be provided. Since most of the required foodstuffs had to be imported, not being available locally, ONUC had to coordinate their importation and distribution. The lack of standardization of equipment and vehicles between and within contingents caused the usual provisioning and maintenance difficulties—problems that stayed with ONUC throughout.

The immensity and complexity of the task required the expertise and skill of professionals to handle it. Because of the political constraints against the use of the major powers in UN peacekeeping, the experienced and skilled logistic support units that might have been provided were not available—or acceptable. It was therefore left to India and Pakistan alone to provide the expert logistic support, but their function was limited. Although ONUC was able to get by without its logistic inadequacy affecting too adversely the direction or character of the operation as a whole, the experience in the Congo, later offset by that of UNFICYP in Cyprus, emphasizes the importance of a sound logistic system manned by an adequate and skilled support group. Since the latter is likely only to be found from those countries professionally experienced in operational administration, the question of availability and acceptability become important factors. It is reasonable to believe that the participation of major powers in international peacekeeping operations is a possibility for the future. One might say that a precedent was set in the Congo, as it had been to a lesser extent in the Middle East, in that it was an American air and sea lift that brought the contingents in in the first place and thereafter assisted with other transportation tasks. It is accurate to say that without that American assistance in the first instance it is improbable that the UN Congo operation could ever have taken place. Certainly, as support troops, contingents from major powers could play acceptable roles in peacekeeping and thereby increase the efficiency of the operational logistic and communication systems.

Much has been written about the changing mandate given to ONUC and the manner in which it was carried out. It has already been shown that certain of the contributing countries withdrew their contingents because of differences of opinion with the secretary-general over the conduct of operations and UN operational policy. It has also been remarked that when ONUC resorted to force to protect its troops against persistent harassment by the mercenary-led Katangan gendarmerie, there was widespread condemnation and outcry from even the major powers, including France and the United Kingdom. It is therefore appropriate at this point to consider the overall mandate and the functions of ONUC in respect to it, which can be broken down into five separate mission objectives. Since the use of force remains a debatable question and one that recurs repeatedly when the character of peaceful intervention is being discussed, this aspect of the Congo experience also needs further exploration.

The initiating Security Council resolution of 14 July 1960 simply authorized the secretary-general to provide the Congolese government with such military assistance as was needed until its own national forces were able to carry out their tasks in full.[10] This resolution was supported by a second on 22 July,[11] but it was not until 20 September that the General Assembly specifically required the secretary-general to "take vigorous action . . . to assist the Central Government of the Congo in the restoration of law and order throughout the territory . . . and to safeguard its unity, territorial integrity and political independence in the interests of international peace and security."[12] This was followed on 21 February 1961 by a Security Council resolution urging, for the first time, the use of force as a last resort to prevent civil war.[13] Nine months later, on 24 November, the Security Council strongly reinforced the terms of the previous resolution but

10. Security Council Resolution S/4387.
11. Security Council Resolution S/4405.
12. General Assembly Resolution A/4510.
13. Security Council Resolution S/4741.

added one significant provision which was "to secure the immediate withdrawal and evacuation . . . of all foreign military, para-military and advisory personnel not under the United Nations command, and all mercenaries." [14]

ONUC's function, therefore, as dictated by the provisions of the Security Council's resolutions, might be categorized under five headings:

1. assistance to the central government in maintaining law and order
2. prevention of tribal conflict and civil war
3. maintenance of territorial integrity
4. prevention of external intervention
5. protection of individual human rights

The whole territory of the Congo was ONUC's operational oyster. Within it the dissident elements opposing law and order included the mutineers in the Congolese army, the tribal factions engaged in the political power struggle within the Congo, the secessionist provinces, and the expatriate infiltration by mercenaries, civilian officials, and businessmen supporting the secessionists against the central government. ONUC's function was to assist the latter in maintaining the territorial integrity of the Congo by preventing these divisive elements, singly or together, from destroying it. This posed major problems of procedure for which there was no precedent. Where an international instrument is introduced in a law-and-order role onto the sovereign territory of a nation-state, there is a need to define the standards to be applied in the actual execution of its functions. Although Security Council peacekeeping resolutions provide for the apprehension and detention of persons in the interests of law and order, no supporting directives are issued as to how this is to be implemented. UN forces in practice therefore have acted within the provisions of the UN Declaration of Human Rights of 1948 and the 1949 Geneva Convention; and, therefore, criticism of the United Nations' handling of detainees has been almost nonexistent. In the Congo, UN troops had to perform police functions in the towns and villages, and a civilian police detachment, provided first by Ghana and later by Nigeria, carried out general functions, including assistance to local authorities in the in-

14. Security Council Resolution S/5002.

vestigation of criminal offenses and traffic control in Leopoldville. This civilian police input had its counterpart in UNFICYP, though as will be shown later, the latter was more sophisticated in its role and more multinational in its composition.

A further problem of a conceptual nature can arise out of an offer of assistance to a government that may be accused of using oppressive measures against individuals or groups inside the nation. A UN force might well find itself involved in a law-and-order operation in which its mandate is to assist in preventing the outbreak of direct violence, only to find itself an instrument of reinforcement of a coercive policy of suppression in the social system. This is a problem needing further study and one that cannot be developed here, but the decision is clearly a political one, and one which of necessity needs to be taken at the very outset of an operation by the appropriate UN body. This body must decide whether or not in the circumstances to use the international instrument or, in the event of the oppressive policy being introduced after the UN force has intervened, whether to withdraw it.

The internal situation in the Congo was such that, with little or no governmental control over tribal areas, ONUC very quickly found itself assisting in the control of intertribal conflict and the warring between the various rival political groups. It cannot be said that ONUC brought an end to such violence, but no intelligent person would have expected it to do so in the light of the complexity of the political scene and the vastness of the territory to be covered by the UN force. But, although the fighting continued during the four years of its presence and at times reached threatening proportions, ONUC succeeded in containing it to the extent of preventing full-scale civil war—a positive effect that can reasonably be attributed to ONUC's presence. The establishment of neutral zones, supervised by UN troops and officials, in areas where there was serious tribal conflict helped to keep the feuding tribes separated and reduce the likelihood of civil war, even though these zones were violated from time to time. In spite of constant pressure from one party or another, the UN force never took the side of any one political group or tribe against another in fulfilling its role as a law-and-order force. Maintaining complete impartiality in its relations with all sides is a major factor in the success of any UN force, but it is not always easy to achieve to the satisfaction of those involved. It requires a balancing act of considerable dexterity to satisfy all the people all the time of the force's impartiality, for it is not only a question of an impartial attitude on the part of the United Nations, but the much more difficult problem of the United Nations' policy and actions being seen to be impartial by all the parties to the conflict. When the United Nations is regarded universally and simultaneously as being impartial, it can be concluded that the United Nations is treating the situation with objectivity to the extent of what is practically feasible in the circumstances.

In the context of the impartiality of a UN force's role it is apposite to note that not least of ONUC's functions was its responsibility for ensuring that the code of human and civil rights was not only accepted but also respected. These responsibilities included the provision of physical security to groups and individuals at risk due to the erupting of political and tribal conflict consequent upon the breakdown in the Congo's social structure. The United Nations established refugee camps for those persecuted for political reasons, regardless of individual political attitudes, and provided secure asylum for them inside these camps against interference and molestation by the government or any other institution, group, or individual who might attempt it. Political asylum in these circumstances was based on a directive laid down by the secretary-general, drafted in accordance with the principles of the Declaration of Human Rights.[15]

ONUC also performed a valuable service in the restoration of political stability to the central government when in July and August 1961, through its good offices and a guarantee of complete physical security, it was able to bring about a meeting of the National Assembly at the Lovanium University outside Leopoldville after nearly a year of political stalemate and virtual standstill in authoritative government. This important initiative by both the civilian and military components of ONUC led to the election of Cyrille Adoula as prime minister and the reestablishment of a normal political administration in a strife-torn country. This may have been one of ONUC's most important and successful achievements of all of its four years in the Congo.

In its efforts to assist in maintaining the territorial integrity of the Congo, ONUC was faced with attempts to secede by three of the provinces, Kasai, Orientale, and, most important, Katanga. Of the three Katanga, as has been shown, under the control and direction of

15. Security Council Report 15th Year, Supplements for July, August, and September 1960, S/4529.

Moise Tshombe, was the most persistent, obdurate, and serious and caused ONUC the greatest problem.

A distinction needs to be drawn here between the function of ONUC in maintaining law and order in the internal security role and that of assisting the central government in opposing the three different secessionist movements. Whereas the former was primarily a military intervention to separate the contestants and once separated to keep them apart, the latter, at least to a large extent, was political. Military intervention followed the persistent armed attacks on UN troops and the induction into the Kantangan gendarmerie of large numbers of mercenaries to lead them. Of all its operations against Katanga, only Round THREE was mounted specifically in support of a political objective—the implementation of U Thant's four-phase program for a new federal constitution; but such implementation depended upon the apprehension and removal of "all foreign military, para-military and advisory personnel and all mercenaries" as directed in the Security Council's resolution of 24 November 1961.

Inherent in operations of this character, where force has to be applied in order to achieve prescribed objectives, there is always the problem of how to interpret policy directives set out in Security Council resolutions and to decide upon the optimum action to be taken in the field. The Security Council resolutions are by design couched in ambiguous or at least vague terms, and it is for the commanders in the field, within the directives given to them by the secretary-general, to decide upon their practical implementation. None of the directives to ONUC were particularly clear, and those of 21 February and 24 November 1961, though authorizing the use of force in the last resort, did not define what was implied by "last resort," leaving it presumably to be decided in the field. The controversy that arose over ONUC's actions in Katanga stemmed from the different interpretations placed on the wording of the Security Council's resolutions. Nor is it easy, when faced with such circumstances as Katanga, to maintain complete and executive control over the UN troops. The pragmatic solution of the problem will depend upon the loyalty and the quality of the professional standards displayed by the contingents from the different contributing countries.

In the end, with the United Nations' assistance, the central government overcame the threats to the territorial integrity of the Congo and reestablished itself. The part that ONUC played in this deserves its rightful recognition—and can clearly be regarded as a justification for the United Nations' overall conflict control policy of combining military operations with political and conciliatory efforts.

Territorial integrity depended not only upon prevention of schisms within the Congo but also on the blocking of external intervention by third parties intent upon destroying or at least disrupting national unity. It was as much ONUC's function to combat the latter as it was to prevent the former. In general the latter function involved the elimination of those foreigners whose presence on Congolese territory had been declared illegal by the Security Council. It necessitated the apprehension, detention (in protective custody), and extradition of those categories of persons mentioned in the respective Security Council resolutions—the mercenaries, former Belgian army officers and officials, and civilian advisers not under UN command. The problem was related primarily to the existence in Katanga Province of some six hundred mercenaries, though they were also found elsewhere in the Congo. As history shows, it took ONUC some time to rid the territory of these unwelcome soldiers of fortune, and it was not helped by the lukewarm and uncooperative attitude of some of the Belgian government officials, both inside and outside Katanga, nor by the open disapproval of its operations by some of the bigger powers. Through its perseverance ONUC eventually mastered the mercenary problem and its attendant evils. In one significant instance at Kabalo in April 1961, thirty mercenaries from South Africa were captured by the United Nations, and their interrogation disclosed the network of a recruitment system operating from centers in a number of South African and European cities. Armed with this information, the secretary-general was able to approach the governments of the respective countries with a view to stopping the traffic. As a result a number of the centers were closed down, and the recruitment of mercenaries was considerably reduced.

ONUC was equally concerned with the halting of illegal trafficking in arms, and in this too it was able ultimately to impose a measure of control, though it was handicapped by not possessing specialists trained in the investigation techniques that are required for this kind of task. This problem of controlling arms smuggling and illicit trafficking is common to all third-party operations of the kind with which the United Nations has been concerned—force level and observer missions. So far no UN force has had a specific mandate forcibly to prevent these activities, because this would necessitate the initiation of the use of force to seize the arms. Yet the influx of arms from outside to either or both of the disputants aggravates and escalates the chances for renewed fighting and operates directly against the purposes of the UN operation. It would appear rational that, in circumstances where the control of illegal arms shipments is an essential factor in the effective handling of an international conflict control intervention, there should be provision in the Security Council resolutions for the apprehension and impounding of arms being brought or sent in from outside sources in this way. The matter of the entry of legal shipments, though of equal importance, must remain a matter of political action.

In the final event the prevention of physical intervention by an outside power is not an impossibility, and though the prevention in this case is a political and diplomatic concern at the highest level, the UN force in the field does have the capability to frustrate any such move—largely through the simple factor of its presence, which can constitute a deterrent in itself, but sometimes through taking action to defeat the attempt. At one point early in the Congo emergency the Soviet Union, in secret agreement with Lumumba, supplied him with both aircraft and ground vehicles in his confrontation with Kasavubu—a unilateral initiative serving to hinder rather than assist the United Nations. The closing of the airport at Leopoldville by the secretary-general's special representative, Andrew Cordier, effectively ended any further attempts by the USSR to supplement the first consignment, at least for long enough to allow international political pressure to be exerted against the Soviet Union to desist from its dangerous and inflammatory action. But it was in its deterrent role that ONUC achieved its greatest effect, because, as Mongi Slim made clear, had the United Nations not intervened in the Congo and had ONUC not been present to act as a deterrent, there is no knowing what the extent of outside interference and intervention would have been and to what degree the major powers would have become involved in an African north/south confrontation. One thing seems certain—the territorial integrity of the Congo would have disappeared, and the birth of the new state, Zaire, would never have come about.

It is questionable whether there will ever be another UN operation on the Congo scale, not so much because of the size of the financial and manpower costs, but because of the complexity and dimensions of the task. The cost of the Congo operation when viewed in perspective with other aid programs was relatively moderate, and as a price for peace it was not so much to pay. The price that would have had to be paid had there been no UN intervention would have been astronomically higher. The manpower cost was equally moderate when considered in relation to the task that ONUC had to perform. The size of ONUC therefore was not such as to preclude the possibility of similar sized peacekeeping forces in future. It was more a question of the immensity of the "real estate" that ONUC had to cover and the multifaceted conflict situations with which it had to deal that determined the extent to which it could operate effectively. Assessed against a background of ad hoc machinery and procedures, the wide extremes of military proficiency among the various national contingents, an uncoordinated military/civilian operating plan of action, and, most important of all, a series of loosely defined operational directives, it is a wonder that ONUC achieved as much as it did. Before another Congo size operation could be considered, the deficiencies of its predecessor would first need to be corrected. It is, however, more rational and realistic to think in terms of smaller scale interventions, certainly so long as these deficiencies remain.

The Congo did spotlight the need for a well-considered philosophy for the use of military force on behalf of an international organization in a third-party role. The outcome of the operation would seem to indicate that the UN peacekeeping effort in the Congo should be judged primarily on the merits of how well it fulfilled its political purpose and secondarily on its military efficiency. It does appear possible, therefore, in certain situations for a UN force to be politically effective despite a lack of professional efficiency in the military sense. This would seem to contradict what has been said in the previous paragraph, but not so. In the Congo the political objective ultimately was achieved; the fact that the military instrument was not as efficient as it might have been merely delayed the achievement.

Even so, as UNEF illustrated the weaknesses in the mounting procedures, ONUC resoundingly underscored the deficiencies in the whole machinery of international peacekeeping and the effects that these defects could have on the operational effectiveness of the force. In the absence of any determined attempt to reactivate the provisions of Article 43 of the Charter, the Congo proved emphatically that some kind of readiness system is essential if the United Nations is to be provided with a well-prepared instrument for implementing Security Council resolutions relating to peacekeeping operations. The implications of this requirement are discussed in a later chapter, but for the moment it will suffice to point out that such readiness needs to be initiated at the national level and on a global basis so that the resources from which the United Nations can select are great enough to forestall any difficulties arising from the host country's right of acceptance. Appropriate training and a clear understanding of operating procedures will go a long way toward offsetting the operational and logistic problems that will inevitably arise, as they did in the Congo, in the early days of an operation mounted under an ad hoc system.

The comparative chaos that attended ONUC's first steps was further aggravated through there being no prenegotiated status of force agreement. In the event it took more than one year for the United Nations to negotiate the terms of ONUC's status, and this long delay created difficulties over cooperation between the force and the Congolese government. Optimally the promulgation of a status of force agreement should be a prerequisite to the establishment of a peacekeeping operation, for it validates the legal and operational standing of the members of the force. Since the agreement provides for complete freedom of movement throughout the territory, the right of self-defense, and immunity from legal prosecution for the UN soldier, it is obvious that the legalizing of the force's status is a matter of extreme importance. Although in Cyprus the problem did not arise, this was due to the time gap between the authorization and arrival of UNFICYP, which points to the fact that a too rapid deployment of a force will cause difficulties that could have long-term repercussions and embarrassing effects. However, "the piper calls the tune," and in an emergency like the Congo the vital factor is to establish a UN presence as speedily as possible and to accept the inevitable problems that follow in its wake—though these would be less serious if a readiness system were developed.

A UN principle that has governed one important aspect of its operations from the beginning has been the discouragement of the use of covert intelligence systems for collecting information and the insistence that only overt means should be employed. The limitation that this places on the sources from which information can be gathered has been felt with varying effects. UNEF and ONUC suffered as a result, while UNFICYP and, generally speaking, the observer missions might be said to have benefited. UNEF was at a disadvantage because of its single-sided deployment, while the ONUC operation was often opposed by hostile forces—in the most part by the Katangese. In contrast, UNIFCYP was welcomed by both Greeks and Turks and respected for its impartial posture; as will be seen, this made a significant difference. In the case of the Congo the lack of a properly structured intelligence system deprived ONUC of much essential information that it needed in order to fulfill its functions with the greatest effectiveness. Being unable to employ covert techniques in the collection of intelligence placed ONUC at a considerable disadvantage. The United Nations' insistence on the principle that its peacekeeping forces should not indulge in covert methods of intelligence collection can be justified on both moral and professional grounds. The adverse effects that it had, however, could be remedied by developing a properly balanced system for the collection and evaluation of pertinent information, openly available, for handling by trained professionals.

Many of the lessons that emerge from the Congo can also to a lesser or greater degree be attributed to the other two force level operations,[16] but it was from the Congo that probably most was learned. UNFICYP certainly benefited from the ONUC experience, and, although the character of the Cyprus conflict was different, it was able to use to advantage the sum of that experience. In retrospect UNEF and ONUC might be styled as pilot projects, but since no one conflict is the same as another, each one needs its own diagnosis and treatment. What the Congo proved was the need for complete flexibility of approach to match the varying patterns of conflict with which any force is involved.

16. UNEF II is yet too young to make a proper or complete evaluation of its lessons.

7

Case Study 3—Cyprus (UNFICYP)

The present Cyprus conflict has persisted for ten years, and for all but a few months of that period the United Nations has maintained a peacekeeping force (UNFICYP) on the island. The conflict was not born overnight as was that of the Congo, but is only the latest outbreak in a long record of Greek-Turkish Cypriot strife that has been a part of Cyprus history since the Turks captured the island from the Venetians in the sixteenth century. Cyprus has had many rulers, among them the Romans, the Lusignans, the Venetians, the Turks, and the British; but throughout, the residual heritage has belonged to the Greeks, who first colonized Cyprus 1,400 years before the birth of Christ. It is little wonder therefore that the twentieth-century descendants of the earliest settlers hold to their deep attachment for Greece and believe in their right to *enosis*.[1]

Since the arrival of the Turks, their relationship with the Greeks has been a stormy one and not without bloodshed. The Turkish ascendancy over Cyprus lasted from 1573 until 1878, when the British acquired control of the island. Since then the Turkish Cypriot share of the island's population has decreased to a mere 18 percent, against the 77 percent of the Greeks. However, equally understandable as the Greek community's strong affinity to Greece is the deep patriotism felt by the Turkish community for their motherland. Turkey's geographical proximity (the mainland is visible only forty miles away across the water) and the insecurity arising out of their minority status, induces the Turkish Cypriots to rely increasingly upon the security and safeguards that Turkey can provide. Out of these two strong affinities have grown the prejudice and mistrust that lie at the root of today's conflict. On the one hand, the Greek Cypriots are jealous of

---

1. Greek word for "union" and in this context meaning "union with Greece."

their position as the majority group and, when Cyprus achieved its independence in 1960, considered it an impertinence that the Turkish Cypriots should have anything but a minor role in government—many remained convinced that independence was but a short step toward *enosis*. On the other hand, so far as the Turkish Cypriots were concerned, it was this last conviction that struck at the security of their freedom and existence. This threat still lies heavily over the community and has become an obsession, which as yet no spoken assurance by the Cyprus government can dispel, and which has colored the actions of the Turkish Cypriot leadership since 1960.

More than anything else it was this distrust that dictated the malfunctioning of the island's administrative machinery during the three years of constitutional government. Unfortunately, the constitution designed in Zurich and London (the Zurich-London Agreements) by the four interested parties—Cyprus, Greece, Turkey, and the United Kingdom—never stood the test of time. From the start its structure creaked, and many of its provisions were too complicated to be implemented. There was a progressive deterioration in confidence between the two communities, and the constitution finally foundered upon a routine question of municipal administration. The Greek Cypriots wanted proportionally representative municipal bodies, integrated as a single authority. The Turkish Cypriots saw in this a further design on the part of the Greeks to control their destinies, so threatening their cherished independence as a separate community. Instead, the Turks insisted upon separate municipalities and the right to collect their own taxes and control their own public services. This in the opinion of the Greek Cypriots would have been unworkable, uneconomic, and inefficient. The impasse that stemmed from this difference of opinion remained unresolved, and the functioning of the collective instrument—the House of Representatives—virtually ceased.

It was not surprising that in this deteriorating situation the opportunists were quick to take advantage. Since the 1950s, when a guerrilla campaign (EOKA[2]) was waged against the British in the cause of self-determination and *enosis,* former members of the movement retained their identity and, analyzing the trend of events, were intent upon preparing for the day when they knew violence would come. They built up an armory of weapons, most of which had never been

2. Stands for the National Organization of Cypriot Fighters.

surrendered after the 1950s emergency, and recruited, organized, and prepared. On a smaller scale, for they had no former military organization to build on, the Turkish Cypriots formed their own underground army. So on the night of 21 December 1963 when the first shots were fired and the first victims died in the capital, Nicosia, the two community sectors of the city became armed camps overnight—a partition that was to be repeated in all the major towns and most of the mixed villages on the island.

Once begun, the violence quickly reached a crescendo where it became impossible for the authorities of either side to control it, let alone halt it. All Turkish Cypriots had withdrawn from government, the House of Representatives, their civil service posts, and the police force, and had shut themselves up inside the Turkish quarter of Nicosia with the rest of their community. The national military contingents of Greece and Turkey, permitted to be stationed on the island under the Zurich-London Agreements, had not hesitated to side with their blood brothers and had moved from their camps to join them on the firing line—a fact that was to complicate the subsequent tripartite policing operation agreed upon by the guarantor powers with President Makarios and the Turkish Cypriot Vice-President Kutchuk. With the breakdown of law and order, both had been seeking the help of their respective mother countries and of the United Kingdom who, by treaty, occupied as a sovereign base two areas in the south of the island for military purposes. The agreement reached was that the two national contingents and a third contingent from the British bases would unite as a peacekeeping force under the overall command of a British military commander to assist the government in maintaining law and order and bringing about an end to violence. The British contingent moved to Nicosia on 26 December 1963, but because the other two contingents were physically involved in the conflict, Britain had to shoulder the whole burden of peacekeeping itself for the next three months—a responsibility that the British government never intended nor wished to assume. Despite their conscientious adherence to their mandate of impartial peacekeeping, the British could not escape antagonism toward its actions by those sections of the press and others who bore no love for the British after the EOKA campaign and had no wish to see them again acting out a peacekeeping role in Cyprus. The British government naturally was sensitive to the growing antagonism and considered it undesirable for its soldiers to continue singlehandedly being responsible for peacekeeping duties. It wished for the responsibility to be more widely borne. Toward this end Britain put forward a plan for an international peace force, drawn from NATO countries, to be sent to the island; but although Greece and Turkey accepted the plan, President Makarios was totally opposed to it.[3] So far as he and his government were concerned, the only kind of force acceptable to them would be one established and controlled by the UN Security Council.

After two months of argument it was agreed somewhat reluctantly to approach the United Nations. On 4 March 1964 the Security Council authorized the secretary-general to raise a peacekeeping force for Cyprus.[4] The mandate, which was initially for a single period of three months, required the force "in the interest of preserving international peace and security, to use its best efforts to prevent a recurrence in fighting and, as necessary, to contribute to the maintenance and restoration of law and order and a return to normal conditions." Subsequently it has been necessary to renew the mandate many times, extending its length to six-month periods. Only once so far in its history of peacekeeping has the United Nations been able to terminate an operation on the originally intended date, and that was the interregnum administration in West New Guinea in 1963.

Two matters of interest appear in the mandate, both of which are worth a comment. First, the declared purpose of the force was to act in the interest of preserving international peace and security; second, the role of the force was defined as contributing to the maintenance and restoration of law and order. Taking first the basic raison d'être, it might be challenged on the grounds that the Cyprus conflict was fundamentally a domestic intrastate conflict between its two communities and that to represent it as a threat to international peace and security was simply a subterfuge to activate a UN peacekeeping operation under Article 39 of the Charter, even though the UN intervention had been requested and was with the consent of the Cyprus government. The challenge, however, can be refuted and the action of the Security Council justified on the grounds that a distinct threat of war between Greece and Turkey would have existed had the Cyprus situation deteriorated, and this would have undoubtedly worsened an already explosive situation throughout the eastern Mediterranean; nor

3. Other NATO countries were not particularly enthusiastic either.
4. Security Council Resolution 5/5575, 4 March 1964.

should the effect of a Greco-Turkish war on the structure of the NATO alliance be dismissed as an inconsequential by-product of the events.

The use of the word *contribute* to describe the intended role of the force is indicative of two things—the desire on the part of the Security Council to leave the provisions of the mandate as flexible as possible, dictating no rigid guidelines nor prescribing any fixed objectives, and the adherence to the accepted principle of UN peacekeeping intervention as one of assistance rather than enforcement—the word *will* does not appear anywhere in the text of the resolution. Commentators on UN peacekeeping actions are the first to point to the weakness and vagueness of the mandates handed to the operational forces and blame the inadequacy of the wording for the ineffectiveness of subsequent field action. It is true that many of those who have been a part of UN peacekeeping have been frustrated by the limitations that have been placed on their actions by the lack of clarity in these mandates. There could be some justification for such criticism in operations where the UN force has a defined line of responsibility and where it mans and supervises an armistice or cease-fire line; perhaps in these circumstances a more definite mandate than those hitherto provided would have been possible. But in a conflict such as that in Cyprus, where the task of each of the six main contingents differs in terrain, scope, and above all in character, anything other than a flexible mandate would be difficult to interpret and implement. This variety of roles is likely to be a common feature of other future operations of the UNFICYP type, necessitating broadly phrased mandates.

Before leaving the question of the mandate and the Security Council resolution that propounded it, a brief comment is relevant to the latter's reference to the government of Cyprus. There are those, and naturally the Turkish Cypriots are foremost among them, who insist that, so long as the Turks are excluded from their rightful positions in the government and are deprived of their constitutional rights in this respect, there is no constitutional government, and that the Greek Cypriots have no legal right to govern in the name of Cyprus. The point, however, is this: the constitution as drawn up under the Zurich-London Agreements is still extant, and though its machinery has broken down, it is still the legal constitution of Cyprus. The reason for the withdrawal of Turkish Cypriot participation in government is also debatable. The Greek Cypriots insist that the Turks withdrew voluntarily and certainly not under duress from them, whereas the Turkish Cypriots are adamant that they left under threat of death and certainly would have been murdered had they remained. Whatever the truth, the government as legally recognized became wholly Greek Cypriot and the only one with which the United Nations could deal. When in 1967 the Turkish Cypriot leadership, which had directed the affairs of the Turkish community in the interim, declared that it had set up its own provisional administration within the Turkish Cypriot enclaves, the United Nations did not then or afterward recognize it either legally or as an official instrument of government.

UNFICYP started forming toward the end of March 1964 when the advance party of the Canadian contingent began to arrive in Cyprus, but it did not become operational until a month later, and even then it was not until the end of June that the whole force was assembled. In comparison with UNEF and especially ONUC, this was leisurely indeed and has been the source of comment in the numerous writings on the United Nations in Cyprus. The important difference between UNFICYP and the other two is that it took over from an ongoing peacekeeping operation, where there were troops (British) already on the ground contributing to the maintenance of law and order. No such situation existed at Suez or in the Congo when the United Nations arrived, and the early days of both operations were bedevilled with administrative as well as operational control deficiencies that are the natural outcome of ad hoc emergency operations. UNFICYP was lucky and probably unique in its advantage of having an existing viable foundation on which to build. It goes without saying that a deliberate buildup of a force over a period of weeks is less likely to suffer from early chaos and growing pains than an operation mounted in the space of a few days. Although Cyprus may be the only experience of its kind, there was wisdom in not rushing the fences, and the benefits to the operational handling of UNFICYP that derived from its steady beginning were incalculable—one must not, however, be lulled into the false position of drawing too many basic lessons from what was after all a rather unique experience.

In composition UNFICYP drew its contingents from Austria, Canada, Denmark, Finland, Ireland, Sweden, and the United Kingdom. All except Austria provided infantry troops of battalion strength, while Austria's contribution was a field hospital. Canada and the

United Kingdom each added a reconnaissance squadron of armored cars to their contingents, and the latter supplemented its contingent still further by providing the transportation, supply, and maintenance units. Recently, Canada has withdrawn its squadron, Ireland has reduced considerably the size of its contingent, while Austria has made available its standby battalion to fill the vacuum left by the Irish. Being almost entirely European in character—Canada being the exception, though as a member of NATO it has a stake in Europe—the problems of adjustment that could have occurred had the force been more multinational did not arise. Nor did the disparity in military experience create any difficulties—on the one hand there were the professional units of Canada, Ireland, and the United Kingdom; while on the other there were the units of Denmark, Finland, and Sweden, largely composed of volunteer reservists, but from countries with a wealth of UN peacekeeping experience behind them. This happy mix was reflected in the staffing of the force headquarters, where the appointments were distributed among the nations contributing contingents to the force. Thanks to the care and the insistence upon high standards with which staff officers have been chosen by their respective governments, there have been few misfits, and the working relations within the headquarters and between the headquarters and contingents have been very good, both operationally and in terms of temperament. Since lessons can be learned from them, two innovations in organization need mentioning here. UNFICYP has a military economics branch for dealing with economic problems arising in the battle zone and a multinational civilian police element. More will be said about these two later, but they quickly proved to be of inestimable value and have contributed a great deal to the humanitarian aspect of the operation.

UNFICYP never exceeded 7,000 in strength and, though there were times when its resources were stretched to capacity, it was possible to reduce its size as operational circumstances altered, so that it is presently half the strength it was at the beginning. Besides the military, there are some fifty UN civilian contract staff members appointed or recruited by the Field Operations Service at UN headquarters in New York, who make up the field secretariat, dealing with the myriad of tasks related to the administrative and legal requirements of UNFICYP.

At the head of UNFICYP are two men, both responsible in their separate right to the Security Council through the secretary-general's office, but very much interlinked in day-to-day decisions—the force commander and the special representative of the secretary-general. Not only does the operational management devolve upon these two men, but also the smooth running and the working effectiveness of the force. It is therefore of fundamental importance to both that they be compatible and share each other's thinking as much as possible. This juxtaposition of these two senior professionals is one of the crucial factors in multinational peacekeeping. Cyprus is the first situation in which the principle of dual control has been applied. As distinct from UNEF and ONUC's commitment, the Cyprus situation made such an arrangement possible. The conflict was small in size compared to the other two, and the military and political fields of action were invariably closely interwoven. In Cyprus it has been rare for a military initiative not to have political overtones and vice versa; this therefore requires the closest collaboration at the decision-making level. The strength of the command and control system in Cyprus can be traced to the realization by the two men concerned of the importance of close collaboration and dual decision taking. Although each has direct access to the secretary-general, most communications regarding action taken, action advised, or action requested are jointly drafted and transmitted. The point has been made that the circumstances in Cyprus permitted this system to operate in UNFICYP; a later chapter looks further into the question of command and control in a wider context, so it is sufficient here only to point to the successful working of one of the patterns used so far in UN force level operations.

The basis of UNFICYP's deployment was to match as far as possible the island's district boundaries—to facilitate the essential relationship that would need to exist between UN contingent commanders and district officers and their senior officials. Conflict pressures did not allow for one contingent per district, but all districts were covered according to the intensity of the armed confrontation. Therefore, while the capital of Nicosia initially had two contingents, and the districts of Kyrenia and Lefka had one each, the remaining two contingents covered the four districts of Famagusta, Larnaca, Limassol, and Paphos between them. The problems and tasks of each were by no means the same. In Nicosia the UN troops were positioned in an observation role along the length of a demarcation line established by the British in the early days of the fighting. Known as the "Green

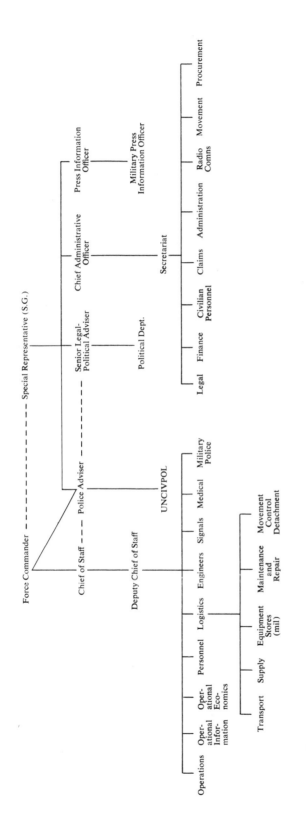

Figure 3. Staff Structure—UNFICYP Headquarters

Line,'' it had become a symbol of partition between the two communities and was certainly seen by the Turkish Cypriot leadership as the dividing line in a partitioned Cyprus of the future. In conception, the line had been intended by the British commander to form a temporary buffer between the two warring communities, along which his soldiers would be stationed to prevent further fighting. In the event, the line was inherited by UNFICYP as a recognized boundary between Turkish and Greek in Nicosia. It has remained such ever since, constituting a major obstacle toward a normalization of relations between the two communities—an example of the dangers inherent in the creation of artificial boundaries, however temporary in intent, without regard to the possible future interpretation of their significance by one side or the other. The area within which the UN soldiers were able to operate was the width of a narrow street on either side of which the opposing armed forces were entrenched. In a situation where a shouted abuse, a thrown brick, or the accidental discharge of a rifle could bring about an immediate shooting response, the UN soldiers on observation duty or patrol could do little to prevent the exchange of fire. Sandwiched in between as they were, they could but observe and report, though this was no easy matter when their field of observation was restricted to tens not hundreds of yards. The technique, therefore, was that of an observer force—to negotiate immediately for a cease-fire, investigate the cause, and apportion the blame. However negative this may sound, in practice, thanks to the vigilance of the UN soldiers, the situation along the Green Line remained reasonably temperate from 1965 onward, despite serious escalations of violence during the same period elsewhere on the island.

A similar responsibility faced the United Nations in two other districts—Kyrenia and Lefka—though here it was open country with the entrenched positions facing each other over distances ranging from one thousand to one hundred yards. Even so the task was the same, with UN posts deployed between the two defense lines from which observation and patrolling took place. The difference was the degree of shooting, sometimes exceeding an exchange of 4,000 rounds of ammunition in a single incident, with the UN posts in the direct line of fire. As in the case of the Green Line, there was not much that the United Nations could do until the shooting ended, and this was liable to take longer, since the distances that the local UN commander had to travel to the respective Greek and Turkish battle headquarters were greater. But once the contact was achieved, the technique was the same—cease-fire, investigation, and apportionment of blame. Because of the mountainous terrain the process took time, but except for a few instances in the early days of the operation, the United Nations was consistently successful in halting the firing and in preventing the shooting from developing into more serious ground fighting.

In contrast, the rest of the island posed a different problem for the United Nations. Instead of lines of armed confrontation, towns and villages were garrisoned by units of the government-raised National Guard or by Turkish Cypriot fighter groups. Camps housing units of the Greek National Army were located at strategic points close to areas where the strength of the fighter groups constituted a threat. These units had come to the island clandestinely in the early months of the emergency. Their presence was never officially recognized, though it was well known that they were there. The problem, therefore, for the UN troops assigned to these open warfare areas was, and still is, to be instantly ready to interpose themselves between the opposing sides whenever and wherever an incident of any size threatened peace and security and provided either side with an excuse to attack the other. It was their job to get there first and place themselves in the middle as an effective buffer force. To do this successfully requires accurate information and quick communications; without these the chances of achieving an interposition are remote. To facilitate the former, observation squads are deployed into those areas known as or thought likely to be potential sources of trouble. The observation squads are backed up by mobile patrols, and all are in communication directly or through relay with the operations room at the contingent headquarters which, in turn, is directly in touch by radio with the force headquarters; so that at any time of crisis at least three levels of command could be negotiating a settlement of the problem or taking action to strengthen the hand of the local UN commander while he continues to negotiate at the place of crisis. There is, of course, much more fluidity in the course that these operations take as compared to those in the direct confrontation areas. The terrain to be covered is greater here and necessitates a wider UN deployment. Fully stretched as they are, the UN troops must be capable of a completely flexible response to counter the frequency and widespread nature of incidents. Whether or not an incident escalates into dangerous dimensions depends very much on the handling of the initial incident by the squad commander (noncommissioned officer) or junior officer on the spot. The speed of reaction on the part of the commanders at all levels, in both the National Guard and the fighter groups, is such that reinforcements of considerable size could be ready and moving at the first scent of trouble. A great deal therefore depends on the ability of the junior commanders to dissipate tense emotions and situations and to persuade the protagonists to leave it to the United Nations to resolve the problem—peacefully and impartially. Negotiation is the primary weapon of the peacekeeper and must be given every chance of succeeding. It also provides a breathing space in which preparatory steps can be taken at the higher echelons of the command chain to ensure prompt action, were the efforts of the commanders on the spot not to succeed. In the event, these tactics have succeeded more often than they have failed, and, except in a few instances, the backup arrangements adequately dealt with those incidents that the local commanders were unable to control.

Though the military economics staff operates through each contingent in every part of the island, it has mounted its most important effort in the confrontation areas of Kyrenia and Lefka. In these two districts the extension and advancement of the two opposing trench systems has meant that small holdings, vineyards, and grazing land belonging to members of either community are now situated in "no-man's land" or, worse still, behind the forward defensive position of the "enemy." So that livelihoods could be maintained and the fruits of harvest gathered in for the benefit of the rightful owner, UNFICYP has throughout its stay in Cyprus escorted the harvesters to and from their fields and vineyards wherever situated and remained as protection while they worked. Similarly, they have ensured the right of the goatherds to graze their flocks safely under the eyes and guns of the opposition. It has been the responsibility of each national contingent to assist economic and social freedom wherever it can and the duty of the economics staff to coordinate and direct its efforts to the best advantage of both communities. Its activities have included health, educational, and relief arrangements for those Turkish Cypriots unable to move freely outside their enclaves because of the political situation, ensuring that they could receive regular and emergency medical attention, education and school examination papers, mail, and the necessities for living—food, clothing, fuel oils, agricultural equipment, building materials, and Red Crescent supplies from Turkey. This contribution has made it possible for the Turks to exist at an acceptable living standard where without it they would have severely suffered.

In close support of the military operations is the relatively small element of civilian police (UNCIVPOL). Its commander also fills the role of police adviser at force headquarters, where he is responsible to both the force commander and the special representative. Although civilian police had been used in previous UN operations, including the Congo, a complete multinational police component had never before been raised; and whereas the police on former occasions had authoritative tasks to perform, those in Cyprus perform in an advisory role, having none of the normal executive powers permitted them in their own national police forces. Though its role is described more fully in a later chapter, at this juncture it is appropriate to emphasize the importance of the contribution that UNCIVPOL has made to the Cyprus peacekeeping operation and to draw some useful conclusions from its achievements. With or without executive powers, a civilian policeman holds a special position vis-à-vis himself and the public. His training is based on civic law and the upholding of civil rights. To the public he is the agent of the law. In a situation like Cyprus, where civil as well as human rights are not always respected, where a reign of terror is a recent memory, and where intercommunal murders, abductions, and victimization are still common occurrences, the presence of an impartial police unit can reduce the sense of insecurity that obstructs any degree of reconciliation. The policeman is far better equipped, both mentally and by training, to fill this psychological vacuum than is the soldier, because he is dealing with a community problem that he has met many times in a different setting in his own home police force. "A round peg in a round hole" is an axiom that can appropriately be applied here, and it is doubly important in the sensitive arena of peacekeeping that the right man should be used. UNCIVPOL has more than proved its worth and has underlined the value of the role that a policeman can perform in a peacekeeping operation. The relatively restricted framework within which UNCIVPOL has had to operate should not be allowed to minimize the importance and the potential of its contribution. UNCIVPOL is a success story that should not be ignored but used as a basis for further development; for as we have said, there are many aspects of international control of violence for which the policeman is better suited than his military counterpart. As conflict requires its proper treatment, so does the treatment require the right person to correctly administer it.

UNFICYP's story falls into two phases, that from 1963 to 1968, when the primary factor was violence and the emphasis was on violence control, and that from mid-1968 to the present day, when political negotiation rather than military action has taken priority. Militarily, during the second phase the island has been quiescent and calm in contrast to the "hot war" that preceded it. Without the daily exchange of fire and constant procession of incidents, any of which could escalate to threatening proportions, UNFICYP's military role has lapsed into one of routine observation, patrolling, and liaison. It is open to question whether UNFICYP as presently structured and operationally oriented is relevant to the current situation on the island—or whether as the character of conflict changes so should its treatment adjust to the new requirements. However, important as the point is, we are concerned at this moment with UNFICYP's military operations in the first phase, and we can leave commentary on the postviolence phase until later.

In the first five years of UNFICYP's time in Cyprus, there was hardly a day when a threat to the peace did not occur. In all that time UNFICYP, with two exceptions, succeeded in maintaining its objective of keeping the peace and preventing a renewal of the fighting, and it did this without firing a shot. The speed with which each single incident could escalate in dimension required the highest degree of alertness and vigilance on the part of each and every UN soldier and a tactical flexibility in force planning and mobility to enable it to intervene swiftly and effectively at the right place at the right time. The number of times that the force achieved this goal is a measure of its success in attaining the third of its objectives—to create an atmosphere within which a settlement could be reached.

The two exceptions referred to relate to the fighting at Kokkina in 1964 and at Ayios Theodoros in 1967. In both cases UNFICYP was unable to persuade the government and Turkish Cypriot leadership to desist from provocative acts that inevitably would lead to fighting and violence. In both instances UNFICYP urged that it should be given the opportunity to bring about a settlement of the immediate dispute that was threatening peace, but the plea was disregarded in the first and unacceptable in the second. The fighting that did break out was contained and limited to the villages concerned, largely due to UNFICYP's continuing efforts to localize the conflict and arrange a cease-fire and, specifically, in the case of Ayios Theodoros, to the insistence of the UN troops on the spot on remaining in position around the village, despite the obvious dangers to their own lives. This deterring presence in the middle of the battlefield had much to do with the brief nature of the fighting and the imposing of a cease-fire after some ten hours. The fact is worthy of record because in the previous incident at Kokkina the UN troops were withdrawn from their battle line positions as soon as the fighting began and therefore were in no position to influence the battle, which lasted seven days. It is interesting to conjecture what would have been the outcome had the UN troops abandoned their positions at Ayios Theodoros.

The fighting at Ayios Theodoros on 15 November 1967 prefaced the end of phase one. It resulted in the killing of twenty-two Turkish Cypriots, but possibly more emphatically it made people realize the senselessness of such an action, where a totally undefended village could be smashed by artillery, mortars, and heavy machine guns. The reaction was immediate. Turkey threatened invasion of Cyprus to secure the safety and freedom of the Turkish Cypriots. International diplomacy prevailed in dissuading Turkey, but at the price of the withdrawal of all the Greek National Army units on the island and the lifting of the blockade that had kept the Turkish Cypriots confined for five years. Although the Greek National Guard and the Turkish Cypriot fighters still operate from their prepared bases and face each other along the Green Line and along their defense lines in the north, since November 1968 the incidence of violence has diminished to negligible proportions, amounting to less than a dozen shooting incidents over a mandate period of six months.

In contrast to the actions at Kokkina and Ayios Theodoros, it should be emphasized that UNFICYP, besides its daily containment achievements, has had its major successes too. One of these was at Melousha in July 1966 when a similar action to that at Ayios Theodoros was precipitated by the National Guard. On this occasion UNFICYP was able to interpose a force between the village and the advancing Greek troops. When negotiations to effect the withdrawal of the Greek forces finally broke down, the UN force was sufficiently strong to represent a considerable deterrent to any attempt to attack the village. When this fact became clear to the commander of the National Guard, and he was told by UNFICYP that were the village to be attacked, the UN troops would oppose the attack with force (since it would have to be made through the latter's positions), he realized that discretion rather than action was the better policy and returned his troops to barracks. One might ask why a similar interposition could not have been effected at Ayios Theodoros. There the circumstances were different in that instead of the guilt being all on one side it was shared, with the initial provocation being from the Turkish Cypriot side. When the attack came, it was therefore difficult for the United Nations to assist those who provoked it in the repelling of it. In retrospect it is true that a physical intervention could have been managed had UNFICYP known of the buildup of forces in the area, including artillery units. The National Guard commander's intentions would then have been clear, and UNFICYP could have legitimately made its dispositions accordingly. This was one instance when covert intelligence sources would have been valuable, since the units were moved into position under cover of darkness on the night of 14–15 November. Even so, it still might have been possible to interpose a force after the first shots had been fired had there been sufficient manpower available to muster a composite force of battalion strength—anything less would have been inadequate. Unfortunately the spare manpower did not exist at short notice.

In a different context UNFICYP recorded another significant success when in Paphos District in August 1967 it resolved a crisis situation that had brought normal life virtually to a halt in that part of the island. In doing so it added another dimension to the role of the peacekeeper—that of "reconciliation through communication." A number of murders of members of both communities, amounting to an intercommunal vendetta, had brought life to a standstill in the rural areas of Paphos District. No one would leave the confines of his own village, even to work in the fields and vineyards on its very outskirts, for fear of being abducted and murdered. No deliveries of food were made from the towns because the tradespeople would not venture into the areas for the same reason. It was therefore necessary for UNFICYP to form convoys to ensure protection for all wishing to travel—an arrangement not popular with the government, which believed that this would encourage greater resistance and delay an early settlement of the problem. UNFICYP's initiative that brought the issue to an end was to carry out an on-the-spot survey in each village,

Greek and Turk, to discover what was at the root of the problem and what might be done to break the existing deadlock. The outcome was a clear admission that they needed assurances that their personal safety and security would be guaranteed in the future before they would begin moving freely again. It seemed that the best way to give them what they wanted was to bring them together face to face to receive these assurances personally. In the course of the next few weeks a series of meetings were arranged at which the leaders from the various villages met, discussed their differences, and gave their assurances—assurances that were honorably kept afterward. Sometimes two villages took part, sometimes as many as eight, but all ended the same way. Each meeting was supervised by an UNFICYP officer and, at most, discussion ranged far wider than the single issue that brought it about, covering a number of areas of interest and concern to those present. The immediate results were a return to normality in the day-to-day life of the villages and a reestablishment of freedom of movement; but the meetings had also provided an opportunity for the villages of the two communities to reopen communication with each other after a break of four years. As a conciliatory effort this initiative of UNFICYP was valuable and constructive.

When setting down the lessons to be drawn from the UNFICYP operation, it is important to reiterate that the circumstances under which it began and the facilities that were available in the way of support backing were exceptional if not unique. Although it is possible that a UN force might in the future take over from an existing national or regional peacekeeping force, it is most unlikely that it would ever again have the advantage of a built-in administrative base, as was provided by the British in Cyprus, to meet all its operational logistic requirements. But this does not stop us from drawing valuable and important lessons from both the structure and the conduct of the operation, which deserve careful study when considering the future handling of international control of violence.

Mention has been made already of the style and form of mandate drawn up for UN peacekeeping forces and the general vagueness with which those given to force level operations have been worded. It is understandable that, apart from the various political reservations that its members may have toward drafting them more firmly, the Security Council is likely to be hesitant to make a mandate too specific at the outset of an operation because of the uncertainty of the situation in the conflict area and of the confused picture of events on which they are required to base their decision. There have been occasions when an original force mandate has been amended or added to, as in the Congo, but so far as Cyprus is concerned, the mandate has remained unchanged through the ten years of UNFICYP's existence. It seems that, providing there is no change for the worse requiring more specific action by the peacekeeping force, the Security Council is content to allow mandates to continue as first prescribed. The Katanga secession required a different initiative from that endorsed in ONUC's initial mandate; but in Cyprus, with one brief exception during the crisis of November 1967, the situation was kept under control and militarily improved rather than deteriorated. For this reason there is no doubt that the mandate was sufficient to the need and required no adjustment. But no emergency ever remains on the same level, and unless the role of a peacekeeping force is constantly being reviewed against the changing circumstances and patterns of the conflict, it can become a negative act; and once it becomes a negative act, it becomes counterproductive. It is open to question whether such a situation has been reached in Cyprus so far as the military action is concerned. No one can deny that the operational emphasis has changed radically from that which pertained in 1964 and that now it is primarily a political and a reconciliation problem rather than one of violence control. As the nature of the conflict altered and politics took the center of the stage, one might have expected the role of the force to be adjusted to meet the needs of the changed circumstances, but this has not happened. The operational tasks have remained fundamentally the same, and soldiers continue to patrol the Green Line and the no-man's land in Kyrenia and Lefka districts and stand in observation posts in those same potentially dangerous areas of the island, despite the fact that the number of shooting incidents in a six-month period is less than a dozen, against the 300–400 during a comparable period in the "hot" years of 1966–67. The unwillingness of the Security Council to consider reviewing and revising the original mandate to suit today's needs does a disservice to the whole structure of peacekeeping, for it disenchants those contributing nations who see their contingents employed year after year in keeping the peace in a conflict where the fighting stopped over five years ago. This disenchantment is echoed in the hearts and voices of the soldiers themselves, especially the professionals, who find their tasks monotonous and irksome and see no point to what they are doing. There is doubt in the minds of member states as to the future of UN peacekeeping operations; this disenchantment could be decisive in their response to new peacekeeping proposals. The flexibility of a mandate, the regular review of its provisions, and the readiness of the Security Council to revise it as circumstances demand could revitalize interest. It is for these reasons that important lessons are to be drawn from UNFICYP.

In 1968 Cyprus might have had a joint police–military observer mission in place of UNICYP, with a civilian directing its operations— it would have amounted to not more than 1,000 in strength, of which the police would have made up half. The proposal was not acceptable then; now, five years later, it could be an answer for Cyprus.

Monotony and boredom are major problems in any operation where observation plays the larger part in the soldiers' daily routine. Days and weeks can pass without any incidents, and yet the demand for vigilance and alertness never diminishes. It is probably more difficult for the professional than for the nonprofessional soldier because he has the added problem of adjusting to a different form of soldiering from the one to which he is accustomed. There is therefore a limited period that a soldier can remain at a peak level doing a task of this kind—ideally not longer than six months. This is normally the length of a volunteer's contract and will be as much as he will do, but for the professional there are often pressures to make his duty tour longer, both from his government and from the force headquarters itself, which has the never ending problem of maintaining continuity. But these pressures should be resisted, except for key staff officers whose operational duties make continuity a top priority. Insomuch as those contingents with regular army battalions come from other operational roles in other theaters, the training factor is all important; a six-month tour with UNFICYP did mean that the remaining six months of the year were available for normal operational training. On the only occasion in Cyprus when 40 percent of the volunteers in one of the contingents were allowed to extend their duty to complete a second consecutive six months, there was a marked falling off in their performance of their duties, and the experiment was not repeated.

The advantages of a military economics department and a civilian police component have been strongly stated and deserve recognition as two essential factors in any peacekeeping operation of similar proportions and character to Cyprus. A third valuable experience to be gained from UNFICYP is the advantage of having the logistic system the responsibility of one country. In Cyprus it was, of course, already positioned and operating on a peacetime basis when UNFICYP arrived, but there is no reason why one country's contribution in other peacekeeping operations should not be made in this way. The advantages are obvious—a single organization is more economic, more efficient, and smoother running, and so long as there can be a standardization of the major items of equipment, problems over provisioning can be considerably reduced. In Cyprus, as in other operations, the national contingents provided their own weapons, radios, and combat vehicles, while the British provided the troop and supply vehicles, food, fuel, backup maintenance organization, and ordnance stores. In a different setting, the massive supply and maintenance available from the British bases would not exist; however, the establishment of a field maintenance depot at the start of an operation could meet the needs of the force during its buildup stage and thereafter as its logistic support. The responsibility for running the depot would be that of the contributing country which undertakes the logistic support role. The same country would provide the equipment and resources not indigenous to the individual contingents, as illustrated above, and the supply and maintenance detachments that operate them. The depot would be expected to handle all incoming and outgoing equipment and stores, including those provided by contributing countries for their contingents. To facilitate the smooth working of the depot, there should be a logistic liaison detachment from each contingent attached to the depot. Any suggestion that a centralized system of this kind would not work can be refuted by the fact that in Cyprus the British supplied the food for all contingents, including special items of national taste. One further benefit that could derive from the concept of a single-nation logistic system is that it could open up the field from which contingents could be selected to include nations that would be otherwise unacceptable in a front line role, countries with sophisticated military logistic organizations.

It has been described in the previous chapter how, from the beginning of force level peacekeeping operations, there has been argument as to the need and desirability for the force to have an efficient intelligence staff, organized and oriented like the standard operational staffs found in national armies at regimental, brigade, and divisional levels. The policy of the United Nations is that field intelligence cells are undesirable and unacceptable in an impartial third-party intervention. This standpoint is not as naïve as it may appear, but its application must take into account the character and circumstances of the conflict in which the United Nations has become involved. Careful consideration has to be given to the advantages and disadvantages to the UN force of a covert system of intelligence. The character of the conflict and the role of the peacekeeping force must dictate the answer. One needs to assess the benefits that will be gained from covert rather than overt methods and set against this the harm that the use of covert methods could do to the relations between the force and the disputants. The equation will be different in every case. In the Congo, where ONUC was in direct confrontation with the mercenaries from the moment of Katanga's secession, there is little doubt that an intelligence staff and network would have been advantageous and justified. In Cyprus, where the relationship between UNFICYP and the two communities is of a more intimate nature, covert intelligence cells would have done more harm than good. The information compiled from overt observation and contacts has been sufficient for UNFICYP to do its job effectively. Covert intelligence obviously would improve on what overt observation could provide, but at the same time it would be more likely to hamper rather than facilitate UNFICYP's work. In an operation where trust, confidence in, and respect for the UN force is such a vital factor to its success, undercover and clandestine methods of operation can close the mouths of those who are normally prepared to talk and turn trust into suspicion. Because UNFICYP has relied on overt methods only, that danger has not had to be faced. The conclusion that one can draw, therefore, is that there should not be a hard-and-fast rule as there is at present, but that the circumstances of the conflict, the role of the peacekeeping force, and the attitude of the disputants toward it should decide the makeup of the system to be used for the collection and evaluation of the overt information available.

In one respect UNFICYP was at a disadvantage where a fuller intelligence structure might have been helpful, though the difficulty was brought about more by its mandate than through the lack of intelligence. As has already been indicated, units of the Greek National Army had clandestinely infiltrated into Cyprus with their weapons

and equipment (including some tanks and guns) from the early days
of the emergency—in all, some 7,000 were on the island. Similarly,
though in lesser numbers, Turkish military personnel had infiltrated
over the years. Since these troops could not be expected to serve on
the island indefinitely, there were regular rotations of individuals similar to the overt rotations of the official Greek and Turkish contingents stationed on the island as part of the treaty arrangements. Although UNFICYP was aware of these clandestine rotations and was
able to monitor those of the Greeks, it had no mandate to prevent
them. The limit of its action in this respect was to report the facts
each time to New York for the question to be raised at the diplomatic
and political levels. These troop movements did nothing to ease the
difficulties of the situation, nor the tensions that emanated from them;
not surprisingly they added to both, yet UNFICYP was powerless to intervene. It would have been an act of enforcement had it done so.
The lesson to be learned from this is that where the possibility exists
in an island conflict or where the country concerned has a seaboard, it
would be an advantage to add a maritime element to the force so that
clandestine seaborne operations of the kind described above could be
investigated and tactfully turned back before reaching the shore. The
manner in which this interception could be effected need not take on
the character of a blockade or an enforcement act. The naval force
required could be expected to operate as an inshore patrol with the
authority to check on all craft inside a prescribed sea limit and not on
recognized entry routes to main harbors.

One experience worth recording from Cyprus, though not specifically a lesson for the future, was the successful grouping of units
from a number of contingents into mixed task forces for special
operations. More than once, because of the size of the problem and
because of the insufficient force available from the contingent in
whose area the problem existed, it was necessary to reinforce the
"home" contingent with elements from the others. In this way it was
possible to interpose a viable force between the contestants, which
was generally superior in size and weaponry to them. This mixing of
national contingents probably would not find favor with the governments concerned were it to be for a prolonged period, nor for good
reason would it be satisfactory—for among other reasons the task
force, once constituted, must be under the operational command of
the contingent commander in whose territory the operation is taking

place. This makes sense when it is recognized that it is he who has the personal contacts and liaison with the local authorities and commanders of the military forces on both sides. Therefore, for short operations, these international task forces can work very well and help to strengthen the total image of the UN force. Sovereignty is sometimes a difficult thing to combat, and the natural tendency is for individual contingent commanders to look on the territory for which they are responsible as their own and resent interference. This can make for difficulties and can work against the best interests of the UN operation.

The Cyprus dispute is not yet resolved, and UNFICYP continues to stand surety for the military peace in the island. It is to be hoped that too protracted a continuance of its presence in its existing form will not offset its considerable achievements of the past through a disillusionment and a dissatisfaction with its role in the present; nor discourage rather than encourage member states, particularly those who have contributed contingents and funds, from taking a wider and more positive look at the benefits that can be derived from such peacekeeping initiatives.

8

United Nations Observer and Supervisory Missions

Force level operations though different in character are, so far as organization and composition are concerned, very akin to standard military operations. This has been demonstrated in the preceding chapters. Observer missions as devised and developed by the United Nations are of a different nature. They can be said to represent an extension of the functional precedents set by the League of Nations in the 1920s and 1930s. During these two decades there were two important occasions when an international force fulfilled an impartial observer role in disputed areas. In 1920 a nine-state "supervisory force" was raised to monitor and observe a plebiscite in Vilna, over which Lithuania and Poland hotly contested sovereignty. In the event, the plebiscite never took place, but it is interesting that in its designation the role of the observer force was laid down by the Council of the League of Nations as being "a peace force, not a fighting force, simply there to perform police duties." Fifteen years later a similar operation was mounted to supervise the plebiscite on the future of the Saarland and was structured on the same principles and directives as that for Vilna. The significant difference was that the Saar force was "entrusted with the maintenance of law and order . . . before, during and after the plebiscite" and therefore assumed the character of a policing force. Foreshadowing their future involvement in UN peacekeeping operations, it is of interest that Denmark, Norway, and Sweden were among the countries that made contingents available to the League for both Vilna and the Saar.

Peacekeeping forces are deployed into active conflict situations to bring an end to fighting and thereafter to maintain an impartial presence between the opposite sides in the dispute, so as to prevent a renewal in the fighting. Observer missions can do no more than act as the eyes and ears of the Security Council, investigating incidents, acting as fact finders, and where possible, by negotiation, preventing incidents from escalating to serious proportions. In this chapter we concentrate on the observer missions of the United Nations and, through case study analysis, assess their effectiveness. We have chosen to categorize them under two heads: (1) supervision of armistice and cease-fire agreements and (2) fact-finding and reporting missions in international disputes. Those in the first category can be long-term commitments—the UN Truce Supervision Organization (UNTSO) and the UN Military Observer Group in India and Pakistan (UNMOGIP) were both set up twenty-six years ago and are still in operation— while those in the second tend to be of short duration, necessitating the checking of particular data which if left unchecked could cause an international dispute; the UN Observer Group in Lebanon (UN- OGIL) is one example.

The problems that face an observer or control mission and the limitations under which they have to operate are not generally appreciated or gauged. Lacking the strength of a backup force and denied adequate freedom of movement [1] in the exercise of their task, they are wholly dependent on the cooperation and assistance of the disputants for the extent to which they can fulfill their mandate. It is not overly surprising that this cooperation is not always forthcoming and that such missions, though accepted or requested by the disputants in the first instance, are subsequently ignored—only being used by either side when it suits its purposes to do so. Despite this the records show that the observers have assiduously performed their unenviable task— unenviable because of the frustrations and dangers attendant upon their role—and have constituted a deterring influence which, though not preventing fighting, has discouraged the more openly hostile acts that undoubtedly would have occurred had there been no observers present. Although some may challenge this claim, political moralities and national images are such that states tend to be embarrassed at being labelled the aggressor in the forum of world opinion, except when the issues are so great that the tide of war swiftly follows, and any embarrassment is submerged in national pride. The opportunities for a successful intervention are likely to be greater in the smaller

1. In UNTSO the observers are restricted to the close confines of their observation posts— in extent approximately 250 square meters.

kind of border incident. Though nothing is wholly trivial in a confrontation across a guarded frontier, here the effect tends to be fragmentary with the action following from a minor harassment raid or reprisal, from which an instantaneous emotional reaction results in an escalation in violence. Such incidents can be and have been peacefully settled by third-party intervention before they could escalate into something much worse. The value of observer missions, therefore, is that they can provide an objective report system that can assist those who have the political ability (and inclination) to react in time to resolve threatening situations. Like force level operations they are not peacemakers, nor in any real sense can they keep the peace; they can only contribute toward a peaceful settlement of disputes. The value of their contribution is relative to the degree of cooperation shown by the disputants. It is as much in the interests of the latter that this cooperation should be readily given; for them subsequently to criticize the observer mission for being ineffective and superfluous is as much a condemnation of their own inadequacy as of any failure on the part of the observers.

The difficulties that these missions face are formidable, and their effective fulfillment of their role is dependent on many factors outside of their control. Can one therefore justify them as being credible in terms of achievement? Possibly not so far as concrete results are concerned, but then is it fair that the assessments should be made on "achievement" alone, when the host countries concerned have obstructed rather than assisted them in the performance of their role? It is more constructive to consider the concept and how these missions can be used to the best advantage by drawing on the experience and performance of past and current missions.

The UN missions have been mounted as a matter of international necessity and not only to meet a request from a particular nation-state. They have been provided for the prime purpose of contributing to the maintenance of international peace and security, either through observation, investigation, or negotiation. This is the perspective in which they should be viewed, not as simply providing a "domestic" service for host countries who may or may not take advantage of their presence to settle their problems—which unfortunately few of them do. International peace and security require the cooperation of all states; therefore, it does not make sense that, having requested or consented to the presence of an observer mission on its territory to assist in preventing conflict or securing an armistice line, a host country should disregard its potential and obstruct rather than facilitate the role the mission has come there to perform. It is not surprising that with this not infrequent attitude toward UN observer missions, there should be a lack of confidence on the part of member states in the degree of ability and viability that such missions have for making any positive contribution to the settlement of disputes. It is little more than a vicious circle with the peacekeeping image of the United Nations suffering a little more each time, until the point is reached where the instrument of the world organization is not used any more, and international missions are mounted independently of it.

Disappointing though this may be, circumstances do arise in regional disputes which better provide the opportunity for third-party observation under regional arrangements than through the United Nations. In the recent confrontation between Tanzania and Uganda, Somalia acted in an investigatory capacity by sending a team to the common frontier to report on any buildup of military forces on either side of it; earlier Somalia had fulfilled a mediatory role by acting as host for a meeting of both countries designed to settle the differences between them. Clearly there are great advantages in bringing the problem solving down to the regional level or even to the level where two states invite an independent observer or investigation team to act as a third party in a dispute between them. However, there are other occasions when the private or independent instrument is not as successful as that which the United Nations can provide—the International Commission for Control and Supervision (ICCS) in Vietnam would seem to be a case in point. Difficulties immediately arise when there is no higher central authority responsible for coordination, support, and direction, and to which the ground missions can report— operationally and logistically the whole affair is likely to become a muddle. What is important about UN missions is that their observation and investigation reports are made public to all member states. It could well be that because of the deficiency in this respect and because the authority of the United Nations is lacking, the ICCS has run into the difficulties that it has, and the agreed upon cease-fire is being so blatantly disregarded. Whatever one may say, the United Nations in all its operations has been more successful in negotiating and supervising cease-fires than the parties to the conflict and the international commissions have been in Indochina. The contribution that UN observer missions have made over the years should not therefore be summarily dismissed as being ineffectual. Any study of the operational facts does indicate that despite the limitations and the difficulties placed in their way, the various missions have carried out the mandates given to them; and in the case of those with supervisory responsibilities over armistice line and cease-fire agreements they have influenced the spread of a more peaceful atmosphere in the areas of dispute.

What follows is a broadly based account of the United Nations' initiatives in this field since 1946. At the end a special section is devoted to the UN operation in West Irian in 1962–63, when a temporary interregnum administration was established during that island's transfer of sovereignty.

Armistice and   PALESTINE   The UN Truce Super-
Cease-fire Agreements   vision Organization (UNTSO) has
                                                   existed in Palestine for twenty-six
years. Its establishment in June 1948, following Britain's withdrawal from Palestine and its relinquishment of the mandate that it had exercised there since 1920, was the culmination of two previous initiatives by the United Nations in Palestine. Since 1946 the British had been involved in a major internal security operation against terrorism. The Jews were demanding a separate autonomous state within Palestine—a demand that the Arab world would not accept. Unable to find a solution, the United Kingdom placed the Palestine problem before the General Assembly with a request that a special commission be set up to make recommendations for its future government. On 15 May 1947 the General Assembly approved a resolution establishing a special committee (UNSCOP) [2] to study the whole Palestinian problem and submit proposals for its solution. The committee consisted of representatives from Australia, Canada, Czechoslovakia, Guatemala, India, Iran, Netherlands, Peru, Sweden, Uruguay, and Yugoslavia. Though the committee's opinions were divided, a submission of proposals was made to the General Assembly in September 1947.[3] These proposals were in part accepted when the Assembly approved a resolution on the future administration of Palestine and the setting up of a

2. General Assembly Resolution 106, 15 May 1947.
3. UNSCOP Report A/364, 21 September 1947.

UN commission to implement its provisions.[4] The commission composed of Bolivia, Czechoslovakia, Denmark, Panama, and the Philippines faced innumerable problems, not least the continuing fighting,
and was in the end forced to report to the General Assembly affirm-
ing "the armed hostility of both Palestinian and non-Palestinian Arab
elements, the lack of co-operation from the mandatory power, the
disintegrating security situation in Palestine and the fact that the Security Council did not furnish the Commission with the necessary
armed assistance . . . made it impossible for the Commission to
implement the Assembly's resolution." [5]

This was not the first time that the commission had expressed the
need for armed assistance,[6] but this time it achieved a result. In a resolution on 16 April 1948 the Security Council called for an immediate truce to the Palestine fighting and set out the measures that needed
to be taken to achieve it.[7] A few days later on 23 April the Council
approved the setting up of a Truce Commission to supervise the
implementation of these measures.[8] It was from these antecedents
and from the framework of the Truce Commission in particular that
UNTSO ultimately emerged in June 1948. In the meanwhile Count
Bernadotte of Sweden had been appointed mediator[9] to act in concert
with the commission in supervising the truce—later he was to continue in this role with UNTSO. No formal resolution establishing
UNTSO was approved by the Security Council; it merely grew from
and assumed the authority and mandate of its predecessor.

On 15 May, a month before UNTSO's birth, the British mandate
came to an end. Simultaneously the Jews proclaimed the establishment of the state of Israel. The reaction of the Arab states was immediate. The armies of Egypt, (Trans-)Jordan, Syria, Iraq, and Lebanon
advanced across their frontiers into Israel, and heavy fighting followed along every border. The Security Council called for an immediate cease-fire and on 29 May succeeded in arranging a four-week
truce; it was to be the first of many. In order to increase the effectiveness of its added responsibilities for supervising the cease-fire, the

---

4. General Assembly Resolution 181(11)A, 29 November 1947.
5. General Assembly Report A/532, 10 April 1948.
6. UN Palestine Commission Report to Security Council S/676, 16 February 1948.
7. Security Council Resolution S/723, 16 April 1948.
8. Security Council Resolution S/727, 23 April 1948.
9. General Assembly Resolution 186 (ES-11), 14 May 1948.

Truce Commission requested the assistance of military advisers and observers. The Security Council agreed, but it was left to Bernadotte to recruit them. The initial observer group numbered twenty-one and came from those countries already forming the Truce Commission—Belgium, France, and the United States. UNTSO came into being a few weeks later. By September the number of observers had increased to three hundred, indicating the extent to which the situation had developed. Fighting had flared up again, and although a second cease-fire was arranged on 15 July, it was to be violated on a number of occasions. However, first Bernadotte and later Ralph Bunche worked unceasingly to effect a more permanent truce. These efforts were tragically disrupted in September 1948 by the assassination of Count Bernadotte. Travelling with the chief of staff of UNTSO, General Lindstrom, and other UNTSO officers on a tour of inspection, the mediator's car was blocked by a jeep in a Jewish-held quarter of Jerusalem. Armed gunmen opened fire on the occupants, killing Bernadotte and one other as they sat in the car.

Bunche took over as acting mediator, and throughout the remainder of that year and halfway through the next he concluded a series of armistice agreements between the newly formed Israeli government and its Arab neighbors. As each agreement was promulgated, UN military observers moved into position along the armistice demarcation line. In addition to the armistice lines two demilitarized zones (DMZs) were established, one in the south around El Auja on Israel's southern border with Egypt, and the other in the north along Israel's border with Syria, between Lake Tiberias and Lake Huleh. These demilitarized zones, being as they were "disputed" territory, were the scene of much skirmishing in the years that followed. This does not mean that the prescribed demarcation lines between Arab and Jew elsewhere were necessarily more peaceful, but in the latter case each side was operating from its own territory, whereas in the DMZ there was a greater tendency (and perhaps incentive) toward violation and trespass. The small teams of UN observers who patrolled the zones were insufficient in strength to observe and prevent all infiltration and violations. It is of great credit to them that they have managed to maintain the reasonable degree of control that they have; even so, the lesson is plain that where demilitarized zones are defined, there must be a sufficient UN military presence to supervise them.

The responsibilities of the observers were arduous and exacting.

They had to be alert to every violation of the truce and, when these occurred, to report them instantly and accurately so that swift action could be taken to correct the situation and ensure that there was no escalation to the point of fighting. It was no sinecure of a job, no cozy passing the time in the "land of milk and honey." It was a task requiring unceasing vigilance and attention to detail; nor was it without its risks.

There were four Mixed Armistice Commissions (MACs), each responsible for one of the interstate armistice lines. The original team of Americans, Belgians, and French had been supplemented by Australians, Canadians, Danes, Irishmen, Italians, Dutchmen, New Zealanders, Norwegians, and Swedes. Equipped with a jeep, a radio, a compass, maps, and binoculars, the observer relied more than anything else on his own personality and powers of persuasion and diplomacy for his authority. To be effective the observer needed to be promptly at the scene of any incident even before it had ended, thereby often exposing himself to the danger of being killed in an exchange of fire. In the case of UNTSO, it is surprising that more were not killed in this way, particularly in its early days when neither Arab nor Jew was especially careful whom he shot in the heat of the moment. This was before the days of the blue beret, when the only visible identification worn by the observers was an armband on the sleeve of his national uniform. Despite the danger, the observer teams tirelessly investigated complaints of alleged violations and sought to effect a cease-fire wherever the shooting started. Despite the danger, the frustration, and sometimes the helplessness, and in spite of the hostility and resentment often shown toward him, it is important for the observer to remain objective. Once he shows partiality, his value as a neutral observer ends. Total impartiality is possibly a naïve expectation, but avoidance of creating double standards is a credible objective. Nevertheless, it is certainly difficult to convince everyone that you are objective and neutral. It is no wonder therefore that a number of observers in UNTSO found themselves persona non grata because of allegations that they were more partial to one side than to the other. To maintain this neutral perspective is probably the most difficult of a peacekeeper's problems. It is a razor's edge on which he performs each day, requiring considerable mental agility if he is not to fall.

The Arab-Israeli war of 1956 and the establishment of the UN

Emergency Force in the Gaza Strip and in the Sinai altered only slightly UNTSO's responsibilities, which basically remained those of supervising the 1949 armistice lines—a task that was only temporarily interrupted by the war. Israel's reluctant withdrawal in 1957 to its former frontiers in no way encouraged a greater sense of security, and the clashes along the armistice lines continued as before. Since the Egypt-Israel border was now covered by UNEF, the main concern of UNTSO's observer teams was along the Israel-Jordon and Israel-Syria borders, respectively. There were eighty-four observers with the Mixed Armistice Commissions responsible for these two areas. There was very little peace in these border areas throughout the next ten years, but, though the skirmishing on occasions developed into short artillery and tank battles, the demarcation lines remained intact and were not erased—as they might well have been had there not been a UN presence.

In the latter part of 1966 the situation in the north became progressively worse with the intensification of Arab activity. The fedayeen were continuing their raids into Israel from Gaza, but there was a more serious situation developing in the north where infiltrators from Syria carried out a series of terrorist attacks in which many Jews were killed and their property destroyed. Despite Syria's denials, there was not much doubt that it was aiding and abetting the terrorists. The Security Council called on Syria to strengthen its measures in order to prevent the incidents, but this resulted in no lessening in activity. A counterclaim by Syria, supported by the USSR, that Israel was massing troops on the Israel-Syria border was strongly refuted, and UNTSO observers found no evidence to that effect. Fighting between Israel and Jordan also flared up again, but the chief area of armed conflict was in the north. The year 1967 opened with further clashes across the border. Attempts by the Mixed Armistice Commission to restore the situation were unsuccessful, for there was no real interest on either side to find a settlement. In April the incident occurred in which the Syrian air force lost four of its six MIG fighters. The engagement arose over cultivation rights in the demilitarized zone. The Syrians had previously opened fire on Israeli tractors plowing inside the zone. The Israelis substituted armored tractors which were then shelled by Syrian artillery. Israeli fighter aircraft attacked the gun positions and were themselves engaged by Syrian fighters, during which the planes were shot down without loss to the Israelis. This display of air superiority might have been taken as a warning, but by now matters had gone too far for the heeding of warnings. A month later Egypt demanded UNEF's removal so as to better support its Arab ally in the event of an attack by Israel. On 5 June the Israeli army attacked on all fronts simultaneously, and the Six-Day War began.

The Middle East war of 1967 solved nothing; if anything it made matters more difficult. The confrontation was simply resited along the Suez Canal, the west bank of the River Jordan, and the Golan Heights, extending considerably the size of the area over which UNTSO had to maintain observation. Besides its existing responsibilities, UNTSO was given the task of policing the canal front. Initially a team of twenty observers was deployed to cover both sides, but this was clearly inadequate, and later the number was increased to ninety. Their presence did not prevent the periodic interchange of commando raids across the canal, nor the almost daily shelling of enemy positions by both sides. On the Jordan front there was a temporary lull while the badly mauled Jordanian army regrouped and reequipped itself; but a new brand of offensive resistance was developing with the upsurge of nationalism among the Palestinian refugees in Jordan, and it was not long before an intense guerrilla war was being fought on the west bank. Syria took the longest to recover, but before long Israel's positions along the Golan Heights were again being threatened.

So the situation continued until October 1973. The cease-fire that came in 1970 only provided an uneasy truce with little calming of tempers. UNTSO's responsibilities remain unaltered, though in extent they have been increased; with the conclusion of the 1973 war they are likely to increase still more. In terms of success it might be supposed that UNTSO has achieved little. Despite its presence, the fighting was forever recurring; certainly in the twenty-five years of its existence there has been little abatement in the unrest, the skirmishing, the blatant violations of the demilitarized zones. Israel's tenacity for preservation and recognition has made it suspicious and intransigent in its attitude toward UNTSO, providing an almost total lack of cooperation. On the other hand, it cannot be said that UNTSO has fared very much better with the Arab states, whose bitter opposition to the Jewish state overrode restraint.

In evaluating UNTSO's contribution to the Middle East crisis, one should start with fundamentals and consider to what extent the purposes for which UNTSO was established have been and are being achieved. One should not judge it on whether it has prevented war or not—of its very nature, the mandate it was given was one of supervision not prevention. Three times in its existence war has broken out in the Middle East—in 1956, 1967, and most recently in 1973. It is doubtful whether any agency on earth could have prevented them at the time; certainly the third-party intervention of Britain and France at Suez exacerbated rather than calmed the situation. But during the years in between, the military conflict was restricted to skirmishing and raids across the armistice lines—and for this relative peace the MAC teams can take much of the credit; nor should it be forgotten that there were many places along the demarcation lines that enjoyed comparative if not total quiet throughout the intervening periods—a circumstance that would not have existed had there been no UNTSO and no UN presence. In a sentence, UNTSO's performance has been one of courageous endeavor. If there is one lesson to be learned, it would seem to be in terms of numerical strength. UNTSO can claim to have lessened the manifestation of violent conflict, but the degree to which it was able to do this would have undoubtedly been greater had the number of observers and observer teams been greater.

JAMMU AND KASHMIR   Of all its operations, that of the UN in Jammu and Kashmir is the one that has been heard of least, though it has been in existence for the same length of time as UNTSO. The fact that after twenty-five years the United Nations Military Observer Group in India and Pakistan (UNMOGIP) is still performing its duties along the Kashmir cease-fire line and thereby underwriting the continuing peace in that state is something that is forgotten by most of the world. There is no news value where there are no fireworks, and so long as UNMOGIP continues successfully to supervise the cease-fire, it and Jammu and Kashmir will remain out of the newspapers and will go on being forgotten. Unlike other UN missions and peace-keeping forces, UNMOGIP does not submit regular reports on the Kashmir situation, so there is no periodic reminder of its existence. For diplomatic and political reasons it was agreed at the start that reporting to the Security Council should be confined to confidential rather than public channels. This was considered desirable because in Kashmir the military observers were constantly being required in the course of their duties to switch from one side of the cease-fire line to the other and back again; any allegation of partiality and bias by either side could have greatly hindered their work. Later, when Dr. Frank Graham was appointed as mediator by the secretary-general, the practice was continued so as not to jeopardize or embarrass his peace efforts. The secretary-general himself made repeated visits to Jammu and Kashmir, and so the United Nations was kept informed through his reports as to the continuing situation, but even so the Security Council appears to have disregarded the warning signals of the deterioration in the interstate relations that prefaced the India-Pakistan war of 1965.

The Kashmir dispute dates from 1947, the year in which India was partitioned and it and Pakistan received their independence. Up to this time the Indian princes had ruled autonomous states, but with independence they were required to accede to one or the other of the two new dominions. Jammu and Kashmir was one of a few states that did not opt either way. Jammu Province is Hindu, while Kashmir is predominantly Muslim. In August 1947, when a revolt in the town of Poonch was suppressed by the state forces, the Muslim tribesmen of neighboring North-West Frontier Province (Pakistan), incensed by reports that their Muslim brothers in the two provinces were being massacred, invaded Kashmir to go to their assistance. Pillaging and murder followed on a substantial scale. The maharaja, a Hindu, appealed to India for help and received it—but in return for his state's accession to India. On 27 October 1947 Indian army units crossed the border into Kashmir.

The fighting that followed was bitter and costly. Diplomatic maneuvers by both sides at first failed to bring the issue to the United Nations, but in January 1948 both agreed to a UN commission [10] to look into the dispute. Inexplicably, the commission (UNCIP) did not reach Kashmir until three months later, by which time the situation had further deteriorated. India claimed that there were 50,000 rebels in Kashmir and another 100,000 being trained in Pakistan; but the real issue was over the timing of the people's plebiscite that would decide Jammu and Kashmir's future. India wanted the plebiscite to be held while the newly appointed government remained in power, but since the prime minister, Sheikh Abdullah, was known to oppose union with Pakistan, that country saw little likelihood of an impartial plebiscite and advocated that it be held under UN auspices.

It took UNCIP almost a year to achieve a breakthrough in the politi-

10. Security Council Resolution S/654, 20 January 1948.

cal and military deadlock, but eventually on 1 January 1949 a cease-fire was arranged, though it depended on mutual goodwill for its effectiveness since there was as yet no agreement on an armistice. On 15 January the two military commanders agreed on a cease-fire line, but it was not until July of the same year that the Karachi Agreement was signed.[11] By this a formal cease-fire came into effect along the agreed upon cease-fire line, which was to be supervised by UN observers stationed on both sides.

UNMOGIP was responsible for supervising the cease-fire and for adjudicating in cases of alleged violations of the Karachi Agreement. Until the India-Pakistan war of 1965, the number of military observers did not exceed fifty at any one time. An additional fifty-nine were provided during the 1965 crisis, but, the 1965 war apart, this relatively small band of observers from eleven countries has deterred a major breach of the armistice during the time it has been in effect. The fact that few people outside of Asia and the contributing countries know of its existence is a measure of its success. Numerous allegations and incidents were investigated in the period between 1949 and 1965. Each one was meticulously examined and in the majority of cases an adjudication made against one side or the other. Each has been recorded and reported, not only to the governments of both sides, but also to the secretary-general. As a brake on escalation UNMOGIP can claim to have been effective.

In 1965 UNMOGIP was rendered temporarily ineffective by the India-Pakistan war that broke the cease-fire agreement and threatened the peace of Asia once again. Early in the year fighting broke out in the Rann of Kutch, a sector of the border between India and Pakistan that had been in dispute for some time. Essentially the conflict was over a territorial claim and was eventually settled by an international tribunal headed by Judge Lagergren of Sweden, which allocated 10 percent of the disputed area to Pakistan and the remainder to India— but that was in 1968, well after the cease-fire had been reestablished. During the first six months of 1965, the number of violations of the cease-fire line multiplied to almost 400—from crossings to artillery exchanges. During August and September major engagements took place in which tanks and aircraft, as well as artillery, took part. Both

11. India/Pakistan Agreement on cease-fire in Jammu and Kashmir, S/1430/Add. 1, 29 July 1949, ann. 26.

armies made advances across the cease-fire line and also across the international frontier in places. But determined efforts by the UN succeeded in arranging a cease-fire on 22 September 1965, and although it was broken on occasions during the succeeding months, the infringements were minor and did not bring about a renewal in the fighting.

On 20 September, when negotiations for a cease-fire were nearing conclusion, the Security Council authorized the secretary-general to provide an additional observer group for outside Kashmir after hostilities ceased. It was established immediately after the cease-fire took effect and remained in existence until March of the following year, its purpose by then having been served. The United Nations India-Pakistan Observation Mission (UNIPOM) had the role of supervising the cease-fire along the international frontier between the two countries and observing the military withdrawals by both sides to within their own boundaries. UNIPOM was eighty-two strong and was deployed almost equally on either side of the frontier. It stayed in position until March 1966 when it was withdrawn on completion of its task, leaving UNMOGIP to continue its duties in Kashmir.

Expectations that a Kashmir settlement might not be far off have not so far been realized. If and when it happens, UNMOGIP will cease its responsibilities and disband. The war of 1970 over Bangladesh further delayed any settlement of the Jammu and Kashmir dispute, and although a peace settlement has been agreed upon for this latest conflict in the subcontinent, no provision seems to have been made for settling the longer-standing issue. It is difficult to assess the extent of UNMOGIP's achievement and whether its presence has prevented the complete destruction of a state—or has preserved a status quo that has been harmful rather than beneficial. But when a settlement is reached and UNMOGIP leaves, it is likely to be remembered for its longevity of stay rather than for its positive accomplishments. UNMOGIP cannot be considered to have failed in its duty, since it has been the lack of any firm will on the part of the two contesting states to settle their dispute that has led to the prolonged but necessary presence of UN observers.

YEMEN The operation conducted by the United Nations in the Yemen in 1963–64 probably is considered to be the least successful of all the UN operations—at least by most political observers and by the international media. Though certainly failing to achieve all of its objectives, the Yemen mission was not the outright failure that those inherently critical of the United Nations' attempts at peacekeeping would have one believe. Admittedly faulty appreciations of what was required were made in the first instance, and the operation once it was mounted was faced with many organizational and administrative problems. The planned operational organization did not suit the needs of the mission; nor was it of sufficient size to cover effectively the vast and difficult terrain over which it was required to operate. Difficulties also arose over the implementation of the commitments agreed to by the UAR and Saudi Arabia, on which the United Nations had based its operation. Though these commitments were honored by both parties in the long run, it took a little time to overcome the initial hurdles.

The Yemen is peopled by two distinct religious sects, the Zaidi and the Shafi. Since the expulsion of the Turks in 1917, the Zaidis had held power with their temporal and spiritual leader, the Imam, as ruler. In September 1962 the old Imam Ahmad died, and he was succeeded by his son Imam Badr. Ahmad had been an autocratic and despotic king who had ruled by suppression; he had survived more than one attempt to overthrow him. His son was more liberal and constitutionally minded and promised to undertake a policy of modern reform—a promise that he was never given the opportunity to fulfill. Only a week after his succession a military revolt drove him from his throne. The rebels were led by a former prisoner of Ahmad, Colonel Sallal, and numbered among their ranks both Zaidis and Shafis. As a military coup it was typical of its kind. The royal palace in the capital, Sana'a, was surrounded by tanks and then shelled into ruins. At first it was supposed that Badr lay dead among the rubble along with the rest of his family and royal bodyguard, but he had managed to survive and, dressed as an ordinary soldier, succeeded in escaping to the mountainous north, the stronghold of the loyal Zaidi tribes. Here with the assistance of King Faisal of Saudi Arabia, Badr collected around him an army and prepared to wage war against the new republic that Sallal had proclaimed.

Throughout the next few months fighting between the two rival groups was widespread and intense with each side claiming victories. The situation was confused, but by the end of the year the two groups remained entrenched and firm in their respective areas, the royalists

(Badr) in the mountains of the north and in the east along the borders with Saudi Arabia and the republicans (Sallal) in the large towns and in the south. But by this time the UAR was supplying Sallal with an increasing amount of material support. By January it was reported that there were between 12,000 and 22,000 UAR troops in the Yemen, and this figure was later to exceed 25,000. With Saudi Arabia strongly supporting the Imam it looked as if it would develop into a long war; for so far international pressures had failed to deter either Nasser or Faisal from interfering.

In March 1963 Ralph Bunche went to the Yemen on a fact-finding mission for the secretary-general. A similar but independent mission was undertaken on behalf of the president of the United States by Ellsworth Bunker, who a year earlier had acted in a similar capacity in the West New Guinea settlement. These two emissaries were between them successful in devising a basis for a solution that was acceptable, at least in principle, to the three interested parties—Saudi Arabia, the UAR, and the Yemen. The secretary-general was therefore able to report to the Security Council the conditions for a disengagement.[12] For its part, the UAR agreed to begin a phased withdrawal of its troops and to desist from taking punitive action against the royalists who had been operating from across the Saudi Arabian border. Saudi Arabia in turn undertook to terminate all aid to the royalists and to deny the use of its territory as a base for royalist operational activity and for the royalist leaders. Both sides agreed that a demilitarized zone should be established, extending 20 kilometers on either side of Yemen's border with Saudi Arabia. Inside the zone UN troops were to be deployed to ensure that there was no infiltration of troops and arms across it. In addition, observers operating outside the demilitarized zone would have the responsibility for verifying that the terms of the agreement were being honored. This plan of disengagement was a constructive attempt to secure a peaceful settlement. There were, however, delays in implementation by each side, partly contrived and partly due to problems not foreseen at the time. The delays resulted in increased suspicion on the part of Saudi Arabia and the UAR as to the genuineness of the other's intentions, raising further obstacles in the way of a final settlement.

The United Nations Observation Mission (UNYOM) arrived in the

---

12. Report of Secretary-General to Security Council S/5298, 29 April 1963.

Yemen on 13 June 1963.[13] Its mandate was for four months. It was 200 strong, of which the largest single elements were a reconnaissance unit from Yugoslavia and an air component of 50 from Canada, operating eight reconnaissance aircraft. Other observers came from Australia, Austria, India, New Zealand, Norway, Sweden, and the United States, mostly drawn from the UN operations in the Congo and Middle East. The reconnaissance unit was intended to secure the demilitarized zone from any violation, while the observers, twenty-two in all, had the responsibility for seeing that aid for the royalists was not coming to them across the Saudi Arabian frontiers and that Egypt was complying with its undertaking of phased withdrawal of its troops from Yemen territory.

The presence of UNYOM, however, made little difference to the situation in the Yemen; the deep-seated nature of the Egyptian and Saudi Arabian military and political engagement was such that, however well intentioned their initial undertakings may have been, the planned disengagement was extremely difficult to achieve. Fighting therefore continued, and the UN observers found themselves unable to fulfill their mandate in respect to their verification role. The UAR was able to make only token withdrawals of its troops and more than once replaced those that had been withdrawn. Saudi Arabia did not take action to halt the traffic of men and arms across the border, and with this continued support the royalists were able to continue their military operations. However, inside the demilitarized zone itself all was relatively quiet, so much so that by November 1963 U Thant was able to recommend the withdrawal of the Yugoslav reconnaissance unit. This left the twenty-two observers to cover the complete task of verification. The Yemen UN operation continued into 1964, its presence being extended on the secretary-general's recommendation at two-to-three–month intervals until September of that year, when at the request of the UAR and Saudi Arabia the mission was withdrawn.[14]

The failure of the UAR and Saudi Arabia to fulfill their undertakings made UNYOM's verification responsibilities meaningless, but even if the withdrawals had taken place and Saudi Arabia had withdrawn its support of the royalists, the size of UNYOM would still have been to-

---

13. Security Council Resolution S/5331, 11 June 1963.

14. Secretary-General's Reports S/5501, 2 Jan 1964; S/5572, 3 March 1964; S/5681, 4 May 1964; S/5794, 2 July 1964; S/5927, 2 Sep 1964; S/5959, 11 Sep 1964.

tally insufficient for such a roving commission. The lesson that the Yemen provides is that if the United Nations mounts an operation requiring comprehensive verification and supervision, then the strength of the mission must be sufficient to its task. This lesson has not been immediately learned, for in 1967 when UNTSO was expanded to cover the Suez Canal, the number of the observers at first deployed was inadequate. In the case of the Yemen the basis of the operation was sound and workable, but it suffered from inadequacy in implementation. As is so often the case in international politics, the instrument itself was not at fault, but the external elements working against it blunted its impact. It is a matter for debate whether the Yemen was a viable operation for the United Nations to undertake under the circumstances. In our opinion the concept was sound enough, and given adequate manpower the mission was a viable one. Its success, however, depended upon the honoring of pledges; and, as we have seen, either through default or insufficiency neither the UAR nor Saudi Arabia found it possible to fulfill its undertakings. The question that then arises is whether, realizing that the whole basis on which the UN operation had been mounted was ephemeral, should the mission have been withdrawn much sooner? The argument on the one side must be that a UN mission, however weak and frustrated in its design, should persevere until all hope of its achieving its purpose has disappeared. On the other hand, there is the whole question of the credibility of the peacekeeping instrument to be considered. If force and mission mandates become inoperative through action or nonaction by either side, global recognition of the fact and of the United Nations' inability to fulfill its role can damage, possibly irrevocably, that credibility. Manpower and equipment deficiencies are relatively easy to overcome; a lack of good faith and the failure to honor declared intentions are problems of a different and more difficult kind. Our judgment is that the effort is worth the disappointment, and the United Nations should intervene in any conflict where its intervention is acceptable or requested—that is the role of the United Nations as required by the Charter. It should not weigh the conflict in the balance of success or failure before deciding on its action. However, the United Nations can help itself. Through proper planning it can obviate the material problems of operational organization and administration, and it can strengthen the image and the standing of its operational endeavors by making better use of the media and the publicity resources available to it around the world. Public opinion on the side of the United Nations is a source of influence yet to be tapped and developed.

INDONESIA   The fourth and final case study in this section is that of the UN intervention in Indonesia in 1947, the first but possibly the least known of the United Nations' cease-fire observer missions. The Indonesian archipelago comprising Sumatra, Java, and Madura had been ruled by the Dutch for more than three hundred years when World War II spread to the Far East in 1942. For the next three years it was under Japanese occupation. During this latter period the Indonesians were permitted to form the Indonesian Independence Preparatory Committee as a first step toward their assumption of the authority of government from Japanese military rule. The United States' atomic attacks on Nagasaki and Hiroshima in August 1945 precipitated these preparatory moves into solid reality. With the capitulation of Japan and the withdrawal of its occupation troops, the Indonesian leaders proclaimed independence and took over administrative authority for the territory. In November of the same year a government was formed with Soetan Sjahrir as prime minister. This was contrary to the declared policy of the Allied nations, that all colonial territories occupied by their enemies during the war would be returned to their former status. The Netherlands government, however, was prepared to accept in principle the de facto situation of an Indonesian government with a Council of Ministers, but insisted that the new state would remain under Dutch rule with a governor-general representing the queen of the Netherlands. This was not acceptable to Sjahrir or his colleagues, since it did not recognize the existence of the Republic of Indonesia. Despite a third-party diplomatic intervention by Britain aimed at assisting the negotiations, the impasse remained. However, in October 1946 talks were resumed after the Netherlands government had set up a commission-general to work on a political structure for the Netherlands East Indies as a whole, and a month later a draft agreement was drawn up and initialled by both parties.

The Linggadjati Agreement contained the recognition by the Netherlands of the Republic of Indonesia as having de facto authority over Java, Madura, and Sumatra; the area of authority was to be extended through mutual cooperation to include those parts of Indonesia at that time under the control of Allied and Netherlands' armed forces. A

United States of Indonesia was envisaged, toward the establishment of which both governments would work. The whole agreement was geared to mutual cooperation requiring mutual consultation and the promotion of the joint interests of the Netherlands and Indonesia. The Linggadjati Agreement was far from being precise on many points, particularly in its omission of establishing the de jure authority of the new republic. The arguments began almost at once on matters in which the Dutch considered that the Indonesians had gone beyond the de facto authority granted to them in the Linggadjati Agreement. The conflicting interpretations of its provisions raised a number of issues, many of which were unacceptable to Indonesia, such as the Netherlands' insistence on the formation of a mixed Dutch-Indonesia police force. When the situation deteriorated, Sjahrir resigned. His resignation was followed by a predictable breakdown in law and order. The Dutch reacted forcibly to restore the situation. To all intents and purposes the Linggadjati Agreement had no further relevance. By the end of July 1947 the Dutch and Indonesians were fighting each other, and the situation was serious.

The Security Council was called into session and on 1 August approved the first of a series of resolutions aimed at bringing about a peaceful settlement to the constitutional problem. In its first resolution the Council called for a cease-fire and the settlement of the dispute by arbitration or by other peaceful means.[15] As an immediate step to assist in the observance of a cease-fire, it was accepted that some kind of neutral observation was required. Wholly opposed to the Security Council assuming any degree of jurisdiction over an affair which it considered to be a domestic matter, the Netherlands suggested that on-the-spot reporting of the situation should be made the responsibility of those countries with "career" consuls in Batavia. Despite an objection by the USSR that the five consuls involved included Britain, France, and the United States but not itself, the Dutch recommendation was incorporated into a Security Council resolution and approved in August 1947.[16] The consuls were "to prepare jointly for the information and guidance of the Security Council . . . reports to cover the observance of the cease-fire orders and the conditions prevailing in areas under military occupation." To assist them in carrying out these instructions the consular commission recommended

15. Security Council Resolution S/459, 1 August 1947.
16. Security Council Resolution S/525(1), 25 August 1947.

that the military assistants provided by the nominated states should undertake the on-the-spot observation, and this was agreed upon by the Security Council, which at the same time set up a Good Offices Commission (GOC) of three of its members to assist in the settlement of the dispute.[17] The three member states of the commission were Australia, Belgium, and the United States; and the consular commission with its military assistants thus became their eyes and ears. The military assistants assumed broad reporting functions related to observation of violations of the cease-fire orders, investigation of allegations of violations, assistance in arranging cease-fires, and provision of operational data for the GOC and Security Council.

In January 1948, six months after the establishment of the GOC and the consular commission with its military observer teams, the two sides agreed on a truce—the Renville Agreement. This agreement stipulated a cease-fire and a standfast of military forces to be fully effective within forty-eight hours of signing. The agreement set down in comprehensive terms the responsibilities and functions of the military assistants in relation to their observance of the cease-fire and standfast. By March of that year the GOC was able to report to the Security Council that it had been concerned with (1) general cease-fire, (2) delineation of the status quo line and demilitarized zones, (3) evacuation of republican forces from Netherlands' controlled areas, (4) release of persons held as prisoners of war, (5) evacuation of families of military personnel and their present welfare, (6) alleged violations of the truce agreement, and (7) the widening of the demilitarized zones. This catalog conceals the wealth of achievement that can be credited to the GOC and its field observer teams. Under (3) their achievement was to evacuate 35,000 republican combatants from behind the Dutch forward positions in the space of one month from the signing of the agreement. Unfortunately the immediate hopes of the Renville Agreement were not to be realized. As 1948 proceeded, despite the efforts of the GOC the political and military situation deteriorated until in December the Dutch abrogated the agreement, citing Indonesia's increasing violations as the cause; interned the republican leaders at Jogjakarta; and began a second police action.

This action by the Dutch lost them the support and sympathy they had hitherto enjoyed from their "friends" in the Security Council,

17. Security Council Resolution S/525(11), 25 August 1947.

who felt that the pretext for their reopening of hostilities was uncon-
vincing in the light of their stated position that they would work to
hand over sovereignty to Indonesia on 1 January 1950. As the result
of continued perseverance on the part of the GOC, which in January
1949 was reconstituted as the United Nations Commission for Indonesia (UNCI), slow but gradual progress was made until in May the
Indonesians stated that they would terminate the guerrilla warfare,
ensure full cooperation in the restoration of law and order, and participate in any conference at The Hague to speed up the transfer of sovereignty to Indonesia. In response to this gesture the Dutch agreed to
the return of republican government to Jogjakarta and to a resumption
of its freedom of action. Hostilities were ended in all parts of Indonesia by 15 August 1949.

The terms of the cease-hostility agreement included the formation
of a Central Joint Board, with subcommittees operating at the lower
levels of administration and communication. The board and each subcommittee was to have an UNCI representative sitting with them.
Their responsibilities were to implement and observe the cease-
hostility arrangements as well as to carry out any other directives
issued to them from time to time. UNCI was able to report in January
1950 that "the joint local committees were all established and functioning." [18]

Another responsibility of UNCI was to assist in the repatriation of
the Netherlands army. This was no simple matter because in addition
to the 80,000-strong Royal Netherlands Army in Indonesia there was
also the Royal Netherlands Indonesia Army, amounting to a total of
65,000 troops. The repatriation of the former posed no great difficulty, since most were organized units and were returning to their
homeland. So far as the latter were concerned, many of whom were
of mixed birth with Dutch fathers, their fighting on the side of the
Dutch against the Indonesians had jeopardized their future in Indonesia. In the event, by the time the agreement on the dissolution of
the Royal Netherlands Indonesia Army had been signed, of the troops
remaining under Netherlands command some 26,000 joined the Indonesian army, while a further 18,750 were demobilized in Indonesia, and only 3,250 departed for the Netherlands along with the
rest.

UNCI remained in existence until early 1951, when it was dis-

18. UNCI 2nd Interim Report S/1449, 16 January 1950.

banded—a little more than a year after the instruments of the transfer of sovereignty had been arranged. In assessing the contribution that it and its predecessor, GOC, made, the most significant factor seems to have been the close-knit interrelationship that existed between the commission and its on-the-spot military observers. As a UN operation it did not exactly relate to any other that had gone before or was subsequently to succeed it. The field observers were not specially recruited by the UN secretariat but were "loaned" by member states with career consuls established in Indonesia. Working through the consular commission, their observation and investigation reports provided the GOC and, through it, the Security Council with the vital on-the-spot assessments and information they needed in their role of negotiation and mediation. The ultimate settlement, though some time in coming, was greatly facilitated by the work done by the GOC and the military observers affiliated with it.

At the outset the observers totalled twenty-five,[19] but through misunderstanding of the terms of commitment this number had shrunk to fifteen within three months. The GOC took immediate steps to check the shrinkage and build up the teams and succeeded in raising their strength to fifty-five.[20] When UNCI was established in January 1949 the figure was increased to sixty-three, where it remained until February 1950 when a gradual and progressive cutback kept step with the progress toward a final settlement. On 6 April 1951 the observer teams were finally disbanded.

It is important that the Indonesian example be well studied, particularly in the light of the recent formation and deployment of the International Commission for Control and Supervision (ICCS) in Vietnam. Besides noting the interrelationship between the ground observation operation and the political mediatory body, which placed military observer teams under the direction of a higher civilian parent body with the overall responsibility for assisting the two disputants to arrive at a peaceful settlement, it is interesting to reflect that the mandate given to the observer teams was adjusted and extended to meet the changing circumstances of the conflict. These adjustments were

19. Australia (4), Belgium (2), China (Taiwan) (4), France (3), United Kingdom (4), United States (8). In addition the resident United Kingdom military liaison officer and the United States naval aide were attached to the commission.

20. Australia (15), Belgium (4), China (Taiwan) (5), France (6), United Kingdom (10), United States (15).

directed by the GOC, the parent body, and provided a flexibility that is not often found in such international operations. Another important factor that should be borne in mind is that, although the military assistance was provided by a specified group of member states and not on a broad UN basis as is usual, and this was done at the express wish of the Netherlands to avoid a direct intervention by the United Nations in what the Netherlands considered to be a domestic matter, the Security Council did set up a parent body (GOC) as a negotiation agent to which the observers could report through the consular commission. It is this lesson in coordination, communication, and control that the International Commission for Control and Supervision might well have followed. The need for coordination and the interrelationship of all peace agencies in the conduct of conflict control initiatives is discussed at some length later in this book. It is true that in the case of Indonesia there were important external factors in the form of big power pressures, and also the internal factor that the Netherlands was willing to grant independence to Indonesia at some future date. At this juncture it is enough to point to the example of Indonesia and the GOC and to reflect on the problems that could well have arisen had that relationship not been established.

Fact-Finding and Reporting Missions Missions that fall under this heading can be said to have relevance at all levels of the geopolitical structure and are probably most effective as interventions when implemented within a regional framework. It is here that disputes between neighbors are likely to be more quickly settled as a result of a third-party investigation by a neighboring state, friendly to both sides. In the next chapter we will study more closely this sector of third-party initiatives; here we will confine our examination to the United Nations' contribution to the settlement of disputes in areas where international rather than regional initiatives have been required.

BALKANS The first example is the mission that went to the Balkans in 1947 at the request of the Greek government to investigate its claim that Albania, Bulgaria, and Yugoslavia were actively supporting the guerrillas who at that time were operating in northern Greece against government forces.

On 3 December 1946 Greece requested the Security Council to consider the situation existing between Greece and its neighbors and asked that an on-the-spot investigation of its complaint be made. Albania, Bulgaria, and Yugoslavia denied the charge and countered that civil strife in Greece arose from the repressive policies of its government. The Security Council responded by establishing a commission of investigation composed of one representative of each member of the Council for 1947 (Australia, Belgium, Brazil, China, Colombia, France, Poland, Syria, the USSR, the United Kingdom, and the United States) to ascertain the causes and nature of the alleged border violations and to make proposals for averting their repetition.[21]

The commission carried out its investigation between January and April 1947 and reported that a majority of the commission had found evidence that Yugoslavia and, to a lesser extent, Albania and Bulgaria had supported the guerrilla warfare in Greece; that Bulgaria and Yugoslavia were supporting separatist movements in Greek Macedonia; that Greek territorial claims against Bulgaria and Albania and Bulgaria's claims to Western Thrace aggravated the situation; that there was no proof that frontier violations had been deliberately provoked by either side; that the large number of incidents showed strained relations; and that the general unrest in Greece helped to explain the situation. The report was hotly contested by a minority of the commission (Poland and USSR) who supported the view that the disorders in Greece were the result of the terrorist and expansionist policies of the Greek authorities.

It was no surprise that, with the USSR objecting, the Security Council was unable to adopt any of the proposed resolutions put forward for the settlement of the question. On 15 September 1947 the Council removed the issue from its agenda, so enabling the General Assembly to deal with the matter. Six days later the General Assembly adopted a resolution calling upon Albania, Bulgaria, and Yugoslavia to do nothing to aid the Greek guerrillas. It further asked these countries as well as Greece to cooperate in settling their disputes through the establishment of normal diplomatic relations, frontier conventions, and cooperation in solving refugee and minority problems. At the same time the Assembly established a UN Special Committee on the Balkans (UNSCOB),[22] consisting of the representatives of Australia, Bra-

21. Security Council Resolution S/339, 19 December 1946.
22. General Assembly Resolution A/109(11), 21 October 1947.

zil, China, France, Mexico, the Netherlands, Pakistan, Poland, the United Kingdom, the USSR, and the United States to assist the four governments in complying with its recommendations and to observe how far they did so. Poland and the USSR declined to participate because they considered that the terms of reference and the functions of UNSCOB violated the sovereignty of the three Balkan states and as such were not in accordance with the principles of the Charter. Since Albania, Bulgaria, and Yugoslavia also opposed the establishment of UNSCOB, it was clear that little cooperation would be forthcoming from that quarter.

UNSCOB remained in existence for four years. During that period it submitted regular reports to the General Assembly, confirming that the claims of Greece were well founded and that the three countries concerned were providing material and moral assistance to the guerrillas in northern Greece on such a scale that the respective governments could not have been unaware of it. These reports prompted the General Assembly to adopt a number of resolutions calling for a cessation of the arms trafficking and for the four countries to renew their existing arrangements for the peaceful settlement of frontier disputes and to settle the growing refugee problem. In this last area, an issue that loomed very large and which was later to become a major preoccupation of UNSCOB was the question of the abduction across the frontier of hundreds of Greek children. All states on whose territory these children were to be found were urged to return them to Greece. The International Red Cross and its national societies were requested to coordinate their efforts to the same end. The majority of the children were never traced; some were returned or subsequently found their way back to Greece, but for the most part they are still missing persons. The countries that had received the Greek children made little or no attempt to comply with the General Assembly's request for their return.

Nor did UNSCOB enjoy much success in terminating the traffic in arms. Having been unacceptable to Albania, Bulgaria, and Yugoslavia from the beginning, UNSCOB received no cooperation from them throughout its existence. This relationship was not helped by the fact that the representatives on the commission were government appointees and acted as such and not in their individual capacities. Albania, Bulgaria, and Yugoslavia, not members of the United Nations at that time, were not disposed to allow any interference in their affairs by such a commission. The situation did not improve; if anything, it deteriorated in that other Central and Eastern European countries, in addition to the original three, began supplying arms to the guerrillas in northern Greece. In 1951 UNSCOB was dissolved, and its work was taken over by the UN Peace Observation Commission, which established a subcommission in the Balkans until 1954 when it too was disbanded.

On the face of it this might seem to have been an abortive mission, but the observers' role was simply to investigate and report, not to impose a solution. In this it did no more than was required of it and provided the data on which the General Assembly and the political arm of the United Nations could act. The fact that the intervention of the United Nations was obstructed can be blamed on the division in the Security Council and the obvious psychological support that the USSR gave to Albania, Bulgaria, and Yugoslavia, which encouraged them to ignore the urgings and resolutions of the General Assembly and not to recognize as valid the presence and authority of UNSCOB. UNSCOB certainly did everything that was in its power to establish the facts and cannot be held to have failed in this respect. But its one-sided posture meant that UNSCOB could never investigate the claims of the three Balkan states that they were not guilty of Greece's accusations. So long as UNSCOB was handicapped in this way, its full effectiveness could never be developed.

LEBANON   The problem that brought a UN observer mission to Lebanon was of a different making. A constitutional crisis in the summer of 1958 threatened to end in civil war and in open conflict between Lebanon and its own Arab allies. The country's population of one and a half million is divided almost equally between Moslems and Christians. The latter held political power at the time, and because of this, foreign policy tended toward an entente with the Western democracies, to which Lebanon looked for support. For some time there had been marked dissatisfaction on the part of the Moslem community and in other Arab capitals with the government's pro-Western policy and with the fact that President Chamoun, a Christian, wished to continue in office for a second term.

Following the murder of a prominent antigovernment newspaper proprietor—allegedly by government agents—serious rioting broke out in the major towns of Beirut, Tripoli, and Sidon, increasing in intensity and violence as days passed. Several people died in the violence, for which Chamoun blamed Syria in particular as being the chief instigator. He appealed to the Security Council to consider Lebanon's charges and to halt the interference in its national affairs. The Security Council delayed action until the Arab League had had an opportunity to settle the dispute, on the basis that it would be preferable if the dispute could be settled under regional arrangements; but when the League proved unsuccessful, the Council met on 11 June and adopted a Swedish resolution calling for the immediate dispatch of an observer mission "to ensure that there is no illegal infiltration of personnel or supply of arms or other material across the Lebanese border." [23]

The UN Observer Group in Lebanon (UNOGIL) wasted no time in forming. Its top tier was a politico-military triumvirate (Galo Plaza, former president of Ecuador, General Odd Bull of Norway, and Rajeshwar Dayal of India). Supporting them were one hundred field observers,[24] who were deployed throughout the country and not only along the Syrian border. To increase the mission's observation capability it was provided with eight light reconnaissance planes and two helicopters by the United States and Sweden—those from America being flown by UN pilots. But UNOGIL's main problem was to gain access to those frontier areas held by dissident tribesmen, into and through which the infiltrations were allegedly being made. The tribes in these areas were on the whole uncooperative, though at times UN observers were allowed to enter under escort. With this handicap and the difficulty of movement generally in the mountainous terrain, UNOGIL was faced with a formidable task, but in its first report, published on 4 July, it stated that it had found no tangible evidence of mass infiltration of arms or of UAR nationals. This report did not please the Lebanese who called it "inconclusive, misleading and unwarranted" [25] and President Chamoun is alleged to have retorted that "If we Lebanese can only tell a Syrian by his dialect, how can a Norwegian or a Swede tell an infiltrator from the Lebanese?" He seems to have missed the point that UNOGIL had reported "no ev-

---

23. Security Council Resolution S/4022, 11 June 1958.

24. This figure had risen to 214 after three months and to 500 by the time that UNOGIL withdrew.

25. Security Council Doc. S/4043, 8 July 1958; Government of Lebanon's official comment on UNOGIL's first report, S/4040, 3 July 1958.

idence of *mass* infiltration.'' The Lebanese government was claiming at this time that there were 3,000 Egyptian, Syrian, and Palestinian rebels inside its borders and that the UAR had supplied the antigovernment forces with 36,000 weapons of various kinds; so it was not surprising that President Chamoun should have been so incensed. UNOGIL, for all its limitations including that of identification, found no proof of what was being alleged, then or later.

On 23 September President Chamoun's term of office came to an end, and he was succeeded by the former army commander in chief General Chehab. With a better-balanced representation in government, life began to return to normal. UNOGIL had made a second report in July which basically confirmed the first, that there was no evidence to support the claim of massive smuggling of arms or armed rebels. Despite the difficulties of observation, over one hundred allegations had been investigated, but in no case had there been explicit confirmation of the complaint to warrant further action by UNOGIL. In short, though smuggling and infiltration were almost certainly going on, these activities were clearly no greater than usual and were confined to small arms and ammunition. When UNOGIL rendered its third and fourth reports, this opinion was maintained.

On 22 November, with Lebanon relatively quiet once again, UNOGIL began its withdrawal, completing it on 10 December. In its six-month existence it had played an important calming role, and, so far as its mandate was concerned, had satisfactorily rebutted the allegations made in the first instance by Chamoun and the Lebanese government, showing them to have been greatly exaggerated. UNOGIL's presence may not have prevented smuggling and infiltration, but it ensured that they were kept within limited bounds.

During UNOGIL's presence in Lebanon events occurred which, though not directly concerned with the country's internal matters, did provide a dramatic counterbalance to its domestic preoccupations. On 14 July 1958 pro-Western King Faisal of Iraq and his prime minister, Nuri es Said were assassinated in a military coup, and Iraq was declared a republic. The repercussions in Jordan and Lebanon, both pro-Western in their foreign policies, were immediate. Both turned to the West for protection; Jordan to the United Kingdom and Lebanon to the United States. Both requests were met, and while British paratroops flew to Amman, United States Marines from the United States

Sixth Fleet began landing across the resort beaches north of Beirut on 15 July. The intention was a show of force; but once having landed, it is not so easy to withdraw without some embarrassment. In its way UNOGIL might be said to have provided the face-saving device for the United States' withdrawal in the following October, in that the United States could point to the continuing existence of UNOGIL as being sufficient in terms of an international presence. UNOGIL never established a working relationship with the Americans and made it very clear from the outset that it had no intention of doing so, since UNOGIL was operating under a specific mandate from the Security Council which had nothing to do with reasons for the United States' presence in Lebanon.

SANTO DOMINGO   The Dominican Republic, with its capital Santo Domingo, occupies the eastern half of the island of Hispaniola in the Caribbean—with Haiti as its western neighbor. In 1965 the republic was ruled by the military-civilian regime led by President Reid Cabral. After the assassination of Gerneralissimo Rafael Trujillo Molina in 1962, the country had returned to democratic rule for the first time in nearly three decades; but the administration of Juan Bosch, a historian, was more visionary than pragmatic, and the "democratic honeymoon" did not last long before being overthrown by Cabral in 1964. Almost at once Cabral himself became unpopular with the military officer corps, most of whom were former Trujillo men, because of his curtailment of their privileges as an elite class—a step made necessary by a need for general economy. Suspecting that Cabral would rig the elections to strengthen his position, the officers set aside their own differences and executed a coup that deposed Cabral and established José Molina Urena as provisional president in his stead. However, it was not long before the military themselves began to disagree, and a rebel group of officers broke away from the rest and set themselves up in opposition. Calling themselves the "Constitutional Government," they seized two military camps close to Santo Domingo, the government radio station in the capital, the president's palace, and parts of Santo Domingo itself, including the important Duarte Bridge across the Ozama River. Their intention was to reinstate Bosch as president.

The United States became increasingly alarmed at the course that events were taking. Its immediate evaluation of the situation was that Reid Cabral would regain power and that the pro-Bosch uprising was communist inspired—an assessment that had to be revised later.

Attacks by pro-Urena units of the army under Colonel Wessin, who had led the movement to overthrow the Bosch government, failed to secure the Duarte Bridge, despite supporting air attacks against the rebel positions. Efforts were made by the Dominican Archbishop Beras and by the diplomatic corps to bring about a halt to the fighting, but these failed. With Wessin's forces still battling to seize the Duarte Bridge, the United States, fearing a second Cuba, decided to intervene, and the Caribbean Amphibious Task Force, led by the helicopter carrier U.S.S. *Boxer* with 1,500 marines on board, was ordered to Santo Domingo to evacuate those American citizens wishing to leave. During the evacuation there was some shooting, and a number of American civilians were roughly handled by the rebels following a report that a key anti-Bosch Dominican was being smuggled out by the Americans. This report proving false, the rebels withdrew.

The rebels' position, however, was becoming increasingly precarious. An army regiment supporting Wessin had managed to enter Santo Domingo avoiding the Duarte Bridge, and the Dominican navy had discarded its neutral position and had also joined forces with Wessin. Realizing that the tide was turning against them, the leaders of the Constitutional Government sought to persuade the United States ambassador to mediate on their behalf, but this appeal led to nothing. The Constitutional Government then informed the Americans that they could no longer guarantee the safety of American and other foreign nationals in Santo Domingo and requested the United States to intervene militarily.

Immediately following this request on 25 April 1965, President Johnson ordered the 1,500 marines ashore from U.S.S. *Boxer,* and they rapidly gained control of the diplomatic residential area of the city. The United States informed the Council of the Organization of American States and the Security Council of the action it had taken. As a fellow member of the same regional organization as the Dominican Republic, the United States had by its action violated the principle of nonintervention by one member state in the domestic affairs of another; but this does not seem to have evoked any reaction from the Council, for that body contented itself simply with a call for an immediate cease-fire and the establishment of an international security zone for the protection of foreign embassies. Despite these moves the fighting continued and the United States further reinforced its troops in Santo Domingo by bringing in the Eighty-second Airborne Division. The paratroops wasted little time in capturing the Duarte Bridge, and the rebel-held positions around it. Fighting, however, continued despite a diplomatic approach by the papal nuncio to the Dominican Republic, Monsignor Clarizio, and another by the United States. Although Wessin and what had now become the "Government of National Reconstruction" were persuaded to sign a cease-fire document, the Constitutional Government refused to do so.

The United States reported all these moves at a meeting of the Security Council on 28 April, at the same time justifying its intervention on the grounds that it was in the interest of law and order, a protective measure for the continued safety of its own and other foreign nationals, and in any case was at the request of one of the parties in the dispute, the Constitutional Government. The USSR hotly contested the United States' interference, while other Council members felt that the situation should be handled by the OAS and that UN involvement was not desirable at that juncture.

Following further appeals by the OAS for an end to hostilities and the arrival in Santo Domingo of its secretary-general, a meeting of Ministers of Foreign Affairs of the American States on 1 May established a special committee comprised of the representatives of Argentina, Brazil, Colombia, Guatemala, and Panama, which was instructed to proceed immediately to Santo Domingo to bring about a restoration of peace and normality in the republic. It was to offer its good offices to the contending factions in an endeavor to achieve a cease-fire and an orderly evacuation of innocent civilians.

At this stage, therefore, there were American troops operating in Santo Domingo, the special committee set up by OAS attempting to bring about a cease-fire, and the Council of OAS and the Security Council both considering the situation. The OAS requested all its member states to make available land, air, naval, or possibly police forces for the formation of an Inter-American Peace Force, which would operate directly under OAS authority (a kind of regional version of Article 43 of the UN Charter!). On 5 May the OAS's special committee succeeded in obtaining the signatures of the leaders of both sides to an agreement (the Act of Santo Domingo) which formalized the cease-fire arrangements that had been initiated by the papal nuncio a few days previously. The agreement, besides providing for a cease-fire, delineated an international security zone with a corridor connecting it with San Isidor, where the Government of National Reconstruction (those opposed to Bosch's return) had its headquarters. But since the corridor bisected the area under the control of the Constitutional Government (those supporting Bosch), it was to prove an aggravation rather than a palliative and was to be the cause of further fighting.

Obtaining signatures is one thing, but getting both sides actually to stop fighting is a different matter, and this the special committee failed to do. On 14 May the Constitutional Government requested an urgent meeting of the Security Council to consider the situation created by the movement of United States troops outside their positions in the security zone and the bombing of Radio Santo Domingo. In the light of these two circumstances, the Security Council approved a call for a cease-fire and invited the secretary-general to send, as an urgent measure, his representative to the Dominican Republic so that the Council could receive a firsthand report on the situation.[26] Wasting no time, the secretary-general sent a small advance party [27] to Santo Domingo and appointed José Mayobre, the executive secretary of the Economic Commission for Latin America, as his representative.

Mayobre's first approaches achieved little. Each side blamed the other for the continued fighting, and Mayobre received a point-blank refusal from the pro-Bosch Constitutional Government to cease hostilities. Trouble also developed from another direction. On 19 May the OAS informed the Security Council of the failure of its special committee to arrange a cease-fire but added that the presence of the United Nations had compromised and interfered with the task of the committee. The UN party's reception certainly was only a little short of hostile and any pretense of courtesy between it and the United States Embassy evaporated with the submission of Mayobre's first report to the Security Council, which the United States considered to be partial to the Constitutional Government. Under the circumstances this relationship problem should not come as a surprise. This was the first time that the world organization and a regional organization had

26. Security Council Resolution 203, 14 May 1965.
27. Led by Major-General Indar Rikhye.

attempted a peacemaking effort in parallel, though each with a different mission. The lack of experience and misunderstanding of each other's role were liable to present problems; but add to this the unilateral intervention of a big power with special interests at stake, and there was every likelihood of disagreement. The OAS of course had the main responsibility, while the UN team was there only with an observation and reporting status within a peacekeeping framework.

On 21 May a twenty-four-hour cease-fire was successfully negotiated by Mayobre to allow the International Red Cross to discover and recover dead and wounded of both sides, but efforts to extend the cease-fire failed. Conciliatory initiatives continued to be sought by all parties, and the Security Council was in repeated session; but little progress was made, and the fighting went on. Not until the second half of June did the varied efforts reap any reward. By then the Constitutional Government forces had lost more ground and were now opposed by a 17,000-strong Inter-American Peace Force (IAPF). It was at this point that the OAS proposed the holding of general elections within six to nine months under OAS supervision. The proposal also provided for a general amnesty for all those who had fought, the surrender of all arms and equipment in unauthorized hands, the establishment of a provisional government, and the convening of a constitutional assembly within six months of the assumption of office of an elected government.

Although the remaining months of 1965 were far from peaceful, and there were repeated violations of the June cease-fire, work toward implementing the OAS's proposals proceeded. The UN observer mission focused its attention on supporting the Inter-American Human Rights Commission, which was dealing with large-scale violations of human rights. These, along with the grave deterioration in the economic situation, had become the serious issues for the Dominican Republic. In November national elections were announced for 1 June 1966, and on that date a new president, Joaquim Belager, and a new government were democratically elected. The Inter-American Peace Force began its withdrawal shortly afterward and completed it by the end of September. In the view of the OAS it was the presence of the IAPF alone that had made it possible for the provisional government to accomplish its task of reconciliation and hold elections in an atmosphere of complete calm.

On 22 October 1966, the UN mission in the Dominican Republic was withdrawn. From the foregoing it might appear to have played a relatively insignificant role, but it should be remembered that its mandate from the Security Council was to observe and report. In this context it had no mediatory role, but the UN representative had been instrumental in bringing about the cease-fire of 21 May 1965 and had throughout exercised a moderating influence in a difficult and dangerous situation, the control of which was primarily the responsibility of the OAS.

The juxtaposition of the various actors in the drama deserves some attention. First there were the two contesting factions, the Government for National Reconstruction and the Constitutional Government, neither of which could be said to have represented the people of the Dominican Republic. Together they had been responsible for the overthrow of the Cabral regime and then had split over the Bosch issue. Then there was the armed intervention of the United States, which could in no sense be described as impartial or peaceful, and which ignored the tenets of the charters of both the United Nations and the Organization of American States by acting unilaterally in response to an alleged "communist-inspired threat," which in the United States' view had the makings of a second Cuba crisis. Thirdly, and belatedly, came the intervention of the OAS, both in a conciliatory and peacekeeping role, which ultimately achieved its objective of ending hostilities and establishing a stable and democratic administration. Alongside these, the UN mission might be said to have had a peripheral role to play, but although limited in scope, it might be commended for its catalytic influence on the actions of the others, since it was the observation and reporting agent of the Security Council and of the world organization.

During the early months of the Santo Domingo affair (the conflict never seems to have spread outside the capital and engulfed the Dominican Republic as a whole), the Security Council met regularly to study Mayobre's reports, but the chief burden of its debates was centered on the action taken by the OAS, particularly in regard to the establishment of its peace force, and on the scope of the mandate of the secretary-general's representative. On the first issue there seems to have been a majority opinion for considering the OAS action as violating the basic provisions of the Charter, particularly Article 53, which requires that "no enforcement action shall be taken under regional arrangements or by regional agencies without the authorization of the Security Council." This, of course, raises a significant issue so far as future peacekeeping in general and the peacekeeping actions by regional organizations in particular are concerned. If, as seems likely, the world peacekeeping apparatus of an international conflict control system will to a greater degree than before depend upon regional arrangements and to a lesser degree on other multinational initiatives, the question of enforcement action will undoubtedly arise—though it is to be hoped that any peacekeeping operations so mounted will conform with the current UN principle of peaceful intervention rather than enforcement.

The other point at issue in the Security Council was Mayobre's mandate. There was a move on the part of France, Jordan, Uruguay, and the USSR to extend his responsibilities to the supervision of ceasefires and the investigation of alleged violations of human rights, since they considered his mandate as originally formulated to be insufficient in scope to cover both tasks. Bolivia, the Ivory Coast, Malaysia, the United Kingdom, and the United States were opposed to any change, since, as the United States pointed out, the Inter-American Human Rights Commission was already in Santo Domingo and was actively investigating any violations. The secretary-general of the United Nations himself was skeptical of the advisability of extending Mayobre's mandate and increasing his staff to cover human rights violations. Since the effectiveness of the investigations would depend very much on the cooperation of the contending parties and on a substantial increase in the number of observers, the secretary-general was not in favor of an extension of his representative's mandate.

It might be wondered why the UN mission to the Dominican Republic is included among the case studies of peacekeeping and peace observation, since it was not constituted nor did it operate exactly as other UN missions in other instances. It is included here because of its observer status and reporting role in a conflict situation.[28] The lesson that emerges centers on the capacity of regional agencies and the United Nations to combine in the settlement of interstate and intrastate disputes. Article 52 calls on regional agencies to "make every effort to achieve pacific settlements of local disputes . . . before referring them to the Security Council." On the other hand, the United Nations cannot remain aloof to any use of enforcement action by a

---

28. Reference is also made to the Dominican Republic in chapter 9 dealing with regional, multinational, and special operations in the OAS context.

regional agency in the settlement of such disputes (Article 53); nor can it in general terms ignore any threat to international peace and security wherever it may occur (Article 39). The experience of Santo Domingo could well be repeated, where a regional agency and the United Nations might be called upon to collaborate in settling a dispute, arranging a cease-fire, or observing that human rights are not violated. *Collaboration* is the essential word, for as with peacemaking and peacekeeping, there needs to be a working interrelationship between all parties concerned with ending conflict. A pattern is required, setting definitive guidelines and precise areas of responsibility for each contributing agency, while at the same time establishing vertical and lateral communication and liaison links to provide the kind of working relationship that is needed. Had such a structure and understanding existed in the Dominican Republic, the long-drawn-out violations of cease-fire and of human rights might have been avoided.

Special Operations:
West New Guinea

The United Nations Temporary Executive Authority (UNTEA) in West Irian, formerly West New Guinea, is the only operation of its kind so far conducted by the United Nations. It is also the only UN operation that has ended on the day on which it had been scheduled to end. UNTEA for eight months assumed responsibility for the administration of the territory during an interregnum between its control by the colonial administration of the Netherlands and its hand-over to Indonesia.

The dispute that necessitated the intervention derived from the long-drawn-out wrangle over sovereignty between the Netherlands and Indonesia following the end of World War II. This had partly resolved itself at The Hague in 1949 with the recognition by the Netherlands of Indonesia as an independent sovereign state. But there remained the question of West New Guinea's future, on which agreement had not been reached. This issue was left open for further negotiation on the understanding that the island's political status would be decided within one year. There was ambiguity over whether or not the Netherlands retained sovereign rights over the territory during the interim period. The Netherlands government insisted that it did, until such a time as the people of West New Guinea were in a position to decide their future for themselves. Indonesia, on the other hand, claimed that by the declaration at The Hague the Netherlands had been given the right merely to administer the territory during the interim period and not the authority to exercise sovereignty over it.

The argument continued far beyond the stipulated one year and still was not resolved in 1954 when Indonesia took the matter to the United Nations. The Indonesians were demanding the incorporation of New Guinea into Indonesia, but at no session of the General Assembly was there a two-thirds majority vote in favor, the minimum necessary for a resolution to be adopted. Not until 1961 did a settlement appear possible. By then the Dutch were finding the continuance of their colonial responsibilities an increasing burden and were actively searching for the means by which they could shed them. Their search was helped by a 1960 General Assembly resolution calling for immediate steps to be taken toward granting independence to the trust and non-self-governing territories still awaiting independence.[29] Using the West New Guinea situation as a test case, the Netherlands proposed that it hand over to the United Nations the responsibility for administering West New Guinea until such a time as the people declared their preference for the future—independence or union with Indonesia. Admirable as this proposal might seem, it did not appeal to the Indonesians, who saw in it an attempt to deprive Indonesia of its rightful territory. In Jakarta on 24 October 1961, Foreign Minister Subandrio claimed that Indonesia reserved the right "to liberate our brothers in West Irian" by force of arms if necessary. This was no idle threat, for it was not very long before Indonesia attempted to implement that intention, which it considered to be its right. In January 1962 a small Indonesian naval force of torpedo boats was intercepted off the west coast of the island by units of the Dutch East Indies fleet. In the engagement that followed, one of the torpedo boats was sunk and the remainder fled. On board the sunken boat, apart from thirty-five soldiers, there had been a quantity of arms including mortars and machine guns. Later in the year a number of Indonesian paratroop landings were made at widely separated points, but most of these attempts at infiltration proved unsuccessful and were liquidated by Dutch marines, though a few of the paratroops remained at large in the jungle.

In May 1962 the secretary-general asked Ellsworth Bunker, a

29. General Assembly Resolution 1514(XV), 14 December 1960.

former United States ambassador to India, to attempt to work out a solution; the result was the "Bunker Plan," which blueprinted the short-term future of the territory. By it the Dutch were to hand over the administration of the territory to the United Nations, which would then administer it for not less than one year with the assistance of non-Indonesian and non-Dutch officials. At the end of the one- to two-year period the administration would be transferred to the Indonesians, who at a future date would give the people of West New Guinea the chance to exercise their freedom of voting on their future. The cost of the UN administration effort was to be shared equally between the Netherlands and Indonesia.

The plan found favor with both sides. The period of the UN administration was agreed to last until May 1963, and 1969 was designated as the year for the self-determination plebiscite. In August the agreement was signed, but since the naval and military activity had continued, it was desirable that a small UN group of twenty-one observers [30] should also be sent to West New Guinea to assist in the implementation of the cease-fire. This they were successful in doing in cooperation with the Dutch and Indonesian authorities. On 1 October 1963, as part of the UN Temporary Executive Authority, a UN security force (UNSF), consisting of 1,500 Pakistani troops, arrived and was deployed in the main towns and districts to deter any attempt to breach the peace and to assist the outlying communities in preparing for the changes ahead.

The concept of a caretaker administration was a new dimension for the United Nations. In the event it proved remarkably successful. From all over the world professional men—industrialists, engineers, technicians, forestry experts, and health advisers—were recruited to take over governmental departments and public utilities from the Dutch and run them during the interregnum. The judiciary posed a special problem, which in the end was resolved by the Dutch judges staying on until the hand-over to Indonesia. On the security side there was a national police force and a militia—the Papuan Volunteer Corps. The rank and file of the police were Papuans, but the officers had all been Dutch. A multinational cadre, under a British officer with Malay police experience, was raised to fill the executive posts so that the force could continue to operate effectively. Senior UN

30. Provided by Brazil, Ceylon, India, Ireland, Nigeria, and Sweden.

secretariat officials arrived to take over senior positions in the administration, and José Rolz Bennett, former deputy *chef de cabinet* to U Thant, was appointed temporary UN administrator until replaced on a permanent basis by Ambassador Abdoh of Iran. To complete the team some 500 former Dutch officials voluntarily remained behind to help. Every opportunity was taken to train suitable Papuans to fill junior posts after the UN had left. Also to ensure that the hand-over to the Indonesians went smoothly when the time came, those Indonesians nominated to take over executive posts in the administration and public and governmental services were brought in early.

The UN Temporary Executive Authority (UNTEA) existed for eight months, transferring responsibility for the administration of West New Guinea to Indonesia on 1 May 1963—the date originally agreed upon for the hand-over. In accordance with the treaty the West New Guineans exercised their "act of free choice" in a UN supervised plebiscite in July and August 1969. The issue for them to decide was whether or not they would remain in Indonesia. They chose to remain.

Certainly in terms of success the West New Guinea experience comes high in the order of merit on the list of United Nations achievements in the sphere of peacekeeping. It also gave a clear indication of how a multinational team of experts (only thirty-five strong) can exercise peaceful and constitutional authority for a prescribed period of time during an interregnum in the political affairs of a small state. This is not to say that problems did not arise in West New Guinea—they did, but in the main they were skillfully handled. UNTEA set a precedent that should not be overlooked; occasions could well arise where the establishment of an international interregnum could provide a stable administration for a period of vacuum in a state's political life—until it is in a position to manage its affairs for itself. The experience of UNTEA should not be wasted but should serve as a model for the future.

9

Regional Arrangements and Operations

Organization of
American States
The development of regional organizations as instruments for collective security followed almost inevitably from the granting to the UN Security Council of the ultimate authority to maintain international peace and security. Such an authority, so far as the Americans were concerned, conflicted with the Monroe Doctrine. Latin America, having an emotional attachment to Pan-Americanism, wanted to safeguard the tradition of regional settlement of intrahemisphere disputes. Thanks to the goodwill and trust that United States policies under the Roosevelt administration had engendered among Latin American countries, the United States was eminently positioned to assume a dominant role in any Latin American initiative for structuring and strengthening regional procedures for keeping the peace. Latin Americans were concerned that in a world organization their special relationship with the United States might be reduced in its effectiveness. There was concern also over the growing power of the Soviet Union and the increasing communist threat in the southern hemisphere. It can be seen that the regional concept for maintaining peace and security was not without its advantages for the United States.

The veto power of the permanent members of the Security Council made it necessary for some provision to be made in the Charter (Article 51) whereby regional authorities could take action to uphold the inherent right of individual or collective self-defense against armed attack. However, so that the authority of the United Nations was safeguarded and the authority and responsibility of the Security Council were in no way affected, a proviso was added to the Charter (Article 53) requiring that any measures taken in the exercise of the right to self-defense shall be immediately reported to the Security Council. The United States recognized as inevitable that the establishment of any regional organization for the Americas would encourage other similar regional organizations in different parts of the world. The subsequent growth of such organizations has more than anything else led to the increasing insistence that peaceful resolution of conflicts be encouraged within regional arrangements.

The Organization of American States, the first regional organization to be established, came into being under the terms of the Rio de Janeiro Treaty in 1948, when a charter was drawn up complementary to that of the United Nations. By this time the United States' relations with the Soviet Union had deteriorated, and the United Nations, so recently established, faced an East-West confrontation. Not unnaturally, the development of OAS to act as a regional security body received great encouragement from its members.

The OAS on a number of occasions, alone and independently from the United Nations, has performed a variety of peacekeeping roles and has succeeded in putting an end to violent conflict. Like the United Nations, it has not always been successful, but its effectiveness in freezing many situations has been demonstrated. Disputing parties have placed complete trust in the impartiality of their regional organization and have been willing to rely on regional methods of settlement. The OAS has been able to provide assistance because regional action to maintain peace was compatible with the varied interests of its membership, especially since the members of the OAS preferred not to bring their problems before the world organization. The American hemisphere, however, could not expect to remain isolated from the issues developing from the cold war, which were inevitably to alter the nature of the OAS-UN relationship and raise many contentious problems.

The purposes of the OAS are somewhat identical to those of the United Nations. Its raison d'être is to strengthen peace and security of the hemisphere, to prevent possible causes of conflict, to assist in the specific settlement of disputes, to provide common action against aggression, and to promote cooperative action within the organization. The seeds of its organization were sown as far back as 1940, when an Inter-American Peace Committee was established with the responsibility for maintaining constant vigilance to ensure that any existing or potential dispute between states of the Americas was quickly resolved, and for proposing methods and procedures by which a settlement might be reached—proposals that in no way sought to impose conditions on either side in the dispute. The committee, however, remained relatively inactive, since its powers of action were dependent upon the consent of all the parties to a dispute—a proviso that subsequently became the yardstick by which UN operations were judged to be acceptable. On the formation of OAS the Inter-American Peace Committee was incorporated as a permanent committee within its framework, but by the provisions of the OAS charter its functions are limited to those of peaceful settlement and do not encompass the wider issues of human rights, economic underdevelopment, and political stability—areas of discord with which IAPC had previously been involved.

The OAS has in its relatively short existence intervened in Latin American disputes in several instances. Its intervention in 1948 in the Costa Rica–Nicaragua border fighting, when the former complained of invasion by the latter, resulted in an amity pact that lasted seven years, after which the OAS once again provided observation patrols in a successful effort to end a renewal of unrest between the two countries. OAS's method of operation has usually been to establish a fact-finding commission to make an on-the-spot investigation and evaluation and report back to its central council. This provides an OAS presence at the point of conflict, which by its very nature helps to cool down tense situations and allows them to be controlled or contained within prescribed limits, as was the case in the 1964 dispute between the United States and Panama. OAS intervened in similar fashion when Cubans invaded Panama in 1959 and in the disputes between Venezuela and the Dominican Republic in 1960, Venezuela and Cuba in 1963, and San Salvador and Honduras in 1969; in each case, in accordance with Article 53 of the UN Charter, it informed the Security Council of its actions. An exception to this list of Article 52 interventions was the Cuban missile crisis in 1962. Since there was a dangerous possibility that that dispute could lead to a global war, its resolution could not therefore be confined to an intervention by OAS alone. Furthermore, the crisis resulted in a confrontation between two superpowers—an additional threat to world peace—and it required the active participation of the United Nations, both in supporting discussions between the two superpowers and within the framework of the OAS, to bring about a peaceful settlement.

Probably the two most comprehensive and determined interventions so far executed by the OAS are those concerned with the Guatemala case of 1959 and the Dominican civil war in 1965. Both required a major effort by the organization to bring them to a settled conclusion; and the latter case, as we have already seen, involved the deployment of an Inter-American Peace Force of 19,000 men (at one time the figure was as high as 23,000). In view of their dimensions these two examples of oas intervention deserve further description.

GUATEMALA   On 19 June 1954 the government of Guatemala reported to the United Nations that Nicaragua and Honduras had attacked it and requested the Security Council to take measures to halt the aggression. Guatemala's specific complaint was that a small band of predominantly Guatemalan nationals, commanded by the exiled Colonel Carlos Castillo Armas, had led the invasion and that it was supported by the United States, which was known to regard the Guatemalan government, headed by Jacobo Arbenz Guzmán, as communist. Guatemala had already appealed to the Inter-American Peace Committee, but now it requested a suspension of consideration of its complaint by the oas and asked for the case to be withdrawn. It was the first instance of a member of the oas attempting to bypass the organization in favor of appealing to the Security Council. A resolution in the Security Council to refer Guatemala's complaint to the oas was vetoed by the Soviet Union, and later the Security Council voted unanimously to call for the termination of the invasion and to request states to refrain from giving assistance to the attackers.

At the request of Honduras and Nicaragua, the Inter-American Peace Committee sent a subcommittee to investigate the situation, also seeking to obtain the consent of Guatemala to this intervention; but Guatemala rejected this move and again attempted to take up the issue with the Security Council. The latter refused to consider this further request and left the oas to deal with the crisis. Having failed with the United Nations, Guatemala accepted the oas intervention and agreed to cooperate with the subcommittee of the Inter-American Peace Committee in settling the dispute; at the same time the oas called a meeting of the Ministers of Foreign Affairs of the American States to consider the situation. However, while this maneuvering was taking place, Castillo Armas's invasion was successful in ousting the Arbenz regime and seizing power for himself. This fait accompli left oas with no alternative but to withdraw its subcommittee and cancel its foreign ministers' meeting, while the new regime of Castillo Armas officially informed the Security Council that the Guatemalan case was closed.

The Guatemalan case had an important impact in developing future relations between the OAS and the UN. The Arbenz regime was in disfavor with the United States as well as with the anticommunist regimes in Latin America. It was to be expected, therefore, that the regime would not wish to have its case dealt with by the OAS, since it believed that the organization would rather help to dissolve the regime than to defend it. The Arbenz regime therefore brought the question to the Security Council hoping that the Council would be able to freeze the situation and thereby permit the regime to survive. It was also to be expected that an issue of this making would be affected by the climate of the cold war between East and West. Western nations rallied behind the United States in its opposition to the Guatemalan crisis being dealt with by the Security Council and instead urged that the OAS should deal with this situation. The Soviet Union and the Eastern bloc countries in the Security Council supported the Arbenz regime's claim that it had the unchallenged right to appeal to the Security Council under Articles 34 and 35 of the UN Charter. Brazil and Colombia, the two Latin American countries in the Council at that time, advocated that it was a matter for the OAS to act on in the first instance, under Articles 52 and 53 of the Charter. In the end, the United States succeeded in having the case referred back to the OAS only by a narrow margin. The significant point here is that the principle was not fully accepted that any American state has the right to appeal to the Security Council whenever its security is threatened.

DOMINICAN REPUBLIC   The circumstances and progress of the Dominican civil war in 1965 and the part that the United Nations played in it have been set out in the previous chapter. It is proper to recognize the prominent role played by OAS in bringing about a peaceful settlement. As we have seen, shortly after the United States' intervention, the OAS established a committee with the mandate to investigate the dispute and to negotiate a settlement; at the same time it raised an Inter-American Peace Force from among its member states to bring an end to the fighting. The committee succeeded in negotiating a cessation of hostilities and, with the help of the IAPF, continued to assist in reducing tension. It performed humanitarian services, undertook extensive economic and fiscal responsibilities, carried out administrative tasks where administrative authority had broken down, and rendered important service in the field of human rights.

The Inter-American Peace Force established in the Dominican Republic was an important first example of how a regional organization could raise a peace force made up of contingents from member states, operating under a unified command and functioning under the authority of the central OAS council. Since the use of ground forces was designed within the framework of peaceful settlement of disputes, the Inter-American Peace Force experience could well set a pattern for the future. There was, however, some sentiment expressed at the United Nations that the organization of peacekeeping forces, as in the case of the Inter-American Peace Force, was a UN function and outside the scope of regional organizations. The Soviet Union and socialist countries particularly supported this viewpoint, but then they have always insisted, along with France, that all peacekeeping forces should be established only with the authority of the Security Council.

The role of the secretary-general of OAS during the Dominican crisis set a new precedent. He accompanied the ad hoc subcommission to Santo Domingo and remained there for a considerable period of time. He not only constituted a continuing presence of the OAS but was directly involved in political and diplomatic activities.

The OAS experience, similar to that of the United Nations, is that it has been able to limit or reduce tensions but not to prevent outbreaks of violence. It has succeeded in bringing an end to hostilities but again, as with the United Nations, has not succeeded very often in resolving those conflicts. The limited effectiveness of OAS in conflict resolution can be attributed to political factors, just as the United Nations has been rendered ineffective in similar circumstances. The OAS does have the advantage of being a more homogeneous organization and is therefore free of some problems that exist within the United Nations—such as the disagreements among the great powers, especially between the two superpowers, and those caused by the differing interests of the various regional groupings and the nonaligned group that exist within the United Nations system.

In the Dominican situation, apart from the small group of the Constitutional Government, who would have been willing to accept a UN presence, the Dominicans were unlikely ever to have agreed to the

United Nations' replacing OAS in its peacemaking and peacekeeping role—in any event, the two superpowers held differing views as to the desirability of a UN intervention, and it was only after considerable discussion that the Security Council agreed that a fact-finding mission should be sent to Santo Domingo. These circumstances would not have encouraged the Dominicans to seek more comprehensive assistance.

The character and composition of the Inter-American Peace Force cannot be considered as an ideal pattern for the future. In numbers it was dominated by the United States which contributed 90 percent of the force—the five other national contingents mustering less than 3,000 altogether. This imbalance of national representation emphasized only too clearly that the presence of troops from the five other nations was nothing more than a token, and that the United States forces really dominated the scene. In the OAS system, however, IAPF sets a precedent in the form that it took, in its operational role, and in its ability to have maintained a cease-fire; but it cannot be looked upon as an ideal example because of the almost unilateral control exercised by the most important partner in the OAS, the United States.

The United States' position in the OAS is an all-important factor, bordering on the unique, and is somewhat parallel to the position of the Soviet Union in the grouping of the socialist states in Europe. The difference, of course, is that in the OAS system there are different political and economic structures and therefore many differences among the member states. Canada, though located in the hemisphere, is not a member of the OAS. This indicates that although the OAS was designed primarily for Latin American nations, the United States, because of its overwhelming power position in the Americas, could not be left out.

An analysis of OAS's development and its relations with the United Nations would seem to indicate that so far efforts to establish a "try OAS first" principle have not been successful. The Guatemalan case of 1954 underlined the belief of many OAS members that the United States was preventing American states from appealing to the Security Council when their security was threatened. It was not until the Dominican crisis that the United States found increasing support among OAS members to rely on the organization and act under Article 53 of the United Nations Charter. The cold war naturally had a great deal to do with the development of the OAS. The Soviet Union often appeared in the unusual role of champion for the United Nations, whereas the United States found itself minimizing the role of the world organization. This has meant that the original concept of developing a suitable relationship between the OAS and the United Nations, which would encourage regional organizations to operate within the framework of the United Nations supervision and control, has been somewhat offset with no immediate likelihood of the concept's taking root.

The OAS has attempted to achieve complete control over the disputes within its own area. On the other hand, the Security Council has not succeeded in regulating or restricting the enforcement operations of the OAS. During the cold war years, the United States attempted every possible means to keep the influence of the Soviet Union out of the American hemisphere. To this end it encouraged within the regional organization enforcement measures in which it could play a dominant role, and in its own self-interest it side-stepped the procedures that would bring in the United Nations.

Organization of African Unity
As its title implies, the Organization of African Unity was created primarily to promote unity and solidarity among African states. As the several independent states emerged in Africa, they found that they had many mutual interests, among them a positive requirement to resolve their conflicts by peaceful means, to which end they established a commission of mediation, conciliation, and arbitration. It is significant that the instruments establishing the commission make no reference to the Charter and jurisdiction of the United Nations, which indicates that the founders of the OAU intended that settlements should be sought within an African framework.

Disputes dealt with by the OAU have been largely concerned with boundary problems, as between Algeria and Morocco and between Somalia on the one hand and Ethiopia and Kenya on the other. It has handled differences over the future of neighboring non–self-governing territories such as those of French Somalia and the Spanish Sahara. It has dealt with situations of friction between member states arising from internal conflicts, as between Rwanda and Burundi, the Nigerian civil war, the Congo civil war and the mercenary problem on the conclusion of UN operations there. The organization has handled other situations of interstate friction between certain West African states including Ghana and Guinea, and Ghana and the Ivory Coast. To analyze these interventions and evaluate their effects one needs to study the specific problems more closely.

The Algerian-Moroccan dispute originated from the fact that only the northernmost sector of the boundary between Algeria and Morocco had been demarcated and that Morocco claimed a part of "Algerian Sahara" on the grounds that it was within its frontiers in precolonial times. The discovery of oil and other mineral deposits within the disputed area added piquancy to the situation. After Algeria had received its independence, political and ideological differences so increased the tensions between the two countries that in October 1963 war broke out between them.

Algeria sought OAU intervention, whereas Morocco preferred bilateral negotiations but, if that were not possible, wished to bring the matter to the attention of the Security Council. The African heads of states persuaded the king of Morocco and the president of Algeria to meet at Bamako in the "neutral" state of Mali, and a peaceful agreement was concluded. The terms of the Bamako Agreement were that hostilities would cease by 1 November and that a commission of Algerian, Moroccan, Ethiopian, and Malian officers would be established to determine the demilitarized zones. The Ethiopian and Malian observers were to supervise the cease-fire and the demilitarized zones, and an extraordinary meeting of the OAU council would be called to set up a commission to determine the responsibility for hostilities, study the frontier question, and make proposals for a settlement of the dispute. Regrettably, these steps did not resolve the situation, and fighting continued. Morocco, therefore, brought the situation to the attention of the UN secretary-general. Counting on the support of those great powers friendly to Morocco—France and the United States—Morocco had hoped for a UN intervention. However, France and the United States preferred that the dispute should be settled through OAU conciliation and that Morocco should not insist on invoking Argicle 35 of the UN Charter and bringing the dispute to the Security Council. Thus encouraged, the OAU went ahead with its attempts to resolve the crisis and by the end of February 1964 had negotiated an agreement between Algeria and Morocco whereby both countries would withdraw their troops and create demilitarized zones agreed to under the Bamako Agreement. The two countries formed a joint committee to settle disputes and harmonize their relations. By May 1970 the two states concluded an agreement on the boundary question.

Somalia's disputes with Ethiopia and Kenya stemmed from the granting of independence to Kenya in December 1963. At the time Kenya's northern boundary with Somalia was in dispute, where a number of Somalis lived and worked within what Kenya considered to be its territory. Many of the Somali settlers were evicted and deprived of their livelihood. Not surprisingly, this expulsion policy led to fighting between Kenyan and Somali groups in the border zone. For similar reasons, and almost concurrently, fighting also broke out between Somalis and Ethiopian troops along Somalia's other border, which in time escalated into a major armed conflict. These border disputes, like many others in the African continent, originated from the arbitrary drawing of the borders by the former colonial authorities.

On 9 February 1964 Somalia requested an urgent meeting of the Security Council, but before any action was taken the secretary-general appealed to both parties to settle their dispute peacefully within an African framework. The Council of Ministers of OAU met at Dar es Salaam and were of the view that "the solution to all disputes between member states be sought first within the OAU." The council, despite strong reservations expressed by Somalia and Morocco, each of whom had sought to adjust international boundaries in its own favor, adhered firmly to the principle that the disputes of member states should be first addressed to the OAU. The council endorsed its charter provision that "all member states pledge themselves to respect the borders as defined and existing at the time of national independence." Somalia accepted the council's ruling and entered into bilateral talks with its neighbors, leading to a series of successful joint ministerial meetings chaired by the president of Zambia. Relations between Somalia and its neighbors were normalized, but following the assumption of power by a military government in October 1969, no further progress has been possible in normalizing relations between Somalia and Ethiopia.

Thus a pattern of peaceful settlement of disputes related to boundary questions has been established by the OAU. Though disputes have been referred to the United Nations, its members as well as its secretary-general have encouraged those concerned to seek a peaceful settlement of their disputes through the framework of OAU. It was the African states themselves who resolved that the borders existing at the time of their independence were international frontiers, and it is broadly true that regardless of the manner in which particular boundary disputes in Africa have been rendered quiescent within the African framework, the OAU machinery—through individual mediation, bilateral negotiation, or other means—so far seems to have obviated the need to resort to the United Nations with regard to such disputes.

In contrast to African boundary disputes, which have been handled almost exclusively within an OAU framework, the problems arising from differences between African states over the future of non–self-governing territories have been handled more frequently by the United Nations than by the OAU. These disputes have related to the question of French Somaliland and Spanish Sahara. The OAU has tended to be more concerned with decolonization aspects of the problem than with resolving questions of rival claims.

In cases where friction between African states arises, as it often does, out of internal conflicts, governments facing a challenge to their authority are reluctant to allow any international involvement in their internal affairs; but since many African frontiers cut right across ethnic lines, these disputes inevitably involve their neighbors and therefore become a matter of international concern. Thus both the United Nations and the OAU have been involved in interstate tensions resulting from internal conflicts in Rwanda and Burundi, in the Democratic Republic of Zaire, and in Nigeria.

The friction between Rwanda and Burundi has been of a recurring nature. The insurgency during 1963, when Rwandese Batutsi refugees in neighboring countries campaigned against the Bahutu-controlled Rwanda government, was followed by massive reprisals. In 1965 there was an attempt by some Bahutu leaders to overthrow the monarchy, which they blamed for perpetuating Batutsi supremacy. And then in 1966 tension escalated between Rwanda and Burundi because of alleged subversive activities by refugees in Burundi. Since then, there have been other occasions when fighting between these two rival ethnic groups has resulted in multiple genocide, requiring humanitarian action on the part of the international community to terminate it. President Mobutu of Zaire succeeded in arranging an agreement between the presidents of Burundi and Rwanda. In this instance the United Nations, through its high commissioner for refugees, played solely a humanitarian role, but since then the UN secretary-general has collaborated with the secretary-general of the OAU in dealing with new and continuing problems.

The major test that the OAU has so far had to face was the renewed civil war in the Congo (Zaire) following the withdrawal of ONUC in June 1964. Even though a government of national reconciliation had been established in August 1961 and the secession of Katanga had been brought to an end by UN troops in January 1963, bitter rivalries remained among Congolese politicians. Nor were the Congolese people in a quiescent mood. Many were openly dissatisfied and showed it. Toward the end of 1963 and before the departure of ONUC, the Congo government found it necessary to impose a state of emergency. This was followed by an outbreak of sporadic disturbances throughout the country. Immediately following the withdrawal of ONUC in June 1964, fighting broke out in Kwilu, Katanga, Orientale, and Kivu. Cyrille Adoula, the prime minister, unable to cope with the situation, resigned and was replaced by Moise Tshombe on 10 July 1964. This appointment heightened the many ideological differences that had remained quiescent under the government of national reconciliation, and fighting broke out with a greater intensity, while at Stanleyville a dissident government was established.

Prime Minister Tshombe sought additional military assistance from the United States and also proceeded once again to recruit foreign mercenaries, including some from South Africa and Southern Rhodesia, in order to regain the territory in the hands of the insurgents. The insurgents, on the other hand, sought assistance from the USSR and the People's Republic of China. By September 1964 the situation had deteriorated considerably, and the Congolese government requested an extraordinary meeting of the OAU Council of Ministers to consider the external aspects of the crisis. The council met early in September 1964 and emphasized the peaceful resolution of conflicts within the OAU framework. It refused Prime Minister Tshombe's request for military assistance from African states through the OAU. It appealed to the Congolese government to stop the recruitment of all foreign mercenaries and to expel those who were already in the Congo, and it called upon Congolese political leaders to seek national conciliation with the help of the OAU. It also called upon all other new member states to refrain from any action that might aggravate the situation and on all other nations not to intervene in the internal affairs of the Congo.

An ad hoc commission of ten states under the chairmanship of Prime Minister (later President) Jomo Kenyatta of Kenya was established to carry out the agreed OAU mandate, that is, to help and encourage the efforts of the Congolese government in the restoration of national conciliation and to help normalize relations between the Congo and its neighboring states, particularly Burundi and Congo Brazzaville.

Since national reconciliation was of primary importance, the ad hoc commission was as much concerned with that aspect as with interstate relations. Tshombe, however, did not accept any interference in domestic issues and refused to meet with insurgent leaders. The ad hoc commission's appeal for cessation of hostilities and for national conciliation went unheeded, but when the insurgents withdrew into Stanleyville, having brought with them several Europeans and Asians as hostages, Prime Minister Kenyatta tendered his good offices.

The OAU secretary-general entered into negotiations with the United States ambassador in Kenya and with Thomas Kanza, representing the insurgents; but before a settlement could be reached, the United States and Belgium, with the cooperation of the British, landed paratroops in Stanleyville. On 1 December Belgium and the United States informed the Security Council that it had completed the rescue of the hostages and had evacuated its paratroops from the Congo. At this point the growing crisis was brought to the Security Council, where a majority of the members agreed that it was a problem that could best be solved within the OAU framework and within the context of Article 52 of the Charter. There was, however, disagreement over the role of the UN secretary-general in his collaboration with the peacemaking efforts by the OAU. In the view of the Soviet Union the secretary-general had no role to play; whereas the two African member states of the Security Council, Morocco and Ivory Coast, in the draft resolution that they submitted to the Council, urged that the secretary-general play a responsible role in the Congo dispute which, if ignored, could escalate to a level where it could threaten international peace and security. In the event, the Security Council did approve a follow-up role for the secretary-general, underlining the premiss that in the first instance it should be the OAU that sought peaceful settlement of disputes in Africa, without prejudice to the role of the UN secretary-general in situations that might affect international peace and security.

The mercenaries in the Congo, recruited by Tshombe's government, were a cause of tension between the Congo and many other African states. The process of their expulsion developed new tensions between the Congo government and Rwanda. In October 1965, Prime Minister Tshombe was removed from office by President Kasavubu, who gave assurances that the mercenaries would be expelled and relations between the Congo and its neighboring African states would be normalized. Within a month, as a result of a military coup d'état, General Mobutu became president of the Congo and began to implement the promises made by his predecessor. The mercenaries had become an integral part of the Congolese National Army (ANC), but before their expulsion could be completed and all their units disbanded, Tshombe was kidnapped and taken to Algeria in July 1967. The kidnapping precipitated a revolt against the ANC by units in Bukavu, and a number of Congolese servicemen loyal to Tshombe joined the rebels. Another group of rebel mercenaries landed at Stanleyville by parachute and established a rebel "government of public safety." This new crisis was brought by the Congolese government before both the Security Council and the OAU. The Security Council condemned the states that gave assistance to the mercenaries and called upon governments to ensure that neither the territories under their control nor their nationals were to be used for subversive activities against the Congo. The OAU General Assembly established a ten-nation ad hoc committee under the chairmanship of President El Azhari of Sudan "to take all steps necessary for the evacuation of the mercenaries." The International Red Cross also intervened to assist in the peaceful evacuation of the mercenaries from Bukavu to Rwanda.

Early in November the Security Council was informed by the Congolese government that a new invasion by mercenaries had taken place; this time from Angola with Portuguese collaboration. The Security Council condemned Portugal and urged all countries to take appropriate measures to prevent Portugal from renewing its activities against any state. At the same time the Council instructed the UN secretary-general to take all possible measures to ensure the implementation of the resolution.

The OAU ad hoc committee established a five-nation commission of inquiry to identify the mercenaries detained in Rwanda as well as the states, organizations, or interested groups behind the mercenary activities in the Congo. Finally, by April 1968, the chairman was able to persuade the government of the Congo to agree to an evacuation as requested by the OAU General Assembly, and with the assistance of the International Red Cross all mercenaries were evacuated from Africa.

The Nigerian civil war provided the second major crisis point for the OAU in the 1960s. It began with the state elections of December 1964, in which the country's northern tribal regions gained a clear majority in the Federal Assembly, causing considerable apprehension among the other regions that the northern tribes would dominate the affairs and administration of the state. The electoral campaign inspired bitter strife with the result that the main political parties, as well as the eastern and western regions, boycotted the elections. As the scale of disturbances, irregularities, and lawlessness increased, a group of junior Ibo officers carried out a coup d'état on January 15, 1966. They assassinated the federal prime minister along with a number of other prominent regional and federal government leaders, including many senior northern army officers. Anarchy was brought to an end by the establishment of a provisional military government under Major General Johnson Aguiyi-Ironsi, the senior Ibo officer. General Ironsi substituted a unitary state for the federal system. This measure was strongly opposed by northern Nigerians, who regarded it as a scheme designed to increase Ibo domination. It did not help that General Ironsi had surrounded himself with Ibo offficers, thus causing further desperation on the part of the northern region. On 29 July 1966 a group of northern soldiers led a coup d'état killing General Ironsi and many of his high-ranking Ibo officers. A few days later Lieutenant Colonel (now General) Yakubu Gowon, a northern officer and a Christian, was appointed to head a national military government. However, before the new government could exercise its control, communal riots spread throughout the country, leading to the killing of many Ibos in the north and a mass exodus of refugees to eastern Nigeria, the traditional home of the Ibos.

General Gowon's government reinstated the federal system and declared that a constituent assembly would be convened and a referendum held to determine an acceptable system of government. Through the good offices of General Ankrah, the head of the Military Revolutionary Council of Ghana, General Gowon met with the four military governors of Nigeria in January 1967 at Aburi, Ghana. The eastern region was permitted control of its security, and it was agreed that there should be some compensation for the loss of life and property of Ibos in the northern region. However, it was made clear that no authority would be given to the Ibo leaders to secede. There were differences of interpretation, and subsequently Colonel Ojukwu, the governor of the eastern region, stopped payments of revenue to the federal government, complaining that no compensation had been paid to the Ibos. The federal government retaliated by imposing economic sanctions. On 27 May 1967 the federal government decentralized the system of government by creating twelve states out of the former regions, thus dissecting the eastern region into one Ibo-dominated state and two other states where Ibos would be a minority. Three days later, Colonel Ojukwu declared the whole eastern region an independent sovereign state to be named Biafra. On 6 July 1967 fighting began between federal government troops and Biafra and continued until the defeat of Ojukwu's troops in January 1970.

The federal government of Nigeria had warned all countries not to interfere in the internal affairs of Nigeria. Therefore intervention by the OAU in this conflict became difficult, and when its council met, it agreed to assure the federal government of Nigeria "of the Assembly's desire for the territorial integrity, unity and peace of Nigeria." OAU appointed a new ad hoc committee, but it was not able to visit Lagos until toward the end of 1967, by which time federal forces had made progress and the Biafran forces were in retreat. The committee did, however, persuade the federal government to establish contact with the Biafrans, though in the event it was not possible to establish the necessary channel of communication.

During the next two months both sides intensified the war, acquiring additional arms stocks from outside sources. Biafran military leaders about this time began to solicit mediation outside the OAU, and in May 1968 both sides agreed that they would start negotiations under the aegis of the British Commonwealth secretariat. The first meeting, held at Kampala, Uganda, under the chairmanship of the Commonwealth secretary-general, did not reach any decision because the Biafrans insisted on a cease-fire and withdrawal of troops to prewar positions as prerequisites to a negotiated settlement.

The OAU realized that it should not allow the settlement of the conflict to take place outside its own forum, but its position was further complicated by the recognition of Biafra by Tanzania, Gabon, Ivory Coast, and Zambia during April and May 1968, contrary to the policy of nonrecognition implied in the OAU's first resolution on the Nigerian conflict. An OAU consultative committee meeting convened by the emperor of Ethiopia in July 1968 persuaded both sides to begin immediate preliminary talks under the chairmanship of the president of Niger. The emperor was able to win the confidence of both sides, and the talks led to an agreement on an agenda that included arrangements for a permanent settlement, terms for the cessation of hostilities, and proposals for the transportation of relief supplies to civilian victims of the war.

When the OAU General Assembly met for its fifth ordinary session, it rejected the view advocated by the four states that had recognized Biafra that unity should never be imposed by force. Instead the General Assembly called upon the United Nations and the OAU "to refrain from any action detrimental to the peace, unity and territorial integrity of Nigeria." This virtually sealed the fate of Biafra and deepened the gulf between the majority of the African states and those four that had recognized Biafra. Fortunately, the antagonism generated by this rift faded away with the defeat of Biafra by federal forces.

Biafra, before losing the war, had attempted to delay the advances of the Nigerian troops so as to arouse world opinion against the genocide that it alleged was being committed against the Ibos. Through press propaganda and the assistance of those governments that had recognized Biafra, the complaint was brought to the attention of the General Assembly of the United Nations. The federal government in the meanwhile had invited observers from the United Nations, the OAU, and the governments of Canada, Poland, Sweden, and the United Kingdom to Nigeria to verify the facts for themselves. These observer teams, after visiting Biafran territory and the federal forces, did not support the charge of genocide.

The Nigerian war was yet another dispute in which the United Nations encouraged the regional organization (OAU) to assume first responsibility for negotiating a peaceful settlement. The UN organs did not themselves play any major peacemaking role. The secretary-general of the United Nations and the various agencies of the UN system did, however, make an important contribution toward the resolution of the humanitarian problems.

In the matter of settlement of disputes and adjustment of differences between OAU member states, relations between the United Nations and the OAU have largely conformed to the principle that a peaceful solution to all such problems should be sought through the OAU. The extent of the United Nations' role has therefore been influenced by the degree of OAU's success. The basic principle of "try OAU first" has been the guiding factor, based on Article 52(2) of the UN Charter. Initially none of the disputes between member states were brought to the United Nations, nor did the Security Council exercise its right to intervene under Articles 34 and 36 of the Charter. Ultimately the Congo question was brought to the Security Council because of extracontinental factors, though at no time was any attempt made to replace the OAU. The Algerian-Moroccan case and the Somalia-Ethiopia and other boundary cases eventually were brought to the United Nations, but even so it was the OAU that finally worked out the answers. This was also the case in the Nigerian civil war, which was mainly dealt with by the OAU and the Commonwealth secretariat. As a result the OAU in its short life has gained considerable experience and has already proved its effectiveness.

Suggestions have been made that some of the political load could be removed from the United Nations through further development of the regional organs. The late Lester Pearson of Canada once suggested a step that he thought would make the United Nations "more united and less national, and therefore stronger." He believed that, similar to regional economic commissions, regional assemblies should be established within the framework of the General Assembly. It was Pearson's recommendation that these assemblies should meet every year and deal with regional problems, at the same time maintaining a tangible link with a Security Council possessed of new powers, new authority, and new (governing) rules and meeting continually in New York.

10

Indochina—A Multinational
Operation outside the United Nations

The war in Indochina started in
1946. Despite two international agreements for ending the war, it still
remains a major unresolved conflict. In 1954, the Geneva Agreement
ended hostilities for the first time. To supervise the subsequent cease-
fire there was established an International Commission for Supervision and Control (ICSC), sometimes referred to as the International
Control Commission (ICC) or International Commission (IC). The
commission was composed of three supervisory and control bodies,
one each for the three countries of Indochina—Cambodia, Laos, and
Vietnam. Notwithstanding France's withdrawal from Indochina consequent upon the signing of the Geneva Agreement (by gradual process the United States took its place), fighting soon broke out again
between North Vietnam and its southern neighbors and continued,
escalating in intensity, for a further nineteen years until, in 1973, a
second peace formula was agreed upon, following the protracted
Paris Peace Talks between North Vietnam and the United States.[1]
For a short while there was hope of peace in Southeast Asia once the
withdrawal of American troops was complete, but this hope was
short-lived; fighting is still going on, and it does not appear that the
agreement reached in Paris will be any more successful in halting the
fighting than was its Geneva predecessor. From the Paris talks there
emerged a new peacekeeping organization, the International Commission for Control and Supervision (ICCS), to supervise the cease-fire in
South Vietnam. This took the place of the ICSC established under the
1954 Geneva Agreement, though the latter remains operative in Laos;

1. There was a short respite for Laos in 1962 as a result of a second Geneva Agreement
relating only to itself, but with the continuing fighting in the rest of Indochina, Laos could not
escape involvement.

the element of ICSC in Cambodia was withdrawn on 31 December 1969.

The ICSC and ICCS[2] are the two largest multinational peacekeeping operations to be established outside the framework of the United Nations. Throughout the war in Indochina the international organization has become involved only when matters relating to human rights or violations of the Cambodian border have been brought to its attention. In January 1966 the United States, under pressure to seek a peaceful resolution of the conflict, brought the matter to the Security Council. However, members questioned the wisdom of the Council considering the problem, preferring that a termination of the conflict be sought through negotiation in a more appropriate forum and one better able to bring about the implementation of the terms of the Geneva Agreement. This view prevailed, and though the item remained on the agenda of the Security Council, it was not debated again in that chamber. In the following October the matter was considered by the General Assembly. A number of its members favored a direct or indirect role for the United Nations, but the majority supported U Thant's view that, apart from what he as secretary-general could do personally, any other role for the United Nations would be undesirable. So the fighting continued, and despite the determined and persistent attempts of U Thant and others to start peace negotiations, the hoped-for end of hostilities remained out of sight. Those negotiations did not get under way until there was a change of mood on the part of the United States and Henry Kissinger became involved.

Vietnam   During World War II the growing independence movement in Indochina received an impetus with the collapse of France and of its colonial administration, at a time when the resources of the Allied nations were limited and their energies entirely focused on the defeat of the Axis powers in Europe.

Following Japan's defeat and its surrender on September 2, 1945, Ho Chi Minh proclaimed the creation of the Democratic Republic of Vietnam, with Hanoi as its capital. Fearing the threat of a communist take-over, General de Gaulle sought and received United States sup-

---

2. To assist the reader the two commissions from hereon will be referred to as ICSC (1954) and ICCS (1973) wherever confusion could arise.

port in sending French troops to Indochina. As might be expected, it was not long before fighting broke out between the French and the Vietnamese nationalists. In an attempt to unite anticommunist dissident groups, the French in 1948 installed former emperor Bao Dai as the chief of state of Vietnam with Saigon as the capital, but this failed to improve the situation for France. Within two years the war in Vietnam was internationalized. First, the armed forces of the People's Republic of China reached the Vietnamese frontier; and then, in 1951, the United States, responding to pressure from France for assistance, agreed to help its Western ally but only to the extent of economic assistance and limited military assistance in the form of an advisory group (MAAG)—a contribution that made but little mark on the conduct of the war. France was itself the subject of increasing internal and external pressures to reach a negotiated peace, but it was not until February 1954 at the foreign ministers' meeting in Berlin, that it was agreed that a conference of interested powers should meet in Geneva during April of that year to discuss Indochina.

The participants at Geneva were Britain, France, the United States, and the French-sponsored states of Cambodia, Laos, and Vietnam on the one hand, and on the other, Vietminh's Democratic Republic of Vietnam, the People's Republic of China, and the USSR. Britain and Russia in the persons of Foreign Secretary Anthony Eden and Foreign Minister Vyacheslav Molotov were appointed co-chairmen. At first, the Saigon delegation insisted on territorial unity for all of Vietnam and national elections under UN supervision. The Vietminh delegation, like Saigon, at first opted for nationwide elections, but later agreed to accept partition into "temporary regroupment areas." The conference did not mean an end to the fighting in Indochina. Both sides were determined to enlarge the zones allotted to them and fought to do so. Almost from the start, therefore, the American delegation, not wishing to give the impression that it approved the surrender of any part of Vietnam to communism, to all practical purposes ceased to participate in the conference. In the event, a military cease-fire agreement was reached, a cease-fire not negotiated by military commanders in the field but at the highest political and diplomatic level.

Although the practical effect of the Geneva Agreement was to divide Vietnam into two independent states, the text of the agreement insisted on the essential unity of the country. No one was more emphatic in regarding Vietnam as one and indivisible than the people most directly concerned—the two rival governments of Vietnam, each of whom demanded unity on terms favorable to itself. With the coming of peace, the Ho Chi Minh government set about the difficult task of transforming a resistance movement based on the countryside into a full-fledged government able to carry on the multifarious functions of administration in town and village alike. This transformation succeeded to such an extent that when the period agreed upon at Geneva for the intertransfer of population between North and South came to an end in mid-1955, no organized opposition to the Ho Chi Minh government remained. This was an indication of the strength of the northern regime, one element among many that differentiated it from the government in the South.

When the war that had engulfed the country for eight years ended in July 1954, it left behind a devastated South Vietnam. Its people, relying as they did upon the French army to preserve their freedom and possessions against the communists, and unable or unwilling to take up arms in their own defense, had lived in a political vaccum during those war years. They had looked to foreigners, who had power, for their support; first to the French, and later to the Americans. This dependence upon foreign powers and factional splits within the country were to be a continuing burden on South Vietnam for many years to come. In July 1954 Ngo Dinh Diem became prime minister of this divided and far from viable state.

Diem took over at a time when the country was in a state of flux and uncertainty. The army and the religious sects were restive. Army leaders sought a strong government that could assert effective leadership in the country, while the sects wanted to keep the privileged position they had acquired during the war against the Vietminh and to play an influential part in the new southern government. On October 1, 1954, President Eisenhower offered to President Ngo Dinh Diem a program of American aid designed "to assist the government of Vietnam in developing and maintaining a strong, viable state, capable of resisting attempted subversion or aggression through military means."

The southern population had no desire to live under communism as practised at that time in the North, but neither did it approve of the government's hostility toward veterans of the resistance and toward nationalism. The Saigon government, therefore, to implement its anticommunist policy turned to the more militant among the northern refugees who were pouring into the South and proceeded to build a regime based on the support of this minority. This course of action, chosen under Washington's guidance, caused grave difficulties for South Vietnam, most of which are still unresolved today. It was into this emotionally and politically unstable situation that ICSC (1954) was precipitated.

Chapter VI of the Geneva Agreement, in particular Articles 29, 34, and 36, provided for the establishment of an ICSC composed of representatives of Canada, India, and Poland, with the responsibility for controlling and supervising the execution of the agreement by the two signatory parties. The functions and duties of the commission (Article 36) included control, observation, inspection, and investigation in the implementation of those provisions concerned with the cessation of hostilities and, in particular, the control of the movement of the armed forces of the two parties effected within the framework of the regroupment plan; supervision of the demarcation lines; release of prisoners of war and civilian internees; and supervision at ports and airfields as well as along the frontiers of Vietnam of the movement and stockpiling of all kinds of arms, munitions, and war material. The costs involved in the operations of the ICSC were to be shared equally between the two parties.

In the first instance the commission was established in Hanoi on 11 August 1954. From there it paid periodic visits to Saigon until it moved to Saigon, whence in turn it paid periodic visits to Hanoi. The commission consisted of three members who had the personal rank of ambassador. The representative of India presided. To better fulfill its functions of supervision and control, the commission set up the following machinery:

1. Each member of the commission was assisted by a delegation from his own country. It consisted of a senior official, to be known as alternate delegate, and military and political advisers. The national delegations, besides providing military and political advisers to the ambassadors, also manned the various committees and inspection teams of the international commission.
2. The Indian member, who was the chairman of the commission, had a dual capacity as he was also ex officio secretary-general, in pursuance of a decision to this effect taken by the three countries constituting the ICSC.

3. There were three main branches in the international secretariat, each in charge of a deputy secretary-general. There was an administration branch responsible for personnel and logistics, as well as for maintaining liaison with the French and the Democratic Republic authorities. An operations branch planned and assisted the commission in controlling the work of the fixed and mobile teams and executing the decisions of the commission regarding the conduct of special investigations. A petitions branch received from individuals and organizations (by mail, through petition boxes, and through the teams) petitions relating to various articles of the Geneva Agreement. These petitions, after examination, were forwarded to the appropriate parties for investigation and report. In addition, there was a public relations branch which publicized the activities of the commission through press releases and maintained contacts with the press.

4. The commission formed three committees to assist it in the more detailed phases of its work: an Operations Committee composed of military advisers to deal with the military operations; a Freedoms Committee composed of political advisers to deal with petitions; and an Administration Committee. From time to time the commission appointed separate ad hoc committees to deal with specific problems.

In accordance with Article 35 of the agreement, fixed teams, composed of an equal number of officers from each delegation, were established at strategic places north and south of the demarcation line. (Some of the locations had to be changed later.) Each fixed team had a mobile team component within itself. Both the North and South Vietnamese were asked to define the zones of action for the fixed teams and the spheres of action within which the mobile teams could operate within their respective fixed team zone. Though in the main the mobile teams operated in this manner, they also from time to time operated under central control. Their tasks were investigation of alleged incidents, supervision of exchange of prisoners of war, supervision of transfer of authority under the regroupment plan, and supervision of the movement of evacuees from the North (Article 14(d)).

Article 28 of the agreement defined the responsibility for the cessation of hostilities as resting with the two parties. To facilitate the implementation of this responsibility through the joint action of the parties, a Joint Commission (JC) was set up. To meet the requirements of Articles 31 and 32, the JC was composed of an equal number of representatives from the high command of each side. To provide further assistance, three joint subcommissions were positioned at Quynh Khe in North Vietnam, Quangtri in central Vietnam, and Pnung Hiep in South Vietnam. The Joint Commission itself had its headquarters outside Haiphong. Since implementation of Article 28 was the joint concern of the parties, ICSC stressed the vital necessity for cooperation by the two high commands in the fulfillment of this obligation and endeavored to retain the cooperation of both parties when controversial matters were under discussion. Apart from discussion with the liaison mission and the chiefs of delegations at the JC, informal approaches were made whenever necessary to members of the two high commands with a view to seeking solutions of problems without making formal recommendations. The day-to-day contact between the ICSC and the parties was maintained, however, through the liaison missions in Hanoi, appointed by the two high commands.

Article 45 of the Geneva Agreement provided that the ICSC in Vietnam was required to act in close cooperation with the ICSCs in Cambodia and Laos, whose headquarters were established at Phnom Penh and Vientiane respectively. The Indian Army Signals provided a radio communications network to link the three commissions and the teams. The French high command arranged an air courier service between Saigon, Phnom Penh, Vientiane, and Hanoi for carrying the personnel and mail of the three commissions. Arrangements for road transport were also made by the parties at both commission headquarters in Hanoi and Saigon and for the fixed and mobile teams.

The question of the ICSC's relationship to the JC was less clearly stated. ICSC was to be informed by the JC of any disputes arising out of differences of interpretation either with regard to a provision or a fact that the latter could not resolve, having the power to make recommendations for their resolution. This power in effect was not of great significance, for quite apart from the limited effectiveness of such a recommendation, there was the problem of majority or unanimous voting within the ICSC. Furthermore, Article 43 recognized the possibility of splits among the three members by providing for majority and minority reports; but these, like ICSC decisions, could be no more than suggestive and, as such, fully dependent upon the cooperation of the conference members who had created the ICSC (1954).

Following upon the implementation of the Geneva Agreement,

some 190,000 troops of the French Expeditionary Corps and 900,000 civilians moved from North to South Vietnam, and more than 100,000 Vietminh soldiers and civilians from South to North. Both states thereby acquired minorities with vital interests in the outcome of the Geneva settlement. In both nations those resettled were to exert an influence over subsequent events well out of proportion to their numbers. Unfortunately, ICSC's early failure to oversee effectively all those provisions of the agreement for which it was responsible greatly prejudiced the chances of a peaceful settlement. Its inability to cope with violations of the armistice, insofar as the handling of would-be migrants was concerned, reduced its competence to supervise the free general elections for which it was also to be responsible.

Equally important to the settlement was the ICSC's mandate to control arms and guarantee against aggression. The commission, soon after being established, reported that the cease-fire was effective and that it was able to arrange with both sides a provisional demarcation line, five kilometers in width. The commission also arranged for the regrouping of the French forces south of the demarcation line and of the People's Army of Vietnam forces north of the line. During this time the bulk of the exchange of prisoners of war and civilian internees was also effected. The ICSC occasionally had to intervene when the JC got into difficulties; however, neither side did much to implement those articles of the agreement dealing with democratic freedoms.

In its second and third reports, issued during 1955, the commission stated that effective implementation required close cooperation between the parties to the agreement, and this had, in various ways, been lacking during the period of the report. The French high command had tried hard to implement the agreement, but there were instances when the government of Vietnam had taken an independent attitude, since it had not been a signatory to the agreement. The commission reported many difficulties with the People's Army of Vietnam over the question of civilian internees and Catholics wishing to go South, and the Canadian member of the commission made a separate and more elaborate report on these difficulties.

The date on which it had been agreed that consultations were to begin between the North and South to prepare for nationwide elections a year later was 20 July 1955; but the Diem government refused to hold any such consultations on the grounds that elections could not be free in the North. Overtures from the North for economic relations and individual contacts between the two zones were also rebuffed.

The government that had emerged in South Vietnam was authoritarian and built around Ngo Dinh Diem and his brother Nhu. Although elections were held at the prescribed intervals, no genuine opposition candidates were permitted to stand, and in consequence the Diem regime became increasingly more politically and administratively powerful. North Vietnam had never accepted the refusal of the South to agree to its terms for reunification of the country. After the general elections had failed to materialize in 1956, the infiltration of communist agents from the North started again, first on a small scale and then as a spearhead of invasion, when it became clear that the Diem government intended to postpone indefinitely discussions on reunification. The agents left behind in the South when the communists had withdrawn in 1954 were reinforced by Cochin Chinese and central Vietnamese from south of the seventeenth parallel, who had gone north after the Geneva settlement. Members of this group formed the nucleus of the Vietcong. Ideologically, they capitalized on the popular feeling that Diem was linked too closely to the United States. Tactically, they resorted to a mixture of propaganda and terror adapted to the specific situation and directed sometimes against arbitrary acts by individual administrators and sometimes against the neglect of the government in the management of rural affairs where competent officials were scarce.

By 1956 the ICSC had to report that there was a majority of opinion among its members that activities on both sides of the demarcation line indicated a further deterioration in the situation. Early in 1957, following the withdrawal of the French, the commission reported that it had been informed by the government of Vietnam that it was prepared to offer effective cooperation to the commission but that it was not prepared to assume responsibility for the implementation of the Geneva Agreement in Vietnam. Since the Joint Commission, which represented an important part of the agreement, had ceased to function with the withdrawal of the French command on 14 September 1956, no consultations between the two parties had been held after that date. This presented the commission with a major difficulty at a time when free nationwide elections aimed at the reunification of Vietnam were not even planned.

The years 1958, 1959, and 1960 saw no improvement in the situation, as the reports of the ICSC clearly show. In a report issued in September 1961 the commission stated that there had been some deterioration during the period covered by the report with regard to the situation in the demilitarized zone. The mounting allegations from both sides of intrusion of the military into the demilitarized zone and other violations were a matter of increasing concern. The commission also reported that there had been no progress in the political field.

At least one member of the commission was becoming disturbed at the military role that the United States was playing in Vietnam. In a report issued on 6 April 1960, the Polish delegation made a statement on the introduction of the United States military mission TERM (Temporary Equipment Recovery Mission) in South Vietnam, subsequent to the signing of the 1954 Geneva Agreement for the cessation of hostilities. The Polish group felt that this mission was inconsistent with and constituted a violation of this agreement. They therefore served a two-month notice on TERM to wind up its affairs. There was no response from Washington to this challenge. However, once given an official airing, the question of the United States' participation could not be conveniently swept under the carpet. In a special report to the co-chairmen (Britain and the Soviet Union) dealing with the continuing deterioration in the situation and the difficulties it was facing with regard to the tendency of both parties to ignore the commission's recommendations and decisions, preferring to maintain their own intransigent stands, the ICSC was obliged to refer to the serious charges of violation of Articles 16, 17, and 19 of the Geneva Agreement by South Vietnam in receiving military aid from the United States.

Fighting had been increasing in intensity during this period, thus precipitating the special report that listed a number of serious allegations of aggression and subversion by North Vietnam against the South.[3] The North Vietnamese strongly rejected all representations made by the ICSC relating to the so-called subversive activities in South Vietnam, which it considered had no relevance to the Geneva Agreement, and informed the commission that "henceforth its Liai-

3. Among the allegations was the complaint by the South Vietnamese that the North Vietnamese forces were allowing the zone in the North to be used for incitement and support for hostile activities in the South, aimed at overthrowing the administration.

son Mission would find itself constrained to resolutely reject all requests for comment of this kind.''

With the refusal of the Democratic Republic of Vietnam (North) to cooperate and to curb its aggressive activities, and the United States' assumption of a more direct military support role in the Republic of Vietnam (South), the continuing effectiveness of the ICSC was coming into question. The commission's own reaction to the United States' policy of direct military support was to question whether it should continue to function. Aware that this complication was making the task of the ICSC more difficult, the United States encouraged South Vietnam in making countercharges of violations by the Democratic Republic. The United States was conscious of the value attached to the presence of the ICSC by the South Vietnamese and therefore attempted to demonstrate that the combat units introduced by the United States were guard duty only and would not fight unless attacked.

As a counter, the North Vietnamese high command complained bitterly about the United States, alleging that its direct military intervention in South Vietnam constituted an ever increasing import of raw material and the introduction of military personnel in violation of the Geneva Agreement—an allegation that could not be ignored.

Accepting the findings of its legal committee, the commission was of the view that beyond reasonable doubt, the authorities in communist North Vietnam had committed the alleged violations. The commission also cited the Republic of Vietnam for its activities in importing military equipment and personnel above the items imposed by the 1954 Geneva Agreement, but the report in this respect clearly demonstrated that these actions were taken by South Vietnam as part of its effort to defend itself against aggression and subversion from the North.

Since December 1961 the commission's teams in South Vietnam had been consistently denied their mandatory right to carry out their control and inspection tasks. Consequently, these teams, though they were able to observe the steady and continuous arrival of war material, including aircraft carriers with helicopters on board from the United States, were unable to determine precisely the quantity and nature of war material unloaded and introduced into South Vietnam. Despite these limitations on its degree of observation, the commission, taking all available facts into consideration and making judgments from its own observations and from the authorized statements made in the United States and the Republic of Vietnam, reported that

> the Republic of Vietnam had violated Articles 16 and 17 of the Geneva Agreement in receiving the increased military aid from the United States in the absence of any established credit in its favour. The Commission is also of the view that, though there may not be any formal military alliance between the governments of the United States and the Republic of Vietnam, the establishment of a United States military assistance command in South Vietnam as well as the introduction of a large number of United States military personnel beyond the stated strength of the advisory group, MAAG, amounts to a factual military alliance which is prohibited under Article 19 of the Geneva Agreement.

The commission also brought to the notice of the co-chairmen a recent and deliberate tendency on the part of both parties to deny or refuse controls to the commission's teams, thereby completely immobilizing their activities and hindering the commission in the proper discharge of its obligations to supervise the implementation of Articles 16 and 17 of the Geneva Agreement. "During the last few months there has been a near complete breakdown so far as this important function of the Commission is concerned. The Commission considered the situation and addressed detailed communications to the two parties, recommending the resumption of normal controls immediately. The Commission, however, regrets to inform the co-chairmen that there has been no improvement in this regard."

The Polish delegation disagreed with the special report signed by the Indian and Canadian delegations. It insisted that "the majority report wrongly admitted unfounded allegations of aggression and subversion brought by the Republic of Vietnam against the Democratic Republic of Vietnam, in spite of the fact that they do not find any legal justification in the stipulations of the evidence." It complained that "these artificial allegations" had been given prominence in the report over that of the United States' military aid to the Republic of Vietnam, which was described in insignificant terms. The Polish delegation added that "in order to cope with this wide-spread national movement, the government of the Republic of Vietnam has asked for military assistance of the U.S.A. which has of late reached a dangerous stage of direct participation of the American armed forces in military operations in South Vietnam.'' A separate report issued by the Indian delegation considered the Polish delegation's statement but did not agree with many of the views expressed.

By 1961 wide areas of the South had been infiltrated by the Vietcong, and many of the best officials in the country had been murdered. Drastic measures were required to halt this campaign of infiltration and liquidation. The government in the South instituted the Strategic Hamlet Program, under which the peasants were regrouped into villages which were then fortified. Beginning in 1962, this program was extended throughout the country.

The increasing guerrilla offensive in South Vietnam had led the United States in 1961 to increase its commitment to train and aid the South Vietnamese army, which, trained by an American mission according to American principles for a conventional war since 1955, was ill equipped for the guerrilla warfare used by the communist aggressors in the South. The Americans envisaged a war of extermination against the Vietcong, in which successes could be measured best by the ''kill rate''—in other words, by the number of Vietcong dead. The Diem government, however, belatedly had come to recognize that the Vietcong too were Vietnamese and that the adversaries of yesterday could change sides tomorrow; but Diem's orders to his military commanders to avoid heavy casualties led to misunderstandings among foreign observers and to a belief in Washington that Diem had become ''soft'' in the conduct of the war.

The gathering tension in Washington's relations with the Diem regime reached a climax with the outbreak of the so-called ''Buddhist affair'' [4] in May 1963. American impatience with Diem increased when it was learned that his brother Nhu was in contact with North Vietnam and with the Vietcong, seeking to strike a bargain whereby Hanoi would let the Vietcong rebellion subside in exchange for a restriction of the American military presence in South Vietnam. These developments had created a disenchantment within the army, which was particularly disturbed by Nhu's self-motivated activities in suppressing the students who were critical of Diem and his government's authoritarian rule. Unrest among the students, who were supported by the army, led to the coup that overthrew the Diem regime on 1

4. Discontent over the government's failure to hold elections and to end the war led to political disturbances and agitation by Buddhists. To suppress the disturbances government troops entered monasteries and arrested the offenders.

November 1963. A military junta assumed power, abolishing the National Assembly and the constitution. No elections were held to reconstitute the National Assembly, nor was a new leader designated to replace Diem. In the general disarray arbitrary purges paralyzed the administration, the Strategic Hamlet Program collapsed, and there were widespread desertions from the army and the militia. During this period of under two years, nine governments succeeded each other by a series of coups. No serious effort was made to replace the abolished constitution, and governmental nepotism and corruption reached unprecedented levels. Taking advantage of the administrative and political chaos, the Vietcong extended their control over large areas in central Vietnam which up till then had been considered secure.

On 7 February 1965 the government of the Republic of Vietnam and the United States ambassador in Saigon addressed a joint communiqué to the ICSC announcing that military action had been taken that day against military installations in North Vietnam. "This action had been taken because these installations had been employed in the direction and support of those engaged in aggression in South Vietnam, culminating in the attacks earlier that morning against installations and personnel in the areas of Pleiku and Tuy Hoa." On the same day the People's Army of Vietnam transmitted a communiqué bringing to the notice of the ICSC that bombing and strafing of a number of places had taken place and requesting the commission "to consider and condemn without delay these violations of utmost gravity and report them to the co-chairmen of the Geneva Conference on Indo-China." In a special report on 13 February the commission stated that it was examining and investigating these complaints. In the meanwhile it advised the co-chairmen that in view of the gravity of the situation, they should consider the desirability of issuing an immediate appeal to all concerned with a view to reducing tension and preserving peace in Vietnam.

In what turned out to be its final report, the ICSC said on 27 February 1965 that some days earlier it had received a communication from the People's Army of Vietnam requesting that steps be taken immediately to withdraw all the fixed teams in the Democratic Republic of Vietnam. This action was urged because of the tension and the gravity of the situation as well as to protect the security of the teams. The commission considered the request and replied to Hanoi that the request had far-reaching implications as it affected the work of the international commission under the Geneva Agreement. The ICSC was prepared to take reasonable risks, but if the People's Army of Vietnam felt obliged to maintain their decision, the ICSC would have no alternative but to withdraw its fixed teams, though with great reluctance. A reply to the commission's telegram, received on 20 February, reiterated the demand for withdrawal. The fixed teams were withdrawn on the night of 20–21 February, after being informed by the local authorities that immediate evacuation must take place for security reasons.

The Polish delegation, in a separate statement, voted against the telegram sent by the commission asking the People's Army of Vietnam to reconsider its request for the withdrawal of the fixed teams north of the demilitarized zone. The Polish delegation felt that because of the imminence of continuing warlike acts by the United States and the Republic of Vietnam, the request of the People's Army for the withdrawal of all teams situated in the Democratic Republic should have been carried out without delay. This view was based on its interpretation of Article 35, which stated that the withdrawal of the teams would be contingent on security reasons. In a further statement the delegation explained that it had always felt that members of the ICSC must be prepared to take some reasonable risks. However, the responsibility for the security of the teams and other members of the ICSC rested entirely with the parties to the Geneva Agreement on the Cessation of Hostilities in Vietnam, and it was quite obvious that because of the attacks previously described, the People's Army of Vietnam was obliged to take the decision that it had and could not be expected to bear such a responsibility when the causes of the danger were beyond its control and when the imminence of further warlike acts existed.

The confrontation with North Vietnam was not the only one with which the South Vietnamese had to contend. The National Liberation Front (NLF) had become solidly established in the South and presented an increasing threat to the political stability and military security of the republic. The Liberation Front operated as a government in the South. It has its own army, the Vietcong, and it levied taxes and carried on administrative and social functions not only through its own agents, but occasionally, by means of persuasion or force, through agents of the Saigon government. In foreign affairs it sent its own missions abroad to both communist and neutral countries.[5]

In June 1965 a new military junta took office in Saigon. General Nguyen Van Thieu, from central Vietnam, became chief of state, and Air Vice-Marshal Nguyen Cao Ky, originally from Tonkin, became the new prime minister. This government was to face new conspiracies from within and increasing resistance from the Vietcong. The Strategic Hamlet Program, intended both to protect the inhabitants from the Vietcong and to discourage them from joining the guerrillas, had backfired badly in the latter respect. This gigantic attempt to uproot a whole countryside of people—including those from the tribal areas in the highlands where they had supported the resistance—and to confine them within village enclaves surrounded by barbed wire and guarded by security teams achieved the opposite psychological effect to that which had been expected. Many thousands of young men joined the ranks of the guerrillas during 1962 and 1963. Guerrilla warfare had begun to take on the character of regular warfare while retaining the characteristic of a people's war, and it was this swelling of the guerrillas' ranks that was the beginning of a whole series of disastrous defeats for the South Vietnamese forces, leading ultimately to Diem's overthrow.

As the level of United States bombing against the North increased, United States ground troops were needed to protect the airfields because the South Vietnamese army was unable to provide effective security. On 1 April 1965 President Johnson approved the dispatch of two United States marine battalions and affirmed that their mission could be expanded to one of a more aggressive and active nature. This signaled not only the entry of the United States combat troops into Indochina, but also a change in the United States mission in Vietnam. From now on, Indochina would witness an increasing involvement by the United States. United States strategy to date had been basically passive in concept, involving material support and enclave defense and security. Now the emphasis had changed to a more active operational role of "search and destroy." Later it was to change yet again to a policy of total attrition.

From here on the Vietnam conflict took on the full dimensions of war. By April 1967 there were 470,000 American troops in South

5. B. A. Fall, *The Two Viet-Nams: A Political and Military Analysis,* pp. 356–61.

Vietnam, and there was a demand for more; but there was mounting dissent at home, and President Johnson rejected the Joint Chiefs of Staff's request to bomb Hanoi and Haiphong. Meanwhile, Ellsworth Bunker, the former special negotiator in the Yemen and in West Irian, had arrived in Saigon as United States ambassador and urged that the Thieu-Ky regime be strongly supported, despite the army's recent poor showing. But division in American public opinion over the war was growing. Under heavy pressure, Lyndon Johnson decided to withdraw from the 1968 presidential race; and with the Democratic party divided, the Republican party's candidate, Richard Nixon, was elected in his place. This change at the top had its effect on the first Paris Peace Talks, which took place shortly before the election. Little was achieved because of the intransigence of Thieu who, aware of the likely political developments in the United States, counted on President Nixon being more helpful.

Soon after his election, Nixon's policy on Vietnam became clear. The war was to be "Vietnamized"—there would be greater support for the Thieu regime, but responding to political realities, Nixon graddually reduced American ground troops as Vietnamization got under way and the air war escalated. Nixon realized that America must get out of Vietnam, but he still adhered to the original United States mission. As the *Washington Post* reported, "What President Nixon means by peace is what other people mean by victory." Four years later American troops in considerable numbers were still in Vietnam.

In 1972, when Hanoi launched yet another offensive, Nixon approved heavier bombing of the North and removed many of the restrictions applied by Johnson. South Vietnamese forces were allowed to enter into Laos and the southern part of Cambodia. Despite this escalation in the use of South Vietnamese forces and of the South Vietnam and United States air forces against both North Vietnam and the communist-controlled areas, Nixon was faced with a mandate to seek peace. He had made this campaign commitment before his first election as president, and with the next elections due in November 1972, he promised not only America but also the international community that he would resort to negotiations instead of continuing to wage war. Well before the elections, because of the change in climate between East and West, Nixon was able to start negotiations to end the fighting in Indochina, and Henry Kissinger, his special adviser for national security affairs, succeeded in transforming

America's relations with the three communist countries [6] because all sides were in the mood for some real "horse-trading." The Chinese appeared ready to trust him to some extent because of his promises to get out of Vietnam, but primarily the bargains were struck on the basis of the hardheaded pursuit of national interests, with all parties eyeing one another critically over the bargaining table. However, this rapprochement between the United States, the Soviet Union, and especially the People's Republic of China, provided the background that facilitated the peace talks between North Vietnam, the Vietcong, South Vietnam, and the United States.

The American-Vietnamese Agreement and Protocols of 27 January 1973 required that "the parties participating in the Paris Conference of Vietnam shall immediately designate representatives to form a four-party joint military commission with the task of ensuring joint action by the parties in implementing the . . . provisions of this agreement.' Article 16 of the agreement described the provisions in detail—the enforcement of a cease-fire throughout Vietnam applicable to all forces, the dismantlement of the United States' military bases in South Vietnam and those of other foreign countries, the repatriation of captured military personnel and foreign civilians by both parties. This article also established that the commission should operate in accordance with the principle of "consultative unanimity." [7] Disagreements should be referred to the International Commission for Control and Supervision. The Joint Commission should begin working immediately after the signing of the agreement and should end its activities in sixty days after the completion of the withdrawal of the United States troops and those of other foreign countries.

Article 17 required that the Republic of Vietnam and the Vietcong should immediately designate representatives to form a two-party military commission whose task would be to ensure joint action by the two South Vietnamese parties in implementing those provisions of the agreement regarding the cessation of hostilities, the question of the return of Vietnamese civilians captured and detained in South Vietnam, the ban on the introduction of troops into South Vietnam, and, lastly, the reduction of the military effectiveness of the two South Vietnamese parties and the demobilization of the troops being

6. North Vietnam, People's Republic of China and USSR.
7. Chapter VI, Article 16.

reduced. The two-party commission would also be required to refer its disagreements to the International Commission for Control and Supervision.

This newly constituted international commission (ICCS [1973]) was established under Article 18 of the Paris Agreement—for Vietnam alone. As has been previously mentioned, the ICSC (1954) still remained operative in Cambodia and Laos. Initially ICCS (1973) had the responsibility for reporting to the four-party commission on all matters concerning the control and supervision of the implementation of the provisions of this agreement.[8] While the ICCS formed itself into control teams to better carry out its operational tasks, the Vietcong and South Vietnamese had to agree between themselves on where the teams were to be located and how they would operate. Having done this, they were required by the agreement to smooth the path for the teams' operations. The four countries selected for the ICCS were Canada, Hungary, Indonesia, and Poland. Poland was already a member of ICSC (1954) and with Hungary represented the Eastern European socialist countries. Canada, also a member of ICSC represented the Western nations, while Indonesia represented Asia. It is worthy of note that India, whose political position had considerably altered since the first ICSC was established in 1954, was excluded this time. India was no longer wanted by South Vietnam in view of the many difficulties that had arisen during the years of India's chairmanship of the ICSC; the Saigon regime had in fact requested the withdrawal of the Indian Embassy from Saigon.

The agreement in Paris in January 1973 made it possible for the United States to begin its withdrawal, but because fighting continued in an effort by all concerned to gain control of more territory before the cease-fire could really be established, the Americans continued to use their aircraft in support of the South Vietnamese and to facilitate the evacuation of their own ground troops. Within a few weeks it became evident that there was going to be little peace in South Vietnam. To further aggravate the situation, fighting had escalated in Laos and Cambodia with the Americans providing air support and supplying their allies with much equipment and munitions. After several attempts to negotiate a new cease-fire, Kissinger, now United

8. Article 19 provided for the calling of an international conference to determine more definitive arrangements for the operational procedures of ICCS.

States presidential adviser, and Hanoi's Le Duc Tho reached agreement on a detailed timetable for a firm Vietnam cease-fire, which called upon both Saigon and the Provisional Revolutionary Government of South Vietnam to order all their units to stop shooting. This agreement was signed on 2 March 1973, but it was agreed that Kissinger and Le Duc Tho would officially announce their agreement on strengthening the original cease-fire at the conclusion of their next round of talks starting on 6 June. Detailed arrangements set out in the agreement were:

1. The United States would halt all air reconnaissance missions over North Vietnam.
2. Twenty-four hours after the agreement was promulgated the Saigon government and the PRG would order their battlefield commanders to cease their fire.
3. Five to ten days later Saigon and the PRG would grant guarantees of privileges and immunity for members of the two-party joint military peacekeeping commission. The two sides would fully deploy observers into the field to keep the peace.
4. Within five to ten days of promulgation the United States would resume operations to remove mines from North Vietnamese waterways and would also resume economic talks with Hanoi.
5. Within three months, zones of control would be delineated.
6. Within six months, a national council of national reconciliation and concord must be established and an election procedure set up to shape the political future of South Vietnam.[9]
7. Military commanders of the opposing parties would meet to establish safety corridors and routes for one party going through areas under the control of other parties.
8. The demilitarized zone was to be respected and all troops and war equipment withdrawn from this buffer zone. There was to be a demobilization of forces by both sides.
9. Legitimate ports of entry would be established for the reinforcement of war materials by each side on a one-for-one basis.

9. Under the terms of the original agreement signed on 27 January 1973, this was supposed to have been accomplished by the end of April.

10. The remaining Vietnamese military and civilian prisoners of war would be released.

Soon after the agreement was announced, the North and South Vietnamese military negotiators agreed to exchange maps showing the areas of control claimed by the two armies in the South. The exchange of maps was intended to lead to the fixing of the limits of the military controlled zones by both sides. One of the major factors of disagreement in the past had been over the exchange of civilian prisoners. The two sides now agreed to go ahead with this exchange.

The arrangements were a comprehensive and positive approach to achieving a disengagement of forces. As a basis for a continuing cease-fire, the agreement was a constructive document. But as in all such cases, its effective implementation was dependent upon the willingness of the parties concerned to make it work. Regretfully, the evidence all too clearly shows that in the South such intent and goodwill does not exist on either side. One year after the truce, fighting still rages in South Vietnam and, if anything, is on the increase. Major-General Duncan McAlpine, commander of the Canadian contingent of ICCS (1973), in August, six months after the truce, described the cease-fire as an illusion. He pointed to the fact that in the six months immediately prior to the cease-fire there were 80,000 casualties, while in the first six months after there were 72,000. As another officer put it, "It is not a cease-fire; it is a less-fire." Few of the requirements of the agreement of 27 January have been met. As yet there is no political agreement; the field commanders have not met and agreed on points of entry, nor have the zones of control been delineated; elections have not been arranged. A political agreement should have been concluded by now. The field commanders should have already met and delineated points of entry and zones controlled by both sides. The National Council of Reconciliation should have arranged elections.

The ICCS (1973) is in general organized along the same lines as ICSC (1954). At the head are the ambassadors who lead the four delegations and are responsible for all policy matters and supervision of the operations and administration. There are a number of advisory committees for political, military, administrative, and financial matters, along with other subsidiary organs. The command and control of the ICCS and its regional headquarters and field teams are directed by the military committee. There is an international secretariat manned by members of all the four delegations.

Ambassador Michele Gouvain of Canada was appointed the first chairman, and this proved to be a wise decision. With their comprehensive experience of peacekeeping, the Canadians wasted no time in establishing the international secretariat and deploying its headquarters and field teams. The headquarters were set up in Tanson Nhut Airbase in Saigon with subordinate regional headquarters deployed in the various geographical areas so as to fulfill the responsibilities ascribed to them in the agreement. Each region has a number of subregional teams. In all there are twenty-six such teams deployed across South Vietnam; twelve are located at potential entry points, with two others at points designated by the South Vietnamese as legitimate points of entry for arms, munitions, and other war materials. The siting of all these teams conforms with the ICCS mandate and the specifications of the Paris Agreement. The teams were required to be in position within fifteen to thirty days after the cease-fire had been arranged, and for the most part this requirement was met. Of the remaining twelve teams, seven are responsible for supervising the release and repatriation of captured and detained persons, while the five others are special teams available for assignment to additional legitimate points of entry designated by one or other of the parties or for any other tasks in keeping with the commission's responsibility for control and supervision. All these remaining twelve teams were established within the thirty-day period as required by protocol.

The ICCS (1973) is deployed at forty-seven different sites throughout the length of South Vietnam. Many of these sites are accessible only by air, while fifteen can be reached only by helicopter. At first, air transportation was provided by the United States Army, but later, as the army's withdrawal got under way, this was replaced by civilian aircraft.[10]

During the first sixty days after the cease-fire, the prisoner-of-war teams visited many locations in Vietnam and supervised the release of 3,273 United States, South Vietnamese, and Vietcong prisoners of war. This program has probably been the most successful aspect of the cease-fire negotiations; but the release of civilian detainees has

10. Air America was awarded the contract and, operating under the name of "ICCS Air Service," has provided twenty-one UHIH helicopters, three Volpar Turbo Beachcraft, and one C-46 Transport. Additional aircraft can be rented from Air America on an "as required" basis.

been beset with difficulties, and the process of their release is considerably slower. Equally, the lack of observance of the cease-fire has been a major disappointment. Up to the time of the departure of the Canadians in July 1973,[11] 18,000 warlike incidents had been reported in South Vietnam and the casualties to both sides between 28 January and 31 July 1973, as already noted, were 72,000. A comparison of the number of incidents reported and investigations requested indicates that requests for investigation were made in very few cases. All that can be claimed one year after the Paris Agreement is that the disengagement and withdrawal of the armed forces of the United States has been achieved and its prisoners of war returned. The ICCS is proving no more successful in its role of peacekeeping than its predecessor, the ICSC, but this was predictable and will continue to be so, so long as the desire for peace among the combatants does not exist. In the latter part of 1973 the overall military situation deteriorated until it had once again become a war situation in all but name with very little prospect of improvement. But before analyzing and evaluating the respective roles of ICSC and ICCS, it is relevant to take a brief look at the other two countries involved in the Indochina conflict—Laos and Cambodia.

Under the terms of the 1954 Geneva Agreement, separate Joint Commissions and International Commissions for Supervision and Control were set up for Laos and Cambodia, with terms of reference similar to those for Vietnam. Although it did not suit either country to have to accept a cease-fire simultaneously with the cessation of hostilities in Vietnam, nevertheless their obdurate and persistent approach to the settlement of other aspects of the truce was largely responsible for settlements highly favorable to their respective interests being arranged. A particular victory for the Cambodians was the recognition of Cambodia's right to self-defense. The royal government vowed not to enter into military alliances which were "not in conformity with the principles of the Charter of the United Nations"; nor, so long as its security was not threatened, would Cambodia permit the establishment of foreign military bases. As for war material and military personnel, the government's delegation at Geneva made

11. Canada's place in the commission was subsequently taken over by Iran.

it clear that there would be no soliciting for assistance before the planned elections in 1955, "except for the purpose of the effective defence of the territory." This left Cambodia free after the elections to take whatever steps it considered necessary for its security, whether or not such steps were absolutely necessary for self-defense. The considerable latitude acquired by Cambodia was wholly in keeping with the royal government's insistence on not being either neutralized or demilitarized. On this point, the Cambodians received indirect assurance from the United States that their security would in some way be covered by the South-East Asian Pact despite their unilateral declaration.

The cease-fire for Laos and Cambodia followed comparable lines. While that for Cambodia called for the removal within ninety days of all French military units and all non-native troops operating with the Free Khmer force, whether they were communist, Vietnamese, or Cambodian, a similar stipulation relating to the withdrawal of Pathet Lao units was applied to Laos, though provision was made for first regrouping them in the provinces of Phong Saly and Samneua.[12] Although Laos was prohibited from seeking to augment its military establishment, the royal government was specifically permitted a maximum of 1,500 French training instructors. Moreover, the prohibition against the establishment of foreign military bases on Laotian territory did not apply to two French bases in operation under a 1949 treaty and employing 3,500 Frenchmen. Laos, like Cambodia, was allowed to import arms and other military equipment essential for self-defense, but the government issued a unilateral declaration making it clear, in terms that nearly duplicated those used in Cambodia's declaration, that its refrainment from alliances and foreign military bases was limited to situations in which Laotian security was not threatened. In view of Vientiane's expressed hope for American protection, the Laotian delegates succeeded admirably in getting a settle-

12. The Cambodian delegation had promised that those insurgents still in the country would be guaranteed the right to rejoin the national community and to participate, as electors or candidates, in the elections scheduled to take place in 1955; but agreement did assure that their demobilization would take place within one month of the cease-fire. The Laotian delegation also issued a declaration averring the government's willingness to integrate former insurgents into the national community without reprisal. Elections in Laos were scheduled for September 1955, and the former Pathet Lao were promised the right to participate in the balloting as electors or candidates.

ment containing terms that restricted, but did not eliminate, Laotian control over their security requirements.

Laos   The achievement of a political set-
                                          tlement between the government
                                          of Prince Sovanna Phouma and the
Pathet Lao was not easy to accomplish; the prince at one time was forced to resign since without Pathet Lao participation all attempts to form a government failed. In 1957 Sovanna Phouma, now back in power, concluded a series of agreements with the Pathet Lao,[13] and with the formation of a coalition government a reconciliation was achieved, and representatives of the Pathet Lao joined the government as ministers.

Under the Geneva Agreement, the United States was prohibited from establishing a military mission in Laos. For a time the United States worked through the French as much as it could to keep the communists from taking over Laos, but this intervention by proxy was of no real substance, and in January 1956 the United States established a military mission, calling it a Program Evaluation Office and attaching it to the United States Aid Mission. A year earlier a United States operations mission had been set up to assist the royal government with economic aid and increased military assistance. Apart from a short period during the months of the coalition government with communist Pathet Lao participation, the aid program mushroomed and by 1958 had provided considerable assistance to Laos.

Over the next few years the situation in Laos was both politically and militarily confused. Sovanna Phouma's coalition government was toppled but was replaced by another coalition headed by General Phoumi. An attempt to overthrow it by a military coup in 1960 failed, but the antigovernment forces, under Captain Cong Lai, were able successfully to escape to the North, where they received supplies and were reinforced with special units by the Soviet Union. The Laos government charged North Vietnam with invasion, but no evidence was found to support this claim when investigated by a team of UN observers. Gaining in strength, Cong Lai, on 31 December 1960, inflicted a severe defeat on the government forces and captured the

13. The Vientiane Agreements.

strategically important Plain of Jarres. Cong Lai was by now receiving regular supplies from the USSR which were being airlifted into the positions on the plain. He had also entered into a defensive alliance with the Pathet Lao.

The United States' overt attitude at this point was one of diplomacy rather than military intervention. Admittedly it had assisted General Phoumi in aborting Cong Lai's attempted coup, but its declared policy was to see in Laos "peace not war, a truly neutral government and not a cold war pawn, a settlement concluded at the conference table and not on the battlefield." [14] A diplomatic settlement suited the mood of the United States at that time. President Kennedy, while reverting to diplomacy and rejecting military intervention, did however agree to covert operations of sabotage and harassment, to the infiltration of commando groups into southeast Laos and Vietnam, while continuing with military aid to guerrilla tribesmen operating against the Pathet Lao; all activities that were to be the biggest factors in militating against the achievement of a negotiated settlement and the establishment of a neutral coalition government.

In Geneva in July 1962 agreement was reached on the setting up of a new government of national union, but this government's life was a short one, all participants in the Laos conflict being responsible for its breakdown. With the end of the Soviet airlift, Cong Lai and the Pathet Lao had turned to North Vietnam for material support, while the United States replaced its military advisers with a military mission. The fighting continued with the Pathet Lao achieving increasing success over the government forces of General Phoumi.

America's military involvement in Laos now took a more positive turn, increasing in substance and in extent. In 1963 it stepped up its supply of aircraft and provided the Laotians with military training facilities in Thailand, where it had dispatched troops the previous year. During 1964 it extended both its ground and air support, particularly in the air, where its main objective was to deny the use of the Ho Chi Minh Trail to the North Vietnamese as a supply link to their forces now becoming increasingly involved in the Laotian war. While America's ground assistance program never reached anything more than a limited participation in support of the field operations against the Pathet Lao and was advisory rather than combat, the air strike

14. President John F. Kennedy, 24 March 1961.

program became and has remained a major factor in the ensuing operations.

From 1964 until the Paris Peace Talks on Vietnam in 1973, the war and the internal political instability remained unresolved. So long as the United States maintained its heavy air strike capacity, the Pathet Lao and North Vietnamese ground operations were contained, but with the lack of stable government any chance of national unity was simply a pious dream. Following the agreement on a cease-fire in Vietnam, however, negotiations began to bring an end to hostilities in Laos, and a cease-fire agreement was reached on 21 February 1973 between Phoumi Vongvichit, the chief Pathet Lao negotiator, and Phen Phong Savan, the chief negotiator for the present government in Vientiane. Although sporadic fighting continued, by the first week of September 1973, Prince Phouma had obtained the approval of King Savang Vatthana. The king, who is recognized by both the Vientiane government and the Pathet Lao and essentially is a nonpolitical figure, had become the focal point of Laotian unity; therefore, his assent was vital. The agreement was finally signed on 14 September 1973. The way was cleared for agreement by a Soviet pledge to support neutralist Prince Sovanna and to refrain from partisan support of the Pathet Lao, who by now could claim to control 80 percent of the country and about one-third of its population. Although the agreement brought the Pathet Lao into the government, this did not have the immediate effect of partitioning the nation of three million people into specific communist, right-wing, and neutralist areas. The agreement meant the departure of nearly 200 American military experts and advisers and some 17,000 mercenaries paid by the United States to fight for the Vientiane government. The estimated 4,000 North Vietnamese troops based in Laos, most of them along the Ho Chi Minh Trail down the eastern side of the country, did not immediately depart nor are they expected to do so at least for some time. The agreement also made provision for the Pathet Lao to station 1,500 of its troops and police in Vientiane, with half that number in the royal capital of Luang Prabang, 150 miles north of Vientiane. The Vientiane government was also permitted to retain an equal number of soldiers and police in the two cities, but the remainder of their armed forces were required to move out.

The other agreements were that a provisional government of national union would be established under the premiership of Prince

Sovanna Phouma, the only political figure who enjoys the respect and confidence of both sides, with his half-brother, Prince Souphanouvong, the nominal leader of Pathet Lao, as deputy premier. The Vientiane government was to have the key portfolios of finance, defense, and interior, with foreign affairs going to the Pathet Lao and the rest being equally divided between the two.

Cambodia   Despite events elsewhere in Vietnam and Laos, Cambodia retained its neutral posture and remained relatively quiet with the political situation reasonably contained. However, as the air war in Indochina expanded, it became inevitable that Cambodia would become increasingly involved. North Vietnam had begun to use Cambodian territory adjacent to the Ho Chi Minh Trail and Cambodian routes to the South to facilitate its support for the Vietcong. In January 1965 the United States decided on direct action against this extension of North Vietnam's supply activities, and air operations were initiated against the "sanctuaries" and trail being used inside Cambodian territory. This was a risk that the United States felt it had to take even though there was every likelihood that the neutralist government of Prince Sihanouk, a government the United States was anxious to support, might not only protest this expansion of operations onto Cambodian soil but even seek to defend its territory. For a time, therefore, the air effort was directed at reconnaissance all along the Cambodian border and carrying out limited tactical strikes to destroy the sancturaries and the supply dumps and to discourage the further use of Cambodia as sanctuary for the North Vietnamese and Vietcong forces. But this effort does not appear to have been sufficient, for by early 1967 the United States was of the opinion that North Vietnam's buildup in Cambodia was complete and represented an important source of supply for its troops in the South. Consequently, the United States felt that it was imperative, and justified, that it step up its efforts to prohibit this use of Cambodian territory, preferably by nonbelligerent political and diplomatic means; but that if these means did not achieve the required result, it would be prepared to use all degrees of force necessary to obtain its objectives.

The speeding up of the Vietnamization of the war in 1970 brought an increase in the fighting in Cambodia. Accused of being procommunist, the neutral government headed by Prince Sihanouk was an early casualty. Prince Sihanouk took refuge in Peking, from where he gave open support to the opponents of the newly established regime of Lon Nol. Though supporting Sihanouk, the People's Republic of China was concerned, as part of its détente with the United States, to bring about a truce in Cambodia within the framework of an overall effort to bring peace to Indochina. As might therefore be expected, Peking did nothing to encourage any fresh offensive or increase in the scale of fighting against the government forces in Cambodia.

As in the case of Vietnam, the conflict in Cambodia is far from over, and since the Paris Peace Talks fighting has reached a new level in the struggle for power in that country. As with the others, the prospect of a peaceful settlement is far from being realized.

Twenty-eight years of war in Indochina, involving in its train the participation on a major scale of two of the great powers, has brought no peace to that area of Southeast Asia. In their turn, France and the United States have failed to impose a settlement by force of arms and have pulled their forces out under negotiated agreements. Both have made use of international commissions as a means of achieving the withdrawal that they sought. It appears reasonable to suspect that France wanted a way out, realizing that nothing would be resolved by war; equally it seems reasonable to suppose that the United States, recognizing that the fighting would continue whatever happened, with the likelihood of an ultimate North Vietnamese victory, also looked for an appropriate facade behind which it could "withdraw with honor." It is not difficult to deduce this single-mindedness of purpose, since neither appears to have given much realistic thought to the structure and operational capacity of the missions that were to assume the truce observation role. One can only conclude that from the start neither France nor the United States was deeply concerned with the character and potential of the multinational operation that was to follow, since it had little chance of being successful. In the event, this is indeed what happened. The nature of the commissions meant that they could only provide a presence, and for a while achieve a deescalation in the fighting, while serving primarily to allow the big powers to disengage. This was the limit to their potential and the extent to which they could proceed in view of the belligerent actions of the parties involved. Throughout Indochina it is as if a truce had never existed.

One may wonder therefore why Indochina has been included here with a chapter to itself, since it in no way represents a positive contribution to the study of peacekeeping possibilities for the future, but rather represents a totally negative answer to the problems of conflict control. However, its inclusion is for a very good reason—its negative value. This negative value derives from the mandate and structure that was given to the two commissions to carry out their prescribed roles, the definition of which has led to misrepresentation. The word *control* included in their designation has given the impression that the commissions were responsible for the implementation of the Geneva and Paris agreements, when, on the contrary, it was the parties to the conflict who had this primary responsibility under the terms of those agreements. The commissions' responsibility was limited to maintaining a watching brief over the implementation by the parties concerned. Even now this differentiation is not generally understood and is the cause of continuing misunderstandings and difficulties—over and above the many functional problems that have plagued the commissions' work.

Neither North nor South Vietnam has displayed any desire to unify, even though they had agreed to do so. With the evacuation to the South of most of the population opposed to communism, Hanoi experienced little threat from any possible opposition within the area under its control. In the South, successive chiefs of state from President Ngo Dinh Diem to President Thieu carved themselves a separate state, the former killing any chance of elections by 1956. As a result it was necessary for ICSC to continue its operations beyond the period originally planned. Its task thereby became more complex, and unavoidably the commission became involved with political issues, besides its responsibilities for supervising the implementation of the military arrangements. This naturally led to numerous disagreements between the members of the commissions and with the parties to the conflict. They received little or no cooperation from either Hanoi or Saigon, and were more obstructed than facilitated in the execution of their responsiblities. Even their freedom of movement was subject to the vagaries of both sides, since they were dependent on both for their transportation. Only in Laos, after 1962, did ICSC teams receive proper, though short-lived, support.

Although ICCS (1973) enjoys satisfactory air transport, its air movement is hampered because clearances are necessary for all flights, and these too are often delayed. This does not make the release of many of the civilian detainees an easy matter when it is carried out at locations that can be reached only by helicopters. Some serious incidents occurred during the early phases when ICCS helicopters were mistakenly fired at, in one instance resulting in the death of a number of ICCS observers. The main responsibility of ICCS (1973) is the supervision of the Vietnam cease-fire. Judging from the enormous number of incidents that have occurred and the very few occasions on which ICCS has been requested to investigate, it would seem quite clear that the parties to the conflict lack faith or desire for seeing that the cease-fire is implemented. However, all the trouble does not lie outside the control of the commissions. There are equally obstructing problems within. High among them has been the adherence to the unanimity rule, which, essential as it may be, has caused its difficulties because of diversity of views among commissioners. Although the rule was intended to apply only to conclusions or recommendations in certain types of situations, it has often been stretched to include decisions on conducting investigations or other operational tasks where only a majority vote was required. This has often frustrated the working of the investigation teams and on occasion, plain fact has been ignored or misrepresented for reasons of political bias.

Many of the inherent problems of the Geneva Agreement and ICSC apply also to the Paris Peace Agreement and ICCS. The mechanism for controlling and supervising the cease-fire remains ineffective. The Joint Military Commissions were and are unable to agree on anything of substance other than the exchange of the prisoners of war.

ICCS (1973), like ICSC (1954), suffers innumerable internal problems. The international secretariat is manned by the delegations represented, and some of its section heads lack expertise. There are difficulties in adopting a common staff procedure. In circumstances where a good rapport between commissions is operationally essential, in neither case can this be said to have been achieved. It is possibly significant that where the member states involved in ICSC (1954) and ICCS (1973) have served together in peacekeeping operations, the working relationship has been better.

ICCS (1973) ran into difficulties right from the start. It was not long before the four parties of the Joint Military Commission individually refused to accept reports of any violations where the party itself was concerned. This led to a division of interests within the Joint Commission, with North Vietnam and the Vietcong siding together on the one side against South Vietnam and the United States on the other. As a result, even had the ICCS (1973) been able to operate smoothly, which it was not able to do, it was never possible for it to report to a body that would listen to its reports and provide cogent direction and advice as to appropriate action.

The very constitution of the ICCS (1973) was based on illusory hopes. The entire past experience of the ICSC (1954) was ignored, maybe in the hope that the political difficulties that the latter had experienced would not exist for the new body. The co-chairmen of the Geneva Conference had neither the authority nor the will to confer and to give guidance to ICSC. The new commission of ICCS suffers from a similar absence of a higher authority. The failure to establish a suitable higher political control echelon in both cases would indicate that the great powers were not seriously interested in procuring a resolution of the conflict through negotiation.

This is possibly the crux of the problem—the lack of an established international body to whom commissions such as those deployed in Indochina can report. This is the fundamental and positive difference between the UN peacekeeping and observer missions and those multinational commissions set up and operative outside the United Nations. Without the higher political authority, without the integrated field formation and organization, the chances of fulfilling a prescribed mandate are slim. It is no reflection on those countries that comprised ICSC (1954) and ICCS (1973) that they failed in the role given to them to perform—the cards were stacked against them from the beginning in the negative attitudes of the belligerent parties toward them and toward their representations. Having no redress to a higher headquarters, they were and remain powerless to influence the situation in Indochina. If one lesson is learned from the Indochina experience, it is that any peaceful international intervention by third parties convened outside the United Nations and the provisions of its Charter is likely to be greatly limited in its effectiveness unless it is established and directed by an independent international political control and is thereby answerable to that control and not individually to the parties to the conflict.

Why was it that the United Nations did not intervene and provide the third-party instrument? In its infancy the Indochina conflict was looked upon by France as a colonial issue and therefore of its concern alone and not that of the United Nations. Later it became in the eyes

of the United States a cold war issue, outside the competence of the
UN. By this time the principle of "by request or with consent" was
the guiding role on which the United Nations based its decisions to
intervene, and since neither Vietnam nor the People's Republic of
China were UN members at that time, this precluded any possibility
of the United Nations' being invited in.

The situation in Vietnam has worsened. The North Vietnamese not
only maintain a large force on their own territory, but also retain a
sizable army in South Vietnam to continue operations in collaboration with the Vietcong. Similarly, the situation in Cambodia has an
influence on developments in Vietnam. With the increase in the scale
of fighting in South Vietnam and Cambodia, the task of the ICCS
(1973) in Vietnam has become almost impossible. Neither the signing of the Paris Agreements nor the joint communiqués issued in
Paris in June 1973 have had any effect on halting the flow of men,
arms, and material from the North to the South. Similarly, infiltration
to the South continues, including that of civilians to the so-called liberated areas of South Vietnam. Under these circumstances there is no
hope of reunification of the two Vietnams except by force. While
fighting has halted temporarily in Laos, there are no indications that
there will be peace in Cambodia.

Peace would seem to be possible in Indochina only if (1) the two
Vietnams agree to live as separate states along the Korean pattern and
consider reunification only after a period of cessation of hostilities;
(2) the present coalition Laotian government proves successful; (3) a
new leadership emerges in Cambodia. In the meanwhile, the United
States, the Soviet Union, and the People's Republic of China must
continue with their efforts to reconcile the warring factions, gradually
reduce military assistance, and increase development aid with the
help of other nations. In the meanwhile all that the ICSC (1954) and
ICCS (1973) can do is to assist in whatever way they can to reduce the
scale of fighting until all fighting ends.

MAPS

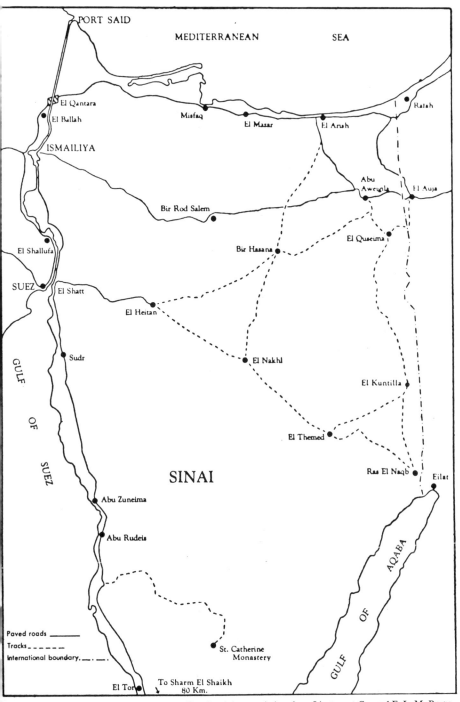

PORT SAID

MEDITERRANEAN   SEA

El Qantara

El Ballah

Misfaq

El Mazar

El Arish

Rafah

ISMAILIYA

Abu Aweigila

El Auja

Bir Rod Salem

El Shallufa

Bir Hasana

El Quseima

SUEZ

El Shatt

El Heitan

GULF

OF

SUEZ

Sudr

El Nakhl

El Kuntilla

El Themed

SINAI

Ras El Naqb

Eilat

Abu Zuneima

Abu Rudeis

AQABA

Paved roads _____
Tracks _ _ _ _ _ _
International boundary._ _ . _ .

St. Catherine
Monastery

GULF   OF

To Sharm El Shaikh
80 Km.

El Tor

Map 2.   The Sinai

Reprinted, by permission, from Lieutenant-General E. L. M. Burns,
Between Arab and Israeli (New York: Obolensky, 1962).

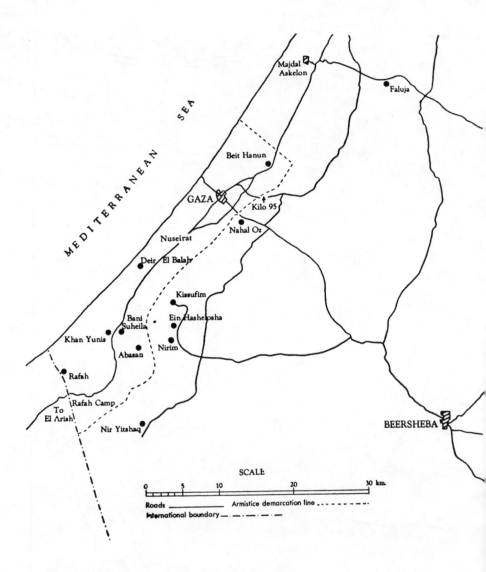

Map 3. The Gaza Strip

Reprinted, by permission, from Lieutenant-General E. L. M. Burns, *Between Arab and Israeli* (New York: Obolensky, 1962)

THE REPUBLIC OF THE CONGO

The boundaries shown on this map do not imply official endorsement
or acceptance by the United Nations.

UN map no. 1274, rev. 2, December 1962

Map 4. The Congo

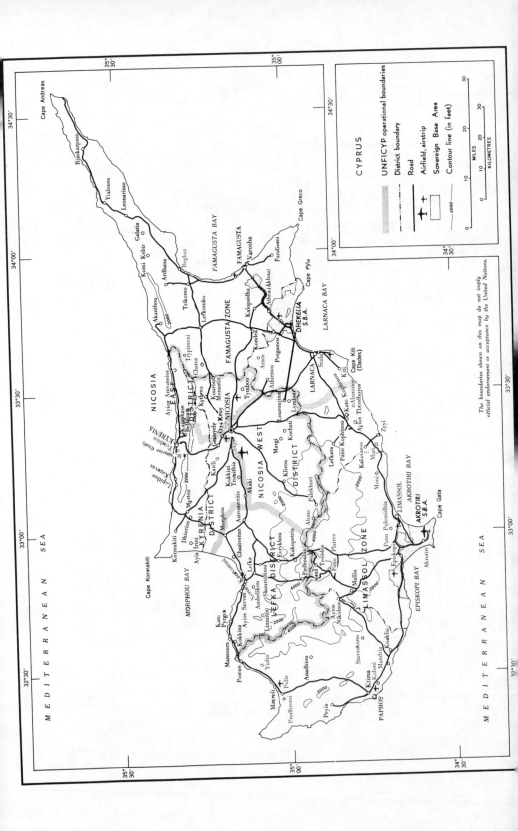

CYPRUS

UNFICYP operational boundaries
District boundary
Road
Airfield, airstrip
Sovereign Base Area
Contour line (in feet)

MILES
KILOMETRES

The boundaries shown on this map do not imply
official endorsement or acceptance by the United Nations.

6. India and Pakistan

UN map no. 1632, December 1965

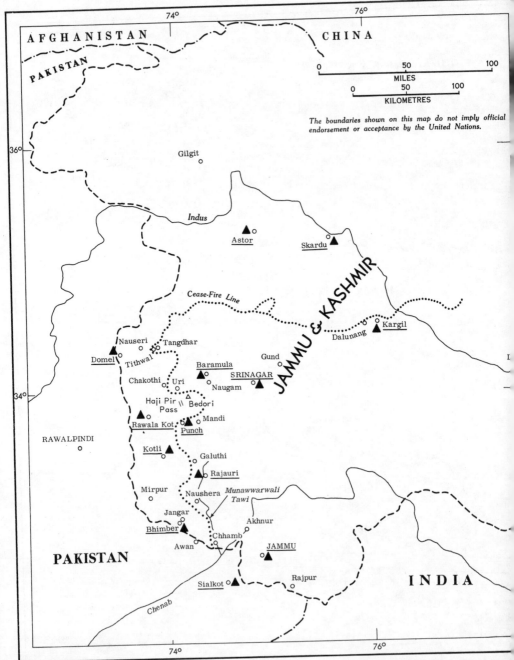

Map 7. Jammu and Kashmir

UN map no. 1609, rev. 2, February

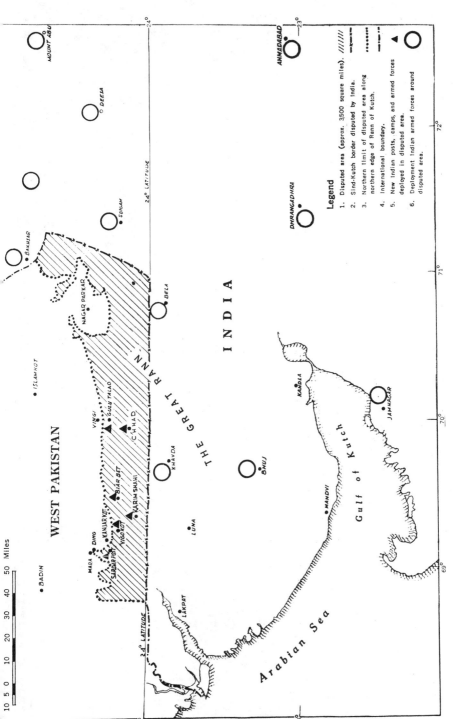

Map 8. Rann of Kutch Dispute

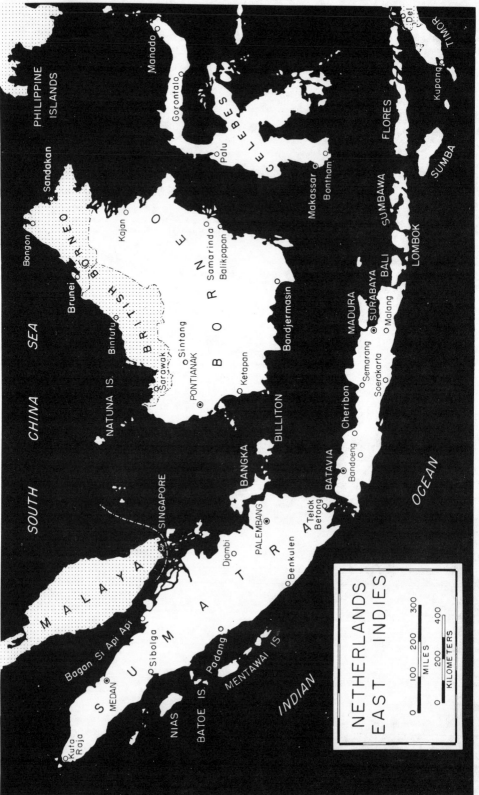

NETHERLANDS
EAST INDIES

MILES
0   100   200   300

KILOMETERS
0   200   400

COMPILED AND DRAWN IN THE GEOGRAPHY DIVISION, OSS

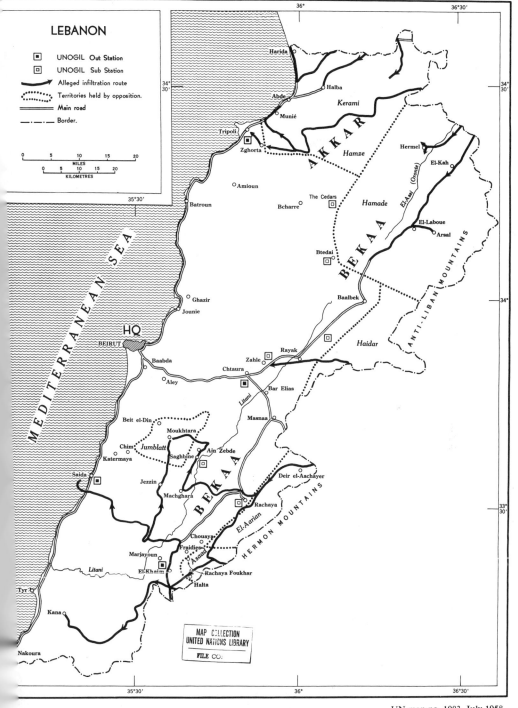

UN map no. 1083, July 1958

0. Lebanon

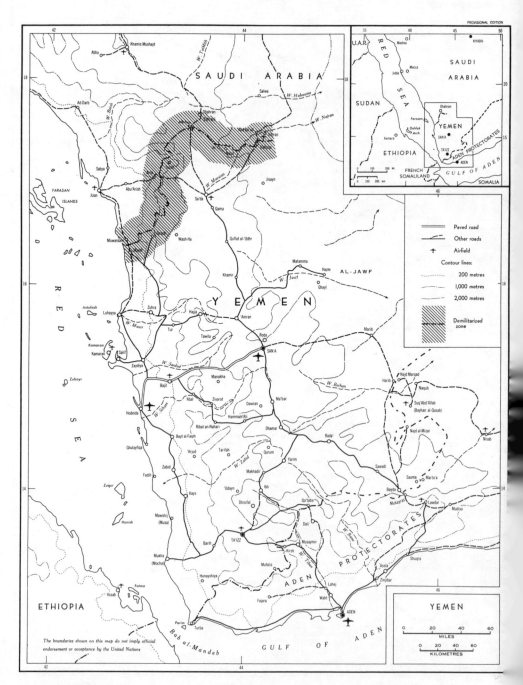

Map 11. Yemen

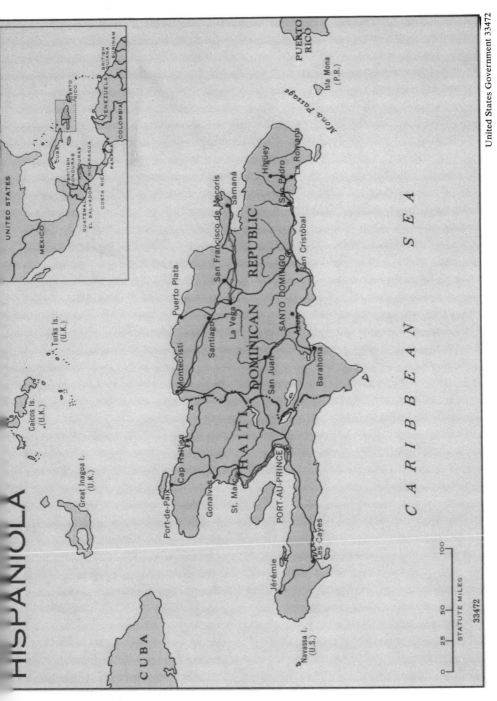

Map 12. Dominican Republic

United States Government 35473 9-61

WEST NEW GUINEA

Legend:
- .... International boundary
- ⊛ Capital
- ⊗ District capital
- ———— Road or track
- ———— Trail

0   100   200 Miles
0   100   200 Kilometers

PACIFIC OCEAN

HALMAHERA

HALMAHERA SEA

PULAU PULAU OBI

CERAM SEA

CERAM

BANDA SEA

REPUBLIC OF INDONESIA

PULAU PULAU DAMAR

PULAU-PULAU TANIMBAR

ARAFURA SEA

PULAU PULAU ARU

VOGELKOP

WEST NIEUW GUINEA

SCHERELAND

BOMBERAI

FAKFAK

GEELVINKBAAI

GEELVINK BAAI

SCHOUTEN EILANDEN

VAN REES-GEBERGTE

MEER VLAKTE

CENTRAL NIEUW GUINEA*

NASSAU-GEBERGTE

ORANJE-GEBERGTE

HOLLANDIA

HOLLANDIA

NEW GUINEA

NIEUW GUINEA ZUID

FREDERIK HENDRIK EILAND

DE JONG'S PUNT

TERR. OF NEW GUINEA (Tr. Terr.-Austr.)

TERR. OF PAPUA (Australia)

TANDJUNG SAWERA

TANDJUNG D'URVILLE

KAAP D'URVILLE

Boundaries are not necessarily those recognized by the U.S. Government.

*Administered from West Irian

128   132   136   140

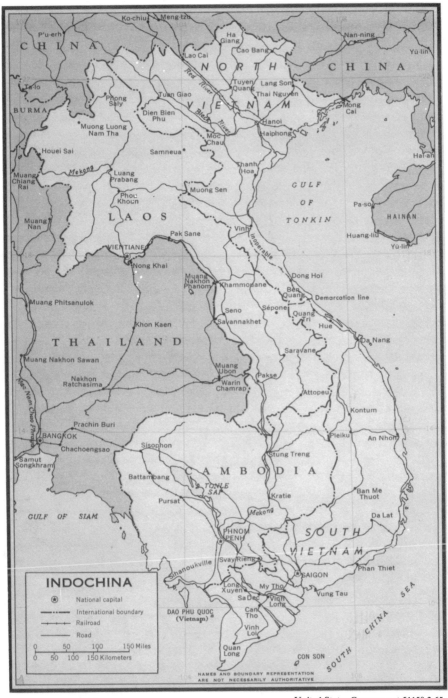

United States Government 51150 2-65

Map 14. Indochina

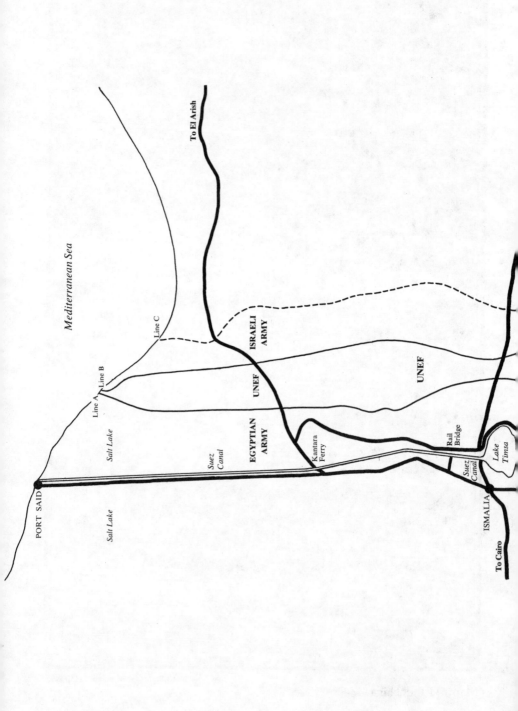

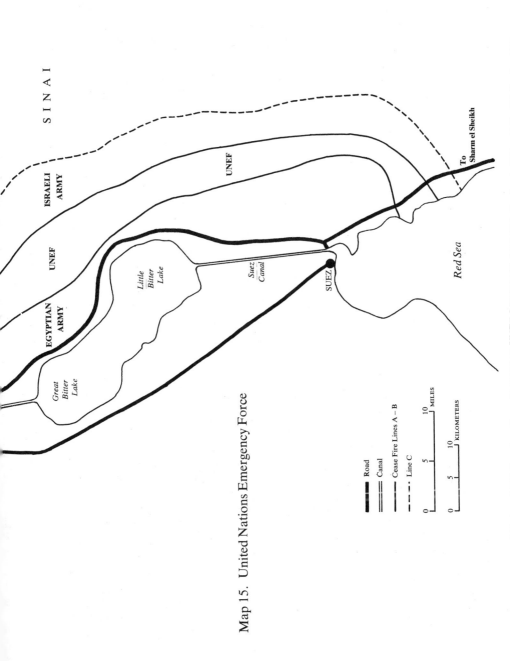

Map 15. United Nations Emergency Force

Legend:
- Road
- Canal
- Cease Fire Lines A – B
- Line C

SINAI

ISRAELI ARMY

EGYPTIAN ARMY

UNEF

UNEF

UNEF

Great Bitter Lake

Little Bitter Lake

Suez Canal

SUEZ

Red Sea

To Sharm el Sheikh

0   5   10   MILES

0   5   10   KILOMETERS

Map issued with Secretary-General's report on UNEF S/11248 of 1 April 1974. It refers to S/Res./340 of 25 October 1973.

PART II

PEACEKEEPING FUTURE

11

The Big Power Complex—
Possible Future Trends and
Their Influence on Peacekeeping

Part II, "Peacekeeping Future,"
will be a functional and practical presentation of what the authors
believe to be a viable concept for international peacekeeping, directed
at the construction of an effective and relevant instrument for containing violence and contributing to the peaceful settlement of disputes.
As will be clear the concept is broad in scope and emphasizes the importance of an interprofessional approach, combining the agencies
required for peaceful settlement into one interrelated effort of peacekeeping, peacemaking, and peace building. But before embarking
upon the presentation of that concept, it is necessary to set out the political framework within which it will have to operate and the levels
at which its treatment can be applied.

The story of the 1960s and the recent entry of the People's Republic of China into the United Nations have influenced the opinions of
member states regarding the advisability and acceptability of formal
arrangements, including signed agreements, for improving international peacekeeping procedures. Those advocating the strengthening
of the United Nations' peacekeeping potential are up against strong
political constraints borne of past experience and procedural disagreements among the big powers. A further uncompromising factor lies in
the conflicting attitudes and understandings that large and small nations have toward an international system for the control of conflict.
The Soviet and Eastern bloc countries tend to see UN peacekeeping as
an anticommunist instrument of the Western bloc—a suspicion that
was only too visibly enhanced during the Congo operation, when the
socialist countries were isolated, their diplomatic representatives ex-

pelled, and Lumumba and his entire political structure, which had been favorably disposed toward socialism, eliminated. In their turn, the Western bloc countries have rationalized their idea of peacekeeping with the UN action in Korea and with their own unilateral interventions—the United States in Lebanon, the Dominican Republic, and Indochina; Britain in Jordan, Kenya, and Tanzania; and France in support of its favored regimes in French-speaking Africa. The developing nations see peacekeeping as a neocolonial device for extending the interests of the big powers and are skeptical that any good can come from it; they lack confidence in it as a viable system of security for them. Last but not least, the nations that contribute troops, equipment, logistics, and finance have their own nagging doubt about the ability of the UN organization to direct and properly manage these operations; but so far this has not deterred them from taking part when the opportunity to do so has arisen.

In facing facts, the advocates of effective peacekeeping machinery must accept that, even with the development of UNEF II, there is no immediate indication that the big powers will reach a firm understanding on what has been a major point of disagreement for a long time. The reticence of the People's Republic of China to participate in the work of the Special Committee on Peacekeeping Operations, and its disassociation from the Security Council's resolutions calling for a cease-fire in the Middle East in October 1973 and the setting up of UNEF II, would seem to preclude the likelihood of any immediate progress. Nor can one discount the low-key approach adopted by the UN secretariat itself, which has taken a hard line against better military and administrative planning, current or advance, so that it can retain control of operations through the existing small staff working directly under the secretary-general. It has clearly become the pattern to blame inadequacies in the peacekeeping machinery, and the resultant operational improvisation, on the prevailing deadlock in the Special Committee on Peacekeeping Operations, and, more especially, on the unresolved differences between the superpowers, rather than to attempt to create an effective control structure; thus the secretariat is left to walk the inevitable tightrope under the constant scrutiny of the member states.

Ostensibly, agreement among the five permanent members of the Security Council is fundamental to the authorization of any UN peacekeeping operation. However, past experience has shown that the

United Nations can act only so long as it has the formal and tacit approval of the United States and Soviet Union. On those occasions when UN forces have been authorized, the support of the United States and a minimal level of acceptance by the Soviet Union were essential to their establishment. While in the past the polarization of the two superpowers has been a crucial factor in the use of international forces and the structuring of an international conflict control system, in the future their agreement will be a necessary prerequisite, as will be the full, or at least tacit, approval of the People's Republic of China.

The United States Because until recently Chiang Kaishek's regime and not the People's Republic has occupied China's seat in the Security Council, the Chinese representation has been ineffective, generally enabling the United States to count on the support or abstention of four of the five permanent members of the Council. On those occasions when the United States has been thwarted by a Soviet veto, it has turned to the General Assembly and invoked the Uniting for Peace Resolution in order to bypass the Security Council. But those days have passed, and the situation has changed; the United States can no longer always rely upon majority support in the Assembly—an Assembly that has changed significantly in membership and in character. The United States is therefore most insistent that matters embedded in the authority of the Security Council be dealt with by the Council and not in the General Assembly, though the United States itself still initiates unilateral action when and where its direct interests are at stake. Whenever this has been the case, the United States has relied upon its own military command, and not the machinery of the United Nations, to effect an intervention. However, it has always been careful to comply with Article 51 of the Charter by reporting its actions to the Security Council, even though this is generally after the event rather than before. Cuba, the Dominican Republic, and Indochina were all instances where the United States acted outside the United Nations, which at best was permitted to play only a peripheral role—and none at all in Indochina.

All this is not to say that the United States is uninterested in the United Nations as an effective peacekeeping institution; it seems to have a genuine desire to develop an efficient peacekeeping system, but there remains the question—for what purpose? In the UN operations in the Balkans, Lebanon, Korea, the Congo, and indirectly in Kashmir, the common denominator was that the operations were anticommunist in their orientation. The United States' decision over the past two decades to meet communist challenges wherever they occurred with all the means at its disposal, including where necessary force to deter force, as in Korea and Indochina, heightened and prolonged the cold war issues until the thaw following President Nixon's visits to Peking and Moscow in 1972. The same power pattern has existed in Europe, with the United States demonstrating its resource capability no less effectively in terms of nuclear sufficiency, until here again in the early 1970s it and the USSR reached a degree of accommodation that helped to ease the tension. The United States, however, reserves its right, when it feels that its interests are jeopardized, to act through a doctrine of controlled and flexible response.

The United States' attitude toward peacekeeping stems from this background. In its actions, either in support of UN operations or in unilateral terms, it has tried to assist emerging nations to achieve independence with minimal sacrifice. In conformity with the influence and hopes of those other founder members who signed the Charter, it remains convinced that not only can peace be kept through negotiations, but that peace may also be enforced. This has been the common theme of successive administrations in their support of the United Nations—a United Nations that was never intended to be a world government and cannot therefore guarantee world peace. While remaining committed to the Security Council's pivotal role of authority in peacekeeping matters, with the General Assembly retaining its authority to recommend action in the event of a veto, the United States, as we have seen, continues to support an active role for the secretary-general. But it is also in favor of a committee, established by the Security Council under Article 29, holding a watching brief over the conduct of peacekeeping operations, advising the secretary-general and receiving his reports; such a committee to be formed and to assume its responsibilities whenever the Council authorizes the secretary-general to undertake peacekeeping operations. In the United States' view the committee, acting as a subsidiary organ of the Council, would provide guidance to the secretary-general in connection with the interpretation of the Council's mandate and remain in close contact and consultation with the secretary-general and key secretariat officials.

The United States' attitude on the financing of peacekeeping operations is that the Security Council should normally, unless it indicates otherwise, establish the means for financing an operation; it being understood that any arrangement so made would not prejudice the General Assembly's authority to apportion expenses among the members. Until a reliable and equitable system for financing peacekeeping is agreed upon, permanent members of the Security Council would undertake to pay their fair share of peacekeeping operations authorized by the Security Council, in addition to what others may contribute.

As a global power, the United States, while supporting the United Nations, has encouraged the development of many regional and multinational peacekeeping arrangements; but primarily the United States has relied on its own power and the deployment of a strategic nuclear weapons system under its exclusive control to maintain its authority. The present Nixon administration has clearly established these attitudes by its direct negotiations with the powers involved in the Indochina conflict, outside the UN framework. (The UN secretary-general was permitted to attend the Paris Peace signing merely as an observer.) As the cold war recedes, the United States appears to have less use for an international security system and has downgraded its relative value. Whether this will continue to be the policy of succeeding administrations remains to be seen.

In Europe, the United States with its tactical nuclear weapons has provided the teeth to the Western military alliance. Since the Americans themselves feel more secure against possible military threat from the Soviet Union with their first line of defense deployed in the heart of Europe rather than along the Atlantic seaboard, it can be expected that a streamlined American troop presence will remain in Europe as a part of NATO. Moves toward achieving balanced reductions in military force have already begun, though their outcome may be some years away.

In the Middle East the United States' future policy also seems clear. Its strong support for Israel, along with its present dependence on oil, and thereby the importance of its relations with the oil-producing countries of the Arab world; its military assistance to Iran, thus creating a new bulwark for defense in the Persian Gulf; and its continued massive assistance to Saudi Arabia, designed to counterbalance the military power of other Arab countries, makes peace in that area very much in the United States' interest. Despite recent moves to bring the latest Arab-Israeli hostilities to an end, major issues still remain and will need to be resolved if there is to be lasting peace in the area. To safeguard American interests, it can be expected that the United States will continue to rely primarily on its own ability; but to keep the peace there would now appear to be a better chance of superpower cooperation in using the United Nations as the instrument for peacekeeping.

In Asia the United States is vying with the Soviet Union, the People's Republic of China, and Japan to gain political and economic influence. Beset with national rivalries, utter poverty, and hunger, Asia will remain a hotbed of intrigue, strife, and violence. The old alliances are disintegrating, and with the end of direct United States presence in South Vietnam, new arrangements will emerge. Although it is unlikely that these will seriously affect the United States' longstanding attitudes toward Asia, they will no doubt require some adjustment.

In Africa the United States will be under increasing domestic and outside pressure to support movements of liberation. This pressure will necessarily influence future American attitudes. In Latin America the United States continues to provide strong support to OAS, and it is learning to deal with leftist regimes and to cope with strong trends against authoritative civil or military regimes. The American hemisphere is caught up with a mood to change its political, economic, and social institutions, and there is a serious possiblity of major and widespread violence developing. A strong and effective OAS would prevent it.

The United States' interest and influence in ensuring peace in the future thus appears to have a diverse quality.

Britain and France   Along with the United States, Britain and France have been the other key members of the Western alliance. Churchill, Roosevelt, and Stalin, as the early architects of the United Nations, were determined that it would be something more than the League of Nations and therefore must have the capability to maintain and restore peace. In the postwar years Britain became increasingly engaged in meeting demands from those members of the

Commonwealth who sought self-determination and sovereign independence. Firmly committed to the development of democratic institutions, the United Nations could have provided the ideal machinery to assist the process of peaceful transfer of power. Disillusionment, however, followed when at Suez in 1956 the joint Anglo-French military intervention was challenged by the world community and threatened with action by the United States and the Soviet Union. The subsequent withdrawal in favor of UNEF was bitterly resented by the British, and, though unjustified, there germinated a lack of confidence in the United Nations' credibility as an agent for strong action in maintaining international peace. The Congo helped but little to revive British enthusiasm. Very sensitive to any threat to its interests in Africa—in its colonial territory of Rhodesia, in the South African problem, and particularly to its copper and other mineral interests—Britain saw only danger in an operation that was dominated by Hammarskjöld in New York and by nonaligned anti-imperialist Indians and Africans in the field. The United Nations attempt to end the secession of Katanga and the actions of Conor Cruise O'Brien only added to Britain's disillusionment and brought the world organization to a new low point in its popularity in the United Kingdom. Yet when the guarantor powers failed to resolve the Cyprus crisis, and the major burden for maintenance of law and order fell on Britain, it was ready to turn to the United Nations for help.

The United Kingdom, however, does continue to support the UN system of peacekeeping, and its support might be said to be more enthusiastic now than at any time since Suez. In general it endorses the United States' position on questions relating to the future of peacekeeping, and its experience in Cyprus and Northern Ireland (though an internal situation) could contribute to the development of a reliable international system. The United Kingdom's support and assistance in the mounting of the current Middle East operation was a major factor in its successful launching.

France's attitude has been largely influenced by its special relationship with its former colonies and the personality of its outstanding former leader, General de Gaulle. Having been initially excluded from the counsels dealing with the development of a world system and retaining a strong desire to deal with French problems itself, France has relied little on the United Nations. The war in Indochina led to only a peripheral role for the United Nations at the Geneva talks in 1954; the

Algerian civil war was an internal problem as far as France was concerned and therefore the United Nations was kept out, as it has been
in other French community problems in other parts of Africa. Although allied to the West, France has differed on a number of occasions with the United Kingdom and the United States and sided
with the Soviet Union on peacekeeping matters. Like the USSR,
France refused to pay for the Congo operation, thereby heightening
the financial crisis within the organization. But when it withdrew
from the Western European Security Arrangement, largely because of
its domination by the United States, and created its own *force de
frappe,* General de Gaulle reached an understanding with U Thant
that ushered in a new era of understanding and support for the UN
system. While firmly upholding the authority of the Security Council
for the authorization, supervision, and financing of peacekeeping
operations, France also has declared in its proposals to the Special
Committee on Peacekeeping Operations that Chapter VII of the
Charter offers broad possibilities that have doubtlessly not been sufficiently probed, and that it is on the basis of its provisions that it
should be possible to determine the role that the various organs of the
United Nations should play in peacekeeping operations. France, independent of United States' domination, has expressed a need for an
effective international peacekeeping system. Apart from approving
the Security Council's decision to establish UNEF II and agreeing to
pay its proportion of its costs, it has not, so far, declared its precise
attitude toward the United Nation's peacekeeping role. However,
there are indications of France's growing interest in international
peacekeeping.

The Soviet Union   The Soviet Union's experience in
                                            Korea and later in the Congo un-
                                            doubtedly established the impres-
sion that a Western-dominated United Nations was being used as an
anticommunist instrument. The downgrading of the authority of the
Soviet under-secretary in charge of political and Security Council
affairs with respect to peacekeeping matters, the bitter controversies
over the role of the secretary-general in the early days of the Congo
operations, and the Khrushchev-Hammarskjöld confrontation only
further established this suspicion in the minds of the Soviet leaders.
These experiences led to the Soviet Union's adherence to the firm

line that the Security Council should tightly control peacekeeping operations, to ensure that it could exercise its veto when necessary. The Soviet Union also opposed institutional improvements in peacekeeping operations so as to prevent any loosening of political control.

During the 1950s and 1960s the central position of the Soviet Union within the socialist bloc precluded any need on its part to use the United Nations' peacekeeping system. When Yugoslavia announced its independence, the Soviet Union resorted to nonmilitary means in an attempt to bring that country back under its full domination. On the other hand, for reasons directly related to East-West politics, it intervened in Hungary and Czechoslovakia, using the Warsaw Pact treaty as its justification, to prevent those countries from following the example of Yugoslavia. The Soviet Union's actions corresponded to those of the other three big powers where their direct interests have been involved. Its support for peacekeeping operations has varied from tacit acceptance to full backing. It has supported the operations in Cyprus, Kashmir, West Irian, and the Yemen; played a key role in ending the India-Pakistan war of 1965; approved the establishment of the UN Truce Supervision Organization; and favored UN Emergency Force operations—but declined to share the costs. Its early support for the Congo operation waned with the removal of Lumumba from power. Its refusal to pay its share of ONUC's costs precipitated the financial crisis in the United Nations and brought about the attempt by the United States to have the Soviets deprived of their voting rights in the General Assembly, which in turn provoked a very real threat to the world organization.

In the Cuban crisis the Soviet Union, like the United States, was glad of the assistance of the United Nations, especially the help the secretary-general was able to provide. But in the main, during the decolonization period and the emergence of many new Asian and African nations, the Soviet Union has been quick to support revolution and change, and it is not likely that this attitude will alter.

The Middle East crisis in 1967 highlighted the degree to which the maintenance of international peace and security depends upon the position of either of the superpowers. The fear of a Soviet veto against any attempt by the Security Council to challenge Egypt's sovereign right to request UNEF's withdrawal aborted any attempt to resolve the crisis. The Soviet Union, like many of Egypt's allies, had counted on the Egyptian armed forces' standing their ground if attacked. Following their failure to do so and the collapse of the Arab armies, the Soviet Union became actively engaged in developing the United Nations' role in the peaceful resolution of conflict in the Middle East. The Russians have a major stake in the Arab world and naturally desire a reduction rather than an escalation of tension in the area. This has been only too clearly borne out in the October 1973 crisis in the Middle East. Elsewhere, in Africa and Latin America, they can be expected to support, at least tacitly, the development of regional systems for conflict control, endorsing UN involvement only where it is necessary.

During the debates of the Special Committee on Peacekeeping Operations, the Soviet Union has firmly maintained not only the supremacy of the Security Council over peacekeeping operations, but also that it is the sole organ empowered to take action to maintain or restore peace. The Soviet Union insists that, having authorized a peacekeeping operation, the Security Council should continue to exercise supreme control over all aspects of its establishment and direction throughout the entire operation. The Security Council, in the Soviet view, must determine the manner in which it will receive advice and assistance on all military aspects relating to a particular operation, including the possibility of establishing a special subsidiary organ for the purpose (Article 29).

So far as the roles of the secretary-general and the secretariat are concerned, the Soviet Union continues to maintain that the former's responsibilities are defined in Article 97 of the Charter and that it is his primary mission to facilitate the implementation of decisions taken by the main organs of the United Nations. Neither he nor the secretariat is empowered to take political decisions and independently implement them.[1] In taking this position the Soviet Union has indicated that it will remain firmly committed in the future to the Security Council as the sole authority responsible for all aspects of UN peacekeeping.

Unilaterally the Soviet Union, like the United States, has placed a heavy reliance on a nuclear deterrent. It has worked to strengthen the defense capability of the European socialist bloc and to keep it unified. But, along with the United States, it has begun to feel the eco-

1. Ambassador Y. A. Malik, permanent representative of the Soviet Union to the United Nations, May 1972.

nomic pinch of the high cost of defense and thus shares with its rival an interest in reducing defense expenditure. The struggle for power and economic gain, however, is certain to continue unabated.

In the Indian subcontinent, the Russians would prefer to avoid a major power confrontation, but they block energetically any Chinese attempt to interfere in that region, as they did in the case of the Bangladesh crisis. The Russo-Chinese border confrontation and China's fear of a Russian preemptive nuclear strike will continue to be major factors in the relations between the two great powers in Asia and will dictate the geopolitical structure and inter-national alignments of the smaller Asian states. In such a major power confrontation, the United Nations or any similar forum could serve only a peripheral peacekeeping purpose, while the United States alone might be expected to play a more significant or effective role.

People's Republic of China   The People's Republic of China until now has not contributed anything tangible to the general debate on peacekeeping practices. This hesitancy is understandable considering the ad hoc and complex way in which those practices have developed within the UN framework over the past three decades. The Chinese naturally first wish fully to understand their many nuances. Their deputy foreign minister, however, in his initial address to the General Assembly, pointed to the fact that the Charter is the product of the world situation prevailing at the end of World War II and went on to say that countries of the Third World are uniting to oppose the superpower policies of aggression, expansion, and war and as a result are playing an even greater role in international affairs.[2] This indicates that China, although one of the five permanent members of the Security Council, wishes to align itself with the nations of the Third World. Since this was the first indication of China's attitude toward current problems of world security, it is worth quoting in some detail from Chiao's maiden speech. In referring to the situation in the Mediterranean, he said that the Chinese government fully supported the call for "a Mediterranean for the Mediterranean countries and the withdrawal of foreign fleets from that region. In discussing security in Europe, he said, "It is necessary to oppose fully the

---

2. Deputy Foreign Minister Chiao, A/PV/2051, 3 October 1972.

aggression, interference, subversion and control by the superpowers, to disband the military blocs, withdraw the foreign armed forces and bring about the peaceful coexistence of the European countries on the basis of respect for independence and sovereignty, mutual non-aggression, non-interference in each others' internal affairs and equality and mutual benefit." He went on, "There are two categories of wars: just and unjust. We support just wars and oppose unjust wars." [3] It is difficult to rationalize the latter statement with China's proved policy in recent years; for while it supports wars of liberation in Africa, its attitude toward Bangladesh has been quite the opposite—it did not give its support to the war of liberation in that country. China's statement leaves little doubt that where issues relating to peace and security are concerned, it can be expected to take a position closely aligned to that of the Third World, thus adding a new element to the power play between the permanent members of the Security Council.

The questions that this raises on matters relating to the Charter have grave implications for the role of the United Nations in maintaining peace and security. It is therefore inevitable that the task of the Special Committee on Peacekeeping Operations is likely to be more complex than before. To underline the difficulties ahead, one only needs to quote Ambassador Huang Hua, the permanent representative of the People's Republic at the United Nations, who has questioned the continuation of peacekeeping operations when they achieve little beyond keeping the peace and in so doing simply preserve the status quo. He has also indicated that China sees little advantage in the establishment of force level operations, since in its opinion, though observer missions may report to the United Nations on observance of peace, peace between warring nations must follow agreements. The United Nations therefore must develop a machinery that not only observes but also assists in making peace through negotiation and conciliation.

Because of their greater acceptability, the medium and small nations have provided the bulk of the UN peacekeeping forces and missions in the past and can be expected to meet the major requirement

3. Ibid.

in the future. Canada, the Nordic countries, India, and Ireland have made the largest contribution, not only to the operations themselves but also toward the development and strengthening of a UN peacekeeping system. It is these middle and small powers particularly, whether they belong to Western or Eastern blocs, the nonaligned and/or the Third World group of nations, who need the United Nations for their protection. The big powers may not depend upon the United Nations for their security, but the other member states do. Of necessity, and for their protection and benefit, they have been prompted to join one of the regional or power security blocs or a politico-economic system. The majority of them probably would prefer not to have to depend on such arrangements and would rather rely upon an international security system. The middle and small powers cannot afford the luxury of power balances. They need a machinery for peacekeeping and for the peaceful settlement of disputes, even though they do generate many of the conflicts that can threaten international peace and security. Unfortunately the dispute over Article 19 in the General Assembly in 1965 and its near disastrous consequences, the United Nations' failure to improve the institutional arrangements for peacekeeping, and the slow rate of progress of the Special Committee on Peacekeeping Operations have all helped to dampen their eagerness and support. The sudden withdrawal of UNEF further added to the disenchantment of many, notably Canada [4] and Denmark. However, despite these setbacks, medium and small powers remain most anxious to resolve the question of peacekeeping. Within the Special Committee on Peacekeeping Operations, in other UN organs, in regional organizations, and in many single or group initiatives, these nations have been actively engaged in seeking means to strengthen the international peacekeeping capability. Their many suggestions to narrow the differences between the great powers are amply demonstrated by the variety of recommendations put forward by them in the Special Committee on Peacekeeping Operations.

By its initiatives Canada particularly has contributed much in a serious attempt to meet the requirements of the superpowers. It has brought its unique practical experience in peacekeeping operations to its work in the committee and, as we have noted earlier, has made

4. Canada, however, has not withdrawn from peacekeeping and is now contributing its unparalleled experience to the logistic management of UNEF II.

positive suggestions regarding the greater employment of the Military Staff Committee and the establishment of firmer links between it and the secretary-general and the secretariat in terms of peacekeeping.[5]

It is unfortunate that the big powers have not set a better example in their encouragement of peaceful resolution of conflicts. Whenever their interests have been involved, they have not refrained from using force. The smaller nations not surprisingly see little wrong in following suit. Many have inherited artificial frontiers, suffered from divided societies, and won independence only at great sacrifice. One can hardly blame them for wanting to protect their hard-won interests by every means possible, including force. They would prefer to fight than have their disputes anesthetized, since this is likely to resolve nothing. However, in spite of conflicts of national and regional interests, they remain anxious to strengthen the peacekeeping systems of the United Nations.

Before that can be accomplished the United Nations must clarify its position in regard to support for liberation movements. Many of these movements are violent in nature, and therefore for member states to give them unlicensed support is to legitimize violence within the framework of the UN Charter. The General Assembly at its Twenty-seventh Session, in a resolution on the granting of independence to colonial countries and people, reaffirmed its recognition of "the legitimacy of the struggle of the colonial peoples under alien domination to exercise their right to self-determination and independence by all the necessary means at their disposal." [6] Since then this attitude toward the use of "all necessary means" has gained greater support in UN deliberations on southern African, Latin American, and Asian conflict problems—to the extent that little or no differentiation is made between those movements that confine their "violence" to direct confrontation with their "oppressors" and those that place no limit on their activities, treating the global scene as their battleground.

The view expressed by the Chinese deputy foreign minister and wide non-European support for the liberation movements in southern Africa, including resort to use of force, are part of the mood of the world today and probably of the future. Violence has not only gained

5. See Canada's Report to Secretary-General on Command and Control of Peacekeeping Operations, A/SPC/152, 10 October 1972.

6. General Assembly Resolution 2908(XXVII), 2 November 1972.

recognition, but has taken new forms hitherto rejected by international law and moral usage. The law itself is under challenge. It is difficult to draw a moral distinction in terms of violence between that committed by Palestinian aircraft hijackers, who have reached the end of their tolerance in reclaiming their heritage, and the actions of the crew of a bomber dropping tons of bombs containing explosives and chemicals, detached in almost every sense from their enemies as well as from the people they are supporting. That is why the United Nations since its inception has not been able to define what aggression is; it means different things to different people. Furthermore, its many interpretations have changed with the course of time. It is a plain fact, however, that while nations in their wisdom are unable to define aggression, they resort to violence when it suits their purpose and decry violence when it does not. This is why an international system designed to reduce conflict and the violence that springs from it is needed more than ever before. The question that remains is: Can it be achieved? We believe it can, provided the institutions that are evolved to manage it are realistic and relevant to the dictates of the Charter. As has been shown, member states with experience in UN peacekeeping are already thinking along these lines, and, although the questions of control, direction, and financing still have to be settled, the gap between the positions of the United States and the Soviet Union has narrowed. It does not seem that control and direction of operations pose insurmountable problems, and once these and the general principles can be agreed upon, one has a right to assume that in accepting these principles, member states would be accepting the legitimacy of the financial obligation.

China's role in all this will be one of considerable significance. It would be guileless to suppose that the People's Republic, now that it has assumed its rightful seat as a permanent member of the Security Council, will not exercise its veto power in support of Third World issues. If it maintains the view that violence, and if necessary counterviolence, constitutes legitimate means for settling disputes, the viability of any international system for the control of conflict comes into question—it certainly places a limitation on the extent to which such a system can be used. It is to be hoped that China will do nothing to oppose the setting up of the system, even though it may not endorse its implementation in any but a restricted level of disputes. Nevertheless, it has to be recognized that China's late arrival at the United Nations can place in jeopardy much of the progress that has been made in reducing tensions and modifying fixed positions between East and West over the last ten years.

The Soviet Union, having reached an approximate parity with the United States in nuclear weapons, has gained sufficient confidence to reduce tensions and make compromises with the Western nations. In exchange, the bitter antagonism between China and the Soviet Union both within and outside the United Nations presupposes that there will be continuing tension between these two permanent members of the Security Council who, together with Japan, are the three most powerful nations in Asia. Ironically this situation alone underscores the need for an international security system, for in its wake could come a polarization of nations, aligned on the one hand with the Soviet Union and on the other with China, along with their attendant interstate problems. China apart, the United States and the Soviet Union are recognized as the superpowers. Though qualifying in every respect for the same recognition, China has made it clear that it has no interest in becoming one. It will remain to be seen whether or not the title will be involuntarily thrust upon China. For the time being at least the superpower structure will continue unaltered, and, as many member states believe, future peacekeeping operations will depend upon agreement between the United States and the Soviet Union on the way in which these operations are to be controlled and directed. There is little doubt that this will require compromises on the part of both. One can expect that the urgency of the crisis and their interest in settling it will influence their actions in the Security Council. This of course is not good enough and simply holds the world to ransom while two superpowers analyze and assess their interests. No security system can operate so long as only the two most powerful members have the ultimate say as to its establishment and use. The system has to be the servant of all the members for their own protection and security—otherwise it will become moribund like the Military Staff Committee. In the final analysis it all boils down to one factor. Any system, any collective security arrangement, any future peacekeeping operation or mission depends wholly on the interest and desire of member states to have a peaceful world and to have an effective conflict control system working in it.

The world community progresses gradually, though slowly, toward the development of viable international institutions. This is not surprising, for after all, three decades—the life of the United Nations—is but a very small fraction of time in the history of man. Hope for the future lies in the attitudes of peoples toward violence and a real concern for their future world. So long as apathy and antipathy to the United Nations and its machinery continues, the full effectiveness of an international system for control of conflict will not be realized. If the majority of member states of the United Nations want the kind of collective security that the United Nations can offer strongly enough to make a supreme and universal effort to bring the system into being, then whether they get it should not depend upon the vacillations and the interests of the two most powerful nations in the world.

Political scientists and others would no doubt say that the world political structure being what it is, it would be unrealistic to believe that it could be otherwise—that it will always depend upon the superpowers whether or not the world organization will play its proper and predetermined role in the maintenance of international peace and security. If this is true, it still does not negate everything that has been recommended here, even though it may make it more difficult to achieve; for the emphasis on action could well shift from the United Nations to regional organizations, where the blueprint can be modified and adapted to meet the specific needs of each region. In 1973 Somalia made available its good offices to ascertain the truth of allegations that armed forces were concentrating along the Tanzania-Uganda border after the border incidents at the beginning of 1972. This was a regional arrangement within OAU and followed Somalia's earlier intervention in making available to the two governments a neutral meeting place where they could discuss and settle their differences. A few months later at the summit conference of the OAU held in Addis Ababa, the heads of state of Tanzania and Uganda were reconciled in a meeting at which the Emperor Haile Selassie of Ethiopia helped to reestablish friendly relations between the two leaders; the outcome of this meeting was a declaration ending the border dispute. Canada, Hungary, Indonesia, and Poland formed the joint International Commission for Control and Supervision to oversee the truce arrangements of the Vietnam War. In this case, the commission was set up by the mutual agreement of the two Vietnams and the United States, independently of the United Nations.

These are but two examples of conflict control arrangements that were made outside the central UN body of the Security Council, but in execution they followed the pattern that has been the hallmark of UN operations in the past. It is certain that so long as the concentration of power remains in the hands of the big powers, the regional and multinational conflict control measures will be more widely used in preference to the UN machinery. With world political patterns changing, past alliances eroding, and new relationships forming, there is every indication that nations will place primary reliance on the strength of their own national and regional security systems. But the general behavior of states in dealing with disputes is unlikely to change much, and there will remain a fundamental dependence upon the United Nations as the recognized guardian of world peace and security—a dependence that will ensure that the United Nations will continue to be confronted with problems requiring its fact-finding, mediatory, and supervisory skills for their settlement.

Whatever may be looked for in an effective system; whatever is required to make the system effective; however desirous and determined the majority of nations are to build a conflict control organism; however much the middle and small nations are prepared to contribute their resources to it when it is established; however constructive and practical people's ideas may be for the structuring of an effective conflict control system—one has to accept that for the present, it is in the hands of two or three major powers to decide whether such a system is to be developed. So long as this remains the prerequisite, one can expect to see few UN interventions, and the onus of peacekeeping will fall on the shoulders of regional organizations. It is here that the strength of the international security system will rest. Most of what is suggested in the second half of this book is as workable at the regional level as it is in the world organization, needing only adjustment and adaptation. Therefore, the structure that we expose is relevant and functional at both geopolitical levels. Though the future opportunities for UN intervention may be rare, this does not mean that the system should not be constructed. It has been shown that it is wanted; it not only would be complementary to those security arrangements at the regional level but would provide the vital backup support that the latter will need; and, most important of all, the United Nations will remain, as the Charter intended it to be, the effective guarantor of international peace and security when all other peacemaking efforts have failed. For future conflict control patterns will depend upon circumstances. Since there is a relationship between domestic and international security, there are risks involved so far as smaller nations are concerned. By placing too great a reliance on the big powers for protection they could lose their independence of action. Therefore, there is all the more need for a multinational security system to preclude such a dependence.

12

Conflict Identification and Control Possibilities

Despite the sophisticated techniques of conflict control and conflict resolution that have derived from academic disciplines (e.g. social psychology), peacekeeping is essentially a practitioner's art. It is, however, just one of the possibilities for conflict control, not the sole panacea for dealing with problems of violence in international society; and it is the task of the statesmen in their collective wisdom to determine in what conflict areas peacekeeping may be applied as a means of diffusing conflict heat and preparing the ground for peaceful settlement. Once areas are identified that lend themselves to the "peacekeeping treatment," it is then a matter of diplomacy to determine the specific "dose" needed. It is the nature and character of application and treatment that we are concerned with in this chapter.

Looking back at the United Nations' peacekeeping record and assessing the variables that determine the applicability of peacekeeping to conflict situations, what strikes one most is that, although the United Nations' peacekeeping efforts have been dictated by considerations that appeared entirely ad hoc at the time, there were really only a few fairly well defined areas in which these efforts ultimately could be applied and implemented. There was, at first, what might be called the "fringe" area between the Western and the Soviet defense parameters; Korea, the Balkans, and Cyprus are examples. Second, there was the general area of decolonization, following the gradual liquidation of the European colonial system; and third, the area provided by the instability within newly emergent states. There were therefore a large range of issues that bedevilled relations between states during the 1945–70 period that did not come within the ambit of the United Nations' peacekeeping operations. They can be categorized as follows:

(1) Issues involving a direct confrontation between the East and West, of which Berlin and the Cuban missile crisis are the two major examples. Over Berlin the United Nations was involved peripherally when it proposed the establishment of a commission to investigate whether or not conditions existed for the holding of free elections there, but because of Soviet opposition the proposal was never acted upon. During the Cuban crisis of 1962–63 the secretary-general of the United Nations did use his good offices in contributing to a settlement.

(2) Issues within the American hemisphere, of which the dispute between Argentina and Uruguay over the ownership of Rio de la Plata Estuary, that between Haiti and the Dominican Republic, and that between the United States and Panama over the status of the Panama Canal are important illustrations. Apart from the Cuban missile crisis, the Dominican Republic crisis of 1965 was probably the only major issue in the hemisphere in which the secretary-general was able to make any contribution, but by and large the area was almost entirely and effectively sealed off against UN penetration.

(3) Issues within the Soviet hemisphere, the most significant being the Hungarian insurrection of 1956 and the Czechoslovakian crisis of 1968. Here again, the United Nations did have a peripheral function during the Hungarian episode when it took upon itself to investigate the situation and give global publicity to alleged Soviet violations of human rights, but this area too has been very firmly in the hands of the Soviet Union.

(4) Issues within Europe, including the civil unrest in Northern Ireland, the dispute over fishing rights between Iceland and Britain and other European countries, as well as other issues between Europe and the Americas, have been outside the purview of the United Nations. Those that did fall within its realm, such as the Balkan and Cyprus problems, were essentially in what we earlier described as the "fringe" areas of the two global systems of the East and the West.

(5) Finally, there have been a number of issues in Asia, involving China especially, in which the United Nations had little or no role to play. These include China's conflict with the Soviet Union; its invasion and occupation of Tibet; the border dispute over Sinkiang and Manchuria; its disputes with India, Nepal, and Bhutan; as well as

disputes with the West (excepting Korea) in Vietnam and Laos and over the islands of Quemoy and Matsu.

This commentary on the limited geographical range of peacekeeping in the past does have its significance when assessing the variables that will condition peacekeeping in the future. That conflicts between global powers, or in regions that fall within their spheres of vital interest, do not lend themselves to the peacekeeping treatment is an empirical statement of fact and can be documented; but it is a nebulous statement in that it starts with the empirical observation itself and does not reveal much about peacekeeping. Does it mean that, by definition, great powers are excluded from peacekeeping? For what reason have they not submitted their disputes to some form of international control in the past? Can one envisage any situations in the future in which they may well be willing to accept some kind of a role for international peacekeeping—the role of supervising arms or armistice agreements, for instance?

To answer these questions, at least as they relate to the past, we have to know whether it is indeed not in the character of the great powers to submit their disputes to international scrutiny and control, or whether there was something about the climate of international affairs over the last two decades that would account for their reluctance to do so. It would seem that a combination of both these factors conspired to limit the horizons of peacekeeping. Great powers are peculiarly sensitive to having their affairs, international no less than internal, pried into by other states. Indeed, the matter has considerable bearing on their international status. States "of status" do not like to be thought of as incapable of looking after their domestic problems, though there are numerous examples in recent history, no less in the present, where it can be shown that some problems can surpass the capabilities of even these states. It was fashionable in the 1950s and 1960s, therefore, to regard only the smaller and newer states of the Third World as fit subjects for international control.

This, of course, is not the whole explanation. There is also the fact, and probably the more significant fact, that during much of the first two decades of the United Nations' life, the superpowers occupied a position of omnipotence, dragging their allies and satellites along with them into conflicts that quickly became bipolarized. In the ensuing cold war, much as each side would have liked to expose the other to global censure by attacking its actions in the United Nations—as the United States did to the Soviet Union over the Balkans, Hungary, and Czechoslovakia—it was hardly reasonable to expect that either party would allow the United Nations to peer over its shoulders. It was not surprising, therefore, that the whole range of issues concerning the great powers, both in relation to each other and in relation to their respective spheres of influence, passed by the United Nations like wind over a maize harvest. The United Nations was ruffled by the cold war, indeed badly ruffled, for many of its promises in the area of collective security, including the activation of a Military Staff Committee, could not be fulfilled as a result; but the United Nations act as no more than a mild windbreaker in the cold war (as witnessed by the Berlin blockade of 1948).

When considering the future of peacekeeping, it is therefore necessary to ask whether the future relations between the great powers are likely to be such as to allow for optimism that there could be any international role for peacekeeping agencies in these relations. That question has been answered, at least in part, by the establishment of UNEF II, first as a guardian of a cease-fire and subsequently as a buffer force between Egyptian and Israeli forces. Besides minimizing the chances of a renewed outbreak of hostilities, UNEF serves the purpose of lessening the possibility of a head-on superpower confrontation. It might not be realistic to conceive of a conflict situation where a UNEF-type buffer force might stand between the armies of the great powers, but might not international peacekeeping perform a more modest function? Might it not perform the tasks of neutral supervision over agreements between the superpowers? Leaving aside the issues of conflict between the superpowers and given the fact of the present limited détente between them, might not international peacekeeping play a role in the collaborative areas of their relations, such as in supervising environmental pollution agreements? These questions are meant to be rhetorical, for it is our submission that circumstances in the future may allow some form of peacekeeping function, even in the relations of the great powers. For already, by assuming peacekeeping roles in the fringe areas between the Western powers and Soviet defense parameters and in the Third World, the United Nations has played a peacekeeping function in areas of immediate concern to the great powers. What seems to be required now is boldness of imagination and a willingness to reexamine and revise those principles inherent to peacekeeping that belong to an earlier era.

There is no question that the United States was the main motivating force behind the UN peacekeeping operations, so far as the fringe areas are concerned. The Balkans and Korea in the 1947–50 period and the Mediterranean in more recent years were especially susceptible to a great power clash because they constituted the "soft ground" for mutual probing and testing by the superpowers of each other's strength. In the Balkans and in Korea the United States policy dictated a somewhat contradictory course of action in the immediate postwar years. In the Balkans the policy was to move in to fill a security gap left by the withdrawing British; and in Korea it was to move out in response to American domestic pressures for withdrawal, while still retaining some kind of a security presence in the area. The United Nations became, in the hands of the United States, a handy tool to implement both these policies. UN involvement in Greece helped the United States administration to "sell" to Congress—and to the American public—new security commitments that it felt obliged to undertake to meet what it saw as a tide of Soviet expansion in Eastern Europe and in the Mediterranean. In Korea, the United States administration managed to get the United Nations committed to preserving the security of South Korea against possible encroachments from the North. This permitted the United States to withdraw a large part of its ground forces from Korea between 1948 to 1950, while still leaving the door open for a comeback were South Korea to be attacked from the North, as indeed happened in the summer of 1950.

The United States was able to attain these objectives within the UN organization because of the considerable, if not total, influence it was able to exert over that organization during the first ten years of its life. Despite vehement protests by the Soviet Union over the United Nations' interventions in the Balkans and in Korea and its attempt to frustrate the intervention by using the veto in the Security Council, the United States was still able to mobilize the United Nations by resorting to the General Assembly. It was through the United States' ability to mobilize support that the UN Special Committee on the Balkans was created in 1947 to observe the borders between Greece and its communist neighbors. In Korea also, the United States was able to persuade the United Nations to send first a temporary commission (UNTCOK), consisting of some thirty observers from the UN secretariat with the task of supervising elections in North and South Korea, and later in 1948 a second commission (UNCOK) to observe the thirty-eighth parallel. It was UNCOK's reporting of the North Korean invasion in 1950 that provided the factual basis for the subsequent Korean military operation of the United Nations.

By the time of the Cyprus crisis a decade and a half later the fear of Soviet expansion had considerably decreased. Nonetheless, the Mediterranean remained the soft underbelly of the Western defense system that made it vulnerable to Soviet penetration, and there were increasing signs of Soviet attempts to establish a naval presence in the Mediterranean. From the West's viewpoint the UN peacekeeping force in Cyprus, besides providing a buffer between the Greek and Turkish Cypriots in the hope that they would reach a negotiated settlement with a minimum of violence, was there to create a peaceful stability on the island and an intercommunal détente that would remove any excuse for penetration by the Soviet Union.

It was, however, in those areas formerly under colonial administration that the United Nations conducted its main peacekeeping operations during the late 1950s and the 1960s. It is worth consideration how this came about and was acceptable. It would be historically incorrect to suggest that the peacekeeping function that the United Nations fulfilled in the emerging Third World was directed solely at controlling the violence generated by the breakdown of the colonial order. Rather, it was a function born of global politics, in which the two superpowers were competing against each other to establish their hegemony in the areas from which the imperial powers were withdrawing. As long as the old colonial power could control the situation itself, the United Nations did not (and could not) intervene. In Algeria, for example, a million people lost their lives in fighting for their freedom, but the United Nations was kept out. The Mau Mau insurrection in Kenya was at times even more violent than that in present-day Rhodesia, but the United Nations was kept out of that too. It is when the administrating power loses control of the situation, thus creating "soft ground" for the cold war to penetrate, that the United Nations sees a legitimate peacekeeping role for itself.

Rather than risk the possibility of Soviet penetration into those "soft ground" situations, the United States sought to involve the

United Nations wherever and whenever such a threat existed. The Soviet Union certainly did not have any interest in maintaining a system based on a Western European colonial order, although it behaved no differently from the Western nations whenever its own hegemony in Eastern Europe was challenged. Thus, the USSR took the side of the anti-colonial Third World countries in making demands for immediate independence for colonial areas. But it could not force the issue of decolonization on the nations of Western Europe so long as the United States stood by the side of its allies. All that the USSR could do was to threaten to subvert colonial regimes by materially or morally assisting the liberation forces and, so far as it was able, to embarrass the United States in the eyes of the Third World.

It is in this Soviet threat, and not in the struggle for liberation by the colonial peoples, nor indeed in the degree of violence used by the colonial powers or by the liberation forces (witness Algeria and Angola), that the United States perceived a danger to "its international order." Given the anti-colonial traditions of the United States (though one should not overlook the fact that it has its own "colonial" administrations in the South Pacific), it might have been expected that it would have actively backed the revolution of the Afro-Asians. In the context of global politics it was, however, generally impossible for the United States actively to support the desecration of the empires of its Western European allies, if this were to pave the way for possible Soviet domination and for weakening of the Western alliance. The United States therefore assisted its allies in resisting the colonial revolution, as indeed it is indirectly doing today along with other Western nations, by supplying arms to Portugal which is using them to suppress the colonial rebellions of Angola and Mozambique. But while the United States has given assistance in some areas, this has clearly not been a wise course of action in every instance. Suppression of colonial revolutions could play into the hands of the Soviets just as much as could over-rapid decolonization. In general, therefore, successive American administrations, with varying degrees of enthusiasm, have preferred the long-term strategy of encouraging an ordered decolonization.

It is in this context that the United States sees UN peacekeeping operations as being useful—as a device to prevent possible Sovietization of a colonial conflict by bringing it within the framework of international action through which the United States can exert discreet pressure over its colonial allies. The various UN mediation and truce supervisory commissions sent to Indonesia during 1948–49 provide excellent illustrations in this respect. In this category would also belong the early Palestinian war; the military interventions of Britain, France, and Israel against Egypt in 1956 following the nationalization of the Suez Canal; and the first Congo crisis of 1960–64. Although these disputes were not strictly colonial, they were either the outcome of an imperial withdrawal (Palestine, 1948, and Congo, 1960) or an attempt to reimpose what has been described as a ''neocolonial'' order (British and French action against Egypt). In these cases the subsequent peacekeeping operations provided the means for preventing Soviet infiltration while at the same time made it possible for the United States to bring pressure to bear on its allies to withdraw their special interests from these areas or at least to reduce them.

The other scenario in which the United Nations operated in its peacekeeping capacity was, of course, where instability within and between new states followed their emergence from colonial rule into independent nationhood. Its opportunities for action in these circumstances have not been total, for these have depended, as in other situations, upon the interests of a global balance of power rather than upon the degree of violence or instability involved.

So far as internal disorders were concerned, there was no question of the United Nations' stepping into the shoes of the colonial powers to maintain a regime of quasi-imperial peace. Only in West New Guinea, because of certain peculiarities of the situation, did the United Nations move in to administer the territory before handing it over to Indonesia. Both in the Congo and in Cyprus the United Nations was concerned primarily with the disruptive global potentialities of the two situations rather than with the substantive aspects of the disputes. In the Congo the United Nations ultimately intervened to break the Katanga deadlock, but until then the emphasis, as in Cyprus, was on helping to maintain internal order so that the parties might reach a settlement through negotiation. The United Nations' role in the Congo expanded as a result of a combination of certain factors that were not anticipated when the operation was launched. Ironically, or perhaps not so ironically, the experience of the United Nations in the Congo had the effect, not of encouraging further such ventures by the United Nations, but of discouraging them (partially in Cyprus; wholly in the Nigerian civil war).

Both in Palestine and in Kashmir, the exigencies of global politics dictated the incidence and mode of the UN peacekeeping operations. During the India-Pakistan war of 1965 there was a possibility, albeit a remote one, of persuading India to accept a settlement on Kashmir or face the predicament of confronting enemies on two fronts, namely Pakistan and China. But nothing came of it; the consensus between the Soviet Union and the Western nations was limited to preventing a possible Chinese take-over of the conflict; and although they were quickly able to concert their policies of arms limitation to stop the hostilities, no peace settlement followed the Tashkent negotiations.

Disagreement among the big powers obstructed any immediate move on their part to intervene to stop the Arab-Israeli hostilities in June 1967. By the time they did attempt to take action, Israel had occupied considerable Arab territory. The Security Council's resolution of 22 November 1967 laid down a possible basis for settlement of the Arab-Israeli conflict, but in the deepening division between the Soviet Union and the United States, aligned respectively on the side of the Arab states and Israel, the two powers were reluctant to compel the parties to implement the United Nations resolution. The United States (there is no evidence of the Soviet Union being similarly inclined) has found itself faced on occasions with the dual predicament of having, on the one hand, to force Israel to accept certain peace proposals made by the UAR and yet feeling compelled, on the other hand, to supply Israel with the badly needed Phantom jets to maintain an arms balance with the MIG fighters supplied to the UAR by the USSR.

In Palestine and in Kashmir, the United States' peacekeeping role was related first and foremost to the demands of global peace under which, no matter how many people died locally and how much territory changed hands, it was important that the conflict should not escalate to involve the great powers in a general war. This is not to deny that the UN Military Observer Group in India and Pakistan (UNMOGIP), the UN Truce Supervision Organization in Palestine (UNTSO), and the UN Emergency Force (UNEF) had a significant local function as well—that of trying to keep the belligerents apart. It is debatable, however, whether or not this latter function was essentially a spin-off from the primary function, that of insulating the conflicts from global repercussions that might lead to general warfare.

It is this broad analysis of conflict strategy and the effect of the superpowers' influence on the peacekeeping actions of the United Nations in the past that concerns us as we turn our attention to the matter of conflict identification and to the possibilities of conflict control. Possibly the most important question to be answered is: Peacekeeping to what end? The world has the choice. Either it can take global peace and international stability as its focal point and then do precisely what the United Nations has been doing in the past—namely, identifying those conflict issues which are likely to endanger that peace and stability—or it can take violence as its focal point and then identify those conflict issues that are likely to lead to violence, whether localized or globalized. It is important to understand the distinction between the two and to appreciate that there is a choice available. Both can be said to have their relevance and their application, but whereas the first is concerned primarily with international stability, the second provides an alternative to enforcement action (counterviolence) as a means of resolving international disputes. Violence in any degree under the first option is itself immaterial, regardless of the numbers killed or maimed in the process, so long as it does not upset the global system or stability. For the second option violence is an anathema; where possible it must be controlled in order that the parties to a dispute can make the attempt to resolve their differences by peaceful means.

It seems to be a valid and reasonable contention that the world should move from the first option to the second, the primary consideration being a moral one. The arguments for doing so have been set out in an earlier chapter, where the point was made that while enforcement may be unavoidable at times, it does not always yield the required results. Indeed, a resort to counterviolence may stiffen the resistance of the adversary, or at worst annihilate him along with the problem itself, which for a variety of reasons including that of morality is most unlikely to bring about the best or even a satisfactory solution. What the peacekeeping instrument might be expected to achieve is a diffusion of violence while the parties to a conflict work out a more equitable adjustment of the situation in which they may have been trapped. In this context, peacekeeping makes no distinction between those instances of violence that threaten to embroil great powers in local conflicts and those that simply kill people. Indeed, if the instrumentality of peacekeeping was found to be useful in containing violence in order to localize conflicts, why should its use not be extended to cover all conflicts with a violent potential, whether or not they endanger international security?

This catholic concept of peacekeeping broadens the horizon of possible situations in which peacekeeping might play a constructive role. Any war would in itself be a justification for action by the world community and its consideration as to whether the particular war was a legitimate area for peacekeeping treatment; peacekeeping intervention would not be conditional on whether or not there was likely to be a great power involvement. In order to arrive at a specific identification of the kinds of conflicts for which control possibilities exist, we need to diagnose conflict symptoms and their potential threat of violence.

In the preceding chapter an attempt was made to analyze the trends in the international system, which would dictate the characteristics of conflict control. Without going into detail as to how conflict situations actually develop, one can classify them into four general categories. The first is *conflict at the global level,* involving two or more major powers. In the past two decades the world has witnessed the cold war between the Soviet and the Western powers, particularly over Berlin and the former's fear of encirclement. But now the cold war has much abated; Eastern and Western Europe are talking of European security; and the world is no longer as bipolarized as it was. China has joined the ranks of the superpowers, politically if not as yet militarily; and on the horizon are two other quasi-superpowers— an integrated Europe and Japan.

The ramifications of the evolution of a multipolarized world are yet to unfold. There are already some signs of these: the possible full military withdrawal of the United States from the Far East and the consequent emergence of China and Japan as the main contenders for political and economic hegemony in Asia; the partial or full military withdrawal of the United States from Western Europe and the much discussed European détente, with the nations of Eastern and Western Europe appearing to be working for a political and territorial stabilization in Europe, a collaboration in the areas of trade, and an exchange of technological know-how; the sharpening of economic rivalry between Europe and the United States; the hostility between the Soviet Union and China over ideological and territorial matters.

These are all issues at the level of superpower politics. The questions looked at from the perspective of peacekeeping are whether there are any signs that these developments are likely to take a violent turn and if so what form the violence will take.

An important and relevant factor in all this is the increasing demilitarization of conflicts in the Western world with the correlation that there is an increasing willingness to adopt diplomatic negotiations as a means of resolving differences. The Soviet–West German negotiations of 1972–73 and the Strategic Arms Limitation Talks are pointers in this direction. There are less obvious signs that Soviet-Chinese relations are taking a similar course in favor of a commitment to negotiated settlements. Indeed, the Soviet Union may well be making its peace in the West in order to prepare itself better for a possible confrontation in the East. A short war on the Sino-Soviet borders may not be ruled out, nor the possibility of continuing border skirmishes, with the ever present danger of escalation. The United States' disputes with Europe, on the other hand, are restricted to economic questions and are highly unlikely to be militarized. All in all, therefore, so far as the superpower relations are concerned, there is little evidence (apart from the Sino-Soviet conflict) that they are likely to settle their disputes, at least in the area of their immediate geographic concerns, by means of violence. This does not rule out their participation, directly or by proxy, in other peoples' wars in other parts of the world.

The second category is *conflict at the regional level,* a localized phenomenon though capable of developing into wider global conflict if one or more of the big powers were to decide to intervene. Innumerable possibilities exist within the world's regional groupings for interstate disputes to escalate into violence. In Africa alone there are already the conflicts in southern Africa between South Africa and the African states (a situation that could easily become an Israel-Arab type of confrontation); the territorial disputes between Somalia and Ethiopia and Somalia and Kenya; the occasional border skirmishes between Tanzania and Uganda and Tanzania and Portuguese-held Mozambique; the possibilities of a clash between the Sudan and Chad or between Zaire and the Congo. In addition, there are the continuing conflicts in the Middle East between the Arabs and Israelis and among the Arabs themselves; and on the Asian continent, between India and Pakistan and India and China. Even Europe itself has witnessed incidents of violence in situations that are difficult to identify. (The Icelandic fishing dispute is a case in point that would have been difficult to anticipate a few years ago.)

In the category of regionally defined conflicts we need to include those that might take place in the relations between the Soviet Union and its East European allies and between the United States and its Latin American neighbors, of which we already have the examples of Hungary (1956) and Czechoslovakia (1968), on the one hand, and Guatemala (1954), Cuba (1958), the Dominican Republic (1965), and Panama (1973), on the other. When the superpowers become involved, they are likely whenever possible to use their economic superiority among other means to enforce obedience and subordination. Past history has shown that they have resorted to violent methods where other means have failed, and in similar circumstances they could be expected to use them again. It could also be that the oppressed nations will become so bold as to challenge the might of the superpowers by increasingly sophisticated methods of organized guerrilla warfare. Though this type of conflict fits more exactly into the next category, it can include economic embargo, such as the withholding of oil by the Arab countries, by which means Third World countries could hold the industrialized powers to ransom.

The third category with which we are concerned is *intrastate conflict,* originating essentially within states even though it may have external causes or may open the way for external intervention. Many observers predict that civil violence will probably be the commonest form of violence in the future world. If true, the reasons for this are not entirely related to the instability of new states, though this is undoubtedly a factor in the equation. The reasons in most cases are far more complex. Underlying most civil strife is the basic feeling of deprivation and injustice felt by sections of society against a dominant class. The commonest variety of this, at least in the Third World, is where the dominant class has become a malleable instrument of the Western powers. Across the world, from the Philippines and Vietnam, through the length and breadth of Africa, to the republics of Latin America, the oppressed are becoming increasingly aware that they are the primary victims of the exploitation in which the rich industrialized states and their own opulent ruling classes are the unholy collaborators. Because in most instances the instruments of peaceful social change are not available, resistance against neoimperialist domination therefore takes the form of violent action against the regimes in power. These latter also retaliate with all the counter-violence at their command, often being backed, in many cases openly, by external powers who have vested interests in suppressing the oppressed.

Of course not all civil strife is caused by this kind of situation. Some is the product of leadership crisis (Uganda in 1971–72), some of tribal antagonism (Burundi in 1972), some of racial conflict (Indonesia in 1967–68), and some of a combination of factors (the Nigerian civil war in 1967–70). Whatever the causes, in terms of sheer violence and brutality, civil strife can often surpass interstate wars.

Finally, there is the fourth category of conflict, which is sometimes referred to as *"north-south" conflict.* It arises out of the feeling of deprivation and exploitation that the peoples of the underdeveloped countries feel about their relations with the developed parts of the world. In an earlier decade this conflict manifested itself mainly in the political arena of colonialism. The whole anti-colonial rebellion was an attempt to break away from the system of imperial order in Africa and Asia. The rebellion found support in the United Nations and derived benefit from the cold war. Now that most of Africa and Asia are politically liberated, they find themselves economically no better off than before, for they are still within the system and dependent upon an economic order directed mainly from Brussels, London, New York, and Paris. This essentially is what the "north-south" conflict is about, but it does not necessarily follow that the conflict in manifest terms will be between the Northern and Southern hemispheres. In fact this is the least likely course that the eruption of violence would take. For one thing, neither the north nor the south is a monolithic bloc, the south even less so than the north. For another, the discontent of the southern hemisphere is likely to express itself mostly in rhetorical terms, as in the periodic meetings of the United Nations Conference on Trade and Development, for it has no military capability to match the power of the northern states. And finally, most of the southern states are, in any case, ruled by regimes that may have vested interests in maintaining a status quo. Therefore any north-south conflict is more likely to express itself in the form of a revolt by the masses in the south against their own oppressive regimes. In the meantime, however, individual countries in the south that fall into the hands of revolutionary regimes may indulge in isolated actions against those northern states who are exercising this economic control and influence over them; however, by so doing, they are likely to become largely isolated as a result of economic boycott. They may then either return to the fold after a successful counter-revolution or become internally totalitarian in order to force the population to make more and more sacrifices for the sake of building a self-reliant economy for future generations. Whichever situation may develop, there is considerable potential for violence.

From the above it must be evident that conflicts cannot be classified into neat compartments. Classification is only a heuristic device to help analysis. Thus, a civil strife that starts as a revolt of the people against an oppressive regime can easily become internationalized through the intervention of a major world power in support of one of the parties to the dispute, and may even escalate into a global war, directly or by proxy, between two or more major world powers.

What then are the possibilities for controlling such categories of conflict and their attendent violence through the international instrument of peacekeeping? We have already advocated the abandonment of the restricted concept of peacekeeping which reduces its function to that of ensuring that a conflict does not lead to general war between the major powers—a form of local anesthetic. Instead we have underlined the point that violence itself, and not just its escalating potential, should be a cause for world concern.

This leads to the question whether any outbreak of violence is a justification for a peacekeeping intervention. Is it justified in the case of communal violence between Flemish- and French-speaking Belgians, or English- and French-speaking Canadians, or Gujarati- and Marathi-speaking Indians? Is this kind of violence and that between the black and white communities of North America and Europe any different from the violence occasioned by the conflicts between the Greeks and the Turks in Cyprus or betweeen the white and the black South Africans? If we abandon the premiss that peacekeeping is only legitimate where conflicts are in danger of being internationalized, do we not open the floodgates for international intervention in all kinds of internal and international disputes?

Clearly there is a need to differentiate between those conflicts that are legitimate matters of a sovereign state and those that are quasi-domestic in as much as they evolve within states still under colonial administrations. Since the latter can be described as imposed rather than elected administrations, there is some justification for the international community to take a serious and active interest in them, even before the disputes have reached such a point of escalation that there is a clear danger of external intervention or of mass genocide. Indeed, while the world waits for a dispute to reach a high point of escalation in order to justify its intervention, the parties concerned may well have taken positions that are so firm that only a military victory by one or the other could conceivably resolve the dispute. Article 39 of the UN Charter provides the authority for action, but it is an authority that has never been invoked.

One must also remember that peacekeeping is not an end in itself. Its primary justification is that it helps to demilitarize a situation so that the parties to the dispute can go back to the negotiating table to work out a peaceful settlement, with or without third-party mediation. Of course, this is easier said than done. The Palestine and Cyprus disputes amply illustrate that negotiated settlements are not easily reached. On the other hand, they also illustrate that the use of military force need not necessarily be the answer either. What is obviously required is that peacekeeping should be associated with vigorous efforts by the world community, as well as by the parties involved, to seek a just and peaceful settlement of disputes.

At no time must a peacekeeping operation become an instrument in the hands of an oppressive regime to insulate itself against the just grievances of the oppressed people. If a peacekeeping force were deployed in a situation where a ruling minority group was beleaguered by liberation forces, its role could only be the humanitarian one of facilitating the evacuation of the beleagured before they were decimated. This would be a legitimate use of a peacekeeping operation. It would be out of the question for the operation to be used to safeguard the position of the regime, for this, by implication, would characterize the peacekeeping force itself as an oppressive agent.

There are, then, two capacities in which a peacekeeping operation can help to diffuse conflict situations—one prior to and the other subsequent upon its deployment. As matters stand, a peacekeeping operation can be implemented only at the request of or with the consent of the host country or countries. The acceptance of a peacekeeping force, therefore, can constitute an important step in cementing a broader agreement between the parties to the dispute. A good example of this was at Suez in 1956 when the establishment of UNEF was instrumental in facilitating the settlement whereby Britain, France, and Israel agreed to withdraw their forces from the canal area. It was the idea of a UN peacekeeping force rather than its actual presence that was the persuasive factor. When UNEF ultimately came to Egypt, it fulfilled its second peacekeeping capacity as a neutral buffer force between the combatants. Similarly, it can be claimed that the proposal to set up an international control commission to supervise the implementation of the Vietnam armistice agreement in 1973 helped to cement the agreement for a cease-fire between the four parties involved in the Vietnam War, even though the commission subsequently found it difficult to carry out its operational functions. It is important, therefore, to recognize the duality of the potential effect that a peacekeeping operation can have on a conflict situation, in that there is value in the idea as well as in the actual presence of a peacekeeping instrument, even when the big powers are physically involved in a conflict.

In future conflict situations it will require boldness and imagination to utilize to advantage the idea and presence of peacekeeping forces as a means of demilitarizing such situations and contributing to a political settlement. The scope of peacekeeping operations need not be confined simply to that of guarding frontiers or occupying buffer zones between two likely combatants, nor to that of supervision and observation of armistice lines and cease-fire agreements. As a later chapter suggests, the range of tasks that third-party initiatives can fulfill is broad, involving civilians as much as soldiers. The examples of ONUC and UNTEA are cases in point. A list of responsibilities could well include supervising of plebiscites or elections (Korea, 1949, and West New Guinea, 1969); supervising of arms control agreements; assisting in land or sea measures as directed by the Security Council to counter arms smuggling and sanction breaking; providing relief services for conflict and natural disaster situations (ONUC civilian operation and Peru earthquake, 1970); establishing temporary administrations in an interregnum (West New Guinea, with Namibia as a possible recipient of this kind of operation in the future). These are but some examples of a typology of peacekeeping action deserving serious consideration for the future. Their objective should always be, first, to assist, in a nonpartisan manner, the parties in a dispute in reaching agreement and, subsequently, if called upon to do so, to help supervise the agreement reached. If this fundamental principle of nonpartisanship were accepted universally, it is not difficult to think of a number of ways in which peacekeeping operations might be used to demilitarize conflicts both between and within states.

This may appear to be too optimistic a view of the potentialities of peacekeeping. We are, of course, not unaware of the numerous political obstacles that all too often hinder the use of the peacekeeping formula as a means to demilitarizing conflict situations. Parties to a conflict usually wish for a partisan third-party intervention favorable to their point of view rather than a neutral buffer force standing between them and their adversary. While one recognizes that specific remedies may not be immediately forthcoming to meet the ills of present-day and future international society, in the mechanism of the peacekeeping force there is a readily available means by which conflict situations can be temporarily insulated from violence while ways are found to reach negotiated settlements.

13

Strengthening United Nations Machinery

In chapter 3 we investigated the Charter and the peacekeeping organs that were designed to implement it and suggested a framework on which a more effective and efficient working machine might be structured. As a preface to a wider study of how that framework could be supported and thereby strengthened from below, we intend at this point to focus our attention again on the UN organization and propose some organic additions to it, which in our view would constructively improve its management of peacekeeping.

Our analysis of case studies has shown the variety of situations in which international peacekeeping has been required to function. It has underlined the fact that peacekeeping is not purely a military responsibility but requires a collection of professional skills. The case studies illustrate emphatically the deficiencies and shortcomings of peacekeeping operations when mounted and conducted on an ad hoc basis. They also illustrate the ability of a multinational force of military and civilians to overcome structural and operational problems despite the ad hoc nature of its creation. Therefore, before we turn to the nuts and bolts of preparedness and preparation outside the United Nations, it is logical to consider what else might be done within the organization to simplify the problems of peacekeeping at the initiation and planning levels.

Although a strong military involvement in the functioning of the United Nations organization has always been resisted and the idea that the secretary-general should be given a military staff to help with the management of peacekeeping operations firmly rejected, experience has shown that the operational handling of peacekeeping forces requires an advisory body of some kind available to the secretary-general, over and above the existing permanent secretariat staff. Until 1969 a military adviser [1] fulfilled the role of military expert on the thirty-eighth floor; [2] the post then lapsed and instead the post of military liaison officer was created. The military adviser acted in a purely advisory capacity to the secretary-general and had no operational planning or coordinating responsibilities. His role therefore did not equate to the kind of staffing that we will be suggesting here. When the opportunity arose, his post was made redundant, giving credence to the fact that the Security Council was prepared to accept the operational shortcomings and disorganization that have beset the initial phases of their peacekeeping efforts, rather than retain the presence of a military adviser in a senior position in the secretariat. This ostrichlike prejudice is just one of the many stumbling blocks that will need to be removed before an effective machine can be evolved.

However desirable contingency planning may be, few would argue that, in the present political climate within the United Nations, preplanning for peacekeeping operations could be in anything but very broad terms, and in no way particular in application. This does not, however, preclude the study of organizational and logistical design, nor necessarily the consideration of the suitability and standard of preparedness of the contribution that any member country can make. This has been hinted at before as a possible area in which the Military Staff Committee might be expected to operate. Alternatively, as we will suggest, planning could be done by an interprofessional body at secretariat level, where it would have the advantage of being a part of the support organization for UN operations of any kind. Wherever the responsibility may ultimately come to rest, such preplanning should be perfectly possible without disturbing any political dovecotes.

Observer missions and force level operations conducted by the United Nations pose a different set of problems from those faced in the more traditional style of military operations and represent a new approach to conflict control within the international arena. The employment of a police force in a third-party role to control internal (national) disturbances is well understood and accepted, but the employment of military force in a third-party role, acting as an instrument of conflict control in international conflicts, has very few precedents.

1. Major General I. J. Rikhye held the post from 1959 to 1968.
2. The floor in the United Nations where the secretary-general and his immediate staff advisers have their offices.

The homogeneous political environment, the common set of values, and the ensuing codified law system form the basis for the use of an instrument of force inside a nation-state. Nothing comparable exists for the global community of nations, and it is therefore not surprising that the use of military force in a third-party role, though accepted by interested parties, does create new problems that cannot necessarily be settled in a purely military fashion.

The scope of problems connected with the command and control of field operations and the work load these problems create warrant a separate staff element to cope with them at the highest political level. The translation of politically initiated objectives and operational orders into practical military objectives is not always easy—and is not made any less complex by the often ambiguously worded resolutions that emerge from the Security Council. Since the resolution is the basic authorizing document of any UN peacekeeping operation, it is of the utmost importance that those responsible for its interpretation get it right. The ambiguity is often deliberate, in order either to achieve consensus at the voting stage in the Council or to avoid defining the mandate too precisely for political reasons vis-à-vis the United Nations and the host country. Nevertheless, this ambiguity can make the task of the commander in the field a difficult one. It would be the job of the staff element mentioned earlier to translate the mandate into more precise terms of reference for him and his subordinate commanders.

Where in the organization the staff component would be located is a matter of opinion; we suggest two possibilities. Whether it would have a permanent or on-call status would also have to be decided. In our view such a staff element must be positioned where the "action" is, that is, where the responsibility for operational command and control is vested, where the operational procurement and deployment of forces are planned and implemented. It is here that expert assistance in the day-to-day management of operations is required; and since, inevitably, much if not all of the responsibility for the operational administrative support of manpower and materials will fall on the shoulders of the secretary-general and his staff, it seems sensible that the staff be located in the secretariat. To be acceptable, however, the staff would have advisory status only and would be primarily responsible to the Security Council for its actions. The alternative, that the Military Staff Committee should act as the sponsoring body, would not necessarily be an impractical arrangement, though the committee's emphasis is on strategy rather than on the tactical nuts and bolts of field operations, for which it is not presently organized. The committee's solely military character is not designed to manage what should be a multiprofessional staff team, but were the committee to be redesigned on a broader base, it could be better equipped to sponsor the kind of staff component envisaged here.

We are concerned not so much with positioning as with the development of a top-level structure that would be viable and acceptable to member states as an international conflict control system. Any staffing of this structure needs to relate to the support requirements of field operations in both military and civilian respects, entailing the inclusion of the whole gamut of professional and technical skills relevant to conflict problems and involving the participation of diplomats, soldiers, civil servants, politicians, international lawyers, police officers, and action-oriented scholars and sociologists. Their responsibilities would include the preparation and coordination of all functional aspects of a peacekeeping operation; the management of the physical requirements of manning, staffing, and organization; the analysis and dissemination of current and background data about the particular conflict situation; and the setting up of the communication and administrative support that is needed. It could be further required to act in an overall coordinating capacity for the field force's requirements once the mounting phase has been completed and the force has become fully operational. Though this proposal may be viewed as overly optimistic and unlikely to be wholly acceptable to member states, it does represent a constructive approach to the establishment of a sound and creative central control system that does not exist at the moment, but that could be developed within the framework of the Charter and within the existing structural institutions of the United Nations. Essentially it needs to be multiprofessional because one cannot separate in practice the political, legal, economic, social, and military aspects of peacekeeping. Any UN operation therefore has to be studied in the widest perspective. In normal military planning at the national level separate staff departments draw up procurement plans (men and equipment); collate information; devise an effective command structure and communications system; develop new ideas on conflict identification, escalation control, and innovative methods for the handling of conflicts. It is therefore reasonable to expect that operations of a more complex and interprofessional nature, like those of the United Nations, require a staffing component that is specifically oriented to their needs. Since this is such an important matter, it is worth spending a little time on a more detailed examination of the requirements of a central staff organization at UN headquarters.

In contrast to what has been recommended, there is at UN headquarters in New York only a small team of experienced diplomats and international civil servants serving the secretary-general as a kind of tactical staff for international crisis. This small staff does not have adequate facilities for analyzing past peacekeeping operations or for making preparations to meet potential new conflict situations. No data bank exists with detailed background information available for easy reference. The UN telecommunications system is notoriously inadequate.

Any realistic approach to the central staff problem has to give due recognition to the understandable apprehension on the part of the UN secretariat to the development of a permanent staff hierarchy based on military formalism. However, this hesitancy should not be allowed to become an overriding factor, to be used against any proposed development of the central control organization; for the emphasis is on the use of the "politically and professionally experienced" and not on establishing a military power base. However, bearing in mind the natural distrust of a "military take-over," the suggestions that follow are modest in scope and flexible in use and fall into three functional categories:

1. conflict control
2. conflict identification
3. communications

Conflict Control   The existing small staff of experts in the secretary-general's office cannot be considered adequate for handling crises when a UN operation of magnitude is organized and sent into the field. Our present proposal provides for a custom-made element to reinforce the permanent team and assist it with the many additional tasks thrown upon the secretary-general's office in moments of international crisis:

—negotiations with host state (or states) on status of forces agreements;

—negotiations with contributing states on manpower and equipment commitments;

—drafting of terms of reference for the force or mission commander, based on the Security Council resolution;

—preparation of standard operating procedures for the field force;

—negotiations with states on rights of overflight and/or staging-through permission;

—structuring the organization for the field command and control machinery;

—planning and arranging for the transportation of the force and its equipment into the operational area;

—preparation of the logistic support in the operational area;

—collection and processing of background information relevant to both the conflict and to the area of operations;

—preparation of a telecommunications network securing rapid communications to and from the field headquarters.

Depending on the nature of the operation, members of the conflict control staff could be drawn from any of the following categories: diplomats experienced in international negotiations; civil servants with experience in governmental departments dealing with matters of conflict and its resolution; politicians experienced in international affairs and international relations; military officers, preferably with previous command or staff experience in peacekeeping operations; international lawyers; senior police officers, preferably with experience of peacekeeping operations. It is expected that the individuals concerned would be selected on a multinational basis from a number of nations so that the different geographical and ideological groupings within the United Nations would be represented. Priority, however, should be given to the inclusion of representatives from those nations with the greatest experience in the field of international peacekeeping, including mediation and negotiation.

The reason for mixing the various professional categories in a conflict control team is to ensure a broad balance of expertise in the evaluation of events as they develop, both in the conflict itself and so far as the field operation is concerned, so that a correct third-party attitude can be maintained throughout the operation. The military skills of organization, technique, discipline, operational aptitude, logistic support arrangements, and, not least, information collection and collation are of paramount importance to the success of any field operation. However, these are not by any means the only skills involved. The other categories of people who we have suggested should make up the conflict control staff have their own valuable skills, and these must be fully utilized in the peaceful settlement of disputes.

Conflict Identification   The last quarter of a century has seen the emergence of many new nations, and almost all of them have been or are involved in one way or another in economic and social conflicts. It is therefore very important to find a means for dealing with these varied and developing conflict situations through institutional peace maintenance procedures. Experience shows that the UN peacekeeping machinery too often is applied only at a late stage in the developmentof a dispute. Apart from the basic lack of unanimity among the permanent members of the Security Council and their power of veto, which often prevents early action and diminishes that organ's capability for exercising its responsibilities, difficulties also arise over the distinction between internal and interstate conflict and the interpretation of an "incipient" dispute, which provoke hesitancy in the United Nations' executive body and delay decision. Were the Security Council to develop a broader structure for dealing with peace maintenance problems and procedures, these difficulties would disappear. But within any broader structure there has to be a built-in early warning system that would alert the Council to the danger potential of any developing conflict situation before it passes the incipient phase and bursts into full-scale violence.

This is not an original thought, since over the years suggestions have been put forward to increase the ability of the United Nations to gather, collate, and disseminate information. It would, however, be wrong to suppose that the United Nations is meagerly supplied with information. Prominent among its sources is the secretary-general himself. The secretary-general frequently meets with permanent representatives of nations and with their foreign ministers and heads of state. He travels a great deal, learning firsthand about many of the developing problems. Not only has he easy access to overt information, but he is the confidant of many governments and organizations, which provide him with information that is not otherwise easily available. Thus, the role of the secretary-general in providing early warning to the United Nations becomes vital, for he can draw attention to emerging situations through quiet diplomacy or through public statements. However, he needs to use his judgment on choosing his approach; he has to guard against contradicting Article 2(7) of the Charter, which prohibits the United Nations from intervening in matters within domestic jurisdiction.

The extent of the information collected in this way must be of a relatively prescribed nature, focused as it is on the secretary-general and his relations with governments and states. It does not emanate from a wide pattern of sources, nor does it necessarily emerge from the deeper strata of conflict or from a broad analysis deriving from specific close studies of potential conflict situations. Although the information so obtained is likely to be superficial, since it is inherent in politics (as it is with human nature) for governments or groups to release only those facts that they wish to be known, nevertheless it is comprehensive and probably as much as anyone could expect from overt sources. The importance of the secretary-general's role in this respect should not therefore be underestimated. Apart from him there are both government and nongovernment agencies providing a constant flow of reliable information to which the United Nations, like anyone else, has access, and not least there is the news media.

Member states have a duty to establish broad criteria for prompt action during the early growth of a conflict. They need to assess the imminence of a threat to international peace and the extent of any violation of human rights that may acquire such an intensity as to arouse the concern of the international community. In the Bangladesh and Biafra conflicts the United Nations and its secretary-general had sufficient information. The Security Council, however, chose not to act. Member states have sometimes wished that the secretary-general would act more often under Article 99, which authorizes him to bring to the attention of the Security Council any matter that in his opinion may threaten the maintenance of international peace and security. The secretary-general has access to quiet or open diplomacy, and the effect of his intervention would depend entirely on which course is best suited for a particular situation.

There have been some UN fact-finding commissions that have

preempted conflict situations, but the majority have been concerned with active conflict and not with preventive diplomacy. Although in the early days of the United Nations it was proposed that the Security Council should form subgroups to consider problems relevant to incipient disputes and explore alternative approaches, nothing ever came of it; and it was left to Brazil to reopen the question in the Security Council.[3] Brazil's foreign minister reiterated his country's former proposal that the Security Council should, whenever the need arose, consider the advisability of setting up ad hoc committees specifically for the settlement of disputes, made up of the disputing parties and other delegations selected by the Council at their behest. This step was necessary in Brazil's view because the consultation processes of the Security Council were directed at collateral aspects of the problem and not toward a search for ways in which to eliminate the cause of the conflict; as a result the Council had been unable to ensure the implementation of its decisions. This appeal did not receive the support it deserved (though the United Kingdom was prepared to take a favorable view), since the permanent members of the Council held that informal consultations were continuing all the time among all of its members. Dag Hammarskjöld attempted to initiate a cabinet system by establishing a team of close secretariat officials, but this led to Khrushchev's demand that the post of secretary-general be replaced by a troika,[4] and the idea was therefore rejected by U Thant when he became secretary-general on Hammarskjöld's death.

There are of course some clearly defined indications of ultimate conflict, though these might only become apparent in the imminent phase; the movement of troops, ships, aircraft, and missiles often follows or precedes heightening of tensions. Increase in the number of incidents provides some indication, as does violation of any agreements. Incidents may lead to movement of population and creation of refugees. Last but not least, discrepancies in the administration of justice, disruptive justice, and nonrecognition of rights may eventually lead to open violence and dispute. There is no lack of indications present in the world today, sufficient to cause concern and calling for some form of action to stem the emerging conflicts.

Regional organizations have an increasing responsibility over the

3. General Assembly Session Twenty-five, Special Meeting of Foreign Ministers of Security Council Member States, October 1970.
4. Khrushchev's speech in the General Assembly on 23 September 1960.

whole spectrum of conflict control in its previolent stage and before it requires international intervention. No one would argue that it is better, if possible, for disputes to be confined and managed within regional control systems than for them to be brought to the United Nations. OAU and OAS have already achieved some successes in this direction, but so far the potential has not been fully developed. Nonpolitical and nongovernmental institutions can also play useful and important roles in the early and developing stages of a dispute by focusing attention on problems of justice, economy, and social needs, thereby counterbalancing the purely political considerations.

Institutions therefore exist that are capable of contributing data to assist in the reduction of world tensions. These institutions, however, are unfortunately all too often rendered ineffective because of the tendency of internal and interstate disputes to overlap, or, in the case of internal situations, due to external overtones. In the UN system, the Security Council, though charged with the primary responsibility for the maintenance and restoration of peace, is also too easily rendered ineffective through the threat of veto by one of its permanent members acting in support of one of the parties to a dispute, or is prevented from even considering certain disputes because they are deemed to be domestic and therefore covered by Article 2(7). In this procedural labyrinth in which the Security Council continually finds itself, the saving grace could be the secretary-general and a well-structured data monitoring system to provide early warning of potential conflicts—the former as a supplier of contemporary top-level information and initiator of preventive action; the latter as a coordinating and reporting body, providing the broadest range of background data.

For the conflict control system to achieve maximum effectiveness it needs to be fed all available data relative to the conflict with which it is required to deal, and which could determine the point at which it should become involved. An important lesson deriving from the study of conflict control during the post–World War II era concerns the timing of international involvement in conflict situations. It has been demonstrated that the earlier the conflict control procedure can start, the greater chance there is of avoiding an armed clash.[5] The timing often does raise insurmountable political difficulties, as it is the privilege of the interested parties to a conflict to request assistance

---

5. Lincoln P. Bloomfield and Amelia C. Leiss, *Controlling Small Wars.*

and not to have assistance imposed upon them. Nevertheless, the considerable experience acquired over the years in the study and handling of conflicts provides incomparable guidance material on which the conflict control team could draw. This material is not, but ought to be, in a central library at UN headquarters. Clearly it should be collected in one place in the hands of a well-qualified research team who could make it available at very short notice.

The conflict control team at the disposal of the secretary-general, in its task of preparing background material for responsible decision-making organs, will need a great variety of data. The requirement for data will comprise geographical, economic, political, and historical facts about the general conflict area and also details about the development of the current conflict. The research team that would be required to provide the data material for the planners and conflict control team should be established as an official UN agency. This "conflict monitoring support team" would include researchers from across a broad field of international conflict study and scholars who have specialized in research into current conflicts. Arrangements should exist to coopt those with a special knowledge of the geographical, economic, social, or political factors existing in the area in which a particular conflict has its setting. A possible breakdown of the staffing of the conflict monitoring support team might be:

1. one sociologist specializing in sociopsychological techniques in peaceful settlement of international disputes;
2. one historian specializing in the collation of documentary evidence in connection with frontier disputes;
3. one political scientist specializing in the use of computer-aided systems for handling information on local conflicts;
4. one information-handling specialist (military or civilian) for data collection and storage;
5. one conflict researcher specializing in internal conflicts, social change, and human rights.

In the search for new approaches to conflict settlement and new processes that might aid peaceful settlement, the value of sociopsychological techniques should not be ignored. Such techniques should be used in an effort to create new problem-solving attitudes in individuals concerned with conflict situations involving the use of armed forces. It is possible that the United Nations might from time to time be called upon to contain, as well as to settle, frontier disputes. The role of the United Nations in this connection may become relatively subordinate, but nevertheless will not be unimportant. The compilation of documentation on frontier disputes will continue, therefore, to have significant value. To assist in collating the data it would be advantageous to include within the monitoring team a small research group specifically for this work. The group could have ready access to copies of treaties, conventions, and protocols governing all present world frontiers and armistice lines. It would be helpful if the historian responsible for this area of research were to be permitted access to national archives in his search for material.

The development of a conflict monitoring support team would certainly be a gradual process with the various functions being shared at the start among two or three persons. To enable the team, when fully constituted, to yield maximum service, it should be supported by a computer-aided system for handling information on local conflicts, such as the one developed at the Massachusetts Institute of Technology in the United States (CASCONII) [6] which could serve as a useful tool for the UN officials engaged in crisis, or preferably pre-crisis diplomacy and decision making. Its capacity would be to store and, at will, reproduce data on an incipient conflict situation along with other stored data on past conflicts having a common denominator with the conflict under study in terms of violence-generating or violence-minimizing facts. Such data would be available to the members of the conflict control team and would be of considerable value to them in evaluating the factors and policy measures necessary to minimize the conflict with which they are currently coping. It is therefore necessary that there should be a close liaison between the conflict control team and the conflict monitoring support team, and it would seem sensible that there should be a physical link between the two. Since the correct interpretation of data information is very important, it would be equally sensible that the conflict control team should include scholars with a background of conflict theory and of its practical application, so that the maximum practical value could be obtained from the information available.

There are nongovernmental organizations that independently work for the peaceful settlement of disputes, both internal and interna-

6. Though still experimental it is hoped that when the system is fully developed it could serve as a backup to the memory bank of a conflict control team as envisaged here.

tional, and there is valuable experience and important information that can be gained through contact with these organizations. It would therefore seem logical that the monitoring support team maintain a close liaison with such organizations, since they are working privately for the same goals as the United Nations—the nonviolent regulation of disputes. This may or may not necessitate a separate liaison group within the conflict monitoring support team, but the important thing is that the liaison should exist.

Data from past conflicts will provide the background research material on which the monitoring support team could base its analysis and evaluation of patterns and trends of similar type conflicts. Equally important is the acquisition of data on current and potential conflicts. Such data could be expected to come from overt sources of observation and as a result of requests made directly to the nation-states concerned. The data bank should contain full and up-to-date information from which the conflict control team can itself provide prompt and frequent conflict assessments for the Security Council. To provide this continuous feedback of up-to-date information the conflict monitoring support team would need to incorporate a processing team, responsible for the collation and dissemination of the material so that it may be made quickly available to those immediately involved as negotiators, mediators, conciliators, or arbitrators.

Communications   The third and final functional category is communications. Quite apart from the information being collected from other sources for analysis and evaluation, there is a paramount need for a constant flow of information providing hour-by-hour, even minute-by-minute, reports on changing conflict situations. This third prerequisite for an efficiently functioning staff organization could be provided only by a satellite telecommunications network. The rapid scientific development and positioning of communication satellites has reached a point where worldwide events can be brought instantaneously to the home. It should be possible, therefore, for the United Nations to have its own telecommunication network to maintain up-to-the-minute coverage of what is happening anywhere in the world, so that it can respond immediately and effectively to disasters or emergencies whenever and wherever they occur. It goes without saying that it is mandatory for the world organization to have a better communications system than it has, so that it can better fulfill its day-to-day responsibilities for the maintenance of international peace and security.

The improvements suggested here for the provision of a more efficient system for the international identification, monitoring, and control of conflict are intended simply as a "bank" of ideas. What is impossible today because of political constraints may be possible tomorrow in different world political circumstances. It is therefore important to look forward with constructive, but controlled, imagination in order to be prepared to exploit the opportunities that progress may present for a more orderly management of conflicts in the international arena.

An effective machinery for the operational control of conflict depends very much on effective political initiatives. As the circumstances surrounding any particular conflict alter, there is a continuing requirement on the part of the Security Council to give political guidance as to the interpretation of the mandate within which a peacekeeping force has to operate. Up till now this guidance has tended to be provided by ad hoc political advisory committees formed for each individual operation and working through the secretary-general and not the Security Council.[7] However constructive that contribution may have been, clearly it is wrong that the political guidance should come from anywhere but the Security Council. A properly organized control system could assist the Security Council in providing the guidance and direction that is needed.

The Security Council, by right of the Charter, is the authorizing body within the United Nations for conflict control measures and operations. Regretfully, its membership does not always match up to this paramount responsibility. Article 23(1) requires that, when electing its nonpermanent members, the Council should pay due regard to the contribution that the countries can make toward the maintenance of international peace and security, besides providing for an equitable geographical distribution. It has been the latter proviso rather than the former that has more recently decided election to the Security Council. One cannot therefore ignore the fact that some of the member

7. E.g. UNEF, Secretary-General's Advisory Committee of representatives of contributing nations; and ONUC, the "Congo Club" consisting of a small group of advisers recruited personally by Dag Hammarskjöld.

states that form the nonpermanent membership of the Council do not always have the experience or capacity to give the political guidance that is so necessary. Therefore, in order to assist the Security Council in its conflict control role, it should have available to it all possible expertise on which it can base its decisions and directives. The kind of supporting structure that this chapter has outlined does therefore have a constructive relevance to the needs of an international conflict control system within the United Nations, based as it is on existing institutions and requiring no more than a realistic application of the Charter.

14

Education, Preparation, and Preparedness

The evaluation of the lessons deriving from the selected case studies and from the analysis of the present international political structure lead one, without much difficulty, to conclude that the incidence, pattern, and character of conflicts are unlikely to change much, if at all, in the foreseeable future. Conflict and violence control therefore will be matters of continuing importance and relevance. A purposeful determination will be required if conflict is not to spread to a point where it escalates into a third world war, with all that that implies in nuclear terms. Therefore the strengthening of the United Nations' capacity to maintain peace and security should be seen as a prerequisite to creating an effective conflict control system, and as a political responsibility requiring the objective support of all member states whatever their size.

The strengthening of the machinery for mounting UN peacekeeping operations will also depend on political intent. It goes without saying that the development and conduct of such operations will depend on the efficiency of the conflict control system. The case studies have underlined the weaknesses inherent in the present machinery, whether it be UN, regional, or multinational. However, our study of world strategic trends and political attitudes has shown us that whatever is built in the way of a conflict control system has to be constructed, and contrived, around the Charter as it stands; it would be unrealistic at this time to think otherwise. This precludes any radical change in the mounting process of future operations and, so far as the United Nations is concerned, patently restricts them to an ad hoc quality. It is yet to be seen whether operations organized under regional arrangements or as multinational initiatives outside the United Nations will prove less hidebound and thereby will achieve greater freedom and flexibility of action. Certainly to date this has not been the case, and there is reason to suppose that they will call for the same instant operational response as has been required from the United Nations; though in the case of multinational operations they will lack the support that the United Nations can give both politically and in operational management and administration. Clearly, there are considerable advantages in structuring an international conflict control system within a tried and experienced organization, such as the United Nations.

Article 43 of the UN Charter provides for standby force arrangements, but since the article has never been acted upon by member states, no standby arrangements exist. Certain countries have promised forces on an earmarked basis, but these are wholly insufficient and not immediately available. Because of this and because it is now generally accepted that the host country has a reasonable right to disqualify any country's contingents from entering its territory, the use of instant ad hoc mounting arrangements has been forced upon the United Nations. For each operation it has collected contingents from those nations that were acceptable and that were willing and sufficiently capable of providing them. It is not surprising, therefore, that when a peacekeeping force is formed, there are broad extremes of experience, military proficiency, and discipline among the various contingents, which makes operational coordination and effectiveness very difficult to achieve. However, UNEF, ONUC, and UNFICYP have shown that such difficulties can be overcome, and in their achievements substantiate the case for developing the multinational peacekeeping concept. What, therefore, can be done to offset the deficiencies resulting from a defunct Article 43, so that there exists in the world an effective reservoir from which multinational peacekeeping forces can be raised? What is needed to ensure that they are adequately and soundly prepared for their task? The answer to both questions would appear to lie in the development of a global concept of education, preparation, and preparedness at the national, regional, and international levels. Let us see how this might be accomplished.

It has been pointed out that extremes of military professionalism among the various national contingents of UN peacekeeping forces can be very wide indeed—the extent of the disparity often being governed by the size of the force and the number of contingents involved. This was particularly the case in the Congo, where over thirty countries provided units or detachments and experience ranged from the highly professional units from India to the less-sophisticated state forces of small African countries such as Mali. In the Middle East and Cyprus, where smaller forces were involved, the disparity was less apparent, mainly due to the fact that the national contingents involved, whether from standing or conscript armies, already had some peacekeeping experience to build on—Canada, India, Ireland, and the Scandinavian countries particularly having taken part in earlier UN observer missions. In Cyprus, with the Middle East and the Congo as "training grounds," the contingents other than that of the United Kingdom had by now a great deal of peacekeeping experience, and the working relationships were better understood. Though the United Kingdom's units had not previously been a part of a UN force or mission (some officers and noncommissioned officers on secondment to the Ghanaian and Nigerian armed forces had been present with their respective contingents in the Congo), they did bring to UNFICYP an unparalleled expertise in operational organization and management. Along with Canada and Ireland, the United Kingdom provided the professional soldiers; whereas Denmark, Finland, and Sweden based their contingents on volunteer reservists and conscripts. Though this made for a disparity in military experience and technique, there were lessons to be learned on both sides.

As the evidence from UNFICYP indicates, the professional career soldier is not automatically the best person for the peacekeeper's role in the intercommunity or intrastate conflicts—conflicts in which it can be expected that international peacekeeping forces will continue to be involved. The military expertise of a well-trained army has invaluable assets and through its well-tried and efficient operational and military procedures can make a considerable contribution to the smooth running of the overall operation of the whole force. However, plain military expertise, though a considerable asset, is not of itself the only prerequisite for peacekeeping; there are other attributes that are not found in military textbooks nor learned on the barrack square. Whether the peacekeeper be of the lowest or the highest rank, his success will depend upon his ability to prevent conflict through every means other than force of arms. Tact, diplomacy, and quiet reasoning when negotiating or mediating between the contestants; complete self restraint, infinite patience, and tireless effort regardless of provocation are the weapons of the peacekeeper's trade—not his self-loading rifle—and through the judicious use of them he can defuse potentially dangerous situations, reduce tensions that could lead to violence, and thereby control and contain the conflict from escalating into something worse. A lost temper, a threatening attitude, excessive persuasion, all can in a moment render useless the attempts of the peacekeeper, and for all the good he will ever do again he might just as well pack his bags and return home. Equally, impartiality and the exercise of a single standard of behavior toward all parties to the dispute will determine the trust and confidence that each side will have in the peacekeeping force. But possibly more important than anything else is the peacekeeper's understanding of the problem at the root of the conflict and of the human relationships involved; for this will determine his attitude and approach to the situations and problems that face him. An understanding of the basic problem can be instilled into a soldier as part of the preoperational briefing he receives before leaving his home country, but until he comes into direct contact with the conflict and the people involved in it, his understanding can be no more than peripheral. It is then and only then that he can fully appreciate the character of the role he is required to play. How quickly he will be able to absorb and adjust himself to the environment, the emotions, and the deep-seated prejudices and hatreds that will color every action and counteraction he will be required to handle will depend upon how thorough his preoperational preparation has been. Impartiality is a key quality, but it requires an identification of the basic problem and an understanding of it.

It is not therefore enough for a peacekeeping soldier to be just a master of his military arts; there are other factors of which he needs to be aware. Since his effectiveness as a peacekeeper depends as much upon his attitude and approach as on his military skill, the former should not be ignored in such a presentation as this; nor is it overstating the case to say that the attitude of the members of a peacekeeping operation and their approach to the role they are called upon to perform can make the difference between the success or failure of their mission. Unless adequately guarded against, their perception of their role can easily assume the character of that of an army of occupation. The use of armed forces in a peaceful third-party intervention is a relatively new development, and, for the inexperienced it can be a confusing one. It is therefore understandable that the British soldiers at

Ayios Theodoros (Cyprus) in 1967 could not reconcile their role as soldiers with that of standing passively by while women and children in the village below their observation posts were being shelled and mortared. Nor is it any wonder that UN observers on the Suez Canal have found it exasperating to be fired at, shelled and mortared, and to have their observation posts reduced to rubble about their ears when their only reason for being on the canal is to assist in maintaining a cease-fire along its banks. As one French professional army officer observed angrily, "I have never been placed in the position before of having to submit to being shot at and shelled without being allowed to fire back." It is asking a great deal of any soldier to react unemotionally in such circumstances. His preparation for peacekeeping has to take account of this very natural attitude, so that the understanding is there from the beginning, and he is attuned to react impartially whatever the situation.

For a soldier not used to basing his attitude and approach on anything but the direct confrontation between soldier and soldier, or soldier and terrorist, this transformation into the role of referee does not come too quickly or too easily; and this is why the psychological adjustment that a soldier is called upon to make in fulfilling his peacekeeping role requires an understanding of the philosophy behind his actions. The adjustment can be more difficult for the professional soldier than for the volunteer or conscript soldier who is his immediate counterpart; for the professional's background, tradition, and whole projection of his image as a career soldier is directed toward one modus operandi—training for war—while the volunteer or conscript, who joins him in the peacekeeping field, lives permanently in a community environment and in a sense has only to move from one civilian environment to another. It would therefore be natural for the latter to adjust more quickly, since he shares an instinctive affinity and a common point of interest with those whom he has come to help; this affinity without doubt helps to establish a relationship and personal communication from the start which, if properly fostered, can generate the trust and confidence that a peacekeeping force requires in order to carry out its task effectively and successfully. From the above it should not be inferred that the professional soldier is at a continuing disadvantage because of his military upbringing. Pure military expertise is still the most important factor in this as in any other military operation. Once the soldier has adapted himself to the operational focus, his worth will be that much greater. Canada, India, and Ireland in their contributions to UN peacekeeping have already shown this to be so, and from their experiences have developed their own preparatory studies and training within their normal military training curricula.

In observer missions, as distinct from force level operations, where individual rather than collective action is the criterion, the difference between the professional and nonprofessional is the most marked. Here it is that the professional's training counts most—not only because of the self-discipline that has been inculcated in him from the moment he became an officer, but more because he better understands the military problems, tactical and strategical, that face the opposing forces in the field. He is therefore better able to deal with the commanders at the respective levels on both sides and create the kind of mutual understanding that is required. Soldiers prefer to deal with soldiers, and in warlike situations this can be advantageous to the success of the peacekeeper's or observer's efforts; however, this "brotherhood of officers" can equally have the disadvantageous effect of developing circumscribed viewpoints, and this is why the wider experience of the nonprofessional is so important.

For equally factual reasons the relationship between the peacekeeping force and the domestic armed forces of the country within which the former is operating has an important bearing on the conduct of the operation. In Kashmir there exists a closer rapport in the relationship between UN soldiers from Commonwealth countries and the national armies of India and Pakistan than the latter have with those from non-Commonwealth countries, no doubt because there is the bond of traditional friendship, understanding, and respect. In similar circumstances in Africa or Latin America, a wholly regional or merely neighbor-state participation in a peacekeeping operation within these continents is likely to be more acceptable for ideological, ethnic, or language reasons than a force composed of Europeans and Asians. However, this would not always be desirable. The Congo showed that there were divisions of support even among African states, some siding with the central government and some with Tshombe's Katanga. There could therefore be a tendency toward partisanship were the third-party forces to be too locally recruited, with a real danger of their becoming a party to the domestic politics of the host state.

Attitude and approach are not the only criteria to be considered. There are language differences that cause problems of communication; cross-cultural differences that exist not only between the disputants themselves and between the disputants and the members of the peacekeeping force, but also among the contingents within a force, adding to the communication problem; and there are the inevitable difficulties over environmental adjustment faced by every peacekeeping soldier. Although so far it has been possible to establish a basic lingua franca that suited the particular UN force and the host country (English in UNEF and UNFICYP and English and French in ONUC), this will not always be the case. Language barriers can cause confusion and mistaken interpretation and might tend to govern the national selection of contingents. Cultural differences are a different matter altogether, and tensions arising out of misunderstandings, or even unintentional tactlessness, could probably result in the withdrawal of the "guilty" contingent. As with an individual, once a contingent loses its credibility in the eyes of any party to the dispute, its effectiveness as a peacekeeping agent goes too. Brashness through lack of preparation could very easily bring this about. Environment, too, can affect a soldier's reaction; and if he is in an unfamiliar environment, he could become temperamentally unsuited for his role. An example of this is the use of troops recruited and trained for special battle operations, such as paratroops and commandos. Because of the nature of their role, they are trained to be hard and tough. It is not surprising that the tenor of their attitude toward conflict is one of ruthlessness. Put such a man in an urban community setting and it is asking a great deal of him to expect him to react in any way other than that instilled in him by his training, unless he has undergone the necessary preparation and adjustment for the role he is going to be asked to perform. In a more general sense, the background from which the soldier comes will also inevitably affect the attitude he adopts. The volunteer soldier, coming as he does from a civilian environment and a civilian job, will have the advantage of a similar working background, even though his standard of living could be much higher. But in the final analysis it is the personality, the understanding of the individual, and his relationship with the community that will dictate the manner of his attitude and approach to his role.

The use of armies for national economic tasks is nothing new. The People's Republic of China has for a long time used its armed forces in an integral role to provide support for civic tasks as well to provide their own requirements in food, clothing, housing, munitions, and so on. But in China everyone has to be self-sufficient in providing for his own needs, including the schoolchildren. Other countries have used their armies for specific nation-building tasks and a new development on this theme is taking place in some of the underdeveloped countries where soldiers work as members of the community over and above the requirements of military training. The army assists as a labor force and is used in community and national projects alongside civilians. They harvest, they build, they work in factories, contributing to the national economy along with everyone else. Clearly, this is both sensible and necessary in small countries, where every man's and woman's contribution is valuable. The system has another effect—probably beneficial under the circumstances—it does not isolate the army from the rest of the community and set it up as an elite body. Though economic and possibly political reasons dictate this policy, nevertheless, it makes the soldier a citizen of his country in the fullest sense of the word and ensures that a common bond of understanding exists between the army and the community; it develops in the soldier a community responsibility that is possibly lacking in the armies of larger countries. Though a direct parallel would not be possible to achieve in countries where the army tends to be something apart, the concept that a soldier is a member of the community needs to be fostered more strongly. This need was never more important than it is today—when the military are looked upon by many nonviolent action organizations as the enemy rather than the ally of society. In the light of the more recent examples of conflict and violence and the increasing involvement of armies in community-type conflicts, there seems to be a commonsense case for adding a new dimension to military training.

It might appear from what has been said that international peacekeeping requires special training on the part of the military. To an extent this may be true at the commander and staff levels, but not so far as the junior commander and soldier levels are concerned. Peacekeeping is a different discipline from war making, and it is therefore important and desirable to train potential field commanders and their counterparts in the diplomatic, political, and international civil service fields for roles within a UN orientation. Like army generals, professional ambassadors are not automatically qualified for the roles of international mediator and negotiator. In some quarters it is considered that a central list of senior military and civilian officers should be maintained in the United Nations and that periodically these officers should be brought to the UN headquarters for the purpose of preparing them for international responsibilities and bringing them up to date on UN thinking and methods. There is sound sense behind this idea, for it could ensure that a pool of expertise would be established and available to the Security Council for use in both emergency and premeditated situations.

Some form of central staff training for senior staff officers earmarked for UN service could also pay a substantial dividend. It is a matter of record that national governments, when selecting officers to fill staff appointments in peacekeeping forces, tend to rate these appointments very highly, viewing the performance of their nominee as reflecting back on themselves and their country—in other words, he will be on display in the "shop window of the world." Therefore, the overall caliber of senior staff officers in UN forces and missions is generally high. Experience and procedure, however, do vary among nations, and this is where a central staff school could play an important role—in standardizing procedures; devising and developing new operational, organizational, and administrative techniques; and familiarizing officers with the differing military characteristics and working patterns of different national armies. Such training should be multiprofessional, embracing all the disciplines involved in the international control and resolution of conflict, so that the foundations of understanding and good working relations so essential in a multinational, multiprofessional operation can be laid in the training and preparation for it. Such a program could also offset the undesirability of force commanders' bringing their own national officers with them in the initial period of an operation.

The development of peacekeeping techniques at the junior level is a matter of adjustment rather than of reorientation. The basic skills already exist—they need only to be adapted to meet a rather different form of soldiering. Some military men argue that one cannot train a soldier for two diametrically opposite roles—war making and peacekeeping—and expect him to be wholly proficient in the primary consideration of being trained for war. This argument confuses the issue; peacekeeping is not a special type of soldiering requiring a different training technique from that in which all armies train. It does not impose an additional burden on a soldier's training capacity. There is, however, some validity in the belief that a period of peacekeeping with the United Nations tends to soften the soldier and that some "toughening up" may be required on the completion of such service. But this is a matter primarily of leadership and reorientation and should not pose any major problem in a professional army. Canada's and India's enduring and successful service in a number of UN operations and missions serves to refute the idea that preparation and training for peacekeeping detracts from an army's warlike ability. Both countries, along with the Nordic countries,[1] have included peacekeeping preparedness in the training curriculum for their armed forces. Peacekeeping, in whatever form it takes, is just another category of special operations for which all professional armies are trained— another dimension to be added to the framework of standard military training, requiring an attitudinal rather than a physical adjustment. In the main it is simply a question of placing greater emphasis on certain fundamental characteristics required of a trained soldier—alertness, vigilance, patience, and acuteness. In his role as an observer he needs to sharpen these personal attributes to a high degree. In his role as a "referee" he must acquire a sense of objective justice and discernment based on his knowledge of the situation and, more important, his understanding of the people concerned and their different motivations. There is no place for double standards in peacekeeping. Both sides expect and should receive equal treatment; each situation must be judged on the facts and the blame attributed accordingly. It is probably true to say that if a peacekeeping force is unpopular with both sides at the same time, then it is carrying out its duties objectively and with impartiality.

Although an understanding of the specific motivations influencing the conflict cannot be fully absorbed or reacted to until the peacekeeper is physically face-to-face with the problem, if his military grounding has included an education in community relations, the peacekeeper's reactions are likely to be more apposite and his handling of the actual problem more competent and constructive. But without that necessary background he is likely to be nonplussed. National police forces, being the guardians of civil law and order,

---

1. Denmark, Finland, Norway, Sweden.

require this understanding for their everyday responsibilities, and some include social studies as an ongoing program for their members from the time they are first recruited right through every stage of their service—a practice that could well be followed by all civilian police forces. It would also appear to make sense for soldiers to follow similar studies throughout their service—at all levels of the rank structure—involving where possible collaboration with all the social and community development organizations in addition to the police. This continuing grounding in and understanding of community life and its problems would instill in an army the correct attitudes of mind and approach to conflicts involving the community. Such training would also develop a psychology and philosophy of conflict treatment that would help to ensure that the treatment prescribed will be the right one.

The technique of peacekeeping with which this book is concerned operates on the principle that peacekeeping can be implemented only with the consent of or at the request of the host country or countries faced with the conflict situation. It is not based on any concept of force or imposition, nor does the force involved play anything but a third-party role. These are constants in international peacekeeping as it is recognized today in the United Nations. But what is not a constant, either in this context or in any other conflict situation, is the character of the conflict itself. No longer can military application to conflict problems be derived from a single blueprint. Although there have been a number of internal security operations conducted by one country or another since the end of World War II, the pattern of the operations themselves has remained remarkably similar. It is interesting that despite the emergence of the UN brand of peacekeeping and the obvious deficiencies in the stylized operational approach to a succession of law-and-order conflicts, little serious thought has been given to the study of conflict treatment and to the lessons to be learned from previous experience. This lack has resulted in the same mistakes being repeated again and again, resulting in unnecessary and sometimes heavy loss of human life. One needs immediately to qualify this last remark by acknowledging the studies that have been carried out, but these have been conducted by those countries whose contributions to UN peacekeeping have been the greatest. Canada's, India's, and the Nordic countries' initiatives in this respect have already been mentioned. Ghana, Indonesia, Ireland, Nigeria, and Pakistan have all used their peacekeeping experience to develop their own patterns and techniques and have applied them to advantage in the subsequent operations in which they have been involved. But they still represent a minority, and more could be done by more states toward developing military thinking in respect to this relatively new concept of soldiering, not only in the UN context but also in relation to their own domestic needs. At present, whenever a local conflict situation arises, the military tend to be committed in a well-practiced and stereotyped enforcement role in aid of the civil power. Past experience has shown that resistance tends to become more determined and better organized the greater the extent of force used against it. This is not to say that force is ineffectual against such resistance, for there are plenty of examples where opposition and resistance have been suppressed by military action; but this is not always the case. Neither suppression nor enforcement necessarily ends the spiral of violence or destroys the opposition, even though the latter's potential may be reduced at the time to an ineffective level. When this happens, one is tempted to question the treatment that has been applied—for the end result is clearly inconclusive; and yet, apart from the use of force itself, the methodology used in the conduct of enforcement operations has something in common with that used in third-party peacekeeping, as do the tactical techniques used in both. However, that is where the similarity ends, and it is important to recognize the difference. The wrong treatment of conflict can be more harmful in the end than no treatment at all.

A too rigid adherence to well-tried methodologies is likely to produce a counterproductive effect. A soldier trained for the single task of war can be expected to react in the same prescribed way in any given situation. Correct treatment and correct preparation dictate the conduct of the action. As with incorrect treatment, a soldier inadequately prepared could well be a counterproductive agent. A soldier who has not been properly prepared for his role is likely to find himself disoriented and out of his depth when he first comes face-to-face with the problem at the point of conflict. Is it fair to put soldiers at this disadvantage and possibly jeopardize an operation simply by failing to see that they receive the necessary training for this type of operation? The answer is obviously no. The training is necessary and important—and must be thorough. For no matter how well trained a soldier may be, and however sophisticated is the army to which he belongs, he cannot be plunged into situations of conflict and be expected to react or perform correctly in his role unless he has been well rehearsed. Of course, no matter how good the preparation may have been, there will still be mistakes, but the better prepared the soldier the less likely and the less dangerous will those mistakes be. Emergencies normally allow little opportunity for preparation for the role of peacekeeping, and skill training tends to be confined to a crash course immediately before the departure of a unit for its theater of operations. The real and lasting skills, however, are learned on the spot and in action after the unit's arrival. It is in this period that most of the mistakes are made, though many of them might be avoided if the preparation were both thorough and more consistent.

No one denies that the prime, and in some cases the only, function of an army is to train for war and for ensuring national security. The idea that an army should also be trained for peace roles is relatively new; though a number of countries have recognized the relevance of it in terms of modern conflict and have adapted training methods to meet this requirement, the concept cannot be said to be generally acceptable in military circles. Those who argue against it do so genuinely on the grounds that a soldier's role—and therefore an army's responsibility—is to defend the nation, if necessary, against external aggression and to fight to maintain peace in the world. For this responsibility the whole projection of military training and the skills of a soldier's trade need to be directed toward the effective use of force to counter opposing force. It is their argument that to distract a soldier from this primary training responsibility, by introducing a secondary or alternative role that runs counter to the whole basic system and purpose of his training, would have the effect of developing a new breed of soldier from whom one could not hope to expect the same high standards of discipline, training, morale, and determination that are fundamental to the high performance of military duty required in present-day operational conditions. To use a common English expression, he would be "neither fish nor fowl."

In fairness to this argument, the idea of training for peace in the military context might appear to be a contradiction in terms, and one can well understand the reluctance with which a great number of military men view the prospect. But is it really a contradiction in terms? Is it not time that we exploded the myth that the vertex of military professionalism and the sole raison d'être for armies is to prepare and train for nuclear war? Surely the role of armies should be to preserve world peace. The word *peacekeeping* has been used in the past two decades to describe all kinds of military actions and operations. None of the actions or operations so described have followed the conventional character of war—of a combat-clad soldier manning his machine gun in his protective foxhole, facing a similarly clad, armed and protected soldier at a distance of a few hundred yards. (This scenario is by no means a relic of the past, as Vietnam, the Middle East, Bangladesh, and Korea have only recently indicated.) Instead, the operations undertaken under the guise of peacekeeping have been of a policing nature and have been concerned with the quelling of terrorists, freedom fighters, or nationalist groups seeking self-determination for themselves. These actions and operations have differed in certain respects from those of the United Nations in recent years—in the use of force, in their character as second-party interventions directed at maintaining law and order through enforcement action, in their support of the existing civil authority, and in their direct confrontation with the opposition—and yet the stage setting is very similar to that in which the United Nations has performed, and the play in all its acts revolves around and within the existing community or communities caught up in the dispute. The military force concerned finds itself as much involved at the different community levels, whether urban or rural, as it does with the violence groups and is unable to ignore either their existence, their interests, or their influence on events.

The counterargument, therefore, to those who believe it is undesirable to train an army to perform both a war and a peace role is this: the most common structure of conflict today is the "small war," whether it be interstate, intrastate, or merely intercommunal; and if this type of war is to be controlled (whether by enforcement or peaceful means), those employed in this role must be qualified in every respect for dealing with the problem situations as they develop. Problems arising out of community conflicts should not and need not pose difficulties in terms of split concepts of action, provided that, as far as possible, the broader dimension of a peacekeeper's role is understood and inculcated into every level of an army's training structure. Throughout his military service, at all levels of promotion and command, the career soldier should be consistently alerted to the skills that this kind of role will require of him and the personal attitude and approach that he will need to develop in order to make the most effective use of them. Today a well-trained, competent soldier is no longer an automaton; he has to be a man of perception, initiative, imagination, and flexibility in thought and action. A man of this caliber should have no difficulty adjusting to these extradimensional skills and superimposing them upon the more traditional training techniques that represent a fundamental part of his profession.

So far we have concentrated on the fact that even the best-trained and most competent soldiers need training in peacekeeping skills if they are to fulfill effectively their tasks as peacekeepers. A greater problem faces those nations with small or newly formed armies. Since it has been to a large extent the smaller nations that have carried the burden of UN peacekeeping through its major operations and observer missions, and since the responsibility for whatever international peacekeeping that is authorized and undertaken in the future is likely to continue to rest on their shoulders, it is important that these skills be as readily available to them as to the others. Since the principle of "consent" by the host country applies as much to the individual national contingents of a peacekeeping force as it does to the force as a whole, the acceptance of a peacekeeping force does not carry with it carte blanche authority for the United Nations to man the force with national contingents of its own choosing. This naturally can make it very difficult for the United Nations to raise militarily adequate and suitable forces. With the size of the force needed in the Congo, the problem was an acute one and became more acute when certain member states withdrew their contingents early in the operation.

The point has been made in an earlier chapter that Article 43 of the Charter requires member states to contribute "armed forces, assistance and facilities" for the maintenance of peace and security. The fact that this article has remained defunct over the years, despite the efforts of successive secretaries-general, is disappointing but not unexpected considering the divisive attitudes in the United Nations toward the use of peacekeeping forces and their cost. However, even if Article 43 remains a dead article of the Charter, this need not mean that nothing can be done toward constructing a viable and effective system for conflict control. The lack of standby forces has not prevented three force level operations from being mounted—it has merely limited the field from which the selection of contingents could be made. Quality has been a greater problem than quantity and accounts for the fact that only a handful of countries have been the providers. It is not to be expected that these few will willingly fulfill this international commitment indefinitely. Another Congo-size operation would be very difficult to mount in terms of manpower alone, unless the field of selection were considerably increased. What therefore is needed is both quality and quantity, but this can only be achieved by developing a global source of manpower and by providing an international exchange of operational techniques and procedures. A precedent for this has already been set by the Nordic countries in the establishment in 1965 of a joint training system to develop unified training courses in each of the four countries,[2] in which different aspects of a UN peacekeeper's role are taught, including staff duties. The need for this special operations training became apparent after officers and contingents from these countries serving with UN forces and missions found that a standardization in training and in operational procedures would improve efficiency, coordination, and technique. The Nordic countries have provided themselves with an institutional system within which the problems and requirements of international peacekeeping can be studied and appropriate techniques and procedures developed.

At the moment the Nordic system is the only one of its kind, but it is a model that could certainly be utilized elsewhere—or even enlarged. It would be a tragedy if it were to remain an isolated group, for it represents a valuable source of experience that should be pooled with others who do not have it. The same can be said of Canada, India, and Ireland, the other most consistent UN peacekeepers. They have the experience and the knowledge of techniques and procedures that are the essentials of effective peacekeeping. The contribution that all these countries could make to the development of an international conflict control system is a significant one, for their experience would help to structure the kind (and character) of system that is needed.

In developing the idea of mutual exchange of experience and expertise, geographical considerations would need to be taken into ac-

2. UN Department of Army Staff, Sweden, *Nordic Stand-by Forces in United Nations Service.*

count; language and climate being only two of the factors involved. Since there are regional structures already existing, it makes sense that the initial exchange should be made at the regional level. The development of regional studies and, later on, joint training courses appears a practical way in which to begin. The studies should not confine themselves entirely to military aspects of peacekeeping, but should embrace the related roles of peacemaking and peace building, thus bringing the interdisciplinary and interprofessional skills into a correct perspective.

The European region in itself combines military maturity derived from centuries of operational experience with major peacekeeping experience. If the expertise and experience in operational procedures and "battlefield management," on the one hand, and the practical skills of third-party peacekeeping, on the other, were shared among all European nations, they could develop and perfect a broader equality in technique and an overall higher standard of quality among all the armies concerned. This could not but improve the effectiveness and efficiency of their contingents when, as member states of the United Nations, they are invited to contribute to a peacekeeping force. The fact that some of the countries concerned might never be involved in force level peacekeeping operations is not important—making the expertise of technique available to all cannot help but raise the standard of military prowess throughout and contribute toward closing the gap in experience and military efficiency that has been one of the major difficulties confronting the United Nations in its operations to date.

Europe has been taken as only an example. The fact that the northern European countries base their military strength on conscript service inclines them toward a close-knit Nordic grouping, but this would not seem to pose insurmountable problems to collective training on a wider scale within Europe. The reluctance of the neutral countries of Finland and Sweden to join in combined studies with NATO countries probably raises the bigger issue, which is most likely to determine the attitude and outlook of those countries toward taking part in a wider-based amalgam for training. Any regional arrangement for Europe, therefore, will need to be set outside the NATO scenario, so that the neutral countries will feel comfortable about being a part of it. But Europe is not the only region within which such a training collaboration could exist. The Organization of American States would appear to form the basis on which another regional grouping could be built. There is much experience available among the Latin American states, collectively in terms of force level and observer operations (Argentina, Brazil, Chile, Colombia, Uruguay, Venezuela), and also in the persons of many outstanding individuals who have played important roles in international mediation and arbitration or have held senior representative military and civilian peacekeeping appointments. Though not part of OAS, Canada's wealth of experience and skills would also be invaluable.

Africa and Asia too have the nucleus from which to develop regional systems of study. The potential is strong with a number of countries—Ghana, India, Indonesia, Nigeria, and Pakistan in particular—having provided contingents, observers, special representatives, and force commanders for UN operations and missions. Geographically there are problems in terms of distance and cost; and because of the relatively small size of some of the national armed forces, there is inevitably a premium on experience in operational procedures and management among the smaller countries. Clearly they will need assistance in developing their potential. The "reasonable prerogative of choice" referred to earlier makes it likely, if only for political reasons, that it will be these states who will continue to be found more acceptable to host countries than contingents from the larger and militarily more sophisticated countries. This, therefore, makes it emphatically more important that these younger military states receive the skill training and benefit from the experience of others. It is to be hoped that this could be achieved within the framework of the parent regional organization; but if this were not possible, other regions or even other countries with greater capabilities might, within their own programs, be willing to provide study and training facilities for these less-experienced countries.

Another means would be to organize and conduct the required training at an international level. The idea of a UN staff training school has already been considered, but equally the training could be provided by some other body independent of any governmental control. An experiment in the shape of the International Peace Academy has already made a successful beginning in this respect. The academy's interdisciplinary programs are designed to give those whose business is the control of conflict and its resolution (soldiers, diplomats, members of defense and foreign ministries, academics, and other practitioners) the opportunity to prepare themselves more effectively for the practical roles of peacekeeping, peacemaking, and peace building. Through its various multinational projects, besides providing for the practitioner, the academy is developing new concepts and techniques for use in the whole field of international conflict control. The more precise training required at unit and individual soldier levels is not part of the academy's curriculum, as this is clearly a national responsibility. The academy represents a higher dimension in skill education and can be said to provide a "construction set" of techniques for others to put together and develop further. The progress of the International Peace Academy so far has shown that an independent transnational training system is possible and can achieve positive as well as creative results. If the system works at this level, then it is reasonable to suppose that it would work at the regional level.

An international conflict control system is a viable concept. There is evidence that without altering the articles or the authorities of the Charter, international peacekeeping can still provide a contributory, practical element in the resolution of conflict. But the effectiveness of the contribution is dependent upon those chosen to carry out the role being adequately and suitably prepared for the task, a factor that must be recognized throughout all strata of military experience. However comprehensive a soldier's or an army's experience and skill may be, learning does not stop. Not only, therefore, must that experience and skill be available and offered to others less well endowed, but it should be used to help improve the skills and techniques already learned.

So, there is the Charter—the legal instrument that empowers the United Nations organization to act in the interest of world peace. There is the Security Council—with the authority to take action to maintain international peace and security. There are the articles of the Charter that provide for the raising of international forces from member states to assist in maintaining that peace and security. There are precedents for the use of such international forces, though not within the strict provisions of the Charter. Despite all this, each successive peacekeeping operation has been mounted on an ad hoc basis with the resultant early chaos, delays, and prolonged teething troubles. Whether or not there will be any change in UN procedure for mounting such operations in the future and whether or not the instant-type operations will remain the standard pattern, we have tried to suggest in this chapter ways and means by which, through national preparation and international/regional collaboration, member states could extend their range of understanding and knowledge of operational procedures, organization, and required skills, thereby achieving a greater standardization in technique, training, and performance which would go a long way toward offsetting the inevitable and inherent problems of the ad hoc system.

The design that has been outlined here is not specifically related to UN operations. The techniques and skills that can be developed within the framework of the design, nationally, regionally, and transnationally, are as relevant to domestic or regional peace efforts as to those of the United Nations. The concept of an international conflict control system embraces all levels of conflict; the models devised as a result of joint study and training, therefore, should be capable of application at each and every level.

The philosophy, and the concepts deriving from it which we present here, have been created out of experience gained in the practical work of peacekeeping. Any response that they may arouse will depend upon the attitude of sovereign states, whether individually or collectively as members of the United Nations, toward the growth of conflict in the world. Whether or not the machinery for international peacekeeping can be made to work will depend upon the willingness of states to concern themselves with the problem and upon their determination to create a fully effective and efficient system for dealing with conflict.

If the existing UN peacekeeping system withers through lack of use, or if the deadlock in the Special Committee on Peacekeeping Operations remains unbroken and Article 43 of the Charter continues to be but a string of empty words, everything that has been suggested might be thought to be superfluous—lacking in value and credibility. But this need not be the case. What has been constructed is a framework of education, preparation, and training that can be implemented nationally, regionally, or internationally within existing training systems. To do this does not require a decision based on a unanimous or two-thirds vote, respectively, in the Security Council or the General Assembly—it is up to governments or regional organizations. The ideas simply provide a methodology by which the military forces of any country can acquire the necessary skill training and, through wider collaboration, can extend their range of expertise. In the process they would better prepare themselves for the role of peacekeeping if and when they are invited or are called upon to fulfill it. By so doing the countries concerned would not make a commitment, nor would they be under any obligation to earmark a proportion of their armed forces for international service as contemplated under the stillborn Article 43; nor, as far as one can see, would it necessitate an increase in their national defense expenditure, for the training required can be superimposed upon the structure of normal military training.

In prefacing our reasons for believing that the need exists for a greater understanding and development of the special skills required in international peacekeeping, we pointed to the undeniable fact that to date the extremes of preparedness, training, and operational experience among national contingents of peacekeeping forces have been very wide indeed. One far-reaching effect, therefore, were the ideas recommended here to be implemented, would be to strengthen and to give more flexibility, both quantitatively and qualitatively, to the United Nations' capability to mount peacekeeping operations.

15

The Broader Picture—
Interprofessional Skills in
Conflict Control

Peacekeeping, whether international or unilateral, has been regarded primarily as a military responsibility. The operational exercise involved has always been looked upon as being the prerogative of the soldier. In broad terms it would be difficult to assess in any other way the category of operations that have been conducted by countries within the context of internal security and counterinsurgency or countersubversion; but where the assessment is misleading is in defining such operations as peacekeeping. It is this that has contributed to much of the existing public misconception regarding the roles and capabilities of the UN peacekeeping forces and to the general misunderstanding of their aims and objectives. The types of military operations referred to are designed to control violence through second-party enforcement action and not through third-party peaceful intervention. However minimal the force used, these operations cannot be considered to be impartial. An earlier chapter described the characteristic difference between the principles on which such operations are based and the guiding principle that has governed UN peacekeeping operations since the Korean War. The latter can more accurately be designated as peacekeeping because of their third-party posture and impartial approach. The distinction rests here, for both typologies are in essence violence control operations and to a degree have much in common; however, it is important that the distinction be kept firmly in mind for it helps to broaden the perspective of the role and character of the operations and the extent of the participation. It also helps to bring into focus the multiprofessional patchwork of skills that are needed, not only to control the violence but to bring the conflict to an end. Since, therefore, the term *peacekeeping* suffers from a number of confusing connotations and since this chapter deals with a wider perspective than the purely military one in its study of the interrelationship between the roles of different participating groups, it is in the context of international control of violence that the chapter has been framed.

The manifestation of violence, and hence conflict itself, may not differ overmuch from a prescribed pattern; the circumstances that bring it about, however, differ in every case—they may be either social, economic, moral, ethnic, religious, or racial. Since no two conflicts are the same, it follows that the treatment necessary to control and dissipate each needs to be flexible and ever changing. A conflict needs the treatment it deserves, and the treatment that is applied must be appropriate and correct for the character and circumstances of the conflict if it is to have a hope of successfully resolving it. If this point has been made more than once, it is because the lesson needs to be learned and recognized. The past is full of instances where stereotyped, repetitive procedures have been used without thought being given to the needs of the particular conflict concerned or to the lessons that have been learned from previous conflict situations and operations. Conflict treatment therefore is no longer a simple matter of procedure, but has become a science that embraces a broad range of peace-related roles and which deserves the careful and profound study of those who have a role to play in the resolution of conflict. The field is indeed wide, for it could include professionals and technicians of all kinds, as individuals and collectively, from nongovernmental, intergovernmental, and international organizations. Prominent among these are the specialized agencies of the United Nations itself, for, through the very performance of their "aid" roles, they are assisting in the improvement of both the social and economic standards of developing countries and contributing to social change, which of itself helps to remove the causes and sources of conflict. It is important that the energies of all such resources be harnessed together so that the roles they perform can be coordinated with the greatest possible advantage to the control of violence. This undoubtedly will not be easy to achieve, but without this coordination and without the needed interrelationship between roles, the overall effect of any violence control operation will be lessened and the effectiveness of the individual agency's contribution could be diminished and even hampered by overlapping and by interagency rivalry and prejudice.

Those who criticize peacekeeping, even the UN typology, as being counterproductive and nonprogressive cannot be disregarded. The single act of peacekeeping, enforced or peaceful, without additional inputs in terms of peacemaking initiatives and peace building action, tends only to preserve the status quo. By the very nature of the mandate given to successive UN force level operations, nothing much more can be expected of them but a dampening down of violence, which puts the clock back to where it was before the force intervened—no doubt to the satisfaction of the dominant power, if there is one, or to the dissatisfaction of all parties concerned in the dispute. In the end, the military action, if not backed up by the other peace agencies, will simply put off the renewal of violence to a later date and will leave unresolved the basic issues at the root of the conflict.

The interrelationship required needs to be adjustable to the changing circumstances of the particular conflict. No conflict remains static. It constantly changes in character and its treatment must be changed to suit it. It follows that the emphasis on roles will alter too and that not surprisingly there will be some overlapping of roles. For instance, in an inter-communal conflict situation, during the initial military action period, it could be that the soldiers, besides performing their primary role of peacekeeping, would carry out both on-the-spot peacemaking and peace building in those areas where the direct armed confrontation make it difficult for civilians to operate. In Cyprus, the assumption by the military of this additional commitment successfully ensured that the Turkish community was economically provided with the essentials for living, despite the economic blockade imposed by the Cyprus government, and its people were able to carry on their agricultural livelihoods in their fields and vineyards under the supervision of UN soldiers. Although this did not of itself bring about a reconciliation, it did establish a human rights precedent that was recognized by the Cyprus government and accepted as being within the responsibilities of UNFICYP. So far there has been no change of practice in Cyprus, and the military continue to fulfill the commitment although the militant phase has long since passed. The situation has become more of a political than a military confrontation, even though the entrenched positions on both sides are still manned.

Those who have taken part in UN peacekeeping operations are well aware of the limitations of the military in many of the capacities in which they are required to act and recognize that there are other civilian organizations better equipped mentally and by training to fulfill them instead. It will be demonstrated later that examples already exist where military and civilian operations have been dovetailed so as to provide a broader and more effective instrument for meeting the particular needs of a conflict situation. However, before citing examples it would be useful to emphasize once more how broad the scope and range of conflict can be, making it impractical to think in terms of a single agency—peacekeeping in this context is one—being expected to deal effectively with all its aspects. The combined and coordinated efforts of any number of agencies are certainly going to be needed, embracing the whole gamut of mediation, negotiation, and maybe arbitration, along with the active economic, social, and development input required to achieve the social change and reconstruction that are fundamental ingredients if the roots of conflict are to be removed. It is unrealistic to suppose that such inputs can be independent and separate, but experience demonstrates that only too often the mix is unsuccessful. However, without an effective interrelationship and the realization that to be successful in the common purpose there has to be a linking of skills and a close working relationship, there will be duplication and omission. Groups and organizations will work at tangents to one another and not in parallel. Prejudices, suspicions, and outright rivalry will grow, to be followed by denigration and condemnation, all disposed to utterly destroy any of the cohesion or collaboration necessary to achieve a successful and lasting effect. If a third-party intervention into conflict is to be constructive and progressive and not in the end counterproductive, the widest range of skills needs to be utilized proportionately to the needs of the situation. In basic terms a peacekeeping operation is as much a relief operation as any required for any other form of disaster, for it is mounted to meet the emergency of a man-made disaster and, like its "natural" counterpart, requires a comprehensive combination of all resources for dealing with it. The ratio between the degree of military and civilian contribution will depend upon the characteristics of the conflict, but one can very well visualize some conflicts requiring primarily a military treatment similar to that of UNEF in the Middle East, whereas others would call for a major civilian presence and effort to reestablish a state's social, economic, and administrative viability and would require only a minimum military input as a security force. The UN Temporary Executive Authority (UNTEA) in West New Guinea provides a good example of the introduction of an international interregnum administration. The examples given illustrate the two extremes, but as has already been said, the changes can be rung in terms of military and civilian content to meet the given circumstances, not only in the initial conception, but also in adjusting to the changing nature of the conflict as the operational situation alters, so that the treatment remains appropriate to the conflict.

Of all the operations that the United Nations has undertaken, that in the Congo (ONUC) best demonstrates in terms of composition how a civilian operation can be mounted in parallel to that of the military. It will be remembered that, following the departure of the Belgians on the Congo's declaration of independence, the subsequent internal disorders virtually brought the country's administration to a standstill and chaos to the social, economic, and judiciary services. Communications and transportation facilities broke down, while intertribal fighting and the harrying of those Belgians remaining along with other Europeans only added to the confusion. A major civilian reconstruction operation was necessary, and the United Nations provided it.

The main objective was to assist the Congolese government in the establishment of a stable economy and social structure, through a comprehensive and long-term program of training and technical aid. However, the immediate requirement was to put the Congo on its feet again administratively and to provide the necessary backup to the maintenance of essential public services—health, education, communications, judiciary, and banking. There was very little for the United Nations to build on, since the Congolese lacked the experience, the necessary preparation, and the training that they needed for the responsibilities of independent statehood. The task that faced the United Nations was daunting indeed but assumed more alarming proportions when, on ONUC's arrival, it was possible to measure the full extent of the social and economic breakdown. Three months after ONUC had been established, in a first report to the secretary-general, his special representative in the Congo reported, "The almost complete lack of trained civil servants, executives and professional people among the Congolese and the striking absence of administrative and political experience . . . . created a serious situation for the young republic." [1] This situation had been made much worse by the total failure on the part of Belgium to arrange for any organized hand-over to the Congolese of the administrative machinery of government and the essential services, but Dayal was able to conclude his report with the comment that "a great deal has been done in the face of insuperable odds . . . there is no doubt whatsoever that the UN presence has had a steadying effect on the situation." [2]

The civilian reconstruction operation lasted seven years, three years longer than its military counterpart. The degree to which the operation achieved its objective must be measured against the extent to which Zaire has now become economically and socially self-sufficient. It is questionable whether the operation could ever have got under way had there been no accompanying peacekeeping operation; even so, it was not until 1963 that a full-scale civilian assistance program could be mounted, because of the serious law-and-order situation that existed. But by the time that the relief operation ended and the UN Development Program took over, a great deal had been done in the way of rehabilitation, on which foundation the new independent state of Zaire was able to reconstruct a viable administrative structure.

One cannot, however, claim that the duality of ONUC—military and civilian—provided a wholly harmonious working relationship. To all intents and purposes they were two separate operations, which suffered from the deficiencies, inefficiencies, weaknesses, and domestic disagreements that are inherent in most comparable ventures, where each component has its own objectives and goes its own way. It would be difficult to assess the extent to which this lack of cohesion aggravated or even damaged the working effectiveness of each component, but there seems good reason to believe that the two operations could have been more closely and effectively linked had the operational structure been better conceived. The Congo was a mammoth operation and mistakes were bound to be made, but it is likely that many of them stemmed from a weakness in the degree of cooperation at the leadership level, which is so vital, especially in the early months of an operation. The initial command structure had a civilian in overall charge of the operation, with the military (force) commander and the director of the civilian operation immediately

1. Rajeshwar Dayal, Report to Secretary-General, 21 September 1960.
2. Ibid.

subordinate to him. When the Katanga crisis developed into an open confrontation with the United Nations, the regional civilian UN representative in Katanga was given a considerable degree of independent authority in matters relevant to the implementation of the Security Council resolution of 21 February 1961. This confusion of roles did not help to promote understanding among the individuals concerned, and as a result they tended to act independently of one another. The establishment of an operational committee or council, where the overall strategy could have been decided and plans coordinated, could have had positive advantages for the ONUC operation and would have ensured greater cohesion.

In Cyprus, though no council or committee was formed, the force commander and the secretary-general's special representative have been in juxtaposition to one another, served by the military chief of staff on the one hand and the senior legal and political adviser on the other. The close working relationship that has been established ensures that action, military or political, is coordinated and when taken represents the dual decision of the military commander and the special representative, even though individually each has direct access to the secretary-general in respect to his own particular responsibilities. The lesson from the Congo was certainly learned in Cyprus, and though there is no parallel civilian operation, were one to be developed the interrelationship could follow the same path that the existing military-civilian relationship has taken. Clearly this would be very much easier to achieve in a small operation like Cyprus, but whatever the size of an operation, the interrelationship structure must be such that it produces the greatest possible potential from all the various components that make up the force; a clear understanding and recognition of one another's roles and limitations must exist, for without it the effectiveness of each will be diminished.

Three separate UN operations—the Congo, West New Guinea, and Cyprus—have included a civilian police element of one kind or another, of which the one in Cyprus has been the most ambitious. ONUC included among its contingents a detachment of Ghanaian civilian police, later to be replaced by a similar detachment from Nigeria, for general law-and-order duties. There was no visible Congolese police force existing at the time of independence and therefore no one to perform the traffic and street patrol duties in the capital, Leopoldville. These duties were performed by the UN police detachments and were about the limit of their responsibilities. They had no judiciary powers of arrest or detention, though they had the right of apprehension. They provided escorts as protection for senior officials of the administration. In West New Guinea a Papuan police force already existed, but the withdrawal of the Dutch police hierarchy left a gap that could be filled only from the ranks of UNTEA. Senior police officers were made available by various countries to fill the vacancies left by the departed Dutch, and the police force operated as before under this multinational group of officers, until Indonesians took their places on the eventual hand-over of responsibilities to their country. Since the UN administration had full powers to exercise its authority in supervising the territory, the powers and duties of the police were similar to those afforded to police forces all over the world. In the case of West New Guinea, the judiciary and court system were able to continue because the Dutch judges agreed voluntarily to continue their duties for the duration of the UN interregnum.

Far and away the most comprehensive police participation was in UNFICYP. It comprised 174 police officers from Australia, Austria, Denmark, New Zealand, and Sweden, formed into one integrated unit known as UNCIVPOL. There is no doubt that it is one of the important successes of the UNFICYP operation and has set a pattern for the United Nations in the future. The role that such an element can perform in a Cyprus-type conflict is an invaluable one, for it can not only be linked to the military operation, as UNCIVPOL is to UNFICYP, but can play a role of even greater significance in a civilian oriented operation. Whether it be a military or civilian operation, whether the disaster is man-made or natural, the use of police within the context in which UNCIVPOL operates cannot be anything but an asset. In the Cyprus context UNCIVPOL's duties are limited to observation, advice, and negotiation. As in the Congo, its members are not permitted any executive authority or direct power of arrest, search, or interrogation; they can detain no one; they can disperse no unlawful crowds. It is therefore surprising, given these limitations, how successful they have been and how greatly respected they have become. Despite the limitations, they have become extremely effective investigators, observers, mediators, arbitrators, and even "father confessors," because they understand the practice of civic law and the importance of civil rights within a community. On numerous occasions it was their efforts rather than those of the military that prevented minor incidents from escalating into something more threatening and dangerous. This third-party presence of the "law" reassured the people of both communities. UNCIVPOL worked as closely with the Cyprus police (wholly Greek Cypriot) as with the Turkish Cypriot police element, which, though not recognized officially, did exercise an authority over its own community and was important to the maintenance of order. Because direct communications between the two communities were impossible, UNCIVPOL in many instances had to assume the negotiator's role; for example, in securing the release of hostages taken by one side or the other. For similar reasons it often undertook the investigation of criminal cases where the circumstances made it impossible for the Cyprus police to investigate a case themselves. Add to this the manning of posts wherever there was tension, the constant checking to ensure that freedom of movement was not unfairly obstructed and that people were not brutally searched when stopped, the supervision and protection of motor convoys whenever they passed through the otherwise closed enclaves of the opposite community, and the reader can have a fair idea of the comprehensive nature of UNCIVPOL's task. The success with which it handled these responsibilities is the measure of its achievements. The commander of this well-knit, multinational unit also acted as police adviser to the force and was responsible both to the force commander and to the secretary-general's special representative for the conduct of his police operations. There can be no doubt that police participation in any operation designed for an intercommunity conflict of this kind is an essential factor and should not be overlooked in the planning and mounting stage of such an operation.

The role of the United Nations' specialized agencies in conflict situations was already touched on briefly at the beginning of this chapter. They had a major role to play in the civilian operation in the Congo, and some of them, including the UN Relief and Works Agency for Palestine Refugees in the Near East (UNRWA), have been active in the Middle East since before the establishment of the UN Truce Supervision Organization in 1948. Though not a UN operation, the Nigeria/Biafra conflict saw the deployment of a number of the agencies in a relief role. One hesitates to criticize the admirable work that these agencies do perform in situations such as that found in Nigeria, but their independence of action and individual control structures afford little decentralization of decision making. This lack of flexibility tends to operate against the best interests of the relief operation and precludes the kind of coordination of effort and degree of effectiveness that is so badly needed. It seems a pity that wherever two or more agencies are deployed in an emergency role, an overall field director with appropriate powers of decision has not been appointed to ensure full coordination and cooperation among all the UN agencies involved.

In the ordinary course of events the specialized agencies are deployed on request to governments of countries to advise and assist with long-term aid projects in the economic, social, technical, and development fields. The nature and extent of the programs evolved are dictated by the governments concerned, and the agency cell provided becomes to all intents and purposes an instrument of the government and responsible to it for the work it does. At any time its services can be dispensed with by that government. Its task is specific, and it has no commitment outside the limits of its directive from the government it serves. The long-term nature of its program requires a cell structure that is not suited for emergency action—nor is it concerned with nor authorized to cooperate with other elements of the United Nations that may be operating on the same territory in an emergency situation. In an attempt to improve coordination an interagency organization—known as the Office for Inter-Agency Affairs—has been established at the United Nations under an assistant secretary-general.[3] This is an important advance and long overdue. A recent example where this coordination was practiced was by the UN Relief Operation in Dacca (UNROD) in 1971.

While this self-sufficiency is understandable—for if agencies were required to switch their priorities to deal with short-term problems created in an emergency, their long-term programs would suffer—it is clear that additional emergency task forces will be needed from those agencies that have a role to play. Such task forces should operate independently from their long-term counterparts and be concerned only with emergency relief. Their activities should be linked closely to the overall operational strategy and coordinated by the field director suggested above, who himself would have a seat on the central operational committee or council charged with the conduct of the operation. The contribution that UN specialized agencies could make

3. Established 1 January 1970, under the authority of Secretary-General Bulletin, 5 February 1970. During 1973 an under–secretary-general has been placed in charge.

in this way is hard to measure, but it is considerable and should not be wasted. Theirs is the role of the specialist professional or technician, which few soldiers are capable of fulfilling. As in the case of the police, it would be advantageous for the United Nations not to ignore the potential of the kind of task forces suggested, when it comes to deciding upon the composition and character of an international force required for a peacekeeping operation of any kind.

While appreciating the difficulties that might arise in absorbing the civilian task forces of the United Nations into a single operational structure of command and control, one should not forget that there are also nongovernmental agencies and organizations, some of whom combine as consortia and in recent years have provided relief task forces, money, and material emergency supplies on an individual national basis for all of the major natural disaster situations. That these have all been natural disasters does not alter the fact that the extent of the contribution has been immense and has become a recognized factor in relief operations of the magnitude described. The comment has been made before that international control of violence is an emergency operation to relieve a disaster situation. It can therefore be suggested that the nongovernmental organizations—particularly those existing within the "disaster" area but not precluding others from outside—could equally well contribute their expertise to such situations, always providing that they are prepared to operate within an overall strategy and under the direction of a "supremo."

Experience seems to show that there has been little or no collaboration so far among these nongovernmental organizations in disaster situations, even after their task forces have been deployed on the ground. Bangladesh is a recent example where there has been no visible linkup between the national voluntary organizations and the newly established UN Disaster Relief Organization. This is hardly surprising since these voluntary agencies themselves prefer to operate independently of each other, rather than to interlink their efforts in order to avoid overlapping and insufficiency. This policy of isolation is difficult to understand. The built-in regard for "sovereignty" and insistence on freedom of action does more to damage than to improve the prospects of the relief operation, but above all it produces not only considerable waste of the material needs provided, but also a comparable waste of human effort. It is strange that this fact is not generally appreciated. As with the specialized agencies, nongovernmental voluntary relief organizations could benefit from a coordinated control structure, interrelated with the central committee or council responsible for the overall direction of the operation. One can visualize many conflict control situations in which civilians rather than military have the primary role (Nigeria/Biafra was one; Namibia could be another in the future) and where voluntary organizations and individual volunteers—medical teams, engineer construction teams, transportation and movement control teams, and voluntary workers of all kinds—could be included.

If the principle is accepted that an interrelationship of roles is essential and that in order to ensure full effectiveness there must be a comprehensive coordination of effort, these factors need to be recognized, not at the time of the emergency, but in the preparation stage. In other words, all agencies—whether nongovernmental, governmental, or intergovernmental (UN)—must be ever aware in their planning, organizational development, and preparation of their field teams of the need to understand the roles of the different agencies involved. They must also be aware of the primary consideration that coordination and cooperation will succeed, where individualism is likely to fail or even add to the confusion. It is a distressing fact that as disaster succeeds disaster, the same mistakes are repeated, the same malfunctions and deficiencies of organization create frustration and disenchantment; and, above all, much of the generous and rapidly provided aid does not reach the victims for whom it is meant because of the lack of coordinated organization.

There is one further act of interrelationship that needs attention— the complementary association that links theory, research, and practice. This linkage is not as difficult to achieve as it is sometimes made to appear, nor is it as irrelevant as some theorists, researchers, and practitioners would have one believe. Yet here again one finds a certain lack of understanding of each other's role in conflict resolution and in some cases a strong supposition that the one is not complementary to the other and does not need to feed upon the experience, skills, or evaluation that the other has to offer. This is really where the whole problem begins, and unless these inborn prejudices can be dispelled and the full benefits of the work in these three disciplinary fields can be shared, most of the value that derives from them will be lost. It is worth repeating that theory and research formulate the design, but it is on the workbench of practice that this design is

given life. Only practical application will discover the faults and the
weaknesses as well as the strengths in the mechanisms of conflict
control; only the drawing board of research and theory can correct or
reinforce them once they are exposed. Not to put too fine a point on
it, international control of violence, conflict resolution, and social
reconstruction need the expertise of a world of experts—the expertise
of Everyman. Nothing less will do, and ways and means must be
found to harness that expertise as a coordinated whole for the benefit
of world peace. It is a matter of fact that in a number of major disasters in the last three decades, technical assistance has been provided
by the armed forces of many countries to assist a victim country with
its relief operations—sometimes independently, sometimes as part of
a UN contribution. In the Peru earthquake disaster of 1970, a special
engineering unit from Sweden carried out major reconstruction work
in the stricken area as part of the United Nations' assistance operation. This now almost accepted and respectable role for soldiers in a
natural disaster setting could foreshadow similar and more comprehensive participation of a like nature in the future. Using the development of an international concept for a natural disaster relief organization as a basis, there would seem nothing to lose but everything to
gain from developing a structure whereby disasters brought about by
conflict would become the responsibility of soldier and civilian alike.

The forum in which this ambitious concept can be achieved is as
yet underdeveloped. It hardly exists. But there are stirrings which,
properly nurtured, could form the basis of a worldwide network of
pooled resources. There is the increasing development of peace studies in the setting of international relations and international affairs at
universities in many countries; there is the growing consciousness
and concern on the part of young people about the state of the world
they live in and the realization that they are the ones who will ultimately inherit a world torn by conflict, unless positive action is taken
to correct the causes of structural violence and to remove the seeds of
the conflict. The creation of institutes for the study of theory and
research on conflict and the slow but discernible recognition by national ministries of defense of the need to study the requirements of
small-scale wars add to the growing body of opinion recognizing that
conflict has reached a dangerous level of universality and has to be
checked. The growing reaction by nonviolent activists and associated
world organizations against violence and war is a visible indication of

the dissatisfaction of so many with the present treatment of conflict and handling of violence. There is an ever widening interest in the search for less violent methods of conflict treatment—alternatives to armed suppression, counterviolence, and enforcement. There is a greater tendency on the part of states and regional groups to consider the violent approach as a last resort, preferring first to attempt all means of peaceful intervention to end conflict. The harmonization of military and civilian operations practised by more and more small states helps to promote just such an attitude.

At first the concept as presented here might seem overambitious to the point of being impracticable. It is not our intention to elaborate to any degree on how a worldwide structure of emergency civilian assistance might be set up; for it is plain that the contribution made by any nation-state will depend on its willingness to participate, its resources, and the extent to which it can mobilize those resources at the proper moment. However, it is at the national level, possibly through a national council, that the coordination of the country's contribution can best be wrought. At the international level one might expect that the overall direction of available assistance would rest with the United Nations, and the responsibility for coordinating the civilian contribution could be delegated to the already established Disaster Relief Organization, working through the UN secretariat or whatever UN body has been entrusted with the conduct of the particular peace-keeping operation. At the regional level, comparable assistance could be provided from both regional and international resources.

Chapter 13 outlined the need for the pooling of experience and expertise among the armed forces of all nation-states at both the regional and the global levels. It is no less important that the preparation and skill training for civilian organizations should follow the same pattern, thus avoiding the lack of coordination that at present occurs when the various agencies first come together on the ground in an active emergency situation. Here again, the kind of studies and preparation carried out by the military could be extended to embrace the broader scope of conflict control involving civilian participation. The International Peace Academy, in its major projects, has already begun to develop this kind of skill training at the transnational level, but it is the only skill training cell of its kind. It is perhaps not too far-fetched to hope that eventually something similar might exist at the national level, where the technical and professional human resources of a country could be trained for emergency roles. Once these national cells were established, consultative and liaison contacts would need to be maintained at the regional level to ensure the exchange of skills and the updating of techniques; while at the supranational or transnational level the establishment of a world university (already envisaged) could include in its structure a training college of the nature of a staff training school, where a world organization for peacekeeping and disaster relief could be developed and where officials from all professions could be trained for roles and responsibilities, both civilian and military, for disasters of any kind.

This idea of world cooperation and coordination for the international control of violence need not be just a fantasy. The International Peace Academy in its small way already has shown that it is possible to bring together people of different professions, interests, and opinion from all over the world—people with different social, racial, ethnic, and religious backgrounds—for the purpose of studying the structure and the treatment of conflict in an open nonpolitical forum and developing the skill training required to ensure that the treatment is correct. The Academy's success lies in the fact that the participants in its seminars are as ready to debate their own national conflicts as openly as any other. It therefore stands to reason that if such skill training and reconciliation of roles can be successfully developed at the multinational level by a private organization, education at a national level should not present great difficulties; while at the other end of the scale, a raison d'être would exist for the establishment of a central UN school for training and development.

An attempt has been made here to excite the reader's imagination to the possibilities of extending the range and the scope of international control of violence outside the existing limited confines of military action, encouraging him to think not only in terms of the interrelationship and interprofessionalism that need to exist among the three main elements of conflict resolution—peacemaking, peacekeeping, and peace building—but also of the important and fundamental role that civilians can play in many capacities. For, as has been repeated more than once, conflict does not take a standard form nor does a single conflict stay static but is forever changing in character. The treatment of it must therefore be flexible and adjustable, and those participating in the application of the treatment should be the best suited for the task. Their skill and proficiency in fulfilling their responsibilities will depend upon their preparation. Whether they be soldiers or civilians, this preparation becomes an essential factor in their training, for it must cover not only the skills required, but also a full understanding of the reconciliation of each other's roles and the paramount need for coordination and cooperation in order to obtain the greatest operational effectiveness. The development of this concept has been linked to the embryonic Disaster Relief Organization. Far more than the international control of violence, it is disaster relief that has captured the imagination and support of world public opinion; but international control of violence and disaster relief have certain significant characteristics in common. It therefore seems sensible to relate the one to the other in terms of civilian participation—and certainly the present weaknesses in coordination and cooperation among the various agencies and organizations involved in disaster relief indicate only too clearly that in this field, also, much needs to be done to improve the machinery of relief.

This chapter represents a blueprint, no more, of what could be achieved in the field of practical application of conflict treatment. Based on national structures and international cooperation, it contains nothing that overrides national sovereignties nor does it raise political issues. It broadens the resources on which the United Nations could draw in times of emergency and it provides a more ambitious perspective for dealing with conflict and its related problems. It also suggests a dual-purpose structure for contending with the needs of "disaster" in its broadest sense. It presents the concept of control of violence as a role for Everyman.

16

A Springboard for the Future

Thomas Hardy, the English poet, once remarked that war was exciting history but that "peace makes dull reading." In contemporary terms one might add the corollary that conflict and violence provide our daily reading but peace is never newsworthy. This view is understandable but is also very much the reason why the UN peacekeeping efforts have had such a critical reception from public opinion. Where conflict and violence have continued or been renewed despite a UN intervention, the critics are quick to react and ridicule; but where the United Nations succeeds in constraining violence and in stabilizing the conflict situation so that an atmosphere exists in which peaceful negotiations can begin, its success tends to pass unnoticed and unheralded, for there is nothing sensational about peace. In a world where double standards could be said to be the rule rather than the exception, one should not really be surprised at this. But the cynical distrust of the United Nations stems less from the lack of understanding and disinterest of peoples than from the tepid support given to it by its member governments.

We do not for a moment claim that what we have written will make any more exciting reading than any other book on peace, but it is an attempt at a constructive approach toward the development of a transnational system for the practical treatment of conflict and violence—transnational, because we have been considering a wide perspective of national, regional, and international effort. The ideas put forward are based on two realities: (1) the international political scene as it is and as we see it continuing to be, and (2) the UN Charter remaining unchanged from its original drafting. No attempt has been made to build political dreamworlds of our own nor to rewrite the Charter to suit our purposes; but within the tight limitations imposed by political realities and the almost rigid antiquity of the Charter's peacekeeping structure, we have offered a formula that is in countenance with the former and does not exceed nor diminish the authority of the latter; a formula that we believe can be worked with advantage within the confines of both.

We are not suggesting that peacekeeping of the UN pattern represents a substitute for enforcement action. We appreciate only too well that at best it can only be an alternative, capable of application at certain levels of conflict. We are aware that these levels are prescribed, and the opportunities for intervention will be limited. We are equally aware that the opportunities that may be available for the United Nations to intervene in the future may be restricted. But none of this alters the fact that an international system for the control of conflicts is needed and, in terms of collective security, is very much desired by the smaller nations, particularly those of the Third World. In the light of its experience over the past three decades the United Nations is the obvious foundation on which such a system should be built. People may argue over the degree of success that it has achieved in its promotion of world peace, but in its peacekeeping operations the degrees of success are high. Those who may contest this point should ask themselves what non-UN operations have been more successful? Certainly not the Vietnam War, certainly not France's unsuccessful campaign in Indochina, certainly not the series of internal security operations of the British since the end of World War II, certainly not Portugal's present confrontation in Africa, certainly not Pakistan's in Bangladesh. And can one with honesty say that where conflict has been ended by oppressive or enforcement measures, there has been peace? Certainly Hungary and Czechoslovakia are not examples of peaceful settlement of disputes, since the dispute in each case has simply been driven underground; Cuba, Goa, Guatemala, and the Dominican Republic are other examples. India's intervention in Bangladesh did not end violence but substituted the violence of reprisal for what there had been before.

There is no doubt that the international machinery of peacekeeping is inadequate and in need of restructuring, but it is worth the perseverance to achieve a more effective and efficient machine and one based on the United Nations. The disappointment of the International Commission for Control and Supervision in the post–Vietnam War period has illustrated only too clearly the difficulties that a non-UN initiative can run into when it does not have an international parent authority to which to report.

To achieve the kind of working coordination that is necessary we have made suggestions as to how the organs of the United Nations, specifically those concerned with peacekeeping, might contribute to the operational mounting and handling of peacekeeping operations. Ideas have also been put forward as to how these organs might be strengthened so that they can better achieve their responsibilities. Nothing that we hâve recommended runs counter to anything that the Charter says, nor do our proposals require major reorganization to be put into effect; what has been suggested is framed on existing structures established by the Charter and would not appear to raise controversial political issues.

Recognizing, however, that political and national considerations could frustrate the implementation of UN peacekeeping operations, we have faced this issue in two ways: first in the context of member state contributions and second in that of acceptability on the part of the parties to a dispute. Since the process of earmarking armed forces under Article 43 of the Charter is to all intents and purposes defunct, some other way needs to be found to make suitable provision for peacekeeping operations. In our view this does not require the setting up of a new recruitment scheme—such a scheme would have to have the authority of the Charter to be effective. On the other hand, by making the demand on member states less formally binding and more flexible in application so that "by arrangement" they may opt to make the kind of contribution to peacekeeping that their national resources permit, a greater response to the requirements of Article 43 might well result. In this way the global resources available for peacekeeping in all its facets could be greatly expanded and strengthened. Moreover it would help to dispose of the recurring difficulty of providing contingents suitable and acceptable to the host country or countries by providing a much wider field of choice.

The framework of our design is not intended to be viewed just in the context of the United Nations. It is a design that could form the basis on which regional peacekeeping machinery could be structured. In cases where regions and the United Nations might collaborate in containing conflicts, whether through peacekeeping, peacemaking, or peace building, having a common design would greatly facilitate the kind of coordination that would be necessary. Nor need the usefulness of the design stop at the regional level. At the national level an understanding of the design and its working could be a guide to the development of machinery for control of internal violence, for which counterviolence would otherwise be the corrective.

We have made a strong point of the value that could come from skill training in preparedness and preparation for active involvement in peacekeeping operations, on the grounds that no one, not even the military, can walk blindly into a conflict situation whatever the setting, interstate or intrastate, and expect to react automatically in the correct manner. Conflict treatment as has been explained takes many forms, as does the conflict itself. Unless care is taken in developing the correct attitude and approach to the peacekeeper's role in any given conflict circumstance, the result could be more destructive than if the conflict were allowed to continue untreated. And since third-party peacekeeping is a multinational venture, the skill training devised should be spread as widely as possible; hence the strong recommendation that the techniques should be studied, developed, and practiced at every geopolitical level, so that a standardization in peacekeeping training can be established. It seems equally evident that if operations are to be multiprofessional in character and composition then the preparatory training should be multiprofessional as well—for efficiency and skill in peacekeeping requires effective coordination of the different professions involved to ensure that the whole operation is successfully conducted. Interprofessionalism is needed in most spheres of life but possibly never more so than in the field of international operations, where the peaceful settlement of disputes will depend upon the effectiveness and elasticity of the multinational, multiprofessional coordination.

We have tried to present a factual picture of what we believe to be possible in the development of a conflict control system and what its ingredients need to be, both inside and outside the United Nations organization. It should, however, be firmly recognized that there has to be two-way traffic between fact and theory. Just as much as the theoretician needs an input of practical experience into his research so that his research can contribute to the needs of the practitioner, so must practical peacekeeping have a theoretical framework within which to develop. Without this understanding there will be no two-way traffic, and the value drawn from practice and research will thereby be wasted.

An old proverb says, "You can bring a horse to water, but you cannot force it to drink." Whether or not a peacekeeping system can be created to provide the kind of effective security safeguards against the threat of conflict and violence that so many of the nation-states are needing, will depend upon the genuine willingness and intent of governments—particularly the big powers. If that willingness does not exist, and the world continues to be subjected to big power politics and international business interests, then the chances of creating that system are slight. But there are indications that there is concern among the smaller nations at the continuing lack of a credible collective security system; therefore, the ideas that have been presented here could form the springboard for the future development of that system.

In his introduction to his annual report on the work of the United Nations in 1960—his last such report before his death—Dag Hammarskjöld said that there were two conflicting basic views of the United Nations, "The first of these envisaged the organisation as a static conference machinery for the resolving of conflicts, interests, and ideologies . . . the second view was of the United Nations as a dynamic instrument of governments through which they could seek reconciliation but through which they should also try to develop forms of executive action undertaken on behalf of all members and aimed at forestalling or resolving conflicts." He went on to say that "the static concept of the United Nations was related to the traditions and national policies of the past. The dynamic concept was related to the needs of the present and future in a world of ever closer international inter-dependence."

The world community must surely make its choice.

PART III

PEACEKEEPING PRESENT

17

An Epilogue—The Return of UNEF to the Middle East

This chapter represents an epilogue in that the events described in it came about after the remainder of the book had been written. Since the establishment of the new UN Emergency Force in the Middle East heralds a possible new era for international peacekeeping forces, it is appropriate to consider it in its present context rather than as an additional case study in part I. For UNEF II represents a fresh opportunity for the world body of the United Nations to examine the potential of the international peace-keeping instrument and the machinery that is needed to make it effective. This latest in the series of UN operations underlines that there are many lessons from the past still needing to be understood and usefully applied, while at the same time it demonstrates the progress that has been made and the improvement in skill and techniques that has come from experience. It proves above all that there exists a capability in an international operation of this kind for a quick and flexible reaction from those who are required to carry it out. In political terms it has a particular significance because it was the nonpermanent members of the Security Council that took the initiative in establishing the peace force when the superpowers found themselves unable to do it alone.

Early in the afternoon of 6 October 1973, while Jews everywhere were observing Yom Kippur, the holiest day in the Jewish calendar, the "quiescent" war in the Middle East once again erupted into bloody battle. The antecedents to this latest round in Arab-Israel hostilities could be traced back more than three years to the day when President Sadat took office after the death of Nasser on 28 September 1970. He is quoted as saying later that he recognized it as his destiny—his inheritance—that he would have to fight to regain what Egypt had lost, though he was prepared to give diplomacy every chance to succeed. In 1972, suspecting that diplomacy was not going to work, Sadat entered into direct and active discussions with his Arab partners, designed to further the prospect of renewing hostilities. When the Russians attempted to restrain him, he expelled the Soviet technicians who had been installing and instructing the Egyptians in the handling of their surface-to-air missile systems (SAM); this move was made in order to give himself greater freedom of action. In November 1972 planning for 6 October began in earnest. There followed continuous meetings between Egypt, Jordan, and Syria at top political as well as military levels, so that there would be full operational and political coordination when the time came to put the planning into effect. It appears that only the date was not an item on the agenda—this remained a matter for Sadat and the Egyptians to decide.

However, the secret planning and political interchanges were not the only activities that were evident during the twelve months preceding October 1973; military maneuvers and redeployments were being carried out by the Egyptian high command, largely in full view of the Israelis in the Bar-Lev line on the east bank of the canal. The Israelis do not claim to have been unaware of what was going on on the Egyptians' side of the canal—nor could they, for much of it was plainly visible.[1] This early warning of Egypt's intentions did not go unrecorded, but it seems unquestionable that the Israelis totally misappreciated and misjudged the Egyptians' timing for the assault. One can only assume that the Israeli high command believed that it could not only deal effectively with any attempt by Egypt to cross the canal, but also would have sufficient time in which to reinforce the Bar-Lev line before a crossing could be achieved. On both counts they were later to find that they had gravely miscalculated. Even up till the last twenty-four hours the Israeli government appears to have been satisfied that it had nothing to fear at that time. Though the armed forces were placed on full alert on Friday, 4 October, the order does not seem in every case to have filtered down through the chain

1. It is said that they even witnessed the experiments carried out to test the effect of high-pressure water jets against banks of sand similar to those guarding the east bank—a method later used by the Egyptians to breach that bank and enable the crossing to be quickly achieved.

of command, so that some of the formations and units remained un-aware of the emergency. The last days before the storm seem to have presented a bizarre picture, with groups of senior Egyptian commanders and staff observing the canal approaches (and, presumably, planned exits) through binoculars, while military units, including missile batteries, moved into position behind them—all apparently in full view of the Israeli units manning the Bar-Lev line. On the Syrian front heavy tank movements toward the Golan Heights were also observed—yet no thought of imminent attack appears to have crossed the minds of the Israeli generals.

It is too early to analyze the causes of this breakdown in tactical judgment and in the intelligence coverage and appreciation of Egypt's and Syria's intentions. Nor is it the concern of this book to attempt this. It is what followed the subsequent fighting that interests us and the reactivation of a UN Emergency Force and how it came about.

When the fighting broke out on 6 October 1973, the only UN presence along the canal and in the Golan Heights were the thinly deployed observer posts of UNTSO, the UN Truce Supervision Organization. Those on the west bank of the canal were immediately rendered obsolete by the advance of the Egyptian army across the canal; those on the east bank were less fortunate, for the majority were quickly engulfed in the fighting and in places came under artillery and mortar shelling before they could be extricated.[2] Eventually, when the Egyptian army had consolidated itself on the east bank, it requested the United Nations to withdraw its observers as they no longer served any purpose. Only two fatal casualties, however, were recorded, a French and an Italian officer whose bodies were found after the cease-fire—the former had been badly injured only one year previously when his vehicle hit a mine.

On the Israel-Syria front the story was much the same. Where the Syrian army advanced across the previous cease-fire line of 1967, the UN observation posts in its path were overrun and the observers taken to the rear. They were held there until after the fighting was halted three weeks later, when they were allowed to return to their posts. On

---

2. In one outpost that received a direct hit, a Canadian officer was on his way to the toilet when the shell struck and he was blown against its door and precipitated unceremoniously onto the seat. Later, when he returned to his room, he found it in a shambles, and the book he had been reading moments before was in shreds.

this northern front there were no fatal casualties, though a Norwegian officer with his wife and child were killed during one of the Israeli raids on Damascus.

Hostilities opened almost simultaneously on both fronts—at 1200 (GMT) on 6 October—with heavy artillery shelling of Israeli positions. UN observers both on the canal and in the Golan reported the shelling and major tank activity over a large section of each front. Their messages to UNTSO headquarters in Jerusalem were timed at 1214, 1221, and 1340 hours.[3] These messages also reported the initial crossing of the canal by the Egyptians and included one report of Israeli return of fire. The reports established beyond doubt that the initiation of hostilities were by Egypt and Syria and in no instance by Israel. This positive reporting temporarily effected a change in the hitherto unequivocal attitude of Israelis toward the United Nations in general and toward UNTSO and its members in particular, with the latter being received with rather greater courtesy and regard than before—a change of attitude that did not survive the subsequent cease-fire, which was felt by many Israelis to have been imposed upon Israel by the United Nations.

The battle waged for three weeks and while it lasted was bloodily fought. Israel, caught unprepared initially, suffered severe losses of men and equipment in the south. It fought a defensive battle, primarily to hold the Egyptians from advancing too deeply into the Sinai until Israel was in a position to mount a counteroffensive. Its immediate and pressing concern was in the north, where the Syrian assault was making inroads into Israeli territory along the Golan Heights. Were Syria to succeed in breaking through into the Upper Jordan Valley north of Lake Tiberias, Israel's territorial integrity would immediately be placed in jeopardy. It therefore concentrated its main effort on preventing such a breakthrough and driving the Syrian army off the Golan Heights. This it very largely succeeded in doing, eventually dislodging the Syrians from the whole of Mount Hermon [4] and advancing into Syrian territory astride the Damascus road.

---

3. Contained in Secretary-General's Reports to Security Council S/7930/Add. 2141 and 2142, 6 October 1973.

4. Syria had retained the summit of Mount Hermon since the 1967 war. In the early days of the October fighting it had driven the Israelis from its lower slopes. It is probable that Israel will seek to retain possession of Mount Hermon along with other strategic points on the Golan Heights as part of any peace settlement with Syria.

Once Israel had secured its objectives in the north, it turned its attention to the Sinai. Here the Egyptian army had advanced little further than the ten to fifteen miles it had covered in the first three days of fighting (it is doubtful whether Egypt intended any deep penetration into the Sinai further than the range of its tactical SAM missiles), though it had continued to build up its strength on the east bank of the canal, especially its armor. As the Israeli army redeployed for its counteroffensive in the Sinai and moved more and more of its armored forces into the battle area, tank engagements increased in size and in consequence. On Sunday 14 October, in what was probably the decisive action of the war, the armored forces of Egypt and Israel met between the Gidi Pass and the Little Bitter Lake in the biggest tank battle in the history of armored warfare. The outcome was a severe defeat for the Egyptians, though tank losses on both sides were heavy, and without doubt considerably affected Egypt's ability subsequently to oppose and liquidate the bridgehead that Israel established on the west bank of the canal in the early hours of 16 October. Claimed to be the "outstanding action of the war," the outcome of this assault across the canal clearly could have gone either way, teetering for some hours on the brink of disaster. It is questionable whether the bridgehead could have survived had the Egyptian high command not put all its armored capacity into the Sinai thrust, but instead had kept a viable component on the west side of the canal to counter any attempt by the Israelis to assault across it. Whatever the final analysis may be, the Israelis became firmly established across the canal and extended their territorial control until, by the time the first cease-fire was arranged, they had virtually cut off Egypt's Third Army in and east of Suez.

Throughout the three-week war, all had been quiet along the Israel-Jordan front. Jordan had not committed itself to joining its Arab neighbors in the simultaneous assault on Israel, and although it sent troops to the Syrian front and fired on any Israeli aircraft violating its airspace, it at no time was engaged directly with Israel. Well aware of its military insufficiencies on the ground and in the air and remembering its defeat in the Six-Day War, discretion certainly would appear to have been the better part of valor; but this did not mean that Jordan did not support Egypt and Syria in their decision to attack. On the contrary, Jordan gave them its full support short of direct participation. This decision may well in the long run be a major factor in settling the Jordan west bank problem as part of an overall Middle East peace settlement. Although Israel manned its positions along the west bank of the River Jordan as a precaution, no fighting took place.

The Security Council met on 7 October to discuss the Middle East situation and heard statements from all permanent member delegations and from representatives of Egypt, Israel, and Syria. This was the first of a series of meetings that the Council held on the Middle East during the course of the next two weeks,[5] but nothing tangible in the form of a cease-fire resolution came out of any of them, because of the lack of a consensus among its members. No initiative was found that might have persuaded either side to cease hostilities; only a not uncommon feeling of inadequacy and frustration pervaded at the United Nations' inability yet again to influence events.

Though the Security Council failed to arrive at a consensus, largely because of the differing views of the superpowers, it was in the end the United States and the Soviet Union that eventually resolved the deadlock and brought about a cease-fire. Soon after the outbreak of the war, the two countries were in contact with each other both through direct communication between President Nixon and Chairman Brezhnev and at a lower level between Kissinger and the USSR ambassador in Washington, Anatoly Dobrynin. The road was not an easy one, and even after Kissinger had visited Moscow at Brezhnev's request, there followed the famous alert when America's total nuclear force was placed on standby because of the Soviets' implied intent to send troops to Egypt. But this emergency was weathered, and the détente between the superpowers was not irrevocably damaged.

On 7 October the United States turned down an appeal from Israel for more arms to meet its war requirement. This refusal was aimed at limiting the extent of the hostilities but was necessarily reversed six days later, after it became clear on 9 October that the USSR was airlifting substantial resupplies of arms and equipment to Egypt. United States arms supplies to Israel were therefore renewed, and the USSR was warned of the serious consequences that could follow from its policy.

Kissinger flew to Moscow on 20 October. The previous two weeks had been spent in continuous consultation with Dobrynin and with the foreign ministers and other representatives of the Egyptian and Israeli

---

5. Subsequent meetings of the Security Council were held on 9, 11, and 12 October.

governments. Brezhnev's invitation was clearly meant to coincide
with the return of Premier Kosygin from Cairo, where he had been
since 16 October. After two days of intensive talks with Brezhnev,
Kosygin, and foreign minister Gromyko, Kissinger went on to Israel
while Kosygin returned to Cairo. It seems clear that both the United
States and the Soviet Union recognized that there was a grave danger
of confrontation were they not to attempt a unified effort to bring
about an end to the fighting. On 21 October this agreement in principle became a reality when they jointly presented a draft resolution
before the Security Council calling for a cease-fire in situ "no later
than 12 hours after the moment of the adoption of this decision," and
that "immediately and concurrently with the cease-fire, negotiations
start between the parties concerned under appropriate auspices aimed
at establishing a just and durable peace in the Middle East." [6] The
resolution was adopted without dissent, apart from the People's Republic of China's refusal to participate in the voting—a position it
has continued to maintain throughout.

This is the first time in UN history that the two superpowers have
together initiated a peace formula for an international conflict. One
recognizes that this collaboration was born of necessity because of
the serious possibility of the two powers becoming involved on opposite sides in the dispute and of the real threat that if allowed to continue unchecked the present war could bring the two countries into
open and direct confrontation—something that neither desired. All
the same, the urgency and subsequent accord with which the superpowers acted does focus attention on the degree to which there has
been a thaw in the cold war and an improvement in East-West relations. One might go further than just hazarding the guess and say that
no such coordination of effort could or would have been possible
seven years ago at the time of the Six-Day War, certainly not a decade ago. But what gives this historic fact greater significance is that
the joint initiative was taken and processed through the Security
Council as the organ of the United Nations, seized as it is with the responsibility for action in relation to the "maintenance of international
peace and security;" tangible evidence that the two superpowers
recognized that if their joint initiative were to succeed, it had to have
the authority of the Security Council. This first resolution was fol-

6. Security Council Resolution S/Res/338, 21 October 1973.

lowed on 23 October by a second, also sponsored jointly by the United States and the Soviet Union, which besides confirming its decision on a cease-fire, requested the secretary-general to arrange for the immediate dispatch of UN observers to supervise the observance of the cease-fire between Israeli and Egyptian forces.[7]

Though Resolution 338 had been accepted by both sides and orders had been issued in accordance with its twelve-hour time limit, the cease-fire was repeatedly broken, as one might expect in the circumstances of such a face-to-face confrontation and high emotion. This prompted Resolution 339 and the attempt to reestablish a UN observer presence in the conflict zone. At first the observers found it difficult to reposition themselves, for by now the cease-fire had completely broken down, with the Israeli army extending its bridgehead on the west bank of the canal. Egypt requested the United States and the Soviet Union to provide a peacekeeping force to supervise the cease-fire, but the United States declined. In order to implement the cease-fire, a group of nonaligned Security Council member states took the initiative; and on 25 October the Council approved Resolution 340, an eight-member resolution proposed by Guinea, India, Indonesia, Kenya, Panama, Peru, Sudan, and Yugoslavia, demanding an immediate and complete cease-fire and a return to the positions occupied by the parties at 1650 GMT on 22 October.[8] The resolution also called for an increase in the number of UN military observers and for the setting up of a second UNEF. The resolution received the full support of the Council, except that of the People's Republic of China, which declined to participate in the voting.

China's attitude is of interest. This was the first test as to what position it would take in the Security Council over peacekeeping and the establishment of peacekeeping forces. Since China believes in wars of liberation,[9] one might have expected it to use its veto powers to forestall any interference in the Middle East conflict. However, Israel had made considerable territorial gains following the first call for a cease-fire; and China, which supported the Arab and Palestinian cause, therefore was eager to bring an end to hostilities. Its head of delegation, Huang Hua, made it plain at the meeting of the Security Council on 25 October that, though the proposed UN emergency

---

7. Security Council Resolution S/Res/339, 23 October 1973.
8. Security Council Resolution S/Res/340, 25 October 1973.
9. See chapter 11.

peacekeeping force was an attempt to occupy Arab territories and one which China was totally opposed to, as it had been to the UN intervention in South Korea, China, "out of consideration for the requests repeatedly made by the victims of aggression, is not in a position to veto it." [10] China maintained its position of not supporting UNEF at subsequent Council meetings when the composition and financing of the new force were discussed.

On 26 October the Security Council met again to receive the secretary-general's report on the action he had taken in accord with the Council's directions to him, contained in its Resolution 340.[11] In his report the secretary-general set down the terms of reference for the force which was to assume the title of its Middle East predecessor, "United Nations Emergency Force." The terms of reference were:

1. To supervise the implementation of the cease-fire and the return of the parties to their respective positions held on 22 October 1973.
2. To use its best efforts to prevent a recurrence of the fighting and to cooperate with the International Red Cross in its humanitarian efforts.
3. In the fulfillment of its task, to receive the cooperation of the military observers of UNTSO.

With regard to the command and control of UNEF, the secretary-general proposed that he himself be responsible for this function under the authority vested in him by the Security Council. Command in the field should be exercised by a force commander appointed by the secretary-general with the consent of the Council and to be responsible to him. In his turn the secretary-general undertook to keep the Council fully informed of developments relating to the function of the force, while all matters affecting its nature and effectiveness would be referred to the Council for its decision.

The secretary-general then went on to enumerate certain essential guidelines on which the functions of UNEF were to be based:

a. UNEF must enjoy freedom of movement, communications, and other facilities necessary to the performance of its tasks.

10. 1750th Security Council Meeting, 25 Oct 1973, and UN Press Release SC/3486 of the same date.
11. Secretary-General's Report S/11052/Rev. 1, 26 October 1973.

b. The force as such and all its members should be granted all relevant privileges and immunities provided for by the Convention of Privileges and Immunities of the United Nations.

c. It should operate at all times separately from the armed forces of the parties concerned, that is, separate living quarters, and, wherever feasible and desirable, buffer zones to be arranged in agreement with the parties. Appropriate status of force agreements should be concluded with both parties.

d. Its composition will be agreed upon in consultation with the Security Council and the parties concerned, bearing in mind equitable geographical representation.

e. It is to be armed with defensive weapons only.[12] No force will be used except in self-defense; *self-defense to include resistance to attempts by forceful means to prevent* UNEF *from discharging its duties under the Security Council mandate.* UNEF is to proceed on the assumption that both parties will take all steps for compliance with Security Council decisions.

f. In performing its functions it will act with complete impartiality and will avoid actions that could prejudice the rights, claims, or positions of the parties which in no way affects implementaton of operative paragraphs of Security Council Resolutions 339 and 340.[13]

As immediate steps the secretary-general proposed the following:

1. Major-General E. Siilasvuo (Finland), presently chief of staff of UNTSO, to be appointed the interim commander of UNEF.

2. UNTSO to provide initially UNEF's headquarters staff.

3. UNEF would need to have a total strength of 7,000.

4. The initial functional period for UNEF should be six months.

5. In the light of the urgency to send UN troops immediately to Egypt, it was the intention to draw upon the Austrian, Finnish, and Swedish contingents with the UN Force in Cyprus (subject of course to the respective governments' approval). At the same

12. This in essence amounted to small arms and personal weapons only. No armored cars nor helicopters were to be included.

13. Res. 339: "Confirms its (SC) on an immediate cessation of all kinds of firing and of all military action, and urges that the forces of the two sides be returned to the positions occupied at the moment the cease-fire became effective." Res. 340: "Demands that immediate and complete cease-fire be observed and that the parties return to the positions occupied by them at 1650 hours GMT on 22 October 1973."

time negotiations would begin with other governments for the provision of contingents. It was further proposed to approach a number of governments to request logistic support, among whom Council member countries might be included.

6. The cost of maintaining a force of 7,000 in the Middle East for six months was estimated at US $30,000,000. This cost should be considered as expenses of the organization, to be borne by members in accordance with Article 17(2) of the Charter.

The Security Council accepted the report and approved a resolution giving effect to its proposals.[14] The approval, with the exception of China, was unanimous. It is interesting to note that despite years of controversy in the Special Committee on Peacekeeping Operations regarding the direction and control of peacekeeping forces, Secretary-General Waldheim acquired the responsibility, as had his predecessors Dag Hammarskjøld and U Thant. Whether or not he retains it as the UN peacekeeping presence in the Middle East develops, it is more than sensible that at this crucial phase in an operation, when speed is all important, that the secretary-general with his team of advisers should take control of the action, even though later he may hand over some of that responsibility to a suborgan of the Security Council. With the outright support given to his report, including that of both superpowers, it could be that a precedent has been set for future peacekeeping.

At 2130 GMT (2330 Cyprus time) on 25 October, UNFICYP headquarters received the first notification from New York that the Security Council had approved the dispatch of a peacekeeping force to Egypt and for its mounting to be undertaken as quickly as possible. The communication from the secretary-general also instructed UNFICYP that, subject to national governments' approval, the contingents of Austria, Finland, and Sweden currently serving with UNFICYP would provide the optimum force to proceed to Cairo for duty along the cease-fire line. Preparations were to be put in hand immediately to have the contingents ready to move. A later signal was more specific in detailing the numbers required from each contingent (a minimum of 200) and the types of equipment they were to take.

Twenty minutes after the receipt of the warning signal, the first of

14. Security Council Resolution SC/Res/341, 27 October 1973.

a number of staff conferences was held at UNFICYP headquarters. From then on the preparations proceeded swiftly and remarkably smoothly. By the time that clearance had been received from national governments for their contingents to be deployed into Egypt (1100 GMT on 26 October), the contingents themselves had already reported to UNFICYP headquarters their readiness to move. Their advance parties began moving to the United Kingdom airforce base at Akrotiri at 1200 GMT, and the first aircraft with 35 Austrians on board was airborne for Cairo at 1832 GMT. Twelve hours later, and less than thirty-six hours after the receipt of the secretary-general's first signal, the 600 troops of Austria, Finland, and Sweden had left Cyprus for Egypt, and not long afterward the Finns were engaged in local negotiations to halt firing along the cease-fire line.

Even these bare bones of the facts make impressive reading, but when all the factors are taken into account, UNFICYP's achievement becomes remarkable—even to the point of moving one UN skeptic, Henry Kissinger, to change his view of the United Nations' potential in the peacekeeping field and to state that no other military system could have reacted so quickly to the establishment of a third-party presence in the canal confrontation area. It is therefore well worthwhile to consider the elements with which UNFICYP had to contend in the process of getting the operation mounted.

In the first instance there were no contingency plans for such an operation; it had never been envisaged that any new peacekeeping force in the Middle East would have its antecedents in Cyprus. Each UN operation is by design wholly independent of any other and fulfills its task in accordance with a specific mandate set down by the Security Council, which would be unlikely to support any idea of the operation being used in any other capacity than that prescribed by its mandate. UNFICYP therefore had to proceed from scratch. Nor were the contingents themselves accustomed to nor prepared for crash moves of this kind. Although UN operations in their initial stages tend to involve rapid deployments of national contingents, they do have a home base and organization from which to set out, and such moves are controlled and programmed within the capabilities of the national organization. To move from one operational theater and role to another poses different problems, particularly as the organization inevitably will be of an ad hoc nature. It requires a major readjustment of mind and attitude to switch in a matter of hours from a quiet, and what might be described as a sedentary, role in Cyprus to a hot war situation in the Middle East. If this were not enough, all three contingents were at the end of their tour in Cyprus and were within days of scheduled rotation; in fact the Austrians and Swedes were due to hand over to relieving contingents only two days later—a circumstance requiring a psychological adjustment in addition to everything else.

Air moves at the best of times require careful planning and detailed knowledge at the unit level. Besides being unused to crash moves, the Austrians, Finns, Swedes, and later the Irish when they followed their colleagues to Egypt, had little experience in the packing and preparation of equipment, stores, and vehicles for air movement and in the compilation of load tables. At headquarters the staff equipment tables setting down what the contingents were to take with them were prepared with the expert assistance of two British officers serving on the headquarters staff. Even more fortuitously the British battalion with UNFICYP at this time was the First Battalion, the Parachute Regiment. In the early hours of 26 October it was instructed to attach a ten-man team to each of the three contingents to advise and assist them in the task of packing and preparation. It was largely thanks to this contribution that the contingents were ready to move so quickly; and we believe it is on record that UN headquarters in New York was considerably surprised (and no doubt delighted) that an operation it expected would take forty-eight hours to implement, indeed took less than half that time.

A matter of particular significance and one important to remember is that UNFICYP's peacekeeping responsibilities in Cyprus were still its priority task and could not be jeopardized by this removal of a fifth of its strength. As a priority consideration it was necessary for UNFICYP to ensure that wherever Austrians, Finns, Swedes, and later the Irish evacuated an operational post, it was taken over by troops from one of the contingents remaining behind. Planning for this contingency began early because the take-overs had to be completed before the outgoing soldiers moved from their posts. This involved (1) a reorganization and a thinning out of posts and positions all over the island, (2) the deployment of the Force Reserve, and (3) an internal airlift by helicopters being required to begin at first light. All this was managed satisfactorily and without fuss, and by 1000 GMT the readjustments were accomplished. Though UNFICYP was temporarily thin on the ground, all existing posts were manned.[15] It requires a high degree of mental flexibility and organizational adaptability to mount an operation within an operation without some loss of cohesion and tempo. What strikes one most is that both objectives were achieved with every degree of success and hardly, if any, lack of momentum in the overall planning.

Not only was national consent necessary before the move could begin, but an added complication was that the majority of the Finnish and Swedish soldiers were reservists and volunteers, while only a few were professional career soldiers. The former had volunteered and undertaken contracts to serve in Cyprus only; therefore, before any of them could be moved to Egypt, they had to be invited to serve there in UNEF II. In the event the response was unanimous, but the legal process had to be gone through and completed along with everything else before the advance parties could move.

The United Kingdom had offered aircraft free to transport the 600 men and their vehicles, equipment, and stores. Here again, the existence of the United Kingdom's operational airbase at Akrotiri in the south of the island, from which the move could be mounted, contributed considerably to the successful outcome of this emergency operation. For not only was the airbase available, but also the aircraft with the required capacity for both passenger and freight movement; what was not immediately available on the ground in the way of aircraft was diverted to Akrotiri to take part in the airlift. Had it been necessary to use the civilian airport at Nicosia, although more approximate to the UNFICYP troops' locations, the operation would have inevitably encountered delays, and the operational facilities and the experienced air staff at Akrotiri would have been lacking. At one moment there was some uncertainty as to whether Akrotiri, as a NATO operational airbase, would be a suitable launching pad for the movement of an international peacekeeping force, but the question was quickly settled, though imposing a slight delay on the move as a whole.

Some sophisticated professional military men might not be particu-

---

15. After two to three days the relief contingents arrived to replace those that had left, and UNFICYP was back to strength. In the meantime both the Cyprus government and Turkish Cypriot leadership had promised full cooperation in the avoidance of incidents, and this pledge was fully honored.

larly impressed by the speed with which the operation got under way. Others more skeptical might claim that had the experts not been there to guide and lead, the move would not have happened. True, the latter claim would be justified to an extent, but only to the extent that the move would not have happened so quickly. Success in putting an operation of this kind together depends as much on those who have to carry out the operation as those who plan it; for the operational organization to be effective and efficient, it is dependent upon every member of the staff at headquarters and in the unit. The results of this crash action UN operation do great credit to the professionals and nonprofessionals alike in UNFICYP, from the force commander and his senior staff officers down to the junior leaders in the contingents. It is doubtful if it could have gone much better had it been a straightforward move involving a single unit, trained for the task. Bearing in mind the circumstances, the limited experience, and the extraordinary complications of which the planners had to take account, Operation DOVE, the code name for the move, does represent a remarkably impressive performance on the part of UNFICYP as a whole and opens one's eyes to the future potential of UN forces in terms of quick action deployment and redeployment of resources.[16] Operation DOVE underlined the need for flexibility, something not always understood and practised among UN forces. It also emphasized the importance of having high-grade and experienced officers at all levels of the headquarters staff. Furthermore, it makes essential the kind of skill training or education that the Nordic countries have devised and the International Peace Academy is developing.

It would be wrong to suggest that this was a classic model for the future and to derive too many lessons from it. As we have been at pains to point out in this book, every UN operation is different, and each needs to be suited to the character of the conflict. Enough, however, has been said to indicate that there are a number of valuable considerations and conclusions to be drawn from this latest experience. Whether circumstances will arise in future to allow for a similar type of operation is questionable; but if they do, there is evidence that it is within the capabilities of the United Nations to act effectively, efficiently, and rapidly—very possibly more rapidly than any other sys-

16. As a short postscript, UNFICYP headquarters made sure that the Egyptian ambassador was kept constantly informed of the progress of the air movement.

tem. What Operation DOVE does show emphatically is that as UN peacekeeping techniques and experience develop and expand, the organization's ability to react quickly and effectively becomes more apparent and substantial.

With the arrival of the first aircraft of Austrians at Cairo Airport late on the night of 26 October, UNEF was officially established. General Siilasvuo, who had already moved from Jerusalem with a staff of 6, assumed command at once. In addition to the 585 UN soldiers, a total of 48 vehicles and 443,591 pounds of stores were flown in in the first thirty-six hours. On 27 October the Finnish contingent established the first UN presence in the Israeli-controlled area west of Suez, and at 2340 GMT the same night a meeting took place between Egyptian and Israeli senior officers in the presence of the Finnish contingent commander and an Irish staff officer from UNEF headquarters to discuss preliminary measures for observance of the ceasefire and matters relating to the supply of essential needs of food and water to the cut-off Egyptian Third Army and the evacuation of their wounded. The meeting took place at kilometer marker 109 on the Cairo-Suez road and resulted ultimately in the UN supply convoys that daily throughout the following three months kept the Third Army alive. By this time, Siilasvuo had accomplished the redeployment of the UNTSO observers on both sides of the canal with a total of fifteen posts—nine on the west controlled from Ismailia Control Center, and six on the east controlled from Kantara Control Center. By this time the Swedish contingent had moved into the Ismailia area, followed after a few days by the Austrian contingent, who were deployed west of the Great Bitter Lake. UNEF was operational and growing in strength.

All this happened while the secretary-general was continuing his approaches to member governments to obtain the necessary contingents to bring UNEF up to the required strength of 7,000. In accordance with the Security Council's directions, these had to be from a broad geographical pattern of representation. First, he obtained the agreement of Austria, Finland, and Sweden to provide additional troops, sufficient to bring their existing contingents in Egypt up to a working battalion strength. Ireland was also approached and agreed to supply a contingent. In order to do this it withdrew 129 of its contingent in Cyprus and airlifted a further 130 direct from Ireland.[17] Having heard the secretary-general's progress report of 31 October,[18] the Security Council, in an informal meeting, adopted a consensus agreement on phase two of Resolution 340, by which the secretary-general was immediately to consult with Canada, Ghana, Indonesia, Nepal, Panama, Peru, and Poland with a view to their dispatching contingents to the Middle East. It was further agreed that contingents from at least three African countries should be included in the force so that there would be a correct geographical distribution within UNEF. As hitherto, China disassociated itself from the consensus, which was agreed to by all other members of the Council.

In the event, all the governments approached agreed to provide contingents. Since the list only included one African country against the three required by the Security Council to give "the correct geographical distribution," Kenya and Senegal were therefore approached and both accepted the invitation. During the succeeding months the contingents began to arrive in Egypt and were deployed on the east bank of the canal and placed temporarily under the Kantara Control Center. On 1 December UNEF's strength, excluding headquarters, was 3,174, with Austria (398), Canada (693), Finland (557), Ireland (260), Peru (404), Poland (324), and Sweden (496) operational, plus small advance parties from Indonesia and Panama. A month later the strength had risen to 5,467 [19] and was only slightly more when the disengagement agreement was signed on 18 January 1974. In addition, UNTSO had 296 observers deployed, 112 on the canal and 124 on the Golan Heights.

In any ad hoc operation the arrangements for the logistic coverage of a force tend to lag behind. In UN terms the exception was UN-FICYP, where the United Kingdom's military supply base on Cyprus was offered immediately by the British government as a source of logistic support. UNEF II, like its predecessor, had to establish its own

17. The Cyprus element was carried in United Kingdom aircraft and that from Ireland by the United States Air Force. In the case of the Austrians and the Finns, their home-based reinforcements were moved in USSR aircraft, while Sweden moved its own with the help of Norway. All moves were at no cost to the United Nations.

18. Secretary-General's Report S/11056/Add. 1, 31 October 1973.

19. Austria (600), Canada (1,012), Finland (615), Indonesia (550), Ireland (290), Panama (409), Peru (497), Poland (803), Sweden (626); Ghana (4) and Senegal (50) had advance parties in Cairo.

logistic system. At a very early stage the secretary-general asked Canada if it would assume the responsibility, which Canada agreed to do. However, the Soviet Union was not satisfied that this responsibility should lie solely in the hands of a Western bloc country but felt it should be shared between Canada and Poland. The USSR's insistence on this point inevitably delayed the establishment of the system and the flow of supplies to the contingents on the ground. Though the later arrivals were not unduly affected, those who had come from Cyprus had brought only thirty-days rations with them, and at one point there was real concern that these might run out before the force maintenance area became operative. For a while some contingents had to purchase supplies locally. An advance party of the Canadians was early on the scene and had begun to organize the system when the USSR objection was lodged; when the strength of the Canadian contingent on the ground was 227, the Poles still only had an evaluation team of 5 in Cairo,[20] and it was not until near the end of November that their main body moved in. The UNFICYP experience had emphasized the advantages in economy and effectiveness that accrue from having a single nation responsible for the field logistic organization in an international force.[21]

The efficient performance of a force's operational duties depends upon an equally efficient logistic backup, and though this rarely will be in existence before the arrival of the force, it must be activated as rapidly as possible afterward. In the case of UNEF II a much more rapid and satisfactory result would have been occasioned had the Canadians initially been given the complete responsibility for setting up the force maintenance area—later, if politics demanded it, it could have become a shared responsibility. Politics, however, seem out of place when it is a question of filling men's bellies and providing the essential needs of soldiers who have come from all over the world into environments to which they are unaccustomed and where the adjustment process is difficult enough. One hopes that the lesson might sink in. It was, at the least, unfortunate that when the Poles first assumed their responsibilities as set out in the Memorandum of Understanding,[22] their efforts were largely obstructed through Israel's refusal to allow any Polish soldiers into Israeli-controlled areas. This

20. Secretary-General's Report S/11056/Add. 4, 14 November 1973.
21. Michael Harbottle, *The Impartial Soldier*, pp. 136–38.
22. United Nations Document Annexure to S/11056/Add. 6, 21 November 1973.

denial of freedom of movement to members of the UN force runs contrary to the status of force agreement that covers the rights of UN forces and those of its members. Previously, it had been the principle that in accepting the peacekeeping force and its composition in the first place, a country accepted its right to freedom of movement without discrimination. Whatever motives lay behind Israel's refusal, it is to be hoped that discrimination in the right to freedom of movement for members of a UN force will not become an accepted practice. It was no fault of the Poles that they were denied the opportunity to fulfill the specific roles they had been given, but one does question how it was that the possibility was not considered in New York when the Memorandum of Understanding was being prepared.

The Memorandum of Understanding recorded the discussions held between the UN secretariat and the delegations of Canada and Poland to determine the organization and composition of the logistic support system for UNEF. These discussions took place in accordance with the Security Council's decisions, taken at its informal meeting on 2 November, and determined the division of responsibilities between the two countries. As a start, Canada was to provide the signal communications and Poland an engineer unit. The logistic base would comprise a road transport unit, including a maintenance unit, from Poland and a composite service unit consisting of a supply company, an aviation unit, a maintenance company, a movement control unit, and a postal detachment, all provided by Canada. Poland later undertook to provide a mine clearance unit and a 100-bed hospital. The whole would be under the direction and control of a chief logistics officer who in the first instance was to come from Canada. He would have command of the whole base but be responsible to the force commander. The manning of the base would be relative to the commitment as divided between the two countries, though the units of each would be administered by their respective contingent headquarters.

Whatever criticism there might be of the manner in which the setting up process was managed, it certainly does not apply to the implementation of the provisions of the Memorandum of Understanding. Once the decisions had been made and the division of responsibilities decided upon, the organization of the logistic base proceeded with commendable speed. Admittedly there were moments of crisis, but the administration succeeded in remaining one jump ahead of the influx of stores and equipment, and any expected chaos did not materialize.[23] The maintenance area was established on the race-course at Heliopolis,[24] a suburb of Cairo, and very quickly took on the appearance of an organized, efficient, and well laid out depot. Although shortages of particular national dietary commodities and comforts, such as beer and cigarettes, still existed in January, most of the needs of individual contingents were being met. The Canadian ration scale, which is a generous one, was used initially as the basic ration scale for the force, which each contingent could adjust to its taste, until supplies allowed for national ration scales to be substituted. In the meantime, additional requirements were bought by local purchase. UNEF's maintenance area at Heliopolis, despite the delay in getting it into operation and the inherent problems arising from ad hoc arrangements, was an impressive functioning component. Much credit is due to the coadministrators, in particular to Canada, who had the burden and the problems of setting it up from nothing but, having the necessary experience born of many UN peacekeeping operations, overcame remarkable difficulties to provide an efficient working logistic support for UNEF.

The arrival and deployment of the first contingents, though having a salutary effect, by no means brought an end to the fighting or to the continuing efforts by the Israelis to improve their positions on the west bank of the canal. At least the relief convoys, agreed upon at the meeting on 27 October at kilometer marker 109, had begun and these, though slow to start with, continued without serious disruption until disengagement took place. On 29 October agreement was reached with Israel for the stationing of UNEF troops on the east bank within Israeli-held territory (on 9 November the Irish moved to Rabah); but all efforts to persuade Israel to withdraw to the positions it had held on 22 October failed to obtain any response. Toward this end, following the Security Council meeting on 2 November, the secretary-general had instructed General Siilasvuo to request the Israeli government to take this action, but the latter had no success.[25] The use of the force commander in the role of political negoti-

23. There were the occasional nonsenses, such as fresh butter being sent unrefrigerated instead of in tins, and the breakfast foods in home delivery cartons being packed at the bottom of a ship's hold under tons of other heavier commodities.

24. In laying out the administrative area, a 900-yard length of race track was left free, available for the race horses to use for sprint training.

25. Secretary-General's Progress Report S/11056/Add. 2, 4 November 1973.

ator must inherently be wrong. The force commander's primary responsibility during the organizational and deployment stage of an operation is for the day-to-day management of his force. This critical phase in the life of the force is a crucial one for its commander; he should not be distracted at this or any other time from his main purpose by having to undertake political initiatives, which with the approval of the Security Council should be delegated by the secretary-general to a special representative. The precedent for this already exists in UNFICYP (and before that operated in the Congo). In the same context it would seem inappropriate and undesirable that UNEF's force commander should have been absent in Geneva for a protracted period during January 1974, chairing the meetings of the military subcommittee of the peace conference, when it was surely more important that he be commanding his force in the field. The cease-fire was undoubtedly precarious and liable to break down at any time unless some more positive diplomatic action was taken to prevent it. Between 29 October and 3 November four further meetings of Egyptian and Israeli military reprsentatives took place at kilometer 109, at which mutual disengagement and the establishment of a UNEF buffer zone were discussed as well as the question of a return to the 22 October positions.

Ever since the initial cease-fire had broken down, Kissinger had been working for a more binding agreement between the two parties, and on 9 November he was able to write to the secretary-general that Egypt and Israel were prepared to accept a six-point agreement.[26] The terms of the agreement were:

A. Egypt and Israel agree to observe scrupulously the cease-fire called for by the United Nations Security Council.
B. Both sides agree that discussions between them will begin immediately to settle the question of the return to the 22 October positions in the framework of agreement on the disengagement and separation of forces under the auspices of the United Nations.
C. The town of Suez will receive daily supplies of food, water, and medicine. All wounded civilians in the town of Suez will be evacuated.

26. Security Council Document S/11091, 9 November 1973.

D. There shall be no impediment to the movement of non-military supplies to the East Bank.

E. The Israeli checkpoints on the Cairo-Suez road will be replaced by United Nations checkpoints. At the Suez end of the road, Israeli officers can participate with the United Nations to supervise the non-military nature of the cargo at the bank of the canal.

F. As soon as the United Nations checkpoints are established on the Cairo-Suez road, there will be an exchange of all prisoners of war including wounded.[27]

The secretary-general immediately instructed General Siilasvuo to call a meeting of the parties' representatives and obtain signed acceptance of the agreement. The meeting took place at kilometer marker 101 on 11 November, and at 1300 GMT both sides signed in the presence of the force commander, who signed on behalf of the United Nations. The agreement was to take effect immediately. It is again of interest to note that although the draft agreement was the result of superpower diplomacy, it was through the organ of the United Nations that it was promulgated and implemented.

This agreement was the first step toward a peace conference. Although meetings in the tent at kilometer 101 were shortly to be discontinued, the scene of negotiations moved to Geneva, where on 21 December the conference to settle the peace of the Middle East began. This was merely a formal meeting at which the opening statement was made by the secretary-general, followed by others from interested parties. The only absentee was Syria, which had refused from the start to take part because of its determination that nothing but the complete withdrawal of Israel to behind its pre-1956 borders was to be tolerated. The conference was adjourned on 22 December until after the beginning of January 1974, but discussions continued in Geneva between military delegations of both sides in the presence of General Siilasvuo. Little progress was made and the achievement of a disengagement appeared just as remote as ever, when Kissinger took a hand once more. In a dramatic series of talks with President Sadat at Aswan and with the Israeli government in Jerusalem between

27. By 23 November, a total of 241 Israeli and 8,305 Egyptian prisoners of war had been repatriated under arrangements initiated and supervised by the International Red Cross and UNEF representatives. The release of Israeli prisoners by the Syrians was not so quickly achieved and was a major obstacle to a peace settlement on the northern front.

11 and 17 January, necessitating a daily shuttle between the two,[28] he was able to devise a formula for the disengagement of forces that was acceptable to both. On 18 January 1974, at the same kilometer marker 101, the instrument of disengagement was signed by the two military commanders in the presence of UNEF's force commander. The terms of the agreement were as follows:

A. Egypt and Israel will scrupulously observe the cease-fire on land, sea and air called for by the United Nations Security Council and will refrain from the time of the signing of this document from all military or paramilitary actions against each other.

B. The military forces of Egypt and Israel will be separated in accordance with the following principles:

1. All Egyptian forces on the east side of the canal will be deployed west of the line designated as line A on the attached map [reproduced in this book as map 15]. All Israeli forces, including those west of the Suez Canal and the Bitter Lakes, will be deployed east of the line designated as line B on the attached map.

2. The area between the Egyptian and Israeli lines will be a zone of disengagement in which the United Nations Emergency Force UNEF will be stationed. The UNEF will continue to consist of units from countries that are not permanent members of the Security Council.

3. The area between the Egyptian line and the Suez Canal will be limited in armament and forces.

4. The area between the Israeli line (line B on the attached map) and the line designated as line C on the attached map, which runs along the western base of the mountains where the Gidi and Mitla passes are located, will be limited in armament and forces.

5. The limitations referred to in paragraphs 3 and 4 will be inspected by UNEF. Existing procedures of the UNEF, in-

28. Reminiscent of another American diplomat's "shuttle" diplomacy. President Johnson's special representative Cyrus Vance, over a period of six days during the Cyprus crisis of November 1967, traveled continuously between Athens, Ankara, and Nicosia in an attempt to prevent war between Greece and Turkey. On this occasion, José Rolz-Bennet, UN under–secretary-general for political affairs and Secretary-General U Thant's special representative, conducted a similar mission, and between them they were successful in their dual attempt.

cluding the attaching of Egyptian and Israeli liaison officers
to UNEF, will be continued.

6. Air forces of the two sides will be permitted to operate up
   to their respective lines without interference from the other
   side.

C. The detailed implementation of the disengagement of forces will
be worked out by military representatives of Egypt and Israel,
who will agree on the stages of this process. These representatives will meet no later than 48 hours after the signature of
this agreement at Kilometre 101 under the aegis of the United
Nations for this purpose.

They will complete this task within five days. Disengagement
will begin within 48 hours after the completion of the work of
the military representatives and in no event later than seven
days after the signature of this agreement. The process of
disengagement will be completed not later than 40 days after it
begins.[29]

D. This agreement is not regarded by Egypt and Israel as a final
peace agreement. It constitutes a first step towards a final, just
and durable peace according to the provisions of Security Council resolution 338 and within the framework of the Geneva conference.

So the door was open for the second phase of UNEF II's role in the
Middle East—the creation of a buffer zone between the forward
defended localities of both sides in the Sinai. It also permitted the
calling forward of those additional contingents who until then had
been waiting in the wings. It should be a less complex problem for
UNEF to organize and deploy itself effectively within a buffer zone
than on either side of the canal with the difficulties of communication.

Whether this second phase will be the last or whether a further
phase will follow, subject upon a substantial withdrawal by Israel
within the Sinai, will depend on the outcome of the Geneva Peace
Conference. Clearly, paragraph D of the disengagement agreement
does not accept this initial withdrawal as final. If further Israeli with-

29. It appears that arrangements also were made for a reduction in weapon strengths by
Egypt on the east bank of the canal and by Israel in the occupied area of the Sinai adjacent to
the UNEF buffer zone.

drawals follow, then one must assume that UNEF, as a buffer force, will continue to be required; though its character, composition, and size might well have to alter with the changing scale of responsibility and could involve the participation of permanent member states of the Security Council, including the superpowers (the latter albeit in a support role only in the communications and logistic fields).

Peace talks wait on an Israeli-Syrian disengagement.[30] Syria will not be easily mollified, and even if it is prepared to go to a settlement, the future of the Golan Heights will be the pivotal point on which any solution will rest. Israel without a doubt received a great shock in October 1973, and it will not readily give up any ground that it has won on the Golan, including particularly the summit of Mount Hermon. It is doubtful that the presence of UNTSO observers will be sufficient or will provide adequate credibility in the eyes of either side, and it seems that a buffer force would be the least that Israel would accept in return for its pulling back from the Golan Heights.

UNTSO's character has undergone a change since the cease-fire of 22 October 1973. It has established new positions to equate with the new forward defended localities but has become more mobile. Whereas before UNTSO was organized on a system of static observer posts, it has now reformed largely on a patrol basis. This gives its observers a wider scope because they are no longer confined strictly to the 250 square meters of their post area. The observers now have recognized and accepted patrol routes; and, though local commanders place restrictions of their own making on their movement, the patrols are able to move freely along the permitted routes.

A development that could be of major significance in the future—not only so far as UNEF is concerned but in terms of future UN peacekeeping missions and operations—is the appearance of United States and USSR observers together in UNTSO. Security Council Resolution 340 specifically barred permanent member states from providing contingents for UNEF. Both the Soviet Union and the United States had consistently stated that there could be no question of their participation in any kind of peacekeeping force in the Middle East. It therefore came as a surprise, and to some a heartening sign of encouragement, when first the Soviet Union and then the United States

30. Agreement signed 31 May 1974. Text UN Doc. S/11302/Add 1.

announced that they would be sending observers to the battle area. Thirty-eight from each joined UNTSO. Those from Russia were deployed solely on the Arab side, with the Americans on both sides. They did not operate independently but in joint patrols or on observation posts with members of other contributing countries—acting no differently from the accepted procedures of UNTSO. In all twenty-six years of its existence, UNTSO possibly has not acquired such a significance as it enjoys today. It has ridden out many storms and taken many knocks, but today on the Golan Heights and in the Sinai it is fulfilling a purpose that has become increasingly important and valuable.

It is of course much too early to make an evaluation of this latest UN peacekeeping operation, as the full effects cannot yet be analyzed; nor could it be a complete evaluation since UNEF II has but begun and may assume more than one dimension before it ends. However, it is possible to ascribe a positive commentary on its progress up to the end of its first phase—the disengagement.

The first thing that has to be said is that we have a new UN peacekeeping operation after a lapse of ten years; a lapse that included Nigeria/Biafra and Bangladesh and a non–United Nations intervention in Vietnam. The only reason for mentioning these latter is that they added strength to the belief among a large section of informed opinion that we would not see another UN peacekeeping force—that UNFICYP was the last. No such claim can any longer be made, for with the rebirth of UNEF a new era in peacekeeping has opened, and the concept of international peacekeeping forces has been strengthened by the joint action of the superpowers in using the instrument of the Security Council to bring about a cease-fire and thereafter supporting the resolution for the establishment of an emergency peace force. It is very doubtful if anyone foresaw that the renaissance of peacekeeping would be achieved in this way.

Apart from the singular act of the superpowers' combining together for the first time in UN history in the submission of a resolution on peacekeeping, it is the first occasion on which the Soviet Union and France have agreed to pay a proportionate share of the costs. China's action in disassociating itself from the voting of the Council is also of considerable significance in future terms. By withdrawing from the voting rather than using its veto power, it recognized the wishes of the majority of Council members (and of Egypt) for an early end to the fighting, though these ran contrary to its own sentiments. Time will show whether China's responsible reaction toward future Security Council resolutions will be governed by the same principles, but remembering the veto-ridden Council debates of the UN's early years, it is a hopeful sign that when the test came, China did not use its right of veto to negate a majority view. Other "firsts" worth noting are:

1. Israel's acceptance of the interpositioning of a UN peacekeeping force.
2. Poland becoming the first Warsaw Pact country to serve in a UN peacekeeping force.
3. Participation of USSR observers in a UN observer mission.

Of the contingents serving with UNEF II, the Canadians, Finns, Indonesians, Irish, and Swedes are seasoned UN campaigners; the Austrians, who had to wait so long before having their standby UN battalion accepted for service in Cyprus in 1973, are fast establishing a reputation for themselves and can be expected to become one of the consistent providers in the future. Of the others, only Ghana has previously participated in a UN peacekeeping operation—in the Congo; Nepal had observers with the UN India-Pakistan Observation Mission in 1965, but three—Panama, Peru, and Senegal—are newcomers.[31] It is encouraging and important that the UN peacekeeping "club" is expanding, with more and more countries becoming experienced and thereby adding to the pool of resources from which the United Nations will be able to select. The larger the club the less becomes the necessity to reactivate Article 43 in its strict Charter interpretation; it will be much easier to encourage the less formal undertaking suggested by us in chapter 3. Skill education or training would still be needed to achieve the required standards in technique and operational performance, but this again is likely to be easier to accomplish as more and more of the smaller nations take part in peacekeeping operations and acquire the practical experience that these will provide. It is certainly heartening that the response to the secretary-general's call should have been so quick and so positive. If nothing else, it shows that small nations do see themselves as having

31. Kenya, finally, did not provide a contingent.

an international role to play in conflict crises where they, and largely only they, are eligible for selection as the keepers of international peace.

But we must not blind ourselves to the inadequacies and inefficiencies that still exist in the peacekeeping machine. We have mentioned the skill education that is necessary to achieve the desired standards of operational effectiveness within a force; hand in hand with this must go the preparation of contingents for the role they will be required to perform. Those unfledged contingents that have joined UNEF II arrived with their own preconceived ideas of what their role would be and what they needed in order to carry it out. As a result a number of domestic problems arose that could only help to detract from the operational effectiveness of these contingents at the start. This was no fault of the contingents themselves, but more that of the United Nations, which had not provided the countries concerned with the information they needed. With ad hoc arrangements, simple things tend to be forgotten, and too much is taken for granted, such as that it is common knowledge that the desert nights in Egypt are cold and not hot as in the Peruvian desert and therefore one blanket per man in the Sinai in December is not enough.[32] An *aide-memoire* of do's and don't's would be easy to circulate, but the problem goes deeper than that. All too often contingents arrive, as they have in UNEF II, with only the haziest idea of what a peacekeeping operation entails, and the period of familiarization is long—representing a dangerous weakness in the force for as long as it takes the particular contingent to adjust itself to the conditions and requirements of the operation. Here again one must blame the organization rather than the individual country. It is one of the inadequacies of the UN secretariat that it does not put the fruits of peacekeeping experience to a more positive use so that national armies can benefit from the lessons learned. The impression obtained from talking to those who are meeting the responsibilities of peacekeeping for the first time is that a basic manual of peacekeeping covering all its operational aspects of organization, administration, standing operating procedures, preparation, and training, as well as status of force agreements and international law as it affects international peacekeeping, would be of inestimable value to all concerned. This impression is just as strongly confirmed by almost

32. At the time of Suez in 1956, one of the contingents from Asia arrived wearing civilian clothes.

all those who have wide experience in international peacekeeping, particularly those in senior command appointments. It would therefore seem appropriate and timely for such a manual to be produced to provide the guidance that is clearly needed and is being sought.[33]

The deficiencies apparent in this latest "instant" peacekeeping operation are far from being insurmountable, despite the inevitable ad hoc system that occasioned its mounting. There is nothing that has emerged so far from UNEF II that obviates any of the ideas put forward in this book for improving the machinery and techniques of peacekeeping. What does emerge only strengthens the case for them.

The concept of placing the logistic support in the hands of one contributing government makes even more sense than it did before. The impressive achievement in terms of the organization and development of the force maintenance area in Cairo must in all fairness be credited to the Canadians, since it was they who bore the burden of its establishment. The political argument must be seen to be irrelevant here; for what is there political about logistics?

The mounting operation from Cyprus should not be looked upon solely as a gratuitous bonus. It demonstrated the value of having experienced UN peacekeepers immediately available with the operational flexibility and the foresight to move contingents from one peacekeeping role to another within a few hours. It overcame the difficulties arising out of the emergency situation and was the reason that the UNEF II operation got off to such an excellent start. UNFICYP's rapid deployment of UNEF underlines the importance and relevance of preparation and training. Fortuitous as it may have been to have had the experts available, it has taught the lesson that by having the knowledge, what could have been a forty-eight–hour operation was accomplished in less than half the time.

Deficiencies there may have been, and no doubt these are being analyzed now in Cyprus, in Cairo, and in the new UN buffer zone in the Sinai, as well as in New York. Deficiencies there will always be, but with the possibility of a new beginning for international peacekeeping and the use of the instrument of the United Nations for the maintenance of international peace and security, let there be no

---

33. If political considerations make it unacceptable for the United Nations to undertake the task, it could equally well be produced by a nongovernmental body, experienced and knowledgeable about what is needed. It is a task that the International Peace Academy will shortly be undertaking.

disregarding them. The mounting of UNEF II was a considerable and positive achievement for which the secretary-general and the secretariat can justly take great credit. An opportunity exists to begin again to work to improve the United Nations' potential in this field and the machinery that is required to make it effective and efficient. Here is the incentive for which the Special Committee on Peacekeeping Operations has been waiting. It would be tragic if this opportunity were to be wasted. The new détente between Russia and the United States could provide the firm base on which to develop the new concepts and techniques. There appears to be enough justification for believing that the good faith and willingness to participate exists on the part of the smaller nations. The varied excursions into multinational initiatives outside the United Nations have met with greater problems of implementation that have their UN counterparts; and when one sets the early achievements of UNEF II against the International Commission for Control and Supervision in Vietnam, one does not need to count the score. Regional organizations could well be encouraged by the UNEF II experience to develop within their own geographical areas of responsibility the same kind of potential for the maintenance of regional peace and security.

This second UN Emergency Force in the Middle East, whatever may be its ultimate fate, has renewed confidence in the ability of the United Nations to mount an effective emergency operation. It has demonstrated that the United Nations has the capability of establishing a force in a confrontation area more quickly than could any other agency, and one which is acceptable to both sides. It has shown that experience from previous operations is beginning to tell, and that the tried peacekeepers are becoming progressively more competent. It has underlined the fact that in terms of conflict treatment peacekeeping with international forces is a reckonable factor that has to be encouraged and developed rather than despised and ignored.

Finally, UNEF II has indicated beyond doubt that major peacekeeping operations of the future will be mounted only so long as the superpowers are in agreement. This is reality, but now that it has happened once, one can be optimistic rather than pessimistic about its happening again. The important thing is that it should, and that it is the Security Council and the machinery of the United Nations that should be used to implement the initiatives agreed to by the superpowers. UNEF II illustrates the fact that for all their political and military strength the two superpowers were unable between them to establish a Middle East peace force and had to leave it to the nonpermanent members of the Security Council to create it.

But care must be taken to ensure that UNEF II does not provide a barren and negative result, which will be the case if it simply fulfills the purpose of keeping apart the armed forces of the two sides. As yet no one knows where UNEF will finally establish its demilitarized zones, but wherever they are they should not become military cantonments, barring access to military and civilian alike, but should be development areas within which a civilian community can live, cultivating and developing the land and, where possible, creating business and industry. Ideally they should provide the opportunity for Arabs and Jews to come together and to live side by side and build up an intercommunity understanding and confidence born of reconciliation achieved through communication. Israel is said to welcome the plans of the Egyptians to reopen the canal and reconstruct and redevelop the east bank for resettlement, since this indicates that Egypt is not determined to look upon the Sinai as a permanent battleground. If therefore confidence can be kindled and fear allayed by such development projects, the reconciliation that could derive from intercommunity relations within a demilitarized zone could make a significant contribution to the strengthening of any peaceful settlement in the Middle East. If the borders of Israel were to be circumscribed by a homogeneous buffer of Jews and Arabs living in harmony, the threat to its sovereignty would be largely dissipated—and eventually would disappear altogether. The United Nations has a clear-cut role to see that, once peace has been made at Geneva, peacekeeping and peace building in the Middle East go hand in hand.

Bibliography

Books

Bar-Yaacov, Nissim. *The Israeli-Syrian Armistice: Problems of Implementation, 1946–66.*Jerusalem: Magnes Press, Hebrew University, 1967.

Bloomfield, Lincoln P., ed. *International Military Forces.* Boston: Little, Brown, 1964.

Bloomfield, Lincoln P., and Leiss, Amelia C. *Controlling Small Wars: A Strategy for the Seventies.* New York: Knopf, 1969.

Bowett, D. W. *United Nations Forces.* London: Stevens & Sons, 1964; New York: Praeger, 1964.

Boyd, Andrew. *U.N.—Piety, Myth and Truth.* London: Penguin, 1962.

———. *Fifteen Men on a Powder Keg: A History of the U.N. Security Council.* London: Methuen, 1971.

Boyd, James M. *Cyprus: Episode in Peacekeeping.* New York: Columbia University Press, 1966.

Brook, David. *Preface to Peace: The United Nations and the Arab-Israel Armistice System.* Washington, D.C.: Public Affairs Press, 1964.

Burns, Arthur Lee, and Heathcote, Nina. *Peacekeeping by U.N. Forces: From Suez to the Congo.* New York: Praeger, 1963.

Burns, E. L. M. *Between Arab and Israeli.* Toronto: Clarke, Irwin, 1962; London: Harrap, 1962; New York: Obolensky, 1963.

Burton, J. W. *Conflict and Communication.* London: Macmillan, 1969.

Calder, Peter Ritchie. *The Agony of the Congo.* London: Gollancz, 1961.

Claude, Inis L., Jr. *Swords into Plowshares.* Rev. ed. New York and Toronto: Random House, 1971.

Cordier, Andrew W., and Foote, Wilder. *The Quest for Peace.* The Dag Hammarskjøld Memorial Lectures. New York and London: Columbia University Press, 1965.

Cox, A. M. *Prospects for Peacekeeping.* Washington, D.C.: Brookings Institution, 1967.

Cruise O'Brien, Conor. *To Katanga and Back: A U.N. Case History.* New York: Simon & Schuster, 1962, 1963.

Davister, Pierre. *Katanga, enjeu du monde.* Brussels: Éditions Europe-Afrique, 1960.

Dinant, Georges. *L'O.N.U. face à la crise congolaise.* Brussels: Éditions "Remarques congolaises," 1962.

Epstein, Howard M., ed. *Revolt in the Congo: 1960–64.* New York: Facts on File, 1965.

Fabian, Larry. *Soldiers without Enemies.* Washington, D.C.: Brookings Institution, 1971.

Fisher, Roger. *International Conflict for Beginners.* New York: Harper & Row, 1969.

Frydenberg, Per. *Peacekeeping, Experience and Evaluation: The Oslo Papers.* Oslo: Norwegian Institute of International Affairs, 1964.

Gerard-Libois, Jules. *Sécession au Katanga.* Brussels: Centre de Recherche et d'Information Socio-politiques, 1963. Translated by Rebecca Young. *Katanga Secession.* Madison: University of Wisconsin Press, 1966.

Goodrich, Leland M., and Hambro, Edvard. *Charter of the United Nations: Commentary and Documents.* Boston: World Peace Foundation, 1949.

Goodrich, Leland M., and Simons, Anne P. *The United Nations and the Maintenance of International Peace and Security.* Washington, D.C.: Brookings Institution, 1955.

Gordon, King. *The United Nations in the Congo: A Quest for Peace.* New York: Carnegie Endowment for International Peace, 1962.

Gross, Ernest A. *The United Nations: Structure for Peace.* New York: Harper, 1962.

Hamzeh, Fuad Said. *International Conciliation; with Special Reference to the Work of the United Nations Conciliation Commission for Palestine.* The Hague: Drukkerij Pasmans, 1963.

Hanning, Hugh. *The Peaceful Uses of Military Forces.* New York: Praeger, 1967.

Harbottle, Michael. *The Impartial Soldier: A Study of the UN Operation in Cyprus.* London: Oxford University Press, for Royal Institute of International Affairs, 1970.

————. *The Blue Berets: A Study of UN Peacekeeping Operations.* London: Leo Cooper, 1971; Harrisburg: Stackpole, 1971.

Higgins, Rosalyn. *International Law and the United Nations.* London: Oxford University Press, 1963.

————. *United Nations Peacekeeping, 1946–67: Documents and Commentary.* Vol. 1., *The Middle East.* Vol. 2., *Asia.* London: Oxford University Press, for Royal Institute of International Affairs, 1969, 1970.

Horn, Carl von. *Soldiering for Peace.* London: Cassell, 1966; New York: David McKay, 1967; Vienna: Molden, 1967.

James, Alan. *The Politics of Peacekeeping.* New York: Praeger, 1969; London: Chatto and Windus, 19619.

Lall, Arthur. *The U.N. and the Middle Ease Crisis.* Rev. ed. New York: Columbia University Press, 1970.

Langenhove, Fernand van. *Le rôle proéminant du secrétaire général dans l'operations des Nations Unies au Congo.* Brussels: Institut Royal des Relations Internationales, 1964.

Lash, Joseph P. *Dag Hammarskjøld, Custodian of the Brushfire Peace.* Garden City, N.Y.: Doubleday, 1961; London: Cassell, 1962.

Lawson, Richard. *Strange Soldiering.* London: Hodder & Stoughton, 1963.

Leclercq, Claude. *L'O.N.U. et l'affaire du Congo.* Paris: Payot, 1964.

Lefever, Ernest W. *Crisis in the Congo: a United Nations Force in Action.* Washington, D.C.: Brookings Institution, 1965.

————. *Uncertain Mandate: Politics of the U.N. Congo Operation.* Baltimore: Johns Hopkins, 1967.

Lefever, Ernest W., and Wynfred, Joshua. *United Nations Peacekeeping in the Congo, 1960–1964: An Analysis of Political, Executive and Military Control.* 3 vols. Washington, D.C.: Brookings Institution, 1966.

Legum, Colin. *Congo disaster.* Baltimore and Harmonsworth, Middlesex: Penguin, 1961.

Lie, Trygve. *In the Cause of Peace: Seven Years with the United Nations.* New York: Macmillan, 1954.

Luard, Evan. *Conflict and Peace in the Modern International System.* Boston: Little, Brown, 1968; London: University of London Press, 1970.

Martin, Andrew, and Edwards, John B. S. *The Changing Charter: A Study in the Reform of the United Nations.* London: Sylvan Press, 1955.

Miller, Richard I. *Dag Hammarskjøld and Crisis Diplomacy.* Dobbs Ferry, N.Y.: Oceana Publications, 1961.

Okumu, Washington A. *Lumumba's Congo: Roots of Conflict.* New York: Obolensky, 1963.

Padelford, Norman J. *The Financing of Future Peace and Security Operations Under the United Nations.* Washington, D.C.: Brookings Institution, for Massachussetts Institute of Technology, 1962.

Pearson, Lester B. *Mike.* Vol. 2. Toronto: University of Toronto Press, 1973; New York: Quadrangle, 1974; London: Gollancz, 1974, under the title *The International Years: Memoirs, 1948–57,* Vol. 2.

Rosner, Gabriella. *The United Nations Emergency Force.* New York: Columbia University Press, 1963.

Russell, Ruth B. *United Nations Experience with Military Forces: Political and Legal Aspects.* Washington, D.C.: Brookings Institution, 1964.

Seyersted, Finn. *United Nations Forces in the Law of Peace and War.* Leyden: Sijthoff, 1966.

Smith, Raymond. *The Fighting Irish in the Congo.* Dublin: Lilmac, 1962.

Stegenga, James A. *The United Nations Force in Cyprus.* Columbus: Ohio State University Press, 1968.

Stephens, Robert. *Cyprus, a Place of Arms.* London: Pall Mall Press, 1966.

Stillman, A. M. *The United Nations and the Suez Canal.* Ann Arbor, Michigan: University Microfilms, 1966.

Trinquier, Roger, et al. *Notre guerre au Katanga.* Paris: Éditions de la pensée moderne, 1963.

United Nations. *United Nations and the Congo: Some Salient Facts.* Official UN "White Book" on the Congo Operation. New York: United Nations, 1963.

————. *General Assembly Official Records (GAOR): 1946 ff.* New York: United Nations, 1947 ff.

————. *Security Council Official Records (SCOR): 1946 ff.* New York: United Nations, 1947 ff.

United Nations Department of Army Staff, Sweden. *Nordic Stand-by Forces in United Nations Service.* Stockholm: Rotobeckman, 1973.

Urquhart, Brian. *Hammarskjøld.* London: The Bodley Head, 1973.

Wainhouse, David Walter, et al. *International Peace Observation: A History and Forecast.* Baltimore: Johns Hopkins, 1966.

————. *International Peacekeeping at the Crossroads.* Baltimore: Johns Hopkins, 1974.

Additional Sources

Adelphi Papers

Rikhye, I. J. *Preparation and Training of United Nations Peacekeeping Forces.* No. 9. London: Institute for Strategic Studies, April 1964.

Disarmament

Egge, B. E. *The Ottawa Conference on U.N. Peacekeeping Forces.* No. 8. Paris: World Veterans Association, 1963.

International Conciliation

Claude, Inis L., Jr. "The United Nations and the Use of Force." No. 532 (March 1961) : 325–84.

Collins, J. Foster. "The United Nations and Indonesia." No. 459 (March 1950) : 115–200.

Mohn, Paul. "Problems of Truce Supervision." No. 478 (1952) : 51–99.

Military Law and Law War Review

Draper, G. I. A. D. "UN Forces (including UNEF)." 5, no. 1 (1966) : 45–61.

————. "UN Force in the Congo (ONUC)." 5, no. 2 (1966) : 377–405.

————. "UN Force in Cyprus (UNFICYP)." 6, no. 1 (1967) : 51–75.

UNITAR Publications

Andemichael, Bertranykun. *Peaceful Settlement among African States: Roles of the United Nations and the Organization of African Unity.* PS/5 1972.

Bailey, Sydney. *Peaceful Settlement of Disputes: Ideas and Proposals.* 3rd rev. ed. PS/1 1971.

Pachota, Vratislav. *The Quiet Approach: A Study of Good Offices Exercised by the United Nations Secretary General in the Cause of Peace.* PS/6 1972.

Younger, Sir Kenneth. *The United Nations Charter and the Challenge of the 70s.* LS/1 1970.

Index

Abdoh, Djalal, UN Ambassador of Iran, 159

Abdullah, Sheikh, 131

Addis Ababa, 229

Adoula, Cyrille, 78, 80, 82, 90, 171

Africa: British interests in, 219; French policy in, 214, 220; liberation movements in, 226; peacekeeping in, 270; Portuguese colonies, 173, 238, 303; regional conflicts in, 243; Soviet policy in, 222, 224; U.S. influence in, 218

African states, possible membership in Security Council, 36

Afro-Asian states, 85

Aguiyi-Ironsi, Johnson, 174

Ahmad, Imam, of Yemen, 134

Air America, 199n

Akrotiri, 320, 322

Albania, UNSCOB and, 143–46

Algeria, 173; dispute with Morocco, 167–69, 177; rebellion in, 50, 220, 237, 238

Angola, 173, 238

Ankrah, General Joseph Arthur, 174

Aqaba, Gulf of, 51, 55, 58

Arab-Israeli conflicts, 124–30, 243; *1948*, 125–26, 218, 239; *1956–1966*, 49–57, 127–28, 239; *1967* (Six-Day War), 30, 61–62, 65, 128–29, 221–22, 240; *1973*, 64n, 129, 222, 309–39; cease-fire agreement, 329–32. *See also* UNEF; UNEF II

Arab League, 147

Arabs: in Gaza Strip, 56, 57, 128; oil embargo, 244; in Palestine, 49; refugees from Israel, 49, 294; and UNEF in peacetime, 67

Arbenz Guzmán, Jacobo, 163, 164

Argentina, 151, 233, 282

Aswan Dam, 50

Atlantic Charter, 19

Australia, 124, 127, 136, 293; and Balkans, 144; and Indonesia, 140, 142n

Austria, 136; Nazi take-over, 19; in UNEF II, 318–21, 324, 325; in UNFICYP, 102, 103, 293

Ayios Theodoros, 110–12, 269

Azhari, Yusuf Omar El, Sudan, 173

Ba'ath party, 59

Badr, Imam, of Yemen, 134–35

Baghdad Pact, 50

Bahutu tribe, 170

Bakwanga, 76

Balager, Joaquim, 153

Balfour Declaration, 48

Balkans, 235, 236; UN observers in (UN-SCOB), 11, 31, 143–46, 216, 232, 233, 236

Baluba tribe, 76

Bamako Agreement, 168, 169

Bangladesh, 22, 133, 223, 224, 257, 278, 303, 334

Bao Dai, 180

Bar-Lev line, 310, 311

Batutsi tribe, 170

Beirut, 55, 56, 57, 146, 149

Belgium: in Balkans, 144; in Congo crisis, 71–74, 76, 78, 79, 84, 92, 172, 290, 291; and Indonesia, 140, 142n; Palestine truce supervision, 126, 127

Beras, Archbishop, 150

Berlin crisis (blockade), 233, 235, 242

Bernadotte, Count Folke, 49, 125, 126

Bhutan, 233

Biafra, 175–76, 257, 294, 297, 334

Bitter Lakes, 313, 324, 331

Bolivia, 125, 155

Bosch, Juan, 149–50, 152, 154

Boxer, U.S.S., 150

Brandt, Willy, 21

Brazil, 144–45, 158n, 164, 282; in OAS, 151; in UN, 36, 38, 258; in UNEF, 54, 57, 58

Brazzaville, 72, 172

Brezhnev, Leonid, 314–15

Britain, 155, 176, 214, 218–19, 233, 258; in Balkans, 144, 145; and Congo operation, 87, 172, 219; in Cyprus (UN-FICYP), 97–100, 102–03, 106, 116, 219, 267–69, 321, 322; at Geneva Conference (1954), 180; in Indonesia, 138, 142n; in Lebanon, 148; Palestine mandate, 48–49, 124, 125; in Suez crisis, 23n, 30, 48–52, 130, 219, 239, 248; and UN, 219; and

DATE DUE